TOEFL 和 SAT 全能书
——夯实基础篇

主　编　苏子进
副主编　李　曦

中国人民大学出版社
·北京·

图书在版编目（CIP）数据

TOEFL 和 SAT 全能书. 夯实基础篇 / 苏子进主编. --北京：中国人民大学出版社，2022.1
ISBN 978-7-300-30087-0

Ⅰ. ①T… Ⅱ. ①苏… Ⅲ. ①TOEFL－词汇－自学参考资料 ②TOEFL－写作－自学参考资料 ③英语－词汇－高等学校－入学考试－美国－自学参考资料 ④英语－写作－高等学校－入学考试－美国－自学参考资料 Ⅳ. ①H313 ②H315

中国版本图书馆 CIP 数据核字（2021）第 261719 号

TOEFL 和 SAT 全能书——夯实基础篇
主　编　苏子进
副主编　李　曦
TOEFL he SAT Quannengshu — Hangshi Jichupian

出版发行	中国人民大学出版社		
社　　址	北京中关村大街 31 号	邮政编码	100080
电　　话	010-62511242（总编室）		010-62511770（质管部）
	010-82501766（邮购部）		010-62514148（门市部）
	010-62515195（发行公司）		010-62515275（盗版举报）
网　　址	http://www.crup.com.cn		
经　　销	新华书店		
印　　刷	唐山玺诚印务有限公司		
规　　格	185 mm×260 mm　16 开本	版　次	2022 年 1 月第 1 版
印　　张	23.5	印　次	2022 年 1 月第 1 次印刷
字　　数	513 000	定　价	68.80 元

版权所有　　侵权必究　　印装差错　　负责调换

PREFACE 序言

本书重点解决的是考生在考试中会遇到的单词问题，帮助考生提高阅读效率，迅速提分。

因为托福只是一项基本英语能力考试，而 SAT 则是美国高考，所以在选词时，作者选了一些比较难的学者用词。本书里的词语都是环环相扣的，仔细看能看出其内在的关联。我们希望读完这本词汇书的考生，不但托福、SAT 可以考高分，上大学之后同样可以读得很顺利，不用总是查字典。学习本书，你留学的时候，美国的教授们会对你另眼相看。

1. 怎样使用本书？

本书单词全部来自托福和 SAT 考题。

（1）主力单词 / 词组选择的是考试中常出现的词，每一个 lesson 的主词条的选择都有作者的小心思在里面，词义相近或相反，帮助考生形成词群记忆的效果。主词条大多配有一个或多个例句，教考生了解单词的不同含义和使用场合，以求精准使用这些单词。

（2）句中单词 / 词组是为了帮助考生在句子的情境中更高效地拓展词汇记忆，降低单独记单词的难度。

（3）补充单词 / 词组是一些高分秘诀词，考频较主词条稍弱，其选择往往是跟主词条出现的文章相关联，考生可作为对主词条的补充来记忆。

（4）识记单词 / 词组是每一个 lesson 的最后一部分，在学习完前面的内容之后，再系统记忆一些关键词。对本部分的要求是记忆、认识即可，不需要掌握例句与不同用法。

（5）在学习本书的过程中，考生需充分使用音频，加强听力训练，掌握单词的正确发音。

（6）本套书分为夯实基础篇（九阳神功）和能力提升篇（九阴真经），考生应该先学基础篇，再学提升篇，达到对托福和 SAT 词汇的全方位掌握。

2. 为什么有大量例句？

大部分托福和SAT考生对单词会读不会用，本书大量例句可以解决这个问题。考生往往只知道单词常用的第一种或第二种意思，但SAT考试却考查第三种或第四种意思，本书例句中的相关词组、同义词及反义词就是为了让考生举一反三，记一个单词等于记住了很多个，对SAT考试的辨词题也会大有帮助。

3. 书中例句为什么没有翻译？

市面上大多数的单词书中例句后面往往跟着中文翻译，这个翻译的存在恰恰让读者产生了一种依赖，而只去记忆关键词，对例句中的其他词语或内在精华不去思考、不去理解，在脑海中还是通过中文去背诵英文，同样的时间内只做了记住关键词这一件事。同时，夹带中文翻译的书浪费了很多的篇幅。本书则不同，例句中不带中文翻译，逼迫学生通过上下文、同义词及衍生词去思考理解，这样做的好处有两个：一是从思考模式中去适应英文语法逻辑，真正习惯用英文思考英文，让考生从内在建立学习外语的环境；二是通过思考，加深印象和理解，同样的时间内既记住了关键词，又联想记忆了衍生词。

4. 目前市场上的书大多是托福和SAT分别出书，本书将两者整合在一起，对考生来说方便之处是什么？

无论是托福语言测试还是SAT美国高考，考试设计的目地都只有一个，帮助考生适应国外的大学学习。本书除了指明考试方向，还可以帮助考生提升英文实力，了解国外文化。实际考试中，托福和SAT的单词有很多重叠的地方，学习托福单词会对SAT有帮助，学习SAT单词亦会对托福有帮助，作者以提升英文实力为主，故将托福和SAT单词整合在一本书中，两门考试用一本书，方便考生携带和使用。

CONTENTS 目 录

Lesson 1 ………………………………………………… 001
Lesson 2 ………………………………………………… 003
Lesson 3 ………………………………………………… 008
Lesson 4 ………………………………………………… 012
Lesson 5 ………………………………………………… 016
Lesson 6 ………………………………………………… 019
Lesson 7 ………………………………………………… 022
Lesson 8 ………………………………………………… 027
Lesson 9 ………………………………………………… 029
Lesson 10 ……………………………………………… 032
Lesson 11 ……………………………………………… 035
Lesson 12 ……………………………………………… 038
Lesson 13 ……………………………………………… 041
Lesson 14 ……………………………………………… 044
Lesson 15 ……………………………………………… 050
Lesson 16 ……………………………………………… 053
Lesson 17 ……………………………………………… 058
Lesson 18 ……………………………………………… 061
Lesson 19 ……………………………………………… 064
Lesson 20 ……………………………………………… 066
Lesson 21 ……………………………………………… 070
Lesson 22 ……………………………………………… 074
Lesson 23 ……………………………………………… 075
Lesson 24 ……………………………………………… 077
Lesson 25 ……………………………………………… 080
Lesson 26 ……………………………………………… 085

Lesson 27	088
Lesson 28	091
Lesson 29	094
Lesson 30	100
Lesson 31	103
Lesson 32	109
Lesson 33	113
Lesson 34	116
Lesson 35	122
Lesson 36	126
Lesson 37	129
Lesson 38	131
Lesson 39	135
Lesson 40	139
Lesson 41	142
Lesson 42	145
Lesson 43	149
Lesson 44	152
Lesson 45	156
Lesson 46	160
Lesson 47	162
Lesson 48	164
Lesson 49	165
Lesson 50	169
Lesson 51	170
Lesson 52	173
Lesson 53	176
Lesson 54	179
Lesson 55	181
Lesson 56	183
Lesson 57	185
Lesson 58	187
Lesson 59	191
Lesson 60	194
Lesson 61	196
Lesson 62	198
Lesson 63	200

Lesson 64	204
Lesson 65	207
Lesson 66	211
Lesson 67	215
Lesson 68	219
Lesson 69	224
Lesson 70	227
Lesson 71	231
Lesson 72	235
Lesson 73	237
Lesson 74	240
Lesson 75	245
Lesson 76	248
Lesson 77	251
Lesson 78	255
Lesson 79	258
Lesson 80	260
Lesson 81	263
Lesson 82	265
Lesson 83	268
Lesson 84	272
Lesson 85	274
Lesson 86	277
Lesson 87	280
Lesson 88	283
Lesson 89	285
Lesson 90	288
Lesson 91	291
Lesson 92	293
Lesson 93	296
Lesson 94	299
Lesson 95	302
Lesson 96	304
Lesson 97	310
Lesson 98	313
Lesson 99	315
Lesson 100	319

- **Lesson 101** ... 323
- **Lesson 102** ... 325
- **Lesson 103** ... 326
- **Lesson 104** ... 330
- **Lesson 105** ... 332
- **Lesson 106** ... 337
- **Lesson 107** ... 340
- **Lesson 108** ... 341
- **Lesson 109** ... 344
- **Lesson 110** ... 349
- **Lesson 111** ... 350
- **Lesson 112** ... 353
- **Lesson 113** ... 357
- **Lesson 114** ... 361
- **Lesson 115** ... 364
- **Lesson 116** ... 366

Lesson 1

Part 1   主力单词 / 词组

aspire [əˈspaɪər]   *v.* 想要（有雄心壮志或企图心）；追求；渴望

I aspire to achieve things of which others dare not to dream.
I aspire to achieve remarkable feats.

aspiration [ˌæspəˈreɪʃn]   *n.* 打算；计划

It appears that every man's insomnia is as different from his neighbor's as are their daytime hopes and aspirations. (F. Scott Fitzgerald, U.S. writer)

The young have aspirations that never come to pass, the old have reminiscences of what never happened. It's only the middle-aged who are really conscious of their limitations. (Saki, British short-story writer)

aspirant [ˈæspərənt, əˈspaɪərənt]   *n.* 有抱负的人   *adj.* 有抱负的；有志向的

Eric is an aspirant biologist.
He is a presidential aspirant.

intend [ɪnˈtend]   *v.* 打算；计划

He intends to grow long hair.

intent [ɪnˈtent]   *n.* 意图   *adj.* 专注的；打算做的

The director's intent was to make her famous.
You could never forget the intent look on her face.
Intent on his study, he lost track of the time.
She is intent on opening Pandora's box.

intention [ɪnˈtenʃn]   *n.* 意图

I have no intention of killing civilians, their deaths are just collateral damage.

purport [pərˈpɔːrt, ˈpɜːrpɔːrt]   *v.* 打算；声称   *n.* 打算；主旨

The new measures purported to subsidize poor students and cut spending as well.
The red Ferrari is purported to be yours.
The purport of this article is about how to develop the domestic economy.

- **Words in sentences 句中单词/词组**

  insomnia [ɪn'sɑːmnɪə] n. 失眠症；失眠
  neighbor ['neɪbər] n. 邻居
  daytime ['deɪtaɪm] adj. 日间的
  reminiscence [ˌremɪ'nɪsns] n. 回忆；旧事
  Pandora's box 潘朵拉魔盒
  damage ['dæmɪdʒ] n. 损害；危害；伤害

Part 2 补充单词/词组

shiftless ['ʃɪftləs] adj. 没志气的
When did he become a shiftless freeloader?

shiftlessness ['ʃɪftləsnes] n. 不中用；无能
Despite his apparent shiftlessness, he became an official.

internecine [ˌɪntər'niːsn] adj. 内讧的；互相残杀的
This year is so unpropitious. Friendly nations are turning into internecine rivals.
The general manager has to solve internecine conflicts in the company.
An internecine war erupted this year.

nerve [nɜːrv] v. 鼓足勇气 n. 勇气；神经
I nerved myself to fight a lion.
She hasn't had the nerve to fire a gun.
The corpus callosum is a thick nerve tract which can only be found in placental mammals.

nervous ['nɜːrvəs] adj. 焦虑的；神经质的
Am I making you very nervous?

energetic [ˌenər'dʒetɪk] adj. 精力充沛的
The once energetic young man sank into shiftless indifference after hearing of his beloved mentor's death.

energy ['enərdʒi] n. 精力；能源
I waste too much mental energy on listening to his whining.

energize [ˈenərdʒaɪz]　v. 使充满热情；使通电
Teammates were energized by the coach's pep talk.

Part 3　识记单词 / 词组

to/for all intents and purposes　实际上；在所有主要方面
reminisce [ˌremɪˈnɪs]　v. 回忆；追忆
reminiscent [ˌremɪˈnɪsnt]　adj. 回忆的；旧事的
collateral [kəˈlætərəl]　adj. 附带的　n. 抵押品
collateral damage　附带损害
artery [ˈɑːrtəri]　n. 动脉
vein [veɪn]　n. 静脉
placental [pləˈsentl]　adj. 胎盘的
mortgage [ˈmɔːrgɪdʒ]　v. 抵押贷款　n. 房贷
bilateral [ˌbaɪˈlætərəl]　adj. 双边的；双方的
press on　继续进行
subsidize [ˈsʌbsɪdaɪz]　v. 给予……津贴；资助
subsidy [ˈsʌbsədi]　n. 津贴；补助金
bravado [brəˈvɑːdoʊ]　n. 虚张声势；逞能；冒险
freeloader [ˈfriːloʊdər]　n. 不劳而获的人
reckless [ˈrekləs]　adj. 鲁莽的；不小心的
callosal [kæˈloʊzl]　adj. 胼胝体的
commissure [ˈkɑmɪˌʃʊr]　n. 接合处；合缝处
whining [ˈwaɪnɪŋ]　n. 哭嚷；抱怨；嘎嘎响
pep talk　激励的话

Lesson 2

Part 1　主力单词 / 词组

extricate [ˈekstrɪkeɪt]　v. 解救；使摆脱
The paramedic extricates me and rushes me to the hospital in an ambulance.

The crane extricated the car from the mud.

rescue [ˈreskjuː]　v./n. 解救；营救
The speleologists make an all-out effort to rescue children trapped inside.
It is too late to rescue her.

rescuer [ˈreskjuːər]　n. 救助者；救星
They have been waiting for rescuers.

savior [ˈseɪvjər]　n. 解救者；救星
She is my savior who lends me money very often.

messiah [məˈsaɪə]　n. 救星
The tribal leader in Africa was regarded as a savior or messiah.

salvation [sælˈveɪʃn]　n. 拯救的途径；救助
Mutual understanding between two hostile nations has become their salvation.
International trading and tourism seem to be the only salvation of the Island's economy.
The elderly lady's delusion was deeply entrenched beyond salvation.
They prayed to God for salvation from hunger, political oppression, and military repression.

deliver [dɪˈlɪvər]　v. 兑现；运送；发布
It is the promise that you fail to deliver.

deliverance [dɪˈlɪvərəns]　n. 解救；解脱
She prayed to a merciful God for the deliverance from poverty.

redeem [rɪˈdiːm]　v. 补救；赎回
He tried to redeem an error he made in the past.
She redeems her watch in a pawn shop.
All the sins can be redeemed, and all the misdemeanors can be forgiven by the almighty God.

redemption [rɪˈdempʃn]　n. 补救；赎回
The major tries many ways to make the redemption of his reputation.
The sinner goes to church every day searching for redemption.

the Redeemer （基督教的）耶稣基督；救赎者
The Redeemer is worshiped by a crowd.

expiate [ˈekspieɪt]　v. 赎罪；补偿
The criminal expiated his crimes by donating all of his fortunes to the victims.

Do you think every wrongdoing can be expiated by a certain amount of money?
By doing volunteer work, the teenager expiates his sins committed during the past year.

liberate [ˈlɪbəreɪt] v. 解放；使自由
Policemen liberate hostages.
The red army liberated China.
The hit squads liberated hostages from their captors.

liberator [ˈlɪbəreɪtər] n. 解放者；解救者
Liberators fought the tyrant.

liberal [ˈlɪbərəl] adj. 自由开放的；开明的
The president was thought of as a liberal figure.

liberal arts 文科
She earned a liberal arts degree.

liberalization [ˌlɪbrələˈzeɪʃn] n. 自由化；放宽限制
She has been a determined champion, fighting for the liberalization of women's voting rights in India for decades.

liberalize [ˈlɪbrəlaɪz] v. 使自由化；放宽对……的限制
The country's trading policies have begun to liberalize.

emancipate [ɪˈmænsɪpeɪt] v. 解放
The fancy is indeed no other than a mode of memory emancipated from the order of time and space.
The best way to emancipate yourself from your parents is to live in a dormitory during college.

emancipation [ɪˌmænsɪˈpeɪʃn] n. 解放
They commemorated the emancipation of slaves on this special day.

manumit [ˌmænjuˈmɪt] v. 解放奴隶
Ironically, the U.S. civil war was meant for manumitting slaves.

manumitter [ˌmænjuˈmɪtɜ] n. 奴隶解放者
He is a manumitter who sets slaves free.

manumission [ˌmænjuˈmɪʃn] n.（农奴、奴隶的）解放
The official manumission of the slaves preceded the Civil War.

● Words in sentences 句中单词 / 词组 ●

paramedic [ˌpærəˈmedɪk] *n.* 护理人员
crane [kreɪn] *v.* 伸长（脖子） *n.* 吊车；起重机；鹤
speleologist [ˌspiːliˈɒlədʒɪst] *n.* 洞穴学家；洞穴探险者
all-out [ˌɔːl ˈaʊt] *adj.* 全力以赴的
mutual [ˈmjuːtʃuəl] *adj.* 相互的
delusion [dɪˈluːʒn] *n.* 谬见；错误的想法
entrench [ɪnˈtrentʃ] *v.* 使根深蒂固
oppression [əˈpreʃn] *n.* 压迫；压制
misdemeanor [ˌmɪsdɪˈmiːnər] *n.* 不检点的举止
almighty [ɔːlˈmaɪti] *adj.* 万能的；有无限权力的
hit squad 雇用的杀手
hostage [ˈhɑːstɪdʒ] *n.* 人质
captor [ˈkæptər] *n.* 劫持者
commemorate [kəˈmeməreɪt] *v.* （用……）纪念；作为……的纪念

Part 2 补充单词 / 词组

serene [səˈriːn] *adj.* 宁静的；安详的
I enjoy the harmonious image of this serene painting.

derelict [ˈderəlɪkt] *n.* 无家可归者；社会弃儿 *adj.* 荒废的；没责任感的
The sailors found a derelict in the high seas.
There is a derelict warehouse.
The derelict security guard fell asleep.
He was fired due to derelict in his duty.

abort [əˈbɔːrt] *v.* 使流产；堕胎；中止
The commander ordered his soldiers to abort the mission.

a spontaneous abortion 自然流产

an induced abortion 人工流产

abortive [əˈbɔːrtɪv]　*adj.* 失败的；无结果的

The king made an abortive attempt to seize back his power.

retrieve [rɪˈtriːv]　*v.* 挽救；找回

We were losing ground and used the atomic bomb as the last resort to retrieve the situation.

retriever [rɪˈtriːvər]　*n.* 寻回猎犬

I once raised a golden retriever.

unfettered [ʌnˈfetərd]　*adj.* 不受约束的；自由的

We are not separatists, but demand unfettered regional autonomy from the central government.

With this VIP card, you can gain unfettered access to every room in the palace.

salvage [ˈsælvɪdʒ]　*v./n.* 救助；抢救

She tried to salvage her property as the fire began to grow larger.

The aircraft carrier was severely damaged beyond salvage.

repression [rɪˈpreʃn]　*n.* 镇压；制止

The violent repression causes a melee between the crowd and the police.

savor [ˈseɪvər]　*v./n.* 享受；品味

Don't savor your victory. You only win the game once.

The movie is an adaptation. However, it has lost the savor of the original novel.

Life has lost its savor since you left me. Day or night seems to be meaningless to me.

savory [ˈseɪvəri]　*adj.* 令人愉快的；名声好的　*n.* 美味小盘菜肴

I will make a savory hamburger.

News articles of atrocity don't make for very savory reading material.

I used to eat some savories before or after dinner.

unsavory [ʌnˈseɪvəri]　*adj.* 不光彩的；不好吃的

I don't associate with him because of his unsavory reputation.

The police chief gets involved in some unsavory business.

A series of unsavory events occur beneath the serene surface of his life.

illusive=illusory　*adj.* 幻觉的；不实际的

Her illusory hopes were shattered after hearing her husband's demise.

Part 3　识记单词/词组

hold off　抵挡住；拖延

caravan [ˈkærəvæn] n. 商队；移民的队伍；车队

swat [swɑːt] v./n. 击打；拍打（尤指昆虫）

squad [skwɑːd] n. 小队；特别行动组；运动队

swat squad 特警队

respondent [rɪˈspɑːndənt] n. 回答者 adj. 被告的

pilaster [pɪˈlæstər] n. 壁柱

redeem a coupon 将优惠券兑换成现金（或物品）

voucher [ˈvaʊtʃər] n. 代金券；保证人；收据

vouch [vaʊtʃ] v. 担保；证实

deed [diːd] v. 转移资产 n. 行为；（尤指房产）契约

title deed 产权证

the Savior 耶稣基督；救世主

speleology [ˌspiːliˈɑːlədʒi] n. 洞穴学

cavern [ˈkævərn] v. 挖空；置……于山洞中 n. 大山洞

deceptive [dɪˈseptɪv] adj. 虚伪的；欺诈的

filial [ˈfɪliəl] adj. 子女（对父母）的；孝顺的

filial affection /duty 子女的亲情 / 孝道

mischance [ˌmɪsˈtʃæns] n. 不幸；厄运

Lesson 3

Part 1 主力单词 / 词组

acquire [əˈkwaɪər] v. 学习（长时间才能学成的事物）；获得

I have acquired fluency in English after several years of study.
I acquire skills of global communication as I continue my work over many years.
Britain acquired trading privileges in Hong Kong.

imbibe [ɪmˈbaɪb] v. 吸收；喝（尤指酒）

Imbibing foreign culture and past life experiences are essential while interacting with foreign associates.

I imbibed six pitchers of beer and had a hangover the next morning.

imbibition [ˌɪmbɪˈbɪʃn] *n.* 吸取

Imbibition of water is a long process for a coconut seed.

absorb [əbˈzɔːrb, əbˈsɔːrb] *v.* 吸收；承受；同化；使……全神贯注

Plants absorb water.

The sponge can absorb the impact.

Let the company pay for it. I don't want to absorb the cost.

The company was absorbed by a multinational corporation.

She was totally absorbed by an outlandish witch-hunt project.

absorption [əbˈzɔːrpʃn, əbˈsɔːrpʃn] *n.* 吸收；同化；全神贯注

His performance is quite well due to his absorption in work.

extrapolate [ɪkˈstræpəleɪt] *v.* 推断；推知

We need a good leader who can extrapolate and learn from the past.

extrapolation [ɪkˌstræpəˈleɪʃn] *n.* 推断；推知

The methods of extrapolation vary widely.

assimilate [əˈsɪməleɪt] *v.* 吸收；同化

She is a quick learner who can assimilate much scientific information in a short amount of time.

It's very difficult to assimilate the Muslim population into the larger culture of the nation.

assimilation [əˌsɪməˈleɪʃn] *n.* 吸收；同化

Assimilation is a requirement for academic success.

The clash of lifestyles and religions has made assimilation difficult.

impregnate [ɪmˈpregneɪt] *v.* 注入；充满；使怀孕 *adj.* 饱和的；怀孕的

I could smell that the steak was impregnated with red wine.

I can sense the atmosphere impregnated with tension.

He impregnated his wife.

I will not consume any fried chickens with impregnated steroids.

osmosis [ɑːzˈmoʊsɪs] *n.* 渗透作用；潜移默化

Osmosis occurs when molecules of the initial liquid pass through a membrane which causes fluid to flow back into the tiny blood vessels.

Kids learn language by osmosis.

osmotic [ɑːzˈmɑːtɪk]　*adj.* 渗透的；潜移默化的

Osmotic pressure causes water to pass slowly through their skin because the body fluids are saltier than the freshwater outside.

The teacher adopts an osmotic approach to teach his students.

• Words in sentences 句中单词/词组 •

pitcher [ˈpɪtʃər]　*n.* 投手；水壶

hangover [ˈhæŋoʊvər]　*n.* 宿醉；[医] 后遗症

outlandish [aʊtˈlændɪʃ]　*adj.* 不寻常的

witch [wɪtʃ]　*n.* 女巫

steroid [ˈsterɔɪd, ˈstɪrɔɪd]　*n.* 类固醇

molecule [ˈmɑːlɪkjuːl]　*n.* 分子

membrane [ˈmembreɪn]　*n.* 膜；膜状物

vessel [ˈvesl]　*n.* 血管；轮船；器皿

Part 2　补充单词/词组

debouch [dɪˈbuʃ]　*v.* 前进；流出

Troops debouched from the military camp into the plain.

The river debouched into the Yellow Sea.

germinate [ˈdʒɜːrmɪneɪt]　*v.* 发芽；生长

Seeds only germinate in the right conditions.

The ancient culture existed before Western civilization began to germinate.

considerable [kənˈsɪdərəbl]　*adj.* 相当多的

The government gave the region considerable autonomy.

amount [əˈmaʊnt]　*n.* 金额；数量

It will take a considerable amount of time to finish this job.

amount to　相当于

Taking without asking amounts to steal.

Supporting enemy amounts to treason.

Studying hard amounts to a high score on your test.

finesse [fɪˈnes] v. 用策略做某事；回避 n. 策略；手腕

He finesses his way through the crowd.
The official is good at finessing hard issues.
By operating with finesse and flexibility, the corporation outstripped its competitors.

stein [staɪn] n. 啤酒杯

The bartender slides beer steins across a table.

snack [snæk] v. 吃点心 n. 零食

She often snacks at three o'clock.
Snacks are impregnated with preservatives.

totalize [ˈtoʊtəlˌaɪz] v. 计算总数；总结

The accountant totalizes receipts at the end of the month.
Some people tend to totalize reality by subsuming it under a single point of view.

summation [sʌˈmeɪʃn] n. 总结

There is a summation at the end of the thesis.
The professor gave a summation of his archaeological discovery.

Part 3 识记单词 / 词组

an acquired taste　　后天养成的嗜好
in the light of sth　　鉴于；因为
savanna [səˈvænə]　n. 无树平原（美国东南部的）
reverse osmosis　　逆渗透
osmotic pressure　　渗透压
aviculturist [ˈeɪvɪˈkʌltʃərɪst]　n. 养鸟贩卖的人
incubate [ˈɪŋkjubeɪt]　v. 孵化；培养
culturist [ˈkʌltʃərɪst]　n. 养殖者；文化主义者
incubation [ˌɪŋkjuˈbeɪʃn]　n. 孵化；繁殖
germination [ˌdʒɜːrmɪˈneɪʃn]　n. 发芽；产生
Islam [ˈɪzlɑːm, ɪzˈlɑːm]　n. 伊斯兰教
Islamic [ɪzˈlæmɪk, ɪzˈlɑːmɪk]　adj. 伊斯兰教的
subsume [səbˈsuːm]　v. 把……归入
trinket [ˈtrɪŋkɪt]　n. 小装饰物；小玩意儿

Lesson 4

Part 1 主力单词/词组

pulchritude [ˈpʌlkrɪtjuːd, ˈpʌlkrɪtuːd]　*n.* 美丽

A woman of pulchritude passes by the classroom window.
Nature's pulchritude of Qinghai Lake has attracted many tourists.

sublime [səˈblaɪm]　*v.* 使升华；使崇高　*n.* 令人赞叹的东西　*adj.* 极美的；非常好的；盲目的

The works of the artist were sublimed by his death.
His work ranges from the sublime to the ridiculous
The sublime beauty of the Mona Lisa was extolled.
His sublime ignorance/arrogance/audacity impressed us.

aesthetic [esˈθetɪk]　*n.* 美感；审美学　*adj.* 美的；审美的

Aesthetic plastic surgery is very popular in South Korea.
They used an aesthetic accessory as a moral touchstone to see whether or not the new employee would steal it.
Different people have different fashion aesthetics.

gorgeous [ˈɡɔːrdʒəs]　*adj.* 美丽的；讨人喜欢的

Although love dwells in gorgeous palaces, and sumptuous apartments, more willingly than in miserable and desolate cottages, it cannot be denied but that he sometimes causes his power to be felt in the gloomy recesses of forests, among the bleakest and rugged mountains, and in the dreary caves of a desert. (Giovanni Boccaccio, Italian writer and humanist)

comely [ˈkʌmli]　*adj.* 英俊的；貌美的

The makeup artist transforms the disheveled gypsy girl into a comely woman.

well-favored [ˈwelˈfeɪvəd]　*adj.* 英俊的；貌美的

She is benevolent and well-favored.

fetch [fetʃ]　*v.* (去)拿来；(去)请来；售得　*n.* 拿来；诡计

Would you please fetch a sweater for me?

The ticket fetched for 200 dollars.

fetching ['fetʃɪŋ]   *adj.* 动人的；迷人的

Her fetching smile has brought her many admirers to the office.

likeable=likable   *adj.* 可爱的；讨人喜欢的

She plays a likable character.

• Words in sentences 句中单词/词组 •

arrogance ['ærəgəns]   *n.* 自大

audacity [ɔː'dæsəti]   *n.* 勇气；大胆

plastic surgery   整形手术

moral ['mɔːrəl]   *adj.* 道德的

touchstone ['tʌtʃstoʊn]   *n.* 试金石；标准

desolate ['desələt]   *v.* 感到凄凉   *adj.* 荒凉的；无人的；孤独的

cottage ['kɑːtɪdʒ]   *n.* 小屋；村舍

gloomy ['gluːmi]   *adj.* 阴暗的；阴沉的

recess ['riːses, rɪ'ses]   *n.* 隐蔽处

bleak [bliːk]   *adj.* 荒凉的

rugged ['rʌgɪd]   *adj.* 崎岖的；态度严厉的

dreary ['drɪri]   *adj.* 阴沉的；枯燥的

dishevel [dɪ'ʃevəl]   *v.* 弄脏；弄乱

gypsy ['dʒɪpsi]   *n.* 吉普赛人；吉普赛语；绞缆筒   *adj.* 吉普赛人的；流浪的

benevolent [bə'nevələnt]   *adj.* 乐善好施的；慈善的

Part 2 补充单词/词组

sumptuous ['sʌmptʃuəs]   *adj.* 奢华的

There was a sumptuous banquet during her wedding.

sumptuary ['sʌmptʃuˌeri]   *adj.* 限制费用的；禁止奢侈的

They passed a sumptuary law to control the colony.

Our budget is sumptuary and limited.

sumptuary tax　　限制消费税

lampoon [læm'puːn]　　*v./n.* 讥讽；挖苦

The reporter had savagely lampooned several politicians.

He is often the target of lampoons in U.S. comedies.

coop [kuːp]　　*v.* 把……关在笼子　　*n.* 笼子

coop up　　监禁；将……禁锢在狭小空间

Women are no longer cooped up in harems, nor are they veiled and silent.

fly the coop　　逃走

A prisoner flew the coop in midnight.

infiltrate ['ɪnfɪltreɪt]　　*v.* 渗透；透入　　*n.* 渗透物

They have massively infiltrated forbidden territory. (Fatima Mernissi, Moroccan writer)

infiltration [ˌɪnfɪl'treɪʃn]　　*n.* 渗透；透入

We destroyed river crossings to make the enemy's infiltration more difficult.

evergreen ['evərɡriːn]　　*adj.* 常绿的；常青的

There are both evergreen and deciduous trees in the forest.

lagoon [lə'ɡuːn]　　*n.* 小而浅的淡水湖

There are many calving and breeding lagoons on the Pacific Coast of Baja for whales.

dweller ['dwelər]　　*n.* （城市、城镇、洞穴等的）居民

Many mountain dwellers still live in hovels or other unsanitary housing.

palatial [pə'leɪʃl]　　*adj.* 富丽堂皇的；宫殿的

The rich woman lives in a palatial mansion.

legalize ['liːɡəlaɪz]　　*v.* 使合法化

Marijuana has been legalized in some states.

tenebrous ['tenɪbrəs]　　*adj.* 黑暗的；晦涩的

I recalled the tenebrous days in prison.

The thief broke into a warehouse during the tenebrous night with no moon.

The legalization of homosexual marriage seems to be tenebrous.

tenebrific [ˌtenɪˈbrɪfɪk] *adj.* 阴沉的；阴暗的

We stayed in the trench during a tenebrific winter.

She portended a coming disaster after having witnessed a tenebrific fight of crows.

sylvan [ˈsɪlvən] *n.* 森林的居民 *adj.* 森林的

The centaur is a sylvan in this forest.

Cameron practices meditation in a sylvan retreat.

dell [del] *n.* 有树林的小谷地

The old couple lives in a sylvan dell.

rout [raʊt] *v.* 击溃；使溃逃；挖掘 *n.* 溃败；惨败；乌合之众

The infantries routed the northern invaders at the border.

Flood routs townspeople.

Pigs tend to rout in the earth.

Her extraordinary talent in painting was routed by another classmate.

fairy [ˈferi] *n.* 小妖精；仙女 *adj.* 小妖精的；仙女的

She encountered a gorgeous sylvan fairy.

The fairy's magic is weak.

Part 3 识记单词 / 词组

hideous [ˈhɪdiəs] *adj.* 不堪入目的；令人惊骇的

grotesque [ɡroʊˈtesk] *n.* 奇形怪状的人；奇异的艺术风格 *adj.* 奇形怪状的；怪诞的

homely [ˈhoʊmli] *adj.* 不好看的；平凡的

ill-favored [ˈɪlˈfeɪvərd] *adj.* 难看的（指人或其脸色）；令人不快的

thin-skinned [ˈθɪnˈskɪnd] *adj.* 皮薄的；易生气的

thick-skinned [ˈθɪkˈskɪnd] *adj.* 厚脸皮的；感觉迟钝的

extol [ɪkˈstoʊl] *v.* 赞扬；赞美

arrogant [ˈærəɡənt] *adj.* 自大的

whippersnapper [ˈwɪpərsnæpər] *n.* 妄自尊大的年轻人

audacious [ɔːˈdeɪʃəs] *adj.* 勇气可嘉的

dwell on 老是想着；一直在说

rug [rʌɡ] *n.* 小块地毯

drear [drɪr] *adj.* 阴沉的
moralist ['mɔːrəlɪst] *n.* 道德家；说教者
dishevelled [dɪ'ʃevld] *adj.* 乱糟糟的
benevolence [bə'nevələns] *n.* 厚道；捐助
deciduous forest 落叶林
coniferous forest 针叶林
broad-leaved ['brɔːd'liːvd] 阔叶树林
pediatrician [ˌpiːdiə'trɪʃn] *n.* 小儿科医师
pediatric [ˌpiːdi'ætrɪk] *adj.* 小儿科的
diplomate ['dɪpləˌmeɪt] *n.* 专科医师；毕业文凭持有者

Lesson 5

Part 1 主力单词 / 词组

cease [siːs] *v./n.* 停止；终止；结束
Both armies ceased fire during negotiation.
The rain ceased.
The free upgrade of this software has been ceased temporarily due to an unidentified loophole which is being fixed.
The whistleblower kept an eye upon her without cease.

cessation [se'seɪʃn] *n.* 结束；中断
An armistice for a cessation of hostilities was agreed upon by both nations.

surcease [sɜː'siːs] *v./n.* 中止；停止
They surceased the project due to a lack of funding.
I watched TV all night long without surcease.
Belarusian army keeps advancing with no sign of surcease.

desist [dɪ'zɪst, dɪ'sɪst] *v.* 停止；中止
The police order the demonstrators to desist from marching further.

respite ['respɪt] *v./n.* 暂缓；缓期执行 *adj.* 暂时看护的
The execution has been respited.

We have worked for eight hours without respite.

The nurse gave me respite care.

recess [ˈriːses, rɪˈses] *v.* 休会；暂停；把……放进壁龛（或壁橱） *n.* 休息

The meeting was recessed at ten o'clock.

The recess of the class is 10 minutes in length.

grind to a halt 慢慢停下来

Life grinds to a halt in the dry season.

Rapid economic growth has ground to a halt owing to trade war.

Severe weather condition causes television broadcasting programs to grind to a halt.

arrest [əˈrest] *v./n.* 逮捕；中止；吸引

He was arrested for theft.

The spread of the disease can be arrested by this new drug.

The general manager failed to arrest the decline of the company.

The commercial minister does whatever he can to arrest the slide in exportation.

The thunder arrested our attention that it was going to rain.

An usual noise arrested security guards' attention.

intermission [ˌɪntərˈmɪʃn] *n.* 中场休息；间歇

There will be a ten-minute intermission in this concert.

After 20 years of intermission, she starts to write again.

stanch [stɑːntʃ] *v.* （使）停止；止血 *adj.* 坚固的

Only his death will stanch the civil war.

She uses cottons to stanch bleeding.

• Words in sentences 句中单词 / 词组 •

whistleblower [ˈhwɪsəlˌbloʊər] *n.* 告发者

armistice [ˈɑːrmɪstɪs] *n.* 休战；停战协定

exportation [ˌekspɔːrˈteɪʃn] *n.* 出口

Part 2 补充单词 / 词组

yellow journalism 夸张的报道

The magazine relies on yellow journalism to make a profit.

etiology [ˌiːtiˈɑːlədʒi] n. 确切的原因

The etiology of the gap between the rich and the poor merits further study.

Sociologists study the etiology of crime.

Doctors examined the etiology of coronavirus.

gap [ɡæp] n. 缺口；隔阂 v. 裂开

The pavement gaped after an earthquake.

There is a gap in her chemical knowledge.

Most parents have experienced the generation gap.

gape [ɡeɪp] v. 目瞪口呆地凝视 n. 张嘴

Would you stop gaping at this pretty waitress for a second? I am going to order something.

The dull story made students gape.

I wondered what was in her mind when I saw her stupid gape.

agape [əˈɡeɪp, ˈæɡəpi] n. 灵性之爱 adj. 大张着的；张大嘴的

He transforms his affection for her into agape.

He was agape after seeing a ghost in the garden at night.

The door was agape, so we could take a look inside.

rift [rɪft] v. 分裂 n. 裂缝；裂痕

Continental fragments were rifted from an immemorial time.

The nation sought to mend the diplomatic rift.

The argument only widened the rift between her and her sister.

spick and span 整洁

I always keep my bedroom spick and span.

virulent [ˈvɪrələnt, ˈvɪrjələnt] adj. 剧毒的；狠毒的

Doctors attempt to eliminate the virulent bacteria in her lung.

The virulent racist attacked several foreign embassies.

The virulent campaign was carried on in the capital city.

hiatus [haɪˈeɪtəs] n. 间隙；裂缝；停滞

The hot spring shot out from the hiatus in the ground.

There is a hiatus between theory and practicality.

He sings again after a two-year hiatus.

journalese [ˌdʒɜːrnəˈliːz] n. 新闻文体；新闻笔调

The editor writes an essay in journalese.

Part 3 识记单词/词组

make one's advent 出现；降生
the innermost recesses of the mind 心灵的最深处
intermittent [ˌɪntərˈmɪtənt] *adj.* 间歇性的
intermittent rain 断断续续的雨
intermittently [ˌɪntərˈmɪtəntli] *adv.* 间歇性地
spasmodic [spæzˈmɑːdɪk] *adj.* 阵阵的；断断续续的
spasm [ˈspæzəm] *n.* 痉挛；抽搐
a stanch supporter 一个忠实的支持者
a stanch friend 一个忠实的朋友
grinder [ˈɡraɪndər] *n.* 粉碎机；白齿
severity [sɪˈverəti] *n.* 剧烈；惨重
subconscious [ˌsʌbˈkɑːnʃəs] *adj.* 潜意识的

Lesson 6

Part 1 主力单词/词组

solace [ˈsɑːləs] *n.* 安慰；慰藉；安慰物 *v.* 安慰
She solaced her mother's grief.
I find solace in my religion.
She found solace in spiritualism despite material deprivation.

comfort [ˈkʌmfərt] *v.* 安慰；使人舒服 *n.* 安慰；舒适
The mother comforts her crying baby.
I enjoy all sorts of comforts in contemporary society.

consolation [ˌkɑːnsəˈleɪʃn] *n.* 安慰
There was a consolation in knowing that his girlfriend was still alive after the earthquake.

• Words in sentences 句中单词/词组 •

deprivation [ˌdeprɪ'veɪʃn] n. 贫穷；丧失
contemporary [kən'tempəreri] n. 同龄人 adj. 现代的

Part 2 补充单词/词组

scout [skaʊt]　v. 侦察；物色　n. 侦察；侦察兵
The squad scouts the area before advancing.
He goes to a club to scout for a singer.

binocular [bɪ'nɑːkjələr]　n. 双筒望远镜
The scout descried the approaching enemy by binocular.

oculist ['ɑːkjəlɪst]　n. 眼科医生；验光师
oculo-=ocul-

ophthalmologist [ˌɑːfθəˈmɑːlədʒɪst, ˌɑːpθəˈmɑːlədʒɪst]　n. 眼科医师

optometrist [ɑːp'tɑːmətrɪst]　n. 验光师
An oculist is an ophthalmologist or optometrist.

optician [ɑːp'tɪʃn]　n. 眼镜商；配镜师
His grandfather is an optician.

with the advent of　随着……的来临

disseminate [dɪ'semɪneɪt]　v. 散播；宣传
With the advent of the Internet, news disseminates more quickly.

inception [ɪn'sepʃn]　n. 开端
At the inception the boss was only a vendor.

boosterism ['buːstərɪzəm]　n. 积极支持

bureaucratese [ˌbjʊrəkrætiːz]　n. 官僚语言
People have become accustomed to governmental bureaucratese and boosterism which verged on the absurd.

convey [kən'veɪ] *v.* 传送；传达

subliminal [ˌsʌb'lɪmɪnl] *adj.* 潜意识的
Scientists wonder how subliminal messages were conveyed.

bereft [bɪ'reft] *adj.* 丧失的；丧亲的
Both sides of the negotiation were bereft of poise.
We were bereft of hope at the sight of his demise.
I did whatever I could to console the bereft mother.

coeval [koʊ'iːvl] *adj.* 同时代的；同年龄的
The origin of this planet is coeval with that of dinosaurs.
The archaeologists found some coeval monuments nearby the excavation site.

Part 3 识记单词 / 词组

letter of comfort 告慰函
comfort station 公共厕所
comforter ['kʌmfərtər] *n.* 安慰者
deprive [dɪ'praɪv] *v.* 剥夺；使丧失
bereave [bɪ'riːv] *v.* 使丧失
bereavement [bɪ'riːvmənt] *n.* 丧失
sort out 解决；分类
flatfish ['flætfɪʃ] *n.* 比目鱼
dinosaurian [ˌdaɪnə'sɔːriən] *adj.* 恐龙的
conveyance [kən'veɪəns] *n.* 运输；运输工具
descry [dɪ'skraɪ] *v.* 看见；发现
pandemic [pæn'demɪk] *adj.* 大规模传染的
dissemination [dɪˌsemɪ'neɪʃn] *n.* 宣传；散播
cardiac ['kɑːrdiæk] *adj.* 心脏的；心脏病的
a cardiac arrest 一次心搏停止
the Scouts 童子军
an arrested tumor 一块中止发展的肿瘤

Lesson 7

Part 1　主力单词 / 词组

distract [dɪˈstrækt]　*v.* 分心；离题
Employing pretty girls might distract soldiers from carrying out their duties.
Don't let video games distract you from your studies.

distraction [dɪˈstrækʃn]　*n.* 困惑；分心
Now I will have less distraction by practicing stoicism.

digress [daɪˈgres]　*v.* 离题；岔开话题
I shouldn't digress from the topic when I get too emotional.
He digressed during his speech.

digression [daɪˈgreʃn]　*n.* 离题
She tried to hide the truth by eloquent digressions.

digressive [daɪˈgresɪv]　*adj.* 离题的
His speech is digressive and discursive from the main topic.

discursive [dɪˈskɜːrsɪv]　*adj.* 离题的；不着边际的
His lofty mind and discursive imagination interest me.

deviate [ˈdiːvieɪt]　*v.* 偏离；背离
Nothing can deviate from the course I've set for myself.
The hydraulic engineer will deviate rivers into the scorched plains.

divert [daɪˈvɜːrt]　*v.* 转移（注意力）；转向
The dictator has been desperately waging war against foreign countries to divert attention from domestic turmoil.
She diverts the investment from mining to banking.
Computer games should divert the kids well.
We have to divert to another road to avoid traffic congestion.

diversion [daɪˈvɜːrʒn]　*n.* 转向；偏离；转移视线的事物；消遣；临时支路
The storm forced the diversion of several flights.

I will create a diversion while I sneak inside the house.
I play chess as a diversion.

divagate [ˈdaɪvəˌɡeɪt] *v.* 离题；偏离；流浪

The monk divagated from his fated path in a time of turmoil. With his willpower, he eventually became a mayor.

divagation [ˌdaɪvəˈɡeɪʃən] *n.* 离题；偏差；流浪

The divagation of the calculated number should maintain under 1%.

tangential [tænˈdʒenʃl] *adj.* 没关系的；正切的

These managers are often given only a tangential role in decision-making in this state-own company.
I don't have the luxury of time to discuss this tangential issue.

deviation [ˌdiːviˈeɪʃn] *n.* 离题；偏差

The deviation is a cornerstone of progress.

sidetrack [ˈsaɪdtræk] *v.* 分心；使转移注意力

She kept on and on in a car and I got sidetracked, almost hitting a deer.

> • Words in sentences 句中单词 / 词组 •
>
> **eloquent** [ˈeləkwənt] *adj.* 雄辩的；有说服力的
> **lofty** [ˈlɔːfti] *adj.* 崇高的；高尚的
> **hydraulic** [haɪˈdrɔːlɪk] *adj.* 水力的；液压的
> **dictator** [ˈdɪkteɪtər] *n.* 独裁者
> **desperately** [ˈdespərətli] *adv.* 绝望地；迫切想要地
> **mining** [ˈmaɪnɪŋ] *n.* 矿业
> **sneak** [sniːk] *v.* 溜；偷拿 *n.* 打小报告的人 *adj.* 突然的
> **turmoil** [ˈtɜːrmɔɪl] *n.* 混乱
> **cornerstone** [ˈkɔːrnərstoʊn] *n.* 基石

Part 2 补充单词 / 词组

devolution [ˌdevəˈluːʃn] *n.* 放权；退化

The efficient corporate operation, however, requires the devolution of real powers to the staff.

airborne [ˈerbɔːrn] *adj.* 空中传播的；空降的
The airborne virus might cause social devolution like a zombie apocalypse.

editor [ˈedɪtər] *n.* 编者；校订者

redaction [rɪˈdækʃn] *n.* 编校
The editor removed some texts in the final redaction.

aphoristic [ˌæfəˈrɪstɪk] *adj.* 简要评论的
His editorial seems to be aphoristic rather than discursive.

mendicant [ˈmendɪkənt] *n.* 乞丐；托钵僧 *adj.* 行乞的

alm [ɑːm] *n.* 救济（品）；施舍金；施舍物
Mendicants usually beg for money and live on alms.

gradient [ˈɡreɪdiənt] *n.* 坡度；倾斜度

temperature gradient 温度梯度
The incubation of birds' eggs is quite sensitive to a temperature gradient.

interstate [ˈɪntərsteɪt] *n.* 州际公路 *adj.* 州与州之间的
Interstates have maintained low gradient and straight routes for maximizing visibility and safety.
Interstate commerce has increased.

aloft [əˈlɔːft] *adj.* 高处的 *adv.* 空中地
The wind aloft is extraordinarily strong.
Sailors went aloft to unfurl the sails.

brackish [ˈbrækɪʃ] *adj.* 微咸的；味道不好的；令人讨厌的
The food from yesterday was brackish.
She has a brackish personality.

palaver [pəˈlɑːvər, pəˈlævər] *v./n.* 空谈；谈判；交涉
She wasted the entire morning palavering about nonentities.
After enough of palaver, we should get down to business.
A palaver between foreign ministers runs smoothly related to global overfishing issues.

turbulent [ˈtɜːrbjələnt] *adj.* 动荡的；混乱的
2020 is a turbulent year for most countries.

We rafted on a turbulent rapid.

turbulence [ˈtɜːrbjələns] *n.* 动乱；湍流

He experienced emotional turbulence as his loyal friend betrayed him.

We all try to survive in the turbulence of the post-war era.

We are experiencing turbulence. Please remain seated.

raft [ræft] *v.* 乘筏；划动筏 *n.* 筏；橡皮艇；大量；许多

The hunters rafted across the river at night.

The old man fished on a raft.

portable [ˈpɔːrtəbl] *n.* 手提电脑 *adj.* 手提式的

I brought a portable for a business trip.

Laptops are portable computers.

vasectomy [vəˈsektəmi] *n.* 输精管切除术

The doctor performs a vasectomy.

vasectomize [vəˈsektəˌmaɪz] *v.* 为……切除输精管

Rapists should be vasectomized.

fallopian tube 输卵管

Salpingectomy is the surgical removal of a fallopian tube.

cursive [ˈkɜːrsɪv] *n.* 草写 *adj.* 草写的

She writes in cursive when in rush.

The American wrote a cursive note for his colleague.

crucifix [ˈkruːsəfɪks] *n.* 有耶稣像的十字架；耶稣受难像

Made a terrible mess of my face with his crucifix. (Joe Orton, British playwright)

luxuriant [lʌgˈʒʊriənt] *adj.* 华丽的；繁茂的；肥沃的

She has a tendency to buy luxuriant goods.

The abandoned land was covered with luxuriant vegetation.

Luxuriant soils are full of organisms.

loft [lɔft] *v.* 高升；向高处击（踢、掷） *n.* 阁楼；顶楼

The spacecraft was lofted by a powerful rocket.

He put some rarely used items in the loft.

antenna [ænˈtenə] *n.* 天线；[动] 触角

The worker adjusted the antenna aloft the building.

ledger ['ledʒər] *n.* [会计] 分类账簿；总账

The accountant retrieved the ledgers while the company building was on fire.

redact [rɪ'dækt] *v.* 编写；校订

The news was redacted before it got the chance to air.

moot [muːt] *v.* 争议；假设　*n.* 辩论会　*adj.* 有争议的；假设的

The issue has been mooted several years ago.

Law students competed in a moot.

It is a moot point whether or not the island belongs to Korea.

Their agreement became moot when the defendant pleaded guilty.

parley ['pɑːrli] *v./n.* 会谈；谈判

The English captain decided to parley with the pirates.

palette ['pælət] *n.* 调色板；主色调

The painter favors a lighter palette.

a palette of 许多

She has a palette of creativity.

The chef can create a palette of flavors.

pallet ['pælət] *n.* 草垫子；托盘

The old man slept in a pallet of mats.

touchy ['tʌtʃi] *adj.* 易怒的；敏感的

She is very touchy about the problem.

The smart staff was asked to deal with the touchy issue.

Part 3　识记单词 / 词组

whitewater [ˌwaɪt'wɔːtə] *n.* 急流

whitewater rafting 泛舟

worth someone's salt 称职的

saline ['seɪliːn] *n.* 盐水　*adj.* 盐的

salinity [sə'lɪnəti] *n.* 盐度

arsenal ['ɑːrsənl] *n.* 军火库

dictatorship [ˌdɪk'teɪtərʃɪp] *n.* 独裁；专政

autocrat [ˈɔːtəkræt] *n.* 独裁者；专制君主
mime [maɪm] *v.* 表演哑剧 *n.* 哑剧
wage [weɪdʒ] *v.* 开始；发动（战争） *n.* 工资
devolutionist [ˌdiːvəˈluːʃənɪst] *n.* 主张放权者
aphorism [ˈæfərɪzəm] *n.* 格言；警句
catchphrase [ˈkætʃfreɪz, ˈketʃfreɪz] *n.* 标语；警句
rapist [ˈreɪpɪst] *n.* 强奸犯
a moot court 一次模拟法庭
nonentity [nɑːnˈentəti] *n.* 不重的人；不重要的东西
mat [mæt] *n.* 垫子；草席

Lesson 8

Part 1 主力单词/词组

upsides and downsides 好处和坏处
Given the upsides and downsides of industrialization, the aboriginal inhabitants have chosen their traditional way of life to restore nature.

pros and cons 正反两方面
Given the pros and cons of initiating nuclear power generation, we adopted ocean power generation.

advantages and disadvantages 优点和缺点
The advantages and disadvantages of going or not going have been posted on our school bulletin.

• Words in sentences 句中单词/词组 •

aboriginal [ˌæbəˈrɪdʒnl] *n.* 土著居民 *adj.* 原始的
initiate [ɪˈnɪʃieɪt] *v.* 采用；开办
bulletin [ˈbʊlətɪn] *n.* 公布栏

Part 2 补充单词 / 词组

untoward [ʌnˈtɔːrd] *adj.* 棘手的；不幸的
The teacher tries to reason with an untoward student.
She had experienced an untoward fate in her childhood.

media literacy 识字；读写能力
Do you think a reporter should have basic media literacy?

meretricious [ˌmerəˈtrɪʃəs] *adj.* 华而不实的；虚有其表的
The boss might have meretricious relationships with his secretary.

trumpery [ˈtrʌmpəri] *n.* 实际价值低的东西 *adj.* 中看不中用的
The clothes were considered to be gaudy trumperies.
The living room was filled with household trumperies.

gimcrack [ˈdʒɪmkræk] *n.* 粗制滥造的东西 *adj.* 华而不实的；粗制滥造的
This gimcrack cookware is rusted only after a couple of weeks.

gewgaw [ˈgjuːgɔː, ˈguːgɔː] *n.* 耀眼而便宜的小东西
My little sister spent a remarkable amount of money on gimcracks and gewgaws.

treatise [ˈtriːtɪs] *n.* 论文；专著
He wrote a treatise on sensors for his graduate degree.
The professor in the law school composed a learned legal treatise.

disquisition [ˌdɪskwɪˈzɪʃn] *n.* 专题论文；学术讨论
His writings include disquisitions on literature and art history.

Part 3 识记单词 / 词组

inhabitant [ɪnˈhæbɪtənt] *n.* 居民

initiator [ɪˈnɪʃieɪtər] *n.* 发起人；创始人

restoration [ˌrestəˈreɪʃn] *n.* 复原；整修

indigenous [ɪnˈdɪdʒənəs] *adj.* 当地的

indigenous plant 当地的植物

diplomatic privilege 外交豁免权

executive privilege 行政官员豁免权

diplomatic immunity　外交豁免权

literacy skill　读写能力

personage [ˈpɜːrsənɪdʒ]　n. 大人物；名人

Lesson 9

Part 1　主力单词 / 词组

assess [əˈses]　v. 衡量；评估

The price and quality will be assessed.

The doctor will assess your health by performing a battery of tests.

The computer assessed the damage of the spacecraft indicating some minor scratches on the hull.

evaluate [ɪˈvæljueɪt]　v. 评估；评价

A performance indicator has been set up to evaluate each individual's performance.

appraise [əˈpreɪz]　v. 评估；鉴定

The artist appraises the painting of the Mona Lisa up to 1 million dollars.

gauge [ɡeɪdʒ]　v. 评估；测量　n. 测量仪器；宽度；口径

Even a fool can gauge your strength which you had better hide before a fight.

GDP is the broadest gauge of a nation's economy.

What gauge of metal wire do you need?

measure [ˈmeʒər]　v. 测量　n. 措施；方法；（一定的）程度

The sea is too deep to measure.

The drastic measure has to be taken to turn the table around.

She felt equal measures of hope and despair.

He was highly motivated to study in large measure by his adoration for his English teacher.

A measure of technical knowledge is preferable in this job.

weight [weɪt]　v. 加上重量；使加权　n. 重量；重物

assessment [əˈsesmənt]　n. 评价

evaluation [ɪˌvæljuˈeɪʃn]　n. 估价；评价

appraisal [ə'preɪzl]　n. 鉴定；估价

measurement ['meʒərmənt]　n. 衡量；尺寸

weigh up　权衡；评估

● Words in sentences 句中单词/词组 ●

hull [hʌl]　v. 剥去（大豆等的）外壳；摘掉（草莓的）花萼　n. 船体；外壳

drastic ['dræstɪk]　adj. 激烈的；剧烈的

turn the table around　扭转局面；转败为胜

adoration [ˌædə'reɪʃn]　n. 崇拜；爱慕

Part 2　补充单词/词组

inaccessible [ˌɪnæk'sesəbl]　adj. 难到达的；难接近的
The ridge of the mountain is an unparalleled, inaccessible setting.

equalizer ['iːkwəlaɪzər]　n. 使平等的东西；均衡器
Coronavirus and education are great equalizers. Even affluents got contracted.

chiaroscuro [kiˌɑːrə'skʊroʊ]　n.（绘画的）明暗对照法
He creates his paintings by chiaroscuro and impasto.

sfumato [sfuː'mɑːtəʊ]　n. 晕涂法
The painting *Mona Lisa* is a consummate example of sfumato and chiaroscuro.

apprentice [ə'prentɪs]　v. 使某人当学徒　n. 学徒
I am an apprentice who needs to be taught.

indent [ɪn'dent, 'ɪndent]　v. 形成锯齿状；缩格　n. 缩格
The coastline was indented by waves.
Begin each paragraph with an indent as you write.

indentation [ˌɪnden'teɪʃn]　n. 凹陷；行首缩进
There is an indentation on the hood of her car.

indenture [ɪnˈdentʃər]　v. 使签约为学徒　n.（旧时的）师徒契约

The slave wanted to end his indentured service.
The apprentice signed an indenture with his master.

daub [dɔːb]　v. 涂；乱画　n. 涂料；拙劣的画

I am going to daub my bread with butter and jam.
The painter daubed pink paint on the wall.

perfume [pərˈfjuːm]　n. 香水；喷香水

She daubs some perfume on her wrist.

perfumery [pərˈfjuːməri]　n. 香水（总称）

denture [ˈdentʃər]　n. 一副假牙

My grandfather ordered a set of dentures.

contract [ˈkɑːntrækt, kənˈtrækt]　v. 订契约；缩小；染病　n. 契约

Metal contracts as it cools.
He contracted a disease in a hospital.
He will sign the contract.

Part 3　识记单词/词组

weigh sth out　称出（一定重量的某物）

weights and measures　度量衡

weigh sb/sth down　压倒；压弯

weigh in　称体重；积极参与

weigh sb's words　斟酌某人的字句

pull sb's weight　负担某人的工作或责任

throw sb's weight around　某人的控制欲强的状态

setting [ˈsetɪŋ]　n. 位置；环境

have the measure of sb/sth　了解……

hulk [hʌlk]　v. 赫然显现；笨重地移动　n. 残骸；巨大笨重的人（物）

impasto [ɪmˈpæstoʊ]　n. 厚涂颜料的绘画法；厚涂的颜料

impaste [ɪmˈpeɪst]　v. 在……上涂厚厚的一层漆；用浆糊封……

Lesson 10

Part 1 主力单词 / 词组

pragmatic [præg'mætɪk] *adj.* 实用的

Most corporation founders are realists who use a pragmatic approach instead of an ideological one.

The pragmatic successor of the corporation has this kind of persona that devotes no time or inclination to deal with social morality.

pragmatist ['prægmətɪst] *n.* 实用主义者

The pragmatist knows that doubt is an art which has to be acquired with difficulty. (C. S. Peirce, U.S. physicist and logician)

practical ['præktɪkl] *adj.* 实用的

This stylish, meretricious book has no practical use regardless of its cover of fig leaves.

The Declaration of Independence...is an eminently practical document, meant for the use of practical men; not a thesis for philosophers, but a whip for tyrants; not a theory of government, but a program for action. (Woodrow Wilson, U.S. president)

realistic [ˌriːə'lɪstɪk] *n.* 现实的；实事求是的

A realistic appraisal of an international landscape is paramount for a diplomat.

feasible ['fiːzəbl] *adj.* 可行的；可用的

The patent will be commercially feasible.

The president wants us to make a feasible plan to land on Saturn next year.

utilitarian [ˌjuːtɪlɪ'terɪən] *n.* 功利主义者 *adj.* 实用的；功利的

Rare metals are mined for utilitarian purposes.

They shouldn't have to justify their existence by utilitarian criteria.

We will destroy museums and libraries, and fight against moralism, feminism, and all utilitarian cowardice. (Filippo Tommaso Marinetti, Italian writer, poet, and political activist)

pragmaticism [præg'mætɪsɪzəm] *n.* 实用主义

practicality [ˌpræktɪ'kæləti] *n.* 实用性；实例

Lesson 10

feasibility [ˌfiːzə'bɪləti]　*n.* 可行性；可能性

utilitarianism [ˌjuːtɪlɪ'teərɪənɪzəm]　*n.* 功利主义

• Words in sentences 句中单词 / 词组 •

ideological [ˌaɪdɪə'lɑːdʒɪkl, ˌɪdɪə'lɑːdʒɪkl]　*adj.* 意识形态的

persona [pər'soʊnə]　*n.* 人物角色；伪装的外表

inclination [ˌɪnklɪ'neɪʃn]　*n.* 倾向；爱好

thesis ['θiːsɪs]　*n.* 论文

tyrant ['taɪrənt]　*n.* 暴君

Saturn ['sætɜːrn]　*n.* 土星；农业之神

moralism ['mɔːrəlɪzəm]　*n.* 道德准则

feminism ['femənɪzəm]　*n.* 女权主义；争取女权的运动

cowardice ['kaʊərdɪs]　*n.* 懦弱

Part 2　补充单词 / 词组

corporation [ˌkɔːrpə'reɪʃn]　*n.* 公司

metallurgical [ˌmetl'ɜːrdʒɪkl]　*adj.* 冶金学的

The corporation produces fissionable material by putting raw uranium through a long series of chemical and metallurgical processes.

saturnine ['sætərnaɪn]　*adj.* 忧郁的

Charlotte has a saturnine temperament.

The hopeless conditions are often found in saturnine dramas.

patent ['pætnt, 'peɪtnt]　*v.* 给予……专利权　*n.* 专利权　*adj.* 专利权的；明显的；可公开调查的

His concept of designing a future car was patented.

She is a patent lawyer.

Everybody knows about his patent lie.

They settled the patent dispute last year.

cathedral [kə'θiːdrəl]　*n.* 大教堂　*adj.* 主教堂的

Universities are the cathedrals of the modern age.

poltroon [pɑːlˈtruːn]　*n.* 懦夫；胆小鬼

We all live in a world of bullies and poltroons.

recreant [ˈrekriənt]　*n.* 懦夫　*adj.* 怯懦的

Grace was upset by her recreant lover.
These recreant soldiers retreat automatically without any order.
He is recreant to the king by conspiring with the enemy.

rakish [ˈreɪkɪʃ]　*adj.* 时髦的；（船）轻快的

There are rakish boys on the rakish yacht.

regatta [rɪˈgætə, rɪˈgɑːtə]　*n.* 划船比赛

The sailor attended the annual regatta in the Mississippi River.

literature [ˈlɪtərətʃʊr]　*n.* 文学；文学作品

I have to read a great deal of literature concerning automobiles.

Part 3　识记单词/词组

infeasible [ɪnˈfiːzəbəl]　*adj.* 不可实行的

theoretic=theoretical　*adj.* 理论上的；空谈的

theorize [ˈθiːəraɪz, ˈθɪraɪz]　*v.* 建立学说；提出关于……的理论

theorization [ˌθiəraɪˈzeɪʃn]　*n.* 理论；理论化

yacht [jɑːt]　*v.* 乘游艇　*n.* 快艇

fig [fɪg]　*n.* 无花果

tyranny [ˈtɪrəni]　*n.* 暴政

tyrannical [tɪˈrænɪkl]　*adj.* 专制的；残暴的

document [ˈdɑːkjumənt]　*v.* 文件；证件

startup [ˈstɑːrtˌʌp]　*n.* 新兴小型企业

criteria [kraɪˈtɪriə]　*n.* 标准；准则

criterion [kraɪˈtɪriən]　*n.* criteria 的单数

metalize [ˈmetlˌaɪz]　*v.* 以金属处理

metallization [ˌmetəlaɪˈzeɪʃn, -lɪˈz-]　*n.* 镀金法

metallurgy [ˈmetələːrdʒi]　*n.* 冶金学

powder metallurgy　粉末冶金学

fission [ˈfɪʃn]　*n.* 分裂

fissionable [ˈfɪʃənəbl] *adj.* 可分裂的；可裂变的
nuclear fission 原子核分裂；核裂变

Lesson 11

Part 1 主力单词 / 词组

congenial [kənˈdʒiːniəl] *adj.* 舒适的；友善的；意气相投的
I enjoy the tourist resort of Thailand with a congenial atmosphere.
The septuagenarian decorates his restaurant with antiquated style and runs it with his equally congenial son.
The dog is vicious, not congenial at all.
I prefer congenial companions to travel with me.

convivial [kənˈvɪviəl] *adj.* 友好的；欢乐的；愉悦的
She plays a convivial character with a sanguine personality.

amity [ˈæməti] *n.* 和睦；友好
The treaty of peace and amity has been signed by both nations.
Positivism has long sought to establish amity with intellectuals.

rapport [ræˈpɔːr] *n.* 友好；和睦的关系
The new regime of the Philippines seeks a closer rapport with China.
The rapport between the horse and its rider can be sensed.

rapprochement [ˌræproʊʃˈmɑːn, ˌræprɑːʃˈmɑːn] *n.* 建立或恢复友好关系；和睦
The possible rapprochement is slim between the Israeli and the Palestinian.
The rapprochement between guerrilla and government has been broken.

• Words in sentences 句中单词 / 词组 •

septuagenarian [ˌseptʃuədʒəˈneriən] *n.* 七十多岁的人
decorate [ˈdekəreɪt] *v.* 装饰；装点；打扮
antiquated [ˈæntɪkweɪtɪd] *adj.* 过时的

positivism [ˈpɑːzətɪvɪzəm] *n.* 实证主义
regime [reɪˈʒiːm] *n.* 政府；政权
Israeli [ɪzˈreɪli] *n.* 以色列人 *adj.* 以色列的

Part 2 补充单词 / 词组

personality [ˌpɜːrsəˈnæləti] *n.* 个性；名人
Don't let the discussion deteriorate into personalities.

emanate [ˈeməneɪt] *v.* 放射；散发出；起源
The ragged beggar emanates a miasma of poverty.
The shivering kids emanate a miasma of fear.

miasma [miˈæzmə, maɪˈæzmə] *n.* 不好的氛围；有害的烟雾
I sniffed a miasma of tobacco.

sniff [snɪf] *v.* 闻；用力吸；抽鼻涕；嗤之以鼻
I catch a cold and sniff.
She didn't take me seriously and sniffed at my idea.

pristine [ˈprɪstiːn] *adj.* 原始的；清新的
I sniffed fresh air in the pristine forest.
I enjoy the pristine beauty of rural areas.

tissue [ˈtɪʃuː] *n.* 面纸；组织（生物）
Do you have any tissues?

bauble [ˈbɔːbl] *n.* 小玩意儿；美观的廉价货
The girl who peddles baubles in the street is my niece.

sphere [sfɪr] *n.* 范围；领域；地位
The tribe tries to preserve its sphere of influence by attacking western invaders.
Ancient women were confined to the domestic sphere.
All points on a sphere have an equal distance from the center.

gamut [ˈgæmət] *n.* 全部；整个范围；音域
She experienced the full gamut of fates from penniless to affluent.
The rich man ran the gamut from praise to contempt.

The song is too high out of my gamut.

ornate [ɔːrˈneɪt]　*adj.* 装饰的；华丽的

His speech is clear and simple rather than ornate and pompous.

The ornate crystal chandelier radiates a splendid light.

rococo [rəˈkoʊkoʊ]　*n.* 洛可可式　*adj.* 洛可可式的

The elaborate work of baroque and rococo buildings in Rome impressed me.

milieu [mɪlˈjuː]　*n.* 出身背景；周围环境

Italy has a milieu of art.

The author depicts a low-class milieu vividly.

The criminologist studies on a criminal's milieu.

mettle [ˈmetl]　*n.* 秉性；气质

All the hardships will serve as nothing, but a touchstone to one's mettle.

He is a man of brave mettle.

The lieutenant has proved his mettle in battle.

Part 3　识记单词 / 词组

congenial company　友善的伙伴

congenial surrounding　令人愉快的环境

convivial atmosphere　欢乐的气氛

convivial host　热情的主人

emanation [ˌeməˈneɪʃn]　*n.* 发出；流出；散发

emanate from　由……而来；由……散发出来

emanationism [ˌeməˈneɪʃənɪzəm]　*n.* 发散说

shiver [ˈʃɪvər]　*v./n.* 发抖；打颤

sniff out　发现

sphere of infuence　势力范围

run the gamut of/from…to　经历……全过程

out of gamut　超出音域范围

server [ˈsɜːrvər]　*n.* 侍者；餐具

wait on　侍候；为……服务

baroque [bəˈroʊk]　*adj.* 巴洛克式的

pompous [ˈpɑːmpəs] *adj.* 浮夸的；壮丽的
chandelier [ˌʃændəˈlɪr] *n.* 枝形吊灯
ambiance=ambience *n.* 周围环境；气氛
companion [kəmˈpænjən] *n.* 同伴
Israelite [ˈɪzriəlaɪt] *n.* 古以色列人；希伯来人

Lesson 12

Part 1 主力单词 / 词组

equivalent [ɪˈkwɪvələnt] *n.* 相等的东西；对应词 *adj.* 相等的；对等物的

Taking without notifying is equivalent to stealing.
Have you taken Math 201? I took the equivalent course at another university.
The two rival companies always manufacture equivalent products.
Samadhi is an ancient Sanskrit word, for which there is no modern equivalent.
He considered the deposition as the equivalent of a death sentence.

synonymous with 与……同义

Extirpating the grassland is synonymous with deprivation of buffaloes' livelihood.

comport [kəmˈpɔːrt] *v.* 举止；行为；相称；合适

The student comports well in the classroom.
The punishment of castration toward a thief in Arabia doesn't comport with human dignity.
My conduct comported with school regulations.

accord [əˈkɔːrd] *v.* 使一致；授予 *n.* 协议；条约；自愿

The two boys' descriptions of the accident accorded with each other.
I came here of my own accord. No one forced me.
The U.S. pulled out of the nuclear accord with Russia and withdrew from the Paris climate accord.
People with different nationalities should be accorded equal respect.
According to what you said, he must be a brute.

accordance [əˈkɔːrdns] *n.* 一致；符合；授予

The police acted in accordance with the law.

amount [ə'maʊnt] n. 数量；总额

amount to 等于；总计

Their statement amounts to nothing more than a slick evasion of the real issue.

The damage amounted to 1 million dollars.

equal ['iːkwəl] v. 等于；与……相等 n. 相等物 adj. 平等的

Two plus two equals four.

Nothing in the world can equal his stupidity.

He treats us as equals.

All men were born equal. Do you think he is equal to the task?

equity ['ekwəti] n. 公平；公正；股本

equality [iˈkwɑːləti] n. 平等；均等；相等

The government has promoted gender equality.

Democracy might bring equality and liberty.

The ruling party has made a commitment to equity, equality and justice.

• **Words in sentences 句中单词 / 词组** •

notify ['noʊtɪfaɪ] v. 通知；告知

rival ['raɪvl] v. 与……相匹敌 n. 竞争对手 adj. 竞争的

Samadhi [sʌ'mɑːdi] n. 三摩地（禅定）

Sanskrit ['sænskrɪt] n. 梵语

buffaloes' livelihood 水牛的生计

castration [kæ'streɪʃn] n. 阉割

brute [bruːt] n. 残暴的人；畜生 adj. 赤裸裸的

Part 2 补充单词 / 词组

climate ['klaɪmət] n. 气候；趋势

I don't like the cold weather and will move to a sunnier climate.

according to 根据；按照

They arranged the spare parts according to size.

spare [speɪ] *adj.* 备用的；多余的

sparing ['speɪrɪŋ] *adj.* 节约的；贫乏的
He is introverted and sparing with words.

spare part 备用零件

apprise [ə'praɪz] *v.* 通知
I apprise my mother I will not be home until 8 o'clock.
Would you keep me apprised of your whereabouts?

expostulate [ɪk'spɑːstʃuleɪt] *v.* 劝告；反对
He was dissatisfied with his integrity and expostulated on his proposal.
Do not expostulate with me. I am going to do it anyway.

expostulation [ɪkˌspɔstjuˈleɪʃən] *n.* 劝告；忠告
She tends to ignore others' expostulation.

inadmissible [ˌɪnədˈmɪsəbl] *adj.* 不允许的；不可接受的
The evidence is too weak, inadmissible in court.

entree ['ɑːntreɪ] *n.* 入场许可；主菜
Do I need an entree to enter this club?
What would you like for your entree? Steak or Salmon?

admissible [ədˈmɪsəbl] *adj.* 有资格进入的；有资格就任的
Her SAT score is admissible to the university.

crusade [kruːˈseɪd] *n.* 改革运动 *v.* 从事改革运动

crusader [kruːˈseɪdər] *n.* 改革者；十字军战士

theocracy [θiˈɑːkrəsi] *n.* 神权政治
The crusaders failed to subdue the Muslim theocracy.

Part 3 识记单词 / 词组

equivalence [ɪˈkwɪvələns] *n.* 等价；均等
identical to 与……相同
tantamount to 等于；相当于

synonym [ˈsɪnənɪm] n. 同义词
antonym [ˈæntənɪm] n. 反义词
comportment [kəmˈpɔːrtmənt] n. 举止
notification [ˌnoʊtɪfɪˈkeɪʃn] n. 通知
medical attention 医护人员的协助
in accord with 与……一致
extirpate [ˈekstərpeɪt] v. 灭绝（斩草除根）
deprive [dɪˈpraɪv] v. 剥夺
bison [ˈbaɪsn] n. 北美野牛；欧洲野牛
contend [kənˈtend] v. 争辩；声称；主张
postulate [ˈpɑːstʃəleɪt, ˈpɑːstʃələt] v. 假定；假设
graze [greɪz] v. 放牧；吃草；轻擦
misconduct [ˌmɪsˈkɑːndʌkt] n. 不端行为 v. 对……管理不善
castrate [ˈkæstreɪt] v. 阉割

Lesson 13

Part 1 主力单词 / 词组

momentary [ˈmoʊmənteri] *adj.* 短暂的；瞬息的

Anger is a momentary madness, so control your passion or it will control you. (Horace, Roman poet)
Apnea is a momentary cessation of breathing.
A momentary slip or lapse in concentration might be fatal during a military exercise.

transient [ˈtrænʃnt] *n.* 暂住者 *adj.* 短暂的

I obsess over her transient beauty.
Propose to her immediately, otherwise, you might miss this transient opportunity.
The life of ephemera, which only lives one day, is transient.

transitory [ˈtrænzətɔːri, ˈtrænsətɔːri] *adj.* 短暂的；转瞬即逝的

The transitory nature of life has reminded us that life is a journey, but not a destination.

fleet [fli:t] *v.* 快速移动　*n.* 舰队　*adj.* 快速的

Time fleets as I look back.

fleeting [ˈfli:tɪŋ] *adj.* 短暂的；迅速的

Seize this fleeting, refulgent moment holding her hand tightly through the treacherous forest while you can.

ephemeral [ɪˈfemərəl] *adj.* 短暂的；极短的

Fashions are ephemeral, as they are constantly changing.

evanesce [ˌevəˈnes] *v.* 消逝

The traditional culture had evanesced.

evanescent [ˌevəˈnesnt, ˌi:vəˈnesnt] *adj.* 短暂的；转瞬即逝的

The chemist imparts the perfume with evanescent fruit odors.

trice [traɪs] *v.* 吊起　*n.* 短暂的时间

in a trice 瞬间

Their amicability recedes in a trice upon knowing our true intention.

- **Words in sentences 句中单词 / 词组** •

apnea [ˈæpniə] *n.* 窒息；无呼吸
refulgent [rɪˈfʌldʒənt] *adj.* 闪闪发光的
impart [ɪmˈpɑ:rt] *v.* 赋予；给予
recede [rɪˈsi:d] *v.* 后退；撤回；降低

Part 2　补充单词 / 词组

coma [ˈkoʊmə] *n.* 昏迷

comatose [ˈkoʊmətoʊs] *adj.* 昏迷的

He has become comatose and terminally ill due to severe brain damage.

megalomania [ˌmegələˈmeɪniə] *n.* 自大狂

The powerful bereaved person didn't shed his tear and had a reputation of selfishness and megalomania.

megalomaniac [ˌmeɡələˈmeɪniæk] n. 自大狂患者；自大狂的人

The megalomaniac differs from the narcissist by the fact that he wishes to be powerful rather than charming and seeks to be feared rather than loved. (Bertrand Russell, British philosopher and mathematician)

interregnum [ˌɪntəˈreɡnəm] n. 空位期；过渡期

Bulgaria was invaded during the interregnum.

armada [ɑːrˈmɑːdə] n. 舰队；机群

patrol [pəˈtroʊl] v. 巡逻；侦察 n. 巡逻；侦察；巡逻机队

An immense armada of German submarines patrolled in the western parts of the Atlantic.

obsess [əbˈses] v. 使着迷

She is obsessed with power.

obsession [əbˈseʃn] n. 痴迷；使人痴迷的人（或物）

I have an obsession with her.
Gamble becomes her obsession since she has nothing to do.

maniacal [məˈnaɪəkl] adj. 发狂的；癫狂的

She tries to reason with a maniacal killer.

saccharine [ˈsækərɪn] adj. 糖质的；故作多情的

The comedic movie tends to have a saccharine ending.

groom [ɡruːm] v. 擦洗 n. 新郎；马夫

overly [ˈoʊvərli] adv. 过度地；极度地

The groom was overly late which cast a blight at the wedding.

blight [blaɪt] v. 破坏；妨害 n. 疫病；不利因素

The divorce of his parents has blighted his academic performance.

terminus [ˈtɜːrmɪnəs] n. 终点；目标；界限

Geologists mapped out the terminus of the glacier.
Neither the river's origin nor its terminus has yet been determined.
The nation moved the terminus secretly at the northern border.

Part 3　识记单词 / 词组

perm [pɜːrm] v. 烫发；卷发

permanent [ˈpɜːrmənənt]   *n.* 烫发   *adj.* 长期的
be/fall prey to sth   成为……的牺牲品；被……欺骗
prey on   捕食；掠夺
lapse into   陷入；显得异常
lapse into silence   陷入了沉默
lapse into a coma   陷入昏迷状态
military exercise   军演
a war correspondent   一名战地记者
fatal virus   致命的病毒
impart the bad news   告知坏消息
urban blight   城市恶化的情况
recede from a promise   背弃诺言
transient government   临时政府
saccharin [ˈsækərɪn]   *n.* 糖精
lapse [læps]   *v.* 流失
mania [ˈmeɪniə]   *n.* 疯狂；狂热
maniac [ˈmeɪniæk]   *n.* 狂人
madness [ˈmædnəs]   *n.* 狂怒；疯狂的行为；精神失常

Lesson 14

Part 1 主力单词 / 词组

sorrowful [ˈsɑːroʊfl]   *adj.* 悲痛的；悔恨的
Wandering through many countries and over many seas, I come, my brother, to these sorrowful obsequies, to present you with the last guerdon of death, and speak, though in vain, to your silent ashes.

sorrow [ˈsɑːroʊ]   *n.* 悲痛；悔恨
With sorrow and despair, the ragged orphan noctivagates along the street feeling like he has been a ghost already.

mourn [mɔːrn] v. 哀悼；悲伤

Will you mourn for his death?

mournful [ˈmɔːrnfl] adj. 悲伤的；哀痛的

She spoke with a mournful tone as if her pet had died.

doleful [ˈdoʊlfl] adj. 悲伤的

Tears dripped down from his doleful eyes as he heard of his mother's demise.

melancholy [ˈmelənkɑːli] n. 忧郁；伤悲 adj. 悲哀的；沮丧的

She has a feeling of melancholy seeing autumn leaves falling down.

disconsolate [dɪsˈkɑːnsələt] adj. 忧郁的；哀伤的；无法平复的

He feels disconsolate that he should be a king, not a prisoner.

My best friend dies. I just have the most disconsolate moment in my life, and you laugh at me.

He betook himself, with a disconsolate widow and bedfellow, to a barn nearby a small river.

dismal [ˈdɪzməl] adj. 悲伤绝望的

I have experienced another dismal night, in the dreamland of which nightmare seems to coexist with me.

despondent [dɪˈspɑːndənt] adj. 郁闷的

Did you recall how despondent and disheartened we were? Returning home seemed to be a distant dream.

plaintive [ˈpleɪntɪv] adj. 伤感的

He is prone to compose a plaintive melody.

Her voice sounds plaintive over her father's death.

sentimental [ˌsentɪˈmentl] adj. 多愁善感的；感情用事的

Some elder Chinese have a sentimental attachment to China's past before economic reform.

She is very sentimental and lachrymose.

sentimentality [ˌsentɪmenˈtæləti] n. 感伤情调；多愁善感

Her cloying sentimentality almost made me puke. I always felt she feigned crying.

maudlin [ˈmɔːdlɪn] adj. 伤感的；容易流泪的

I can see not one ray of brightness, not one flash of gaiety, only maudlin joviality, or grim despair on her face.

I like maudlin lyrics more than jovial ones.

I always have maudlin sentiment toward the poor.

The old man cracks open another beer and becomes maudlin.

mawkish [ˈmɔːkɪʃ] *adj.* 多愁善感的；自怜的；无味的

He is used to having mawkish sentiment towards the homeless.

I like mawkish love stories.

They disliked the mawkish dish.

lugubrious [ləˈɡuːbriəs] *adj.* 忧伤的

The cello is not one of my favorite instruments. It has such a lugubrious sound, like someone reading a will.

grieve [ɡriːv] *v.* 悲痛；悲伤

She grieves over her son's death.

aggrieve [əˈɡriːv] *v.* 使悲痛；使受委屈

aggrieved [əˈɡriːvd] *adj.* 受委屈的；怨愤的

We all felt aggrieved that an innocent man was sentenced to jail.

The government encourages the commonalty not to dread or be aggrieved at the loss of their property in the fire.

wistful [ˈwɪstfl] *adj.* 伤感的；渴望的；留恋的

She gave me a wistful look before she said goodbye.

elegy [ˈelədʒi] *n.* 哀歌；挽歌

He works in the funeral industry, good at writing elegy and eulogy.

eulogy [ˈjuːlədʒi] *n.* 悼词；赞词

She wrote an incredible eulogy for his father.

elegiac [ˌelɪˈdʒaɪək] *n.* 挽歌 *adj.* 挽歌的；哀伤的

I can't stand the elegiac tone of the erhu.

The movie portrays the wistful, elegiac mood of a lost orphan.

atrabilious [ˌætrəˈbɪljəs] *adj.* 心情不好的；忧郁的

The bereft person has a gloomy, atrabilious mood.

Atrabilious maladies include lovesickness and melancholia.

threnody [ˈθrenədi] *n.* 挽歌；哀悼

She sang a brooding threnody.

bilious [ˈbɪliəs] *adj.* 坏脾气的；恶心的

The bilious white looks like a dead man's face.

Lesson 14

lachrymose [ˈlækrɪmoʊs] *adj.* 催泪的；悲伤的；易落泪的
It was a lachrymose movie. The leading actress died at the end for a noble cause.

lugubriousness [luːˈguːbrɪəsnəs] *n.* 忧伤；悲伤

grief [griːf] *n.* 悲伤

eulogistic [ˌjuːləˈdʒɪstɪk] *adj.* 赞颂的

elegiacal [ˌeliˈdʒaɪəkəl] *adj.* 挽歌的；哀悼的

threnodist [ˈθrenədɪst] *n.* 挽歌之作者；唱挽歌者

bile [baɪl] *n.* 胆汁；不开心；坏脾气

• Words in sentences 句中单词/词组 •

obsequies [ˈɑːbsəkwiz] *n.* 葬礼；丧礼

guerdon [ˈɡɜːdən] *n.* 报酬；奖赏

ragged [ˈræɡɪd] *adj.* 衣服破烂的

drip [drɪp] *v.* 滴下

widow [ˈwɪdoʊ] *v.* 使丧偶 *n.* 寡妇

bedfellow [ˈbedfeloʊ] *n.* 伙伴；同床之人

coexist [ˌkoʊɪɡˈzɪst] *v.* 共存

disheartened [dɪsˈhɑːrtnd] *adj.* 绝望的

lachrymose [ˈlækrɪmoʊs] *adj.* 催泪的；悲伤的；易落泪的

cloy [klɔɪ] *v.* 感到腻烦；倒胃口

puke [pjuːk] *v.* 呕吐 *n.* 呕吐物

lyric [ˈlɪrɪk] *n.* 歌词；抒情诗 *adj.* 抒情的

erhu [ˈɜːrhuː] *n.* 二胡

lovesickness [ˈlʌvˌsɪknɪs] *n.* 相思病

melancholia [ˌmelənˈkoʊliə] *n.* 忧郁症

Part 2 补充单词/词组

jubilate [ˈdʒuːbəˌleɪt] *v.* 扬声欢呼；欢喜

jubilation [ˌdʒuːbɪˈleɪʃn] *n.* 欢腾；欢庆

This is a day of jubilation, a day of remembrance and gratitude. Our common task now is to establish a new European order.

jocund [ˈdʒɑːkənd, ˈdʒoʊkənd] *adj.* 欢乐的；快活的

Kids have a jocund day in an amusement park.

jocundity [dʒoʊˈkʌndəti] *n.* 欢乐；快活；欢乐的话

The gloomy movie is lacking in jocundity.

mete [miːt] *v.* 分配；给予 *n.* 分配；给予；边界；界石

The judge metes out severe punishment to the felon.

peter out 逐渐结束；逐渐消亡

Their romantic relationship petered out as her husband worked abroad.

presentiment [prɪˈzentɪmənt] *n.*（尤指不祥的）预感

I have a presentiment that she will study biology for the rest of her life.

noctivagant [nɒkˈtivəgənt] *adj.* 晚间徘徊的；夜游的

There are noctivagant prostitutes.

tatter [ˈtætər] *v.* 撕碎 *n.* 碎布

China rebuilt the tattered political and economic system after the Warlord Era.
The soldier wearing a tattered uniform looks like a bandit.

tatterdemalion [ˌtætədəˈmeiljən, -ˈmæ-] *n.* 穿着褴褛衣服的人 *adj.* 衣服褴褛的

A tatterdemalion walked along the street asking for food.

saccharine [ˈsækərɪn] *adj.* 甜腻的；过于殷勤的

The viewers consider the television special too saccharine and cloying.

coy [kɔɪ] *adj.* 装腼腆的；含糊其词的

Anderson is coy about the company's investment.
I don't know if she loves me or not from her coy response.
Her coy trick has won her the attention of many gentlemen.

flashy [ˈflæʃi] *adj.* 华丽的；闪耀的

Richard likes to show off his flashy luxurious car.

sanguine [ˈsæŋgwɪn] *adj.* 乐观的；乐天的

The fashion model who has a sanguine personality is a sweet, jocund companion.

Lesson 14

exhort [ɪɡˈzɔːrt]　*v.* 激励；规劝；告诫

He exhorted his warriors to fight to the very end.
I exhorted him not to go into the enchanted forest.

exhortation [ˌeɡzɔːrˈteɪʃn]　*n.* 讲道词；训词；劝告

He has become a champion by his coach's exhortation and guidance.

hortatory=exhortatory　*adj.* 劝告的；激励性的

I like the hortatory movies more than the comic ones.
My friend wrote me a hortatory epistle.

uniformity [ˌjuːnɪˈfɔːrməti]　*n.* 一致；单调；相同

Soldiers repeated the patriotic slogan with promptness and uniformity.

constant temperature　恒温

They secured the metal quality and uniformity by constant temperature.

Part 3　识记单词/词组

a forlorn figure　一个孤独的身影
a forlorn ghost town　一个空旷的鬼城
lorn [lɔːrn]　*adj.* 孤独的；郁郁寡欢的
be sb's pet　是某人的宠儿
dole [doʊl]　*v.* 发放　*n.* 赈济物
metes and bounds=boundary　边界
betake [bɪˈteɪk]　*v.* 使前往；致力于
lyrical [ˈlɪrɪkl]　*adj.* 抒情的；适于歌唱的
malady [ˈmælədi]　*n.* 疾病；（社会的）弊病；腐败
lovelorn [ˈlʌvlɔːrn]　*adj.* 单相思的；失恋的
forlorn [fərˈlɔːrn]　*adj.* 孤苦伶仃的；绝望的
nocturnal [nɑːkˈtɜːrnl]　*adj.* 夜间的
nocturnal animal　夜行动物
diurnal [daɪˈɜːrnl]　*adj.* 白天的；每天的
diurnal predator　白天的捕食者
prey [preɪ]　*v.* 捕食　*n.* 受害者
predation [prɪˈdeɪʃn]　*n.* 掠夺；掠食

console [ˈkɑːnsoʊl, kənˈsoʊl]   *v.* 安慰   *n.* 操纵台
extant [ekˈstænt, ˈekstənt]   *adj.* 至今尚存的
extant artefacts   至今尚存的手工艺品

Lesson 15

Part 1 主力单词 / 词组

privilege [ˈprɪvəlɪdʒ]   *v.* 给特权   *n.* 特权；荣幸

Obligations and privileges should be shared equally.

He was quite sure that he had been wronged. Not to be wronged is to forgo the first privilege of goodness. (H. G. Wells, British writer)

entitle [ɪnˈtaɪtl]   *v.* 给予权利；使有资格

Africans are entitled to all the rights, and privileges, and immunities by the constitution of the United States.

entitlement [ɪnˈtaɪtlmənt]   *n.* 权利；资格

The affluent politician has an arrogant sense of entitlement to the election.

prerogative [prɪˈrɑːɡətɪv]   *n.* 特权

Killing a slave with immunity was a prerogative of the aristocracy.

The president enjoys constitutional prerogative with derogatory attitudes toward developing countries.

vest [vest]   *v.* 给予……权力   *n.* 内衣；背心

The police were vested by the court to search his house with a warrant.

• Words in sentences 句中单词 / 词组 •

obligation [ˌɑːblɪˈɡeɪʃn]   *n.* 义务；责任；必须要做的事情

immunity [ɪˈmjuːnəti]   *n.* 豁免；免疫

aristocracy [ˌærɪˈstɑːkrəsi]   *n.* 贵族

derogatory [dɪˈrɑːɡətɔːri]   *adj.* 贬低的；诋毁的

Part 2　补充单词 / 词组

opiate [ˈoʊpiət] v. 用鸦片麻醉；使迟钝　n. 麻醉药　adj. 含鸦片的；催眠性的
Music and movies are opiates of his nostalgia.

opioid [ˈoʊpiˌɔɪd] n. 类鸦片药物　adj. 类鸦片的
Some teenagers suffer from opioid addiction.

obligatory [əˈblɪɡətɔːri] adj. 有义务的；必须的
The U.S. doesn't require obligatory military service.
The obligatory death scene has been overused.

peremptory [pəˈremptəri] adj. 独断的
The general talked to a soldier with a peremptory tone.
His peremptory disregard of the objection offends the public.

mandamus [mænˈdeɪməs] n. 执行令；命令书
The chief police received a peremptory mandamus to apprehend the suspect at once.

confidante [ˈkɑnfəˌdænt] n. 知己女友

butcher [ˈbʊtʃər] n. 屠夫；肉贩；屠杀

covet [ˈkʌvət] v. 觊觎；垂涎
She had become the confidante of a butcher which was not a privilege that others coveted.

thrall [θrɔːl] n. 束缚；奴役；吸引
He was in thrall to his emotional scars and misery.
The wonderful music held the audience in thrall.
The girl with sublime beauty held me in thrall.

warrant [ˈwɔːrənt] v. 保证；担保　n. 证明
It doesn't warrant your time on this lost cause.

arraign [əˈreɪn] v. 传讯；指责
He was arraigned on bribery charges dating back three years.
The religious leader was arraigned in the tabloids for misusing the donated money.

arraignment [əˈreɪnmənt] n. 传讯；提审
The judge presided over his arraignment.

omnipresent [ˌɑːmnɪˈpreznt] *adj.* 无所不在的；遍及各处的
Fungi are omnipresent organisms which cause mucor.

omniscient [ɑːmˈnɪʃnt] *adj.* 全知的；似乎全知的
Do not do bad things because God is omnipresent and omniscient.
The psychic who knows about your past seems to be omniscient.

omniscience [ɑːmˈnɪʃəns] *n.* 全知

omnivore [ˈɑːmnɪvɔːr] *n.* 杂食动物；杂食的人

omnivorous [ɑːmˈnɪvərəs] *adj.* 杂食的
Bears and pigs are omnivorous animals.

carnivore [ˈkɑːrnɪvɔːr] *n.* 食肉动物；食虫植物

carnivorous [kɑːrˈnɪvərəs] *adj.* 肉食性的
Lions are carnivorous animals.

herbivore [ˈɜːrbɪvɔːr, ˈhɜːrbɪvɔːr] *n.* 食草动物

herbivorous [ɜːrˈbɪvərəs, hɜːrˈbɪvərəs] *adj.* 食草的
Buffaloes are herbivorous animals.

pansophy [ˈpænsəfi] *n.* 无所不知；广博的知识

pansophic [pænˈsəfɪk] *adj.* 智慧的；知识的；科学的
I like the pansophic Indian guru.

pansophism [ˈpænsəfɪzəm] *n.* 自称无所不知

encyclopedia [ɪnˌsaɪkləˈpiːdiə] *n.* 百科全书
Some professors wrote a new pansophic encyclopedia.

vested interest 既得利益
The private company has a vested interest in buying this public chemical factory.
The Ministry of Finance would never really allow market supply and demand to determine exchange rates when political comrades have a vested interest in either high or low currency values.

Part 3　识记单词/词组

omnipotent [ɑːmˈnɪpətənt] *adj.* 万能的

omnificent [ɔm'nifisənt] *adj.* 创造万物的
omnirange [ˈɑːmnɪˌreɪndʒ] *n.* 多向导航系统
serf [sɜːrf] *n.* 农奴
slavery [ˈsleɪvəri] *n.* 奴隶制度
bondman [ˈbɑːndmən] *n.* 农奴
subpoena [sə'piːnə] *v.* 传唤
dishearten [dɪs'hɑːrtn] *v.* 使沮丧；使气馁
respondent [rɪ'spɑːndənt] *n.* 答复者；被告
correspondent [ˌkɔːrə'spɑːndənt] *n.* 记者
sentimentalize [ˌsentɪ'mentəlaɪz] *v.* 感伤地对待……
dowager [ˈdaʊədʒər] *n.* (继承财产、爵位的孀居) 贵妇
moody [ˈmuːdi] *adj.* 喜怒无常的；闷闷不乐的
moodiness [ˈmuːdinəs] *n.* 喜怒无常
ephemeron [ɪ'femə,rɑːn] *n.* 蜉蝣
ephemora=ephemerons *n.* 蜉蝣（复数）
cello [ˈtʃeloʊ] *n.* 大提琴
violin [ˌvaɪə'lɪn] *n.* 小提琴
jovially [ˈdʒoʊviəli] *adv.* 快乐地
jovial [ˈdʒoʊviəl] *adj.* 快乐的；好交际的
terminal cancer 晚期癌症

Lesson 16

Part 1 主力单词 / 词组

furtive [ˈfɜːrtɪv] *adj.* 秘密的；鬼鬼祟祟的
The glance of Mr. John's eye was furtive.
His furtive attempts to fix the door lock are foiled.

surreptitiously [ˌsʌrəp'tɪʃəsli] *adv.* 秘密地；偷偷地
The cat surreptitiously approached a rat.

She intercepted her lover's letter surreptitiously.

covert [ˈkʌvərt, ˈkoʊvɜːrt] *n.* 小树丛；藏身处　*adj.* 隐秘的；秘密的

America's support of covert operations and aid in the Middle East has continued to reveal itself.

clandestine [klænˈdestɪn, ˈklændəstaɪn] *adj.* 秘密的；暗中的

The clandestine cult has generally been a minuscule group, legally barred from participation in public affairs as outsiders.

esoteric [ˌesəˈterɪk] *adj.* 难懂的；秘密的

Esoteric knowledge of Buddhism has stumped many western philosophers.

arcane [ɑːrˈkeɪn] *adj.* 难懂的；神秘的

Arcane incantation and lore have passed down to a few people.

abstruse [əbˈstruːs, æbˈstruːs] *adj.* 难解的；深奥的

Agnosticism, resting on psychological and scientific findings, is too abstruse for the laity to appreciate.

The solution is simple. It is not an abstruse or difficult question.

recondite [ˈrekəndaɪt] *adj.* 深奥的；不易懂的

The recondite hieroglyphs can only be understood by a few archaeologists.

Searching for aliens is a recondite subject.

impalpable [ɪmˈpælpəbl] *adj.* 难懂的；触摸不到的

Growth is a greater mystery than death. All of us can understand failure, we all contain failure and death within us, but not even the successful man can begin to describe the impalpable elations and apprehensions of growth. (Norman Mailer, U.S. novelist and journalist)

A homeless orphan and a political grandee meet on a deserted road only to discover that each is an impalpable ghost of the other.

convolute [ˈkɑnvəˌlʊt] *v.* 弯曲；曲折　*adj.* 曲折的

Grama grass has convolute leaves.

convoluted [ˈkɑːnvəluːtɪd] *adj.* 复杂的；盘绕的；弯曲的

The scholar's sentence is too convoluted for kids to comprehend.

The disputes in this rich family are very convoluted.

The tree has convoluted branches.

Could you please untie this convoluted knot for me?

These wire coils are tightly convoluted.

convolution [ˌkɑːnvəˈluːʃn] *n.* 错综复杂

Extensive convolutions create a large surface area of the brain cortex.

occult [əˈkʌlt] *v.* 掩蔽；遮掩 *n.* 神秘学；神秘仪式 *adj.* 神秘的；超自然的

The light of the moon will be occulted during a lunar eclipse.

We found an occult underground passage in the ancient temple.

• Words in sentences 句中单词/词组 •

foil [fɔɪl] *v.* 挫败；阻止 *n.* 箔；衬托

reveal [rɪˈviːl] *v.* 揭露；泄露

minuscule [ˈmɪnəskjuːl] *adj.* 微小的；极小的

stump [stʌmp] *v.* 语塞；被难住；迈着沉重的步子走

incantation [ˌɪnkænˈteɪʃn] *n.* 咒语

lore [lɔːr] *n.* 知识；传说

agnosticism [æɡˈnɑːstɪsɪzəm] *n.* 不可知论

psychological [ˌsaɪkəˈlɑːdʒɪkl] *adj.* 心理的；精神的

laity [ˈleɪəti] *n.* 外行人；普通信徒

hieroglyph [ˈhaɪərəɡlɪf] *n.* 象形文字；象形符号

grandee [ɡrænˈdiː] *n.* 显要人物；（旧时西班牙或葡萄牙的）大公

cortex [ˈkɔːrteks] *n.* （尤指大脑或其他器官的）皮层

a lunar eclipse 一次月食

Part 2 补充单词/词组

incondite [ɪnˈkɒndɪt, -daɪt] *adj.* 粗劣的；生硬的

Your incondite writing has to be revised.

penumbra [pəˈnʌmbrə] *n.* 半影；（绘画）交接处

The sun eclipse casts a penumbra on earth.

A penumbra of desolation fell upon us after we got lost in the remote forest.

The novel resides in the penumbra area between literature and merchandise.

In the penumbra of dream and dawn, she recollected her first love.

intercept [ˌɪntərˈsept] *v.* 拦截；截住

It waited in a perfect position to intercept its prey.

agnosia [æɡˈnəusiə] *n.* 失认症

She suffers from agnosia and is unable to recognize her husband.

ceiling [ˈsiːlɪŋ] *n.* 天花板

profession [prəˈfeʃn] *n.* 职业

We are firefighters. Ceiling collapses at the sites of fires are one type of great peril in our profession.

amateur [ˈæmətər, ˈæmətʃər] *n.* 业余爱好者

discalced [disˈkælsd] *adj.* 不穿鞋的

You made me look like a discalced, second-rate amateur.

dilettante [ˌdɪləˈtænti] *n.* 业余爱好者 *adj.* 业余的

She is an elegant piano dilettante who didn't receive any formal training.

collapse [kəˈlæps] *v.* 倒塌；崩溃 *n.* 垮掉；虚脱

The disabled man collapsed his wheelchair and put it in the corner of the room.

You are in great peril. The entire building is about to collapse.

leukemia [luːˈkiːmiə] *n.* 白血病

progenitor [prouˈdʒenɪtər] *n.* 祖先；前辈

abnormal [æbˈnɔːrml] *adj.* 反常的；变态的

Blood cells are made in the bone marrow. Leukemia begins to grow when an immature blood cell in the marrow, known as a progenitor cell, becomes abnormal, dividing uncontrollably and overriding the body's normal restrictions on cell division.

pterosaur [ˈterəˌsɔːr] *n.* 飞翼龙

The pterosaur is the progenitor of this bird.

progeny [ˈprɑːdʒəni] *n.* 后代；后裔

imminent [ˈɪmɪnənt] *adj.* 即将发生的；（危险等）逼近的

The progeny of ISIS terrorists, imminent threats to the United States, are different in important ways.

gnosis [ˈnoʊsɪs] n. 灵知

The world can be saved by gnosis.

compartment [kəmˈpɑːrtmənt] n. 区划；划分；隔间

cubicle [ˈkjuːbɪkl] n. 小卧室；小隔间

A pupil lies on a comfortable cot in a cubicle.

bullion [ˈbʊliən] n. 金条；银块

The airplane has a special compartment for mail and bullion.

palmistry [ˈpɑːmɪstri] n. 手相术

Palmistry and astrology are occult knowledge.

scion [ˈsaɪən] n. 后裔；子孙；嫩枝

He is a scion of a nobleman.

seedling [ˈsiːdlɪŋ] n. 幼苗；秧苗

The scion is inserted into the stem of a seedling.

boustrophedon [ˌbuːstroʊˈfiːdən] n. 牛耕式转行书写法

Boustrophedon can be found in ancient Egypt.

divide [dɪˈvaɪd] v. 划分；分发

He divides profits into equal shares.

flagship [ˈflæɡʃɪp] n. 旗舰；佼佼者

She is the flagship in the realm of rocket engineering.

Apple company will launch its flagship product soon.

Part 3　识记单词/词组

compartmentalize [kəmˌpɑːrtˈmentəlaɪz] v. 划分；区分

palmist [ˈpɑːmɪst] n. 看手相的人；手相家

revelation [ˌrevəˈleɪʃn] n. 被揭示的真相

Revelation [ˌrevəˈleɪʃn] n. 圣经

chant [tʃænt] v. 反复念诵

chanting incantation 念咒

agnostic [æɡˈnɑːstɪk] adj. 不可知论的　n. 不可知论者

sideline [ˈsaɪdlaɪn]　v. 使退出比赛；使停止参赛
from the sidelines　旁观
elation [ɪˈleɪʃn]　n. 很高兴
perilous [ˈperələs]　adj. 危险的
abnormality [ˌæbnɔːrˈmæləti]　n. 不正常
hieroglyphic [ˌhaɪərəˈɡlɪfɪk]　n. 象形文字　adj. 象形文字的；难解的
battleship [ˈbætlʃɪp]　n. 主力舰；战舰
flagship store　旗舰店
chiromancy [ˈkaɪroʊmænsi]　n. 手相术
somatosensory [ˌsoʊmətəˈsensəri]　adj. 身体感觉的
somato=somat　身体
marrow [ˈmæroʊ]　n. 骨髓；精华
lunar [ˈluːnər]　adj. 月球上的；阴历的；苍白的
imminent war　即将来临的战争
imminent death　即将来临的死亡

Lesson 17

Part 1　主力单词/词组

educate [ˈedʒukeɪt]　v. 教育
In a Fortune 500 company, I was at a certain disadvantage among highly educated and cultivated people.
He was always an immoderate lover of the Scottish nation, having not only been born there but educated by that people and besieged by them always, having few English about him till he was King. (Edward Hyde Clarendon, English statesman and historian)
A nutritionist educated her parents about nutrition.

coach [koʊtʃ]　v. 培训　n. 教练；长途汽车
It is an oddity to see a proctor coaching an examinee during the college entrance exam.

cultivate [ˈkʌltɪveɪt]　v. 培养；栽培
Brazil begins to cultivate soybean and maize during the trade war.

nourish [ˈnɜːrɪʃ] v. 培养；养育

Hardship serves nothing but to nourish your spirit.

nourishment [ˈnɜːrɪʃmənt] n. 营养；营养品

inculcate [ɪnˈkʌlkeɪt] v. 反复灌输；谆谆教诲

A reviewer believes the movie scenario should be subservient to morality, inculcating ethics as well.
The government inculcated students with patriotism and jingoism.

indoctrinate [ɪnˈdɑːktrɪneɪt] v. 向……灌输（信念、教条）

Kamikaze was indoctrinated in destroying U.S. fleets with a suicide attack.

brainwash [ˈbreɪnwɔːʃ] v. 对……洗脑；向……强行灌输

The despot has brainwashed and dehumanized his mild civilians into puppets of a military machine.

pedagogy [ˈpedəɡɑːdʒi] n. 教学法

Curriculum, heuristics, pedagogy, and teacher training are crucial elements in education.

imbue [ɪmˈbjuː] v. 使……充满……；沾满

The anthem of China imbues a strong sense of patriotism.
His hand imbued with her blood.

predispose [ˌpriːdɪˈspoʊz] v. 使受……的影响；使易于患（某种病）

Highly academic environments predispose children to learn better.

● Words in sentences 句中单词 / 词组 ●

immoderate [ɪˈmɑːdərət] adj. 过度的；不合理的
nutritionist [nuˈtrɪʃənɪst] n. 营养师
oddity [ˈɑːdəti] n. 怪人；怪事；反常现象
proctor [ˈprɑːktər] n. 监考人员；监考
entrance [ˈentrəns, ɪnˈtræns] n. 入口
maize [meɪz] n. 玉米
reviewer [rɪˈvjuːər] n. 评论家
scenario [səˈnærioʊ] n. 剧情；可能发生的事态
subservient [səbˈsɜːrviənt] adj. 次要的；恭顺的；屈从的

> **ethic** [ˈeθɪk] n. 行为准则；伦理
> **kamikaze** [ˌkæmɪˈkɑːzi] n. 神风特攻队
> **despot** [ˈdespɒt] n. 专制者；暴君
> **dehumanize** [ˌdiːˈhjuːmənaɪz] v. 使无人性；剥夺……的人性
> **puppet** [ˈpʌpɪt] n. 傀儡；木偶

Part 2 补充单词 / 词组

monologue [ˈmɒnəlɒɡ] n. 独白；独角戏
There was a monologue at the beginning of the show.

interior monologue 内心的独白
The screenwriter forfeits action in favor of interior monologue.
Stream of consciousness is often confused with interior monologue, a flow of thoughts inwardly expressed, similar to a soliloquy, talking when alone.

inward [ˈɪnwərd] n. 灵魂中；内脏 adj. 里面的 adv. 内心里

forfeit [ˈfɔːrfɪt] v. 丧失；被没收 n. 没收物；罚金 adj. 被没收的
The team reaches playoffs by winning three consecutive games, one of them by forfeit.

commandeer [ˌkɑːmənˈdɪr] v. 征用；征募；[口] 霸占；没收
I am going to commandeer your car to chase the criminal.

incontinent [ɪnˈkɑːntɪnənt] adj. 不自制的；无节制的
I divorced her because of her incontinent spending on luxury goods.
The adult diaper is for incontinent patients.

despotic [dɪˈspɑːtɪk] adj. 暴君的；专制的
Do you think the tyrannical and despotic policy will last long?

despotism [ˈdespətɪzəm] n. 暴政；君主专制
People suffering under his despotism are observable.

bland [blænd] adj. 温和的；淡而无味的
Her bland smile melts my frozen heart.
The bland music was sold in a white market.
Bland food doesn't have much flavor.

onward [ˈɑːnwərd] *adj.* 向前的 *adv.* 在前面

The train will carry me onward.
We have lived in Seattle from 2010 onward.

Part 3 识记单词/词组

forfeiture [ˈfɔːrfɪtʃər] *n.* 没收物；罚金；丧失
confiscate [ˈkɑːnfɪskeɪt] *v.* 没收；将……充公；征收
confiscation [ˌkɑːnfɪˈskeɪʃn] *n.* 没收；充公；征用
playoff [ˈpleɪɔːf] *n.* 最后决赛阶段；延长赛；锦标赛
screenwriter [ˈskriːnraɪtər] *n.* 编剧家
screenplay [ˈskriːnpleɪ] *n.* 电影剧本
soliloquy [səˈlɪləkwi] *n.* 独白；自言自语
stream of consciousness 意识流；自由意识
biennial [baɪˈeniəl] *adj.* 两年一次的
doctrine [ˈdɑːktrɪn] *n.* 信条；教义
white market 白市（合法交易市场）
pedagogue [ˈpedəgɑːg] *n.* 死板的教师
pedant [ˈpednt] *n.* 书呆子；学究
pedantic [pɪˈdæntɪk] *adj.* 学究式的；迂腐的；卖弄学问的

Lesson 18

Part 1 主力单词/词组

persevere [ˌpɜːrsəˈvɪr] *v.* 不屈不挠；坚持不懈

China persevered through Japan's ruthless invasion with great endurance and fortitude during World War II.
The scientist has persevered in the field of paleontology and tried to find the origin of ancient life.
We set out to oppose Tyranny in all its strides, and I hope we shall persevere. (Abraham Clark, U.S. politician)

perseverance [ˌpɜːrsəˈvɪrəns] n. 毅力
He continues to work with untiring perseverance.

perseverant [ˌpɜːrsəˈvɪrənt] adj. 有毅力的
She is waiting for the exam result with hope perseverant.

persist [pərˈsɪst] v. 坚持不懈；存留
The reporter persisted with his questioning about the widespread strikes from different professional industries in Hong Kong.
The superstition has persisted to this day.

pertinaciously [ˌpətɪˈneɪʃəsli] adv. 坚决地；坚忍不拔地
The judge pertinaciously refused to be dislodged.

indefatigable [ˌɪndɪˈfætɪɡəbl] adj. 不懈的
Doctors were indefatigable in the effort to relieve the injured.
His indefatigable exertions and toils have procured me an exceptional skill of embroidery.

indomitable [ɪnˈdɑːmɪtəbl] adj. 不屈不挠的；意志坚定的
The space adventure requires indomitable spirit and courage.
The indomitable old soldier fought to the very end.
The indomitable gelding might win the race.

impregnable [ɪmˈpreɡnəbl] adj. 难以攻陷的；坚定不移的
The corporation has an impregnable firewall.
Destroying this impregnable fortification required extreme tactics.

invincible [ɪnˈvɪnsəbl] adj. 无敌的；不屈不挠的
Spanish fleets seemed to be invincible at the start of the Age of Discovery.

unassailable [ˌʌnəˈseɪləbl] adj. 无懈可击的；没有争论余地的
Their troops were not unassailable.
Poverty seems to be an unassailable barrier for me to further my education.

insuperable [ɪnˈsuːpərəbl] adj. 不能制胜的；不能克服的
He was faced with insuperable obstacles in his attempt to revive Egyptian culture.

fortitude [ˈfɔːrtɪtuːd] n. 坚韧；刚毅

pertinacity [ˌpɜːrtnˈæsəti] n. 固执

Lesson 18

> • Words in sentences 句中单词/词组 •
>
> **endurance** [ɪn'dʊrəns]　*n.* 忍耐力；承受力
> **paleontology** [ˌpeɪliɑːn'tɑːlədʒi]　*n.* 古生物学
> **stride** [straɪd]　*v.* 迈大步走　*n.* 进展；进步
> **exertion** [ɪg'zɜːrʃn]　*v.* 努力；费力；运用
> **toil** [tɔɪl]　*v.* 苦干　*n.* 辛苦活
> **gelding** ['geldɪŋ]　*n.* 阉马
> **the Age of Discovery**　海权时代

Part 2　补充单词/词组

handover ['hændoʊvər]　*n.* 交接；转移
The handover of Hong Kong began in 1997.

pregnable ['pregnəbl]　*adj.* 易受攻击的；弱的
They captured a pregnable fort within an hour.

juggernaut ['dʒʌgərnɔːt]　*n.* 强大力量；重型货车
The terrorist organization has developed into a regional juggernaut.
The U.S. is a juggernaut with which no nation wants to fight.

interest group　强大力量
You will be crushed by an invisible political juggernaut if you keep disregarding the interest group.

scourge [skɜːrdʒ]　*v.* 惩罚；鞭打　*n.* 苦难的根源
Hitler was the scourge of World War Two.
My drunken father was the scourge of my childhood.

scour ['skaʊər]　*v.* 擦净　*n.* 洗涤；除垢剂
He scoured the drawer for his silver fork before dining.

geld [geld]　*v.* 阉割

eunuch ['juːnək]　*n.* 太监；无男子气概的人
You have to be gelded in order to become a eunuch.

assailable [əˈseɪləbl] *adj.* 易受攻击的；有隙可乘的

There is one assailable point in her argument.

travail [ˈtræveɪl, trəˈveɪl] *v.* 艰苦劳动 *n.* 分娩的阵痛；艰苦劳动

Art is the stored honey of the human soul, gathered on wings of misery and travail. (Theodore Dreiser, U.S. novelist)

She finally passed the Certified Financial Accounting exam after years of travail.

Scientists travailed year after year to create ultimate weapons.

Rachel travailed in pain.

Part 3 识记单词 / 词组

hand over　交出

superable [ˈsupərəbl] *adj.* 可胜过的；可征服的

give in　认输

Paleo [ˈpeɪlioʊ]　古；史前

struggle [ˈstrʌɡl] *v./n.* 努力；奋斗

dislodge [dɪsˈlɑːdʒ] *v.* 使免职；使……移动

Lesson 19

Part 1 主力单词 / 词组

appreciate [əˈpriːʃieɪt] *v.* 感激；欣赏；鉴赏；理解；涨价

If you can give me a discount, it would be highly appreciated.

We went to the museum to appreciate ancient art and paintings.

The U.S. government doesn't appreciate or fully understand the value of environmental conservation.

Once U.S. currency appreciates, Asian currency depreciates.

appreciation [əˌpriːʃiˈeɪʃn] *n.* 欣赏；理解；感谢

oblige [əˈblaɪdʒ] *v.* 强迫；帮忙

Will you oblige me to close the door.

The U.S. obliged the U.N. to sanction the nation whose leader was obliged to negotiate with the U.S. delegates in Singapore.

obliged [əˈblaɪdʒd] *adj.* 被迫的；非常感谢的

I was very much obliged to you for the presents you sent me last autumn.

gratitude [ˈɡrætɪtuːd] *n.* 感激之情

The victim expressed gratitude for the police's assistance.

Part 2 补充单词/词组

stoic [ˈstoʊɪk] *n.* 克制感情的人   *adj.* 克制感情的；坚忍的

He has been an honest, stoic, hard worker.

The monk has a stoic indifference to cold and poverty.

The stoic spirit of migrant workers was tested by adverse circumstances.

chimpanzee [ˌtʃɪmpænˈziː] *n.* 黑猩猩

intellect [ˈɪntəlekt] *n.* 智力；知识分子

Chimpanzees' intellect is higher than that of other animals.

He is a man of superior intellect.

From your demeanor, I know that you are an intellect.

take the plunge 断然采取行动

At midnight, the general will take the plunge to attack the enemy down the hill.

jilt [dʒɪlt] *v.* 遗弃（情人）

traumatize [ˈtrɔːmətaɪz, ˈtraʊmətaɪz] *v.* 使……受损伤

The mortification of being jilted leaves him emotionally traumatized.

assail [əˈseɪl] *v.* 攻击

The U.S. launched several missiles to assail its enemy.

sentient [ˈsentiənt, ˈsenʃnt] *adj.* 有感觉的；有情感的

The general is sentient of danger and asks his soldiers to withdraw immediately.

cognizance [ˈkɑːɡnɪzəns] *n.* 审理；标志；认知

Brazil didn't take cognizance of the potential pandemic.

The judge who gave him a lenient sentence has no cognizance of his true criminal nature.

cognizant [ˈkɑːɡnɪzənt]　*adj.* 已认知的；注意到的

Is the president cognizant of the impending danger?

amenable [əˈmiːnəbl]　*adj.* 易接受建议的；适合的

The old man is not amenable to change and advice.
I was amenable to spending more time with my grandmother.
The data is amenable to further analysis.
All students are amenable to school regulations and laws.

Part 3　识记单词/词组

ingratitude [ɪnˈɡrætɪtuːd]　*n.* 忘恩负义
ungratefulness [ʌnˈɡreɪtfəlnəs]　*n.* 忘恩负义
currency appreciation　货币升值
currency depreciation　货币贬值

Lesson 20

Part 1　主力单词/词组

stubborn [ˈstʌbərn]　*adj.* 固执的；坚持的

The bandits who were surrounded by commandoes had to choose between more stubborn resistance and capitulation.
Facts are stubborn things. (Tobias Smollett, Scottish novelist)
Her ex-husband was convincingly impetuous and stubborn.

obstinate [ˈɑːbstɪnət]　*adj.* 顽固的；难以对付的

The sage found it hard to shake cults out of a vague but obstinate belief of karma.

adamant [ˈædəmənt]　*adj.* 固执的；坚持的

His adamant refusal of deployment to the northern frontier has offended the king.

adamantly [ˈædəməntli, -mænt-]　*adv.* 坚决地；顽固地

tenacity [təˈnæsəti]　*n.* 固执；坚持

He persists in going on the treacherous mission with great tenacity.

They defended their freedom with indomitable tenacity.

tenacious [tə'neɪʃəs] *adj.* 非常固执的；记忆力很强的

Your tenacious grasp of my hand has caused me to bruise.

The accountant has a tenacious, retentive memory for financial details.

tenaciously [tə'neɪʃəsli] *adv.* 坚持地；坚韧不拔地

Hanging onto the lost cause tenaciously might be a foolish act.

obdurate ['ɑːbdərət] *adj.* 固执的；铁石心肠的

The most malicious and obdurate tyrant of Zimbabwe has made people's lives like a living hell.

intractable [ɪn'træktəbl] *adj.* 难驾驭的；倔强的

Ethiopia continued to suffer this year from persistent and intractable problems of drought.

Venereal disease is intractable, difficult to be cured.

This metal has an inherent intractable property.

He won't go out with his intractable friend anymore.

recalcitrant [rɪ'kælsɪtrənt] *adj.* 不易顺从的

On a few occasions, the boss encountered some recalcitrant employees.

intransigent [ɪn'trænzɪdʒənt] *adj.* 固执的；不妥协的

The intransigent rebels have decided to fight to the very end. Their motto is "never surrender."

impervious [ɪm'pɜːrviəs] *adj.* 不为所动的；不能渗透的

Helen was an ebullient girl, impervious to minor criticisms.

The stainless steel is strong, impervious to rust.

Glass is an impervious substance.

impassive [ɪm'pæsɪv] *adj.* 面无表情的；无动于衷的

His face remains impassive. I don't know what he thinks.

restive ['restɪv] *adj.* 不听话的；焦躁的

He disciplined the restive child with a small stick.

The restive horse just won't budge.

I spent a restive night worrying about the exam results.

perversity [pər'vɜːrsəti] *n.* 反常；任性；倔强

Perversity is the muse of modern literature. (Susan Sontag, U.S. writer.)

Words in sentences 句中单词/词组

bandit [ˈbændɪt] n. 土匪
commando [kəˈmændoʊ] n. 突击队
capitulation [kəˌpɪtʃuˈleɪʃn] n. 投降
convincingly [kənˈvɪnsɪŋli] adv. 令人信服地
impetuous [ɪmˈpetʃuəs] adj. 冲动的；鲁莽的
sage [seɪdʒ] n. 智者（尤指老人）
cult [kʌlt] n. 异教徒；邪教
karma [ˈkɑːrmə] n. 业力（佛教和印度教用语）
deployment [dɪˈplɔɪmənt] n. 部署；调动
grasp [ɡræsp] v./n. 抓紧；握紧
bruise [bruːz] n. 瘀伤 v. 受伤
retentive [rɪˈtentɪv] adj. 记忆力好的；容易保留的
lost cause 不会成功的事；没希望的人
drought [draʊt] n. 旱灾
venereal disease 性病
motto [ˈmɑːtoʊ] n. 座右铭；格言
ebullient [ɪˈbʌliənt, ɪˈbʊliənt] adj. 活泼热情的
substance [ˈsʌbstəns] n. 物质；实质；根据

Part 2 补充单词/词组

genuflect [ˈdʒenjuflekt] v. 单膝下跪；顺从；崇敬
We have genuflected before the god of science only to find that it has given us the atomic bomb, producing fears and anxieties that science can never mitigate. (Martin Luther King, U.S. civil rights leader)

altar [ˈɔːltər] n. 圣坛；祭坛
Worshippers genuflected before the altar.

prostrate [ˈprɑːstreɪt] v. 使俯卧；使疲惫 adj. 被征服的；疲惫的
Prostrate shrubs cover the entire land.

Soldiers were prostrate from the heat under the scorching sun.

rule [ru:l]　*v.* 统治；（用尺）划（线）　*n.* 规则；建议

ruler ['ru:lər]　*n.* 统治者；直尺

Down to the present day, subjects prostrate themselves in awe of the ruler's majesty and dare not speak out, wives are held down as inferiors and being uneducated, are kept in ignorance. (Kang Youwei, Chinese reformer and scholar)

follower ['fɑ:louər]　*n.* 追随者；信徒

Followers prostrate themselves in front of the Indian guru.

slip [slɪp]　*v.* 使滑倒　*n.* 滑跤；纸片；错误

opulence ['ɑ:pjələns]　*n.* 丰裕；奢侈

opulent ['ɑ:pjələnt]　*adj.* 奢侈的；丰饶的

affluent ['æfluənt]　*n.* 富裕的人；支流　*adj.* 富裕的

hearth [hɑ:rθ]　*n.* 壁炉

I enjoyed the comforts beside a hearth in the winter.

prehension [prɪ'henʃən]　*n.* 掌握；理解

The eagle captures the prey with jaw prehension.

prehensible [pri'hensibl]　*adj.* 能缠绕的；可以领悟的

Monkeys have prehensible arms.

prehensile [prɪ'hensl]　*adj.* [动] 适于抓握的；有理解力的；贪婪的

The elephant has a prehensile trunk.

The dog has a prehensile tail.

contusion [kən'tu:ʒn]　*n.* 挫伤；瘀青

He has a contusion on his left leg.

contuse [kən'tju:z]　*v.* 打伤；捣碎

His arm was contused due to a car accident.

clench [klentʃ]　*v./n.* 握紧；咬紧

He clenches his fists and prepares to fight.

I clenched my teeth when I heard she spoke ill of me.

ossify [ˈɑːsɪfaɪ] v. 骨化；硬化；僵化

The cartilage and bone are ossified with age.
It is an ossified Christian high school.

texture [ˈtekstʃər] v. 使具有某种结构 n. 结构；质地；神韵

Each type of wood has its own texture.
The texture of this silk cloth is smooth.
The texture of this movie is quite violent.

Part 3 识记单词 / 词组

a sense of occasion　　一种隆重的（或特别的）气氛

tractable [ˈtræktəbl]　adj. 易处理的；顺从的

intransigence [ɪnˈtrænzɪdʒəns]　n. 不妥协；不调和

half-hearted [ˌhæf ˈhɑːrtɪd]　adj. 不热情的；兴趣不大的

hang on　坚持做某事；紧握

nirvana [nɪrˈvɑːnə]　n. 涅槃

offense [əˈfens]　n. 冒犯；犯罪；攻击

calcify [ˈkælsɪfaɪ]　v. 硬化

calcification [ˌkælsɪfɪˈkeɪʃn]　n. 石灰化；钙化物质

ebullience [ɪˈbʌliəns, ɪˈbuliəns]　n. 沸腾；（感情等的）奔放；兴高采烈

textural [ˈtekstʃərəl]　adj. 质地的；组织的

Lesson 21

Part 1 主力单词 / 词组

scheme [skiːm] n. 阴谋；诡计；方案；计划

The scheme of overthrowing the government was devised by revolutionists.

The chancellor of Germany thought of various schemes of expanding territory in Middle Africa.

The swindler made schemes and collected money by faking religious providence.

conspire [kənˈspaɪər]　v. 密谋；一起运作

They conspired to defraud the old lady who was asked to pay ransom for her family.

It seems that fate conspires with misfortune. I got the offer from the university but was unable to attend due to lack of money for the tuition.

complicity [kəmˈplɪsəti]　n. 同犯；同谋；共犯

He and a reprobate were convicted of complicity in kidnapping a rich kid.

intrigue [ɪnˈtriːg]　v. 使很感兴趣；迷住　n. 阴谋

The leery atmosphere of intrigue and instability gave rise to the phenomenon of fleeing investors.

connive [kəˈnaɪv]　v. 密谋；纵容；放任

The inhuman killer connives to take the philanderer's life very slowly.

He connived with a committee to rig the result of the election.

connivance [kəˈnaɪvəns]　n. 默许；纵容

Three syndicates were tarnished by backroom deals and connivance of paparazzi to infringe upon the privacy of others.

machinate [ˈmækɪneɪt]　v. 密谋

It is not a good idea to machinate against the president.

machination [ˌmæʃɪˈneɪʃn]　n. 阴谋诡计

Backstage machinations seemed to have dominated the court life entirely for the crown prince.

plot [plɑːt]　v. 密谋；绘制　n. 阴谋；故事情节

His plot to blow up the presidential palace has been discovered.

cabal [kəˈbæl, kəˈbɑːl]　v. 密谋；策划　n. 阴谋

He was accused of being a ringleader in the insurgents' cabal.

A cabal plotted to assassinate the prime minister.

There is a cabal of artists examining the exquisite painting.

skulduggery=skullduggery　n. 欺骗；[口] 阴谋诡计

Disclosure of political espionage and skullduggery got him killed.

He was accused of accounting skullduggery.

Words in sentences 句中单词/词组

ransom [ˈrænsəm] n. 赎金

leery [ˈlɪri] adj. 疑神疑鬼的；有戒心的

instability [ˌɪnstəˈbɪləti] n. 不稳定；不稳固

inhuman [ɪnˈhjuːmən] adj. 无人性的

philanderer [fɪˈlændərər] n. 玩弄女性的男人

rig [rɪɡ] v. 操纵；安装 n. 钻井设备

syndicate [ˈsɪndɪkeɪt, ˈsɪndɪkət] v.(文章、图片、节目）出售给多个媒体 n. 财团

tarnish [ˈtɑːrnɪʃ] v. 诽谤；（使）褪色

backroom [ˈbækˌruːm] n. 后面的房间 adj. 后台的；私下的

paparazzi [ˌpɑːpəˈrɑːtsi] n. 狗仔队

infringe [ɪnˈfrɪndʒ] v. 违背；触犯（法规）；侵害（合法权益）

backstage [ˌbækˈsteɪdʒ] adj. 秘密的；后台的；幕后的

ringleader [ˈrɪŋliːdər] n.（做坏事的）头目；元凶

Part 2 补充单词/词组

conspiracy [kənˈspɪrəsi] n. 密谋者

conspirator [kənˈspɪrətər] n. 共谋者

complicit [kəmˈplɪsɪt] adj. 串通的；同谋的

collude [kəˈluːd] v. 共谋；串通
The agent had colluded with the United States for too long.

collusion [kəˈluːʒn] n. 密谋；勾结
The party member faces allegations of collusion with the Russians.

reprobate [ˈreprəbeɪt] v. 指责 n. 恶棍；拒绝救赎 adj. 堕落的
There was a reprobate gangster who tried to blackmail a civilian.
The brutal enforcement of the police was reprobated.

reprobation [ˌreprəˈbeɪʃn] n. 责备；遗弃；反对
The president's reprobation of the accursed nuclear pollution should be made known

internationally.

technician [tekˈnɪʃn] n. 技师；技巧纯熟的人
The technician adds some ballasts to increase the stability of the hot air balloon.

ballast [ˈbæləst] v. 使稳定 n. [船]压舱物；沙袋
The president's calm remark and his subsidiary policy will provide ballast to the whole society.
The fisherman ballasted the canoe with rocks.

jurisdiction [ˌdʒʊrɪsˈdɪkʃn] n. 管辖权；司法权；审判权
The policemen had been connived through bribery into smuggling goods under their jurisdiction.

parvenu [ˈpɑːrvənuː] n. 暴发户

hierarchy [ˈhaɪərɑːrki] n. 统治集团；等级制度
The interloping parvenu does things wantonly and is sure to upset the town's social hierarchy.

primogenial infant 初生婴儿

dirge [dɜːrdʒ] n. 送葬曲；挽歌
She wrote the dirge for the death of her primogenial infant.

requiem [ˈrekwiəm, ˈrekwiem] n. 安魂曲；挽歌
The requiem was created by Mozart.

Part 3 识记单词 / 词组

immediate family [法律]近亲属
pecking order 长幼尊卑制度；权势等级；啄序
peck [pek] v. 啄食；连续敲击；吹毛求疵
spouse [spaʊs, spaʊz] n. 配偶
attendant [əˈtendənt] n. 服务员 adj. 护理的；到场的；伴随的
attendee [əˌtenˈdiː] n. 出席者；参加者
accursed [əˈkɜːrsɪd, əˈkɜːrst] adj. 可恶的；应受诅咒的
blackmail [ˈblækmeɪl] v./n. 敲诈
lee [liː] v. 逃走；逃跑
interlope [ˌɪntərˈloʊp] v. 侵害他人权利；闯入；干涉

Lesson 22

Part 1　主力单词/词组

protect [prəˈtekt]　*v.* 保护

Applying sunscreen protects us from the sun's ultraviolet radiation.

Movies for me are a heightened reality. Making reality fun to live with, as opposed to something you run from and protect yourself from. (Steven Spielberg, U.S. film director)

safeguard [ˈseɪfɡɑːrd]　*v./n.* 保护；保卫

Massive military construction on islands of the South China Sea may have political implications designed to safeguard China's sea territory.

defend [dɪˈfend]　*v.* 保护；防卫

Will you stand to defend your country or evacuate at the sight of an enemy?

enshrine [ɪnˈʃraɪn]　*v.* 保护；保留；珍藏

The rights of speech and belief are enshrined in the new law.

aegis [ˈiːdʒɪs]　*n.* 庇护；保护；宙斯的盾牌

under the aegis of　在……的保护或支援下

Gangsters coerce locals to sell drugs under the aegis of the mafia.

indemnify [ɪnˈdemnɪfaɪ]　*v.* 保障；赔偿

The insurance indemnifies the house against the earthquake.

The government indemnified the losses of fishermen.

• Words in sentences 句中单词/词组 •

sunscreen [ˈsʌnskriːn]　*n.* 防晒油

ultraviolet [ˌʌltrəˈvaɪələt]　*adj.* 紫外线的

radiation [ˌreɪdiˈeɪʃn]　*n.* 放射线；增强

as opposed to　而不是

implication [ˌɪmplɪˈkeɪʃn]　*n.* 意味；暗示；可能的影响；牵连

evacuate [ɪˈvækjueɪt]　*v.* 撤退；撤离
mafia [ˈmɑːfiə]　*n.* 黑手党；帮派

Part 2　补充单词 / 词组

violet [ˈvaɪələt]　*n.* 紫罗兰　*adj.* 紫色的；紫罗兰的
Violet and crimson lights shed upon my face alternately in the disco.

duress [duˈres]　*n.* 强迫；禁锢
She accepted the deal under duress.
Japan's military expansion is still held in duress by the treaty with the United States of America.

imply [ɪmˈplaɪ]　*v.* 暗示；必然包含
The doctor implied his death was unnatural.
Higher positions imply greater responsibility.

beat around the bush　拐弯抹角地说
Just say what you mean. You don't have to beat around the bush.

winch [wɪntʃ]　*v.* 吊起；拉起　*n.* 绞车；卷扬机
He winches me up from the well.
The injured survivor was winched by helicopter.

Part 3　识记单词 / 词组

crimson [ˈkrɪmzn]　*v.* 变得绯红　*n.* 深红色　*adj.* 深红色的
defendant [dɪˈfendənt]　*n.* 被告人
plaintiff [ˈpleɪntɪf]　*n.* 原告
enshrinement [ɪnˈʃraɪnmənt]　*n.* 珍藏
indemnification [ɪnˌdemnɪfɪˈkeɪʃn]　*n.* 赔偿；补偿

Lesson 23

Part 1　主力单词 / 词组

temporary [ˈtempəreri]　*adj.* 临时的；暂时的
Do you prefer a permanent job or a temporary one?

The setback to German troops was only temporary.

There was a temporary decline in Russian power after the death of the emperor.

provisional [prə'vɪʒnl]　*adj.* 临时的

Italy forms a coalition as a provisional government before the new president is elected.

interim ['ɪntərɪm]　*adj.* 临时的；过渡的

The military has formed the interim government of Thailand only for six months.

pro tem=pro tempore　暂时地；目前地

He became the leader pro tempore before a more suitable candidate showed up.

tentative ['tentətɪv]　*adj.* 不确定的；不肯定的；暂定的

There is no guarantee. His words were tentative and contingent.

Part 2　补充单词 / 词组

betroth [bɪ'trəʊð]　*v.* 把……许配给

His father betrothed her to a noble.

emeritus [ɪ'merɪtəs]　*n.* 荣誉退休者　*adj.* 荣誉退职的

She is an emeritus professor at the University of Washington.

face the consequence　承担后果

If you do not release my daughter, you will face the consequence.

consequential [ˌkɑːnsɪ'kwenʃl]　*adj.* 随之发生的；重要的

I would like to pay insurance against consequential loss.

He made a consequential decision to launch a nuclear bomb.

forthright ['fɔːrθraɪt]　*n.* 直路　*adj.* 直率的

convenance ['kɑnvə,nɑns]　*n.* 习俗；礼节

She is forthright with little regard for the convenances.

descant ['deskænt]　*v.* 伴唱；伴奏；评论　*n.* 详细的评论

The financial specialist loves to descant on various business activities.

soprano [sə'prænoʊ, sə'prɑːnoʊ]　*n.* 女高音歌手；女高音

I would like to see the soprano descanted above the melody line.

shambles ['ʃæmblz]　*n.* 混乱；废墟；屠宰场

What is there now but a vast shambles of the heart?

Brazil tries to climb out of its economic shambles left by its deposed president.

shamble [ˈʃæmbl] v. 摇晃地走 n. 摇晃的脚步

The drunkard shambled into the room.
They shambled back to the school after being defeated in a wrestling contest.

Part 3 识记单词/词组

musical interlude 音乐插曲
political interlude 政治插曲
tentative plan 临时计划
prelude [ˈpreljuːd] v. 演奏前奏曲；开头 n. 前奏曲；序幕
interlude [ˈɪntərluːd] n. 插曲；间歇
setback [ˈsetbæk] n. 挫折；退步；阻碍
a pro tem committee 临时委员会
incident [ˈɪnsɪdənt] n. 事件
incidence [ˈɪnsɪdəns] n. 影响

Lesson 24

Part 1 主力单词/词组

disquiet [dɪsˈkwaɪət] adj. 焦虑的；不安的

The terror attack has caused public disquiet.

disquieting [dɪsˈkwaɪətɪŋ] 令人不安的；令人忧虑的

The Criminal rate declines in comparison with last year but is nevertheless disquieting.
I have no concern about this disquieting political report since integrity is a rarity among politicians.

distraught [dɪˈstrɔːt] adj. 极其不安的

My aunt is distraught because her children have been kidnapped.
She is so distraught that she can't really answer my question.

disconcert [ˌdɪskənˈsɜːrt] *v.* 使不安
Neither fame nor fortune can exasperate or disconcert the holy person.

overwrought [ˌoʊvərˈrɔːt] *adj.* 过度紧张的
The defendant became too overwrought as the verdict came out.

anxious [ˈæŋkʃəs] *adj.* 不安的
Examinees become anxious about the test.

abject [ˈæbdʒekt] *adj.* 糟透的；极其苦恼的
People are in abject poverty in some remote mountain.

stressed [strest] *adj.* 压力重的；紧张的
The demanding teacher makes us all very stressed.

> • Words in sentences 句中单词 / 词组 •
>
> **in comparison with** 和……比较
> **integrity** [ɪnˈtegrəti] *n.* 操守；正直；诚实；完整
> **rarity** [ˈrerəti] *n.* 罕见的东西（或人）；稀有；罕见
> **exasperate** [ɪgˈzæspəreɪt] *v.* 使恼怒；使恶化；使加剧
> **demanding** [dɪˈmændɪŋ] *adj.* 要求很高的

Part 2 补充单词 / 词组

psychiatric hospital 精神病院
She has an epiphany about how to escape from the psychiatric hospital.

wound [wuːnd, waʊnd] *v.* 使受伤 *n.* 伤口；伤害
A doctor treated his wound properly before it mortified.

suture [ˈsuːtʃər] *v.* 缝合 *n.* 缝合处；缝线

incision [ɪnˈsɪʒn] *n.* 切开；刻痕
The doctor sutured the incision.

surgical [ˈsɜːrdʒɪkl] *adj.* 外科的
I saw a surgical suture on his abdomen.

jet propulsion 喷气推进
Is there any way to increase jet propulsion?

traumatic [trəˈmætɪk] adj. 创伤的；令人痛苦的
The orphan reminds her of a traumatic past.

conventionality [kən,venʃəˈnæləti] n. 惯例；恪守常规
Conventionality is not morality.

recherché [rəʃerˈʃei] adj. 罕有的；矫揉造作的
The jewel merchant has a collection of recherché stones.
I enjoyed the recherché banquet providing proboscises and bear's palms.
I am an easy-going person without a recherché manner.

rarefied [ˈrerɪfaɪd] adj. 变稀薄的；纯化的；怪异的
It is difficult to breathe in the rarefied air of high altitude.
The meal has been refined to cater to the clients' rarefied tastes.

flocculent [ˈflɑːkjələnt] adj. 绒毛状的；覆以绒毛的；松散的
Her flocculent hair looks like a bird's nest.
There are brown flocculent precipitates at the bottom of the river.

flock [flɑːk] v. 聚集；蜂拥 n. 一群人
Birds of a feather flock together.

Part 3 识记单词/词组

birds of a feather 一类人；志趣相投者（指负面的）

abject misery 凄惨

rare [rer] adj. 稀少的；罕见的；不常发生的

rarefy [ˈrerəˌfaɪ] v. 使变稀薄；使纯化

proboscis [proʊˈbɑːsɪs, proʊˈbɑːskɪs] n. 象鼻

anthropology [ˌænθrəˈpɑːlədʒi] n. 人类学

ideology [ˌaɪdiˈɑːlədʒi, ˌɪdiˈɑːlədʒi] n. 意识形态；思想观念

ideological [ˌaɪdiəˈlɑːdʒɪkl, ˌɪdiəˈlɑːdʒɪkl] adj. 思想的

ideo [ɪˈdiːəʊ] n. 观念；意想

capitalist ideology 资本主义意识形态

Lesson 25

Part 1 主力单词/词组

infer [ɪnˈfɜːr] *v.* 推断；推论

I can infer he is not a worker from his thin finger.

Be true! Be true! Be true! Show freely to the world, if not your worst, yet some trait whereby the worst may be inferred. (Nathaniel Hawthorne, U.S. novelist and short-story writer)

She inferred from that the gigantic cave must have been the cyclops' hideout.

deduce [dɪˈduːs] *v.* 推断；推论

I can deduce her age around sixty by her wrinkled complexion.

Indeed, it's always a paltry, feeble, tiny mind that takes pleasure in revenge. You can deduce it without further evidence than this, that no one delights more in vengeance than a woman. (Juvenal, Roman poet)

ratiocinate [ˌrætɪˈɑːsɪneɪt] *v.* 推理；采用三段论法

I ratiocinated the unsolved murder case in isolation.

ratiocination [ˌreɪʃɪˌoʊsɪˈneɪʃn] *n.* 推理；推论

I am not impressed by the detective's ratiocination.

ratiocinative [ˈreɪʃəʊˈɒsɪneɪtɪv] *adj.* 推理的

Mia likes to read ratiocinative crime novels.

vaticinate [væˈtɪsɪneɪt] *v.* 预言；预断

The financial expert vaticinates the course of the stock market quite accurately.

vatic [ˈvætɪk] *adj.* 预言的

Many locals escaped the town due to the vatic apocalypse.

conjecture [kənˈdʒektʃər] *v./n.* 推论；推测

Bias has influenced their conjecture.

To die for an idea is to place a pretty high price upon conjectures. (Anatole France, French novelist, poet, and critic)

These culprits' voices rose in a chorus of conjecture and alarm, repeating the selfsame remark, "What are you gonna do about it?"

speculate ['spekjuleɪt] v. 推测

She speculates about his motives.
The lieutenant speculated as to whether the reinforcement will arrive on time.
Scientists speculate that our fates are predetermined.

surmise [sər'maɪz] v./n. 臆测

Local police surmised that the victim must have been drunk as he fell off the precipice.
It was surmised that the boss cut his managers' salary to offset his losses.

guess [ges] v./n. 猜测

I guess the financial reform is meant to protect our frail economy from sordid cases like the president's financial fraud.

divine [dɪ'vaɪn] v. 猜到；领悟 n. 牧师；神学家 adj. 天赐的；非凡的；极美的

I tried to divine the intention of what she told me. However, I believed there was not a jot of the truth of her saying.
The relic of Jesus was supposed to have divine power.

syllogism ['sɪlədʒɪzəm] n. 三段论；演绎推理；推断

I won't believe the fallacious conclusion of his syllogism.
His syllogism of the murder case was intriguing.

● Words in sentences 句中单词/词组 ●

whereby [wer'baɪ] adv. 由此；在……的情况下；处于……的位置

gigantic [dʒaɪ'gæntɪk] adj. 巨大的；庞大的

cyclops ['saɪklɑːps] n. 独眼巨人

hideout ['haɪdaʊt] n. 隐匿处

wrinkle ['rɪŋkl] v. (使)起皱纹 n. 皱纹；(布料上的)褶皱

paltry ['pɔːltri] adj. 不重要的；无价值的

bias ['baɪəs] n. 偏见

culprit ['kʌlprɪt] n. 犯人；罪犯；肇事者

chorus ['kɔːrəs] v./n. 异口同声地说；齐声背诵；合唱

selfsame [ˈselfseɪm] *adj.* 完全一样的；相同的
reinforcement [ˌriːɪnˈfɔːrsmənt] *n.* 援军；加强
predetermined [ˌpriːdɪˈtɜːrmɪnd] *adj.* 事先决定好的
precipice [ˈpresəpɪs] *n.* 悬崖
offset [ˈɔːfset] *v.* 抵消；补偿；把……并列 *n.* 抵消；补偿；开端；出发 *adj.* 胶印的
frail [freɪl] *adj.* 身体虚弱的；易损坏的
sordid [ˈsɔːrdɪd] *adj.* 不道德的；不诚实的
not a jot 一点也没有；丝毫没有

Part 2 补充单词 / 词组

jot [dʒɑːt] *v.* 匆匆记下 *n.* 一点；少量
He jotted down her name.

scripted [ˈskrɪptɪd] *adj.* 内定的；按照剧本的
The whole dancing show is scripted. Your team will never be a champion.

kismet [ˈkɪzmet] *n.* 命运；时运
Our kismet is in the king's hands.
She prayed to God for having good kismet.

cache [kæʃ] *v.* 匿藏；贮藏 *n.* 贮藏所；高速缓冲存储器
They cached stolen goods in a remote cave.
The web designer cached the website to increase speed.
A farmer discovered a cache of weapons from a previous dynasty.

crinkle [ˈkrɪŋkl] *v.* 卷曲 *n.* 波纹；沙沙声
Autumn leaves crinkle on the ground when a breeze passes by.
The skin of the old man is crinkled.

breeze [briːz] *v.* 轻松完成（获得）；轻快地走 *n.* 微风
He breezed through the medical certification test.
She breezes past the protesters.

corrugate [ˈkɔːrəɡeɪt] *v.* 使起皱；使成波状 *adj.* 起皱的
Sheets of corrugated iron make the roof of the temporary building.

puny [ˈpjuːni] *adj.* 微小的；弱小的

I saw the puny arms of a baby.

His puny attempt at an apology infuriated the victims' families.

versatile [ˈvɜːrsətl] *adj.* 多才多艺的；多种用途的

The versatile garment can be worn on various occasions.

eclectic [ɪˈklektɪk] *adj.* 不拘一格的；兼容并蓄的；博采众长的

She adopts an eclectic approach combining the elements of traditional Chinese and contemporary French clothing in her fashion design.

eclecticism [ɪˈklektɪsɪzəm] *n.* 兼容并蓄

The composer embraces musical eclecticism.

precipitous [prɪˈsɪpɪtəs] *adj.* 陡峭的；急躁的；急促的

Below us is a precipitous gorge.

There has been a precipitous decline in tourism.

frailty [ˈfreɪlti] *n.* 脆弱；虚弱；弱点

Do you think frailty is a women's privilege?

No one is perfect. Love is how much you can embrace your spouse's frailties and faults.

infirm [ɪnˈfɜːrm] *adj.* 体弱的；意志薄弱的；不稳固的

Rarely does the insurance company insure infirm people.

expire [ɪkˈspaɪər] *v.* 满期；终止；呼气

The license is infirm and expired.

infirmity [ɪnˈfɜːrməti] *n.* 体弱；虚弱

The young man has been smart and ambitious but he suffers from infirmity since childhood. He gets sick easily.

atherosclerosis [ˌæθərouskləˈrousɪs] *n.* 动脉硬化（症）

cardiovascular [ˌkɑːrdiouˈvæskjələr] *adj.* 心血管的

arthritis [ɑːrˈθraɪtɪs] *n.* 关节炎

cataract [ˈkætərækt] *n.* 白内障；大瀑布；激流；豪雨；洪水

osteoporosis [ˌɑːstioupəˈrousɪs] *n.* 骨质疏松

diabetes [ˌdaɪəˈbiːtiːz] *n.* 糖尿病

hypertension [ˌhaɪpərˈtenʃn] *n.* 高血压

Alzheimer's disease 阿尔兹海默症

Atherosclerosis, cardiovascular disease, cancer, arthritis, cataracts, osteoporosis, type 2 diabetes, hypertension, and Alzheimer's disease are infirmities of old age.

condescension [ˌkɑːndɪˈsenʃn] *n.* 高傲的态度；优越感

His infirmities are arrogance and condescension.

factotum [fækˈtoʊtəm] *n.* 家务总管；杂役

He performed as a versatile factotum and general manager.

zephyr [ˈzefər] *n.* 和风；微风

Coastal zephyrs stirred up the girls' hair.

windswept [ˈwɪndswept] *adj.* 被风吹扫的；迎风的

The Indians traveled in the windswept region of treeless plains and thin vegetation.

verity [ˈverəti] *n.* 事实；信念；准则

The verity of this assumption has been refuted by many scientists a long time ago.
The verity of the legend is questionable.
The eternal verities among people are love, altruism, righteousness, patriotism…etc.

Part 3 识记单词 / 词组

inference [ˈɪnfərəns] *n.* 推断的结果；结论；推断

deduction [dɪˈdʌkʃn] *n.* 演绎；推论；推理

deducible [dɪˈduːsəbl] *adj.* 可推论的

refute [rɪˈfjuːt] *v.* 驳斥；否认

reality [riˈæləti] *n.* 事实；真实

actuality [ˌæktʃuˈæləti] *n.* 事实；真实

script [skrɪpt] *v.* 把……改编为剧本 *n.* 手迹

an eclectic taste in art 一种对艺术广泛的兴趣

divining rod 探矿杖

Titan [ˈtaɪtn] 泰坦；太阳神

demography [dɪˈmɑːgrəfi] *n.* 人口统计；人口状况

lieutenant [luːˈtenənt] *n.* 中尉

Lesson 26

Part 1 主力单词 / 词组

emperor [ˈempərər] n. 皇帝；君主

I bowed to the emperor but refused to kneel down.
The history of Germany is a history of wars between the emperor and the princes and states...of the licentiousness of the strong, and the oppression of the weak, of foreign intrusions, and foreign intrigues...of general imbecility, confusion, and misery. (Alexander Hamilton, U.S. president)

monarch [ˈmɑːnərk, ˈmɑːnɑːrk] n. 君主；帝王

The monarch was enthroned.

potentate [ˈpoʊtnteɪt] n. 帝王；统治者

The guerrilla potentates implacably committed to an apocalyptic showdown rather than to continued efforts at a negotiated modus vivendi.

regal [ˈriːgl] adj. 帝王的；庄严的；豪华的

The president's wife has a regal bearing.

regalia [rɪˈgeɪliə] n. 王位标志

Each royal family has its own unique regalia.

monarchy [ˈmɑːnərki, ˈmɑːnɑːrki] n. 君主政体

regal power 王权

• **Words in sentences 句中单词 / 词组** •

licentiousness [laɪˈsenʃəsnɪs] n. 荒淫；放荡
intrusion [ɪnˈtruːʒn] n. 侵入；闯入
imbecility [ˌɪmbəˈsɪləti] n. 愚蠢行为；低能
enthrone [ɪnˈθroʊn] v. 登基
implacably [ɪmˈplækəbli] adv. 无法被安抚地

apocalyptic [ə,pɑ:kə'lıptık]　*adj.* 预示大灾难的；启示的
modus vivendi　妥协；折中

Part 2　补充单词 / 词组

balk [bɔ:k]　*v.* 受挫折；（突然）停止　*n.* 挫折；停止；粗木材；投手犯规
His plan was balked due to lack of manpower.
Investors balked at the idea of investing more funds.
Soldiers and their horses balked at the sight of the immense enemy.

oaf [oʊf]　*n.* 笨蛋
He is a thoughtless, chubby oaf at school.

idolatrous [aɪ'dɑ:lətrəs]　*adj.* 极端崇拜的；崇拜偶像的

rendering ['rendərɪŋ]　*n.* 翻译方式；译文；表现；描写；演出
The various interpretations of the Bible were considered to be idolatrous renderings of living things.

plutocrat ['plu:təkræt]　*n.* 财阀；富豪

reactionary [ri'ækʃəneri]　*n.* 反动分子；反动派　*adj.* 极端保守的；反动的
How am I supposed to fight these plutocrats and reactionary nobles?

magnate ['mægneɪt]　*n.* 富豪；大亨
She is married to a shipping magnate.

supposititious= suppositious　*adj.* 假冒的；假定的
His supposititious heir tried to inherit his fortune alone by eliminating other heirs.

patrician [pə'trɪʃn]　*n.* 贵族；上流社会的人　*adj.* 贵族的；上流社会的
He was born into a patrician family.
The billionaire leads the life of a patrician.

pamper ['pæmpər]　*v.* 溺爱；姑息
Patrician women pampered gladiators.
The mother pampered her son too much.

uxorious [ʌk'sɔrɪəs]　*adj.* 溺爱妻子的
He is a perfect husband, uxorious and hard working.

prism ['prɪzəm]　*n.* 棱镜；棱柱

prismatic [prɪz'mætɪk]　*adj.* 多彩的；棱柱的；棱镜的
The prismatic portrait of a coddled daughter interested all of us.

kettle ['ketl]　*n.* 水壶

boil [bɔɪl]　*v.* 使激动　*n.* 煮沸；沸腾

boil over　沸腾而溢出；非常恼火
She coddled the kettle to prevent the water from boiling over.

retinue ['retənu:]　*n.* 随员；扈从
The president travels with his retinues.

Part 3　识记单词/词组

a rule of thumb　一种实用的估算方法；一种经验工作法（常依据经验而非准确测量）

imbecile ['ɪmbəsl]　*n.* 愚蠢的人；低能的人

crown prince　王储；皇太子

idolator [aɪ'dɒlətə]　*n.* 崇拜者

idolatress [aɪ'dɑ:lətrɪs]　*n.* 女性的偶像崇拜者

deity ['deɪəti, 'di:əti]　*n.* 神；女神

opal ['oʊpl]　*n.* 蛋白石；猫眼石

affluence ['æfluəns]　*n.* 丰富；涌入

nobility [noʊ'bɪləti]　*n.* 贵族；崇高

coddle ['kɑ:dl]　*v.* 娇惯；用文火煮

regicidal [ˌredʒɪ'saɪdl]　*adj.* 弑君王的

goose step　正步走

genuflection [ˌdʒenju'flekʃn]　*n.* 跪拜；屈膝

slip of the tongue　口误

slip sb's memory/mind　被某人忘记

slip through sb's fingers　机会或某人被错过

slip into sth　迅速穿上……

slip out　被无意说出

slip out of sth　快速脱下……

slip up 犯错误；疏忽
a slip of paper 一张纸条
slip through the net 漏网；被漏掉
slip away 秘密地离开；很快地过去

Lesson 27

Part 1　主力单词 / 词组

venial [ˈviːniəl] *adj.* 可被原谅的
These peccadilloes are venial.
Souls can be purified from venial sins or remitted from mortal sins by undergoing temporal punishment in the purgatory.

forgivable [fərˈɡɪvəbl] *adj.* 可被原谅的
These minor faults are forgivable.

excusable [ɪkˈskjuːzəbl] *adj.* 可被原谅的；可免除的
The psycho's tendency to anthropomorphize squirrels as humans is excusable.

pardonable [ˈpɑːrdnəbl] *adj.* 可被原谅的；可宽恕的
Politicians who ignore the economy and only focus on political ideologies are not pardonable.

• Words in sentences 句中单词 / 词组 •

peccadillo [ˌpekəˈdɪloʊ] *n.* 小错
remit [rɪˈmɪt, ˈriːmɪt] *v.* 减轻；恢复；汇款；取消；驳回
mortal [ˈmɔːrtl] *n.* 普通人　*adj.* 致命的
temporal [ˈtempərəl] *adj.* 世俗上的；短暂时间的；现世的
anthropomorphize [ˌænθrəpəˈmɔːrfaɪz] *v.* 人格化；赋予人性
squirrel [ˈskwɜːrəl] *n.* 松鼠

Part 2 补充单词 / 词组

prosimian [prəuˈsimiən] n. 原猴亚目的猴

anthropoid [ˈænθrəpɔid] n. 类人猿 adj. 似人的；似猿的

They research on prosimians and anthropoid apes.

experiment with 用……进行试验

simian [ˈsimiən] n. 类人猿；猴子 adj. 类人猿的；(像)猴的

The medical research has experimented with simians for the SARS vaccine.

secure [siˈkjuər] v. 取得；拴牢；保护 adj. 安心的；牢靠的

She pleases her boss to secure her position.
Her reckless remark secured her father's displeasure.

latitude [ˈlætitjuːd] n. 纬度；选择的自由

Some Eskimos live in the high-latitude Arctic.
The father gave his children considerable latitude in course selection.
There won't be any latitude for me to save your life.

latitudinal [ˌlætiˈtjuːdinəl] adj. 纬度的

The latitudinal range and topographical variations produce unusual diversity of climate and species.

latitudinarian [ˌlætətuːdəˈneəriən] n. 不拘泥于教义和形式的人 adj. 能容纳不同意见的

The principal is an open-minded latitudinarian.

flaccidity [flækˈsidəti] n. 软弱；没气力

flaccid [ˈflæsid, ˈflæksid] adj. 松弛的；无活力的

My uncle has not exercised for years and has flaccid muscles.

chastise [tʃæˈstaiz] v. 惩戒；鞭打

insolence [ˈinsələns] n. 傲慢；无礼

The slave was chastised for his insolence.

array [əˈrei] v. 布置；排列；穿着 n. 大量；陈列

Warriors arrayed in front of invaders and then charged.
I need the data arrayed in ascending/descending order.

She were arrayed her best-looking clothes before a dancing show.

Students wore a splendid array of formal attire for the prom.

ascend [əˈsend]　　*v.* 上升；攀登

The balloon ascends slowly into the sky.

legend [ˈledʒənd]　　*n.* 传说；铭文

The legend ascends to the 12th century.

descend [dɪˈsend]　　*v.* 下来；突然到访；沿……向下；降临

He is descended from a king of the War Period.

A large number of visitors descended upon the beach today.

The mountain river descends into the basin.

descendant [dɪˈsendənt]　　*n.* 子孙；后裔　　*adj.* 降落的；祖传的

The folklore of his time was passed on to his descendants.

rope [roʊp]　　*v.* 用绳子捆　　*n.* 绳；丝状黏质物

The climber descends the cliff by a rope.

The little kid drooled a rope of saliva as he saw a delicious cake.

posterity [pɑːˈsterəti]　　*n.* 后裔；子孙

The tradition has been handed down for posterity.

Think of your posterity! (John Quincy Adams, U.S. president)

forefather [ˈfɔːrfɑːðər]　　*n.* 祖先；祖宗

Think of your forefathers!

libretto [lɪˈbretoʊ]　　*n.* 剧本；歌词

Flaccid libretto made me very sleepy.

fair [fer]　　*n.* 庙会；露天游乐场　　*adj.* 公正的；相当好的；白皙的　　*adv.* 公正地；相当好地

Adalynn doesn't believe his fair promises.

The company received a fair amount of responses to the advertisement.

The weather is fair.

Caucasians have fair skin.

His oral French is fair.

Serious sport has nothing to do with fair play.

equitable [ˈekwɪtəbl]　　*adj.* 公平的；公正的

This is an equitable solution to settle the dispute.

Part 3　识记单词 / 词组

mortal enemy　死敌

porm ['pɔm]　n.（学校的）班级舞会

legendary ['ledʒənderi]　n. 圣徒传　adj. 传说的；著名的

basin ['beɪsn]　n. 盆地；洗涤槽

The Taipei Basin　台北盆地

The Amazon Basin　亚马逊河流域

folklore ['foʊklɔːr]　n. 民间传说；民俗学

infernal heat　酷热

plumber ['plʌmər]　n. 管子工；铅管工

play fair　按规则行事

Caucasian [kɔː'keɪʒn]　n. 高加索人；白种人　adj. 高加索地方的；白种人的

longitudinal study　纵向研究

punitive import duties/tariffs　惩罚性的进口税

punitive action　惩罚的举动

punitive raid　惩罚的袭击

tomb raider　盗墓者

raid [reɪd]　v. 搜捕；劫掠　n. 袭击

anthropomorphism [ˌænθrəpə'mɔːrfɪzəm]　n. 神人同形同性论

reprehensible bombing　应受谴责的轰炸

lax security　松懈的警戒

reprehend [ˌreprɪ'hend]　v. 指责；责备

reprehension [ˌreprɪ'henʃn]　n. 非难；指责

Lesson 28

Part 1　主力单词 / 词组

essential [ɪ'senʃl]　n. 基本要素　adj. 重要的；本质的

It is essential to build a strong foundation.

We are firm believers in the maxim that for all right judgment of any man or thing it is useful, nay, essential, to see his good qualities before pronouncing on his bad. (Thomas Carlyle, Scottish historian and essayist)

cardinal [ˈkɑːrdɪnl] *n.* 深红色 *adj.* 很严重的；鲜红色的

The shrine, placed at the intersection of the cardinal axes of the pedestrian precinct, is colossal.

vitality [vaɪˈtæləti] *n.* 活力；生命力

vital [ˈvaɪtl] *adj.* 至关重要的；生气勃勃的

The heart, liver, spleen, bladder, lungs and kidneys are the body's vital organs.

pivotal [ˈpɪvətl] *adj.* 关键的；中枢的

Little progress has been made on the pivotal issue of food containing radiation.

imperative [ɪmˈperətɪv] *n.* 规则 *adj.* 必要的；不可避免的

Taking immediate action is imperative to the company's success.

significance [sɪɡˈnɪfɪkəns] *n.* 意义；重要性

significant [sɪɡˈnɪfɪkənt] *adj.* 重要的；值得注意的

That picture with my wife is significant to me.

momentous [moʊˈmentəs] *adj.* 重大的；重要的

The First Sino-Japanese war was a momentous event recorded in history.

It is a momentous decision that I am faced with.

● **Words in sentences 句中单词/词组** ●

nay [neɪ] *n.* 反对（票） *adv.* 而且；不但如此；不

shrine [ʃraɪn] *n.* 圣坛；纪念地

precinct [ˈpriːsɪŋkt] *n.* 步行区；警察辖区

colossal [kəˈlɑːsl] *adj.* 巨大的

liver [ˈlɪvər] *n.* 肝

spleen [spliːn] *n.* 脾

bladder [ˈblædər] *n.* 膀胱

radiation [ˌreɪdiˈeɪʃn] *n.* （核）辐射

Part 2 补充单词 / 词组

paramount [ˈpærəmaʊnt]　*adj.* 最重要的；最主要的

paramount importance　重中之重

Speed for a race car is paramount/of paramount importance.

subservient [səbˈsɜːrviənt]　*adj.* 用来辅助的；有用的；屈从的

My achievement is subservient when compared with Bill Gates's.
All the foreign policies we have made are subservient to the unification of China.

therapeutic [ˌθerəˈpjuːtɪk]　*adj.* 治疗的；有益于健康的

therapeutics [ˌθerəˈpjuːtɪks]　*n.* 治疗学；疗法

negligible [ˈneɡlɪdʒəbl]　*adj.* 微不足道的；可忽略的

The spectacular advances made in therapeutics by industry during recent years tend to make us forget the medicinal value of plants. Their usefulness is far from negligible; their active principles are manifold and well-balanced. (Paul Fruictier, French writer)

reclamation [ˌrekləˈmeɪʃn]　*n.* 开垦；改造

apace [əˈpeɪs]　*adv.* 高速地；迅速地

Land reclamation continues apace in India.

sulfanilamide [ˌsʌlfəˈnɪləˌmaɪd]　*n.* 磺胺

derivative [dɪˈrɪvətɪv]　*n.* 衍生物；衍生字　*adj.* 拷贝他人的；差别的；有区别的

Work on the research project concerning sulfanilamide and its various derivatives is proceeding apace.
Shakespeare's script may be derivative of others' work.

pedestrian [pəˈdestriən]　*n.* 行人　*adj.* 步行的；平淡的

He lives an uneventful, pedestrian life.
I don't know what the point is of this pedestrian movie.

Part 3 识记单词 / 词组

cardinal rule　重要的规则
cardinal sin　严重的罪

coefficient [ˌkoʊɪˈfɪʃnt] n. 系数
differential [ˌdɪfəˈrenʃl] n. 差别；差额；分速器
cog [kɑ:g] n. 轮齿
finch [fɪntʃ] n. 雀鸟
flinch [flɪntʃ] v. 畏惧 n. 退缩
theraphy [ˈθerəpi] n. 治疗；疗法

Lesson 29

Part 1　主力单词 / 词组

indolent [ˈɪndələnt] adj. 懒惰的；懒散的
He who is used to going for a saunter becomes a parasite on society, useless and indolent.
This indolent rascal, who by a strange mischance, had broken his leg instead of his worthless neck, brought suit for malpractice.

faineant [ˈfeɪnɪrnt] n. 无所事事者；懒惰者　adj. 无所事事的；懒惰的
He is too faineant to do his home assignment.
My faineant brother has been lying on the couch all day long.

lethargy [ˈleθərdʒi] n. 昏睡；嗜眠症
The mysterious illness has a physical symptom of lethargy.

lethargic [ləˈθɑːrdʒɪk] adj. 昏睡的；不关心的
The lethargic patient can't walk for a long time.
Most legislators are lethargic to issues relating to those who identify as homosexual.

idle [ˈaɪdl] v. 使空转　n. 空转　adj. 空闲的；懒惰的
I enjoyed the idle pleasures of my school days.

listless [ˈlɪstləs] adj. 倦怠的；没兴趣的
She got bored and listless answering in monosyllables.

lackadaisical [ˌlækəˈdeɪzɪkl] adj. 不热心的；没活力的
The statistics of GDP indicate a booming economy, not a lackadaisical one.

I serenaded her below her window in a lackadaisical tone.

sloth [sloʊθ]   *n.* 懒散；怠惰；树懒

His fat sister who eats a lot and has an aversion to work has the sins of gluttony and sloth.

slothful [ˈsloʊθfl]   *adj.* 懒惰的；不活跃的

The department has been unproductive due to too many slothful workers.

She is not lazy but moderately slothful.

languid [ˈlæŋgwɪd]   *adj.* 疲倦的；萧条的

I was famished with my languid eyes half-open.

I enjoyed the charm of dolce vita on a languid summer afternoon.

languorous [ˈlæŋgərəs]   *adj.* 怠惰的；没精打采的；沉闷的

The major turned the languorous port into an international resort.

languor [ˈlæŋgər]   *n.* 倦怠；慵懒；消沉

The dehydrated patient experienced the languor of convalescence.

Intense languor arises on summer days on the tropical island.

droop [druːp]   *v.* 使……下垂 *n.* 下垂；枯萎；弯曲

The child yawned and his eyelids drooped while listening to a boring story.

Plants droop during a severe drought.

droopy [ˈdruːpi]   *adj.* 下垂的；无精打采的

The toddler wore droopy pants.

drowsy [ˈdraʊzi]   *adj.* 沉寂的；催眠的；呆滞的

The drugs make me drowsy.

His sermon seems to have a drowsy effect in which I almost fall into a peaceful slumber.

somnolent [ˈsɑːmnələnt]   *adj.* 使人想睡的

Teaching a somnolent student on a very hot day is taxing.

The somnolent hum of insects as a lullaby makes me very sleepy.

hebetude [ˈhebɪˌtjuːd]   *n.* 没精神

The education minister expected to rekindle teachers' passions in heuristics in a miasma of apathy and intellectual hebetude.

torpor [ˈtɔːrpər]   *n.* 麻木；蛰伏

Only could he greet the recent bad news with a resigned fatalism and torpor.

lassitude [ˈlæsɪtuːd] n. 无精打采；懒怠

The lassitude was occasioned by fatigue and insomnia.

soporific=soporiferous adj. 催眠的；想睡的

His boring lecture makes me very soporific.

• Words in sentences 句中单词/词组 •

saunter [ˈsɔːntər] v. 闲逛；漫步

rascal [ˈræskl] n. 无赖；坏蛋

couch [kaʊtʃ] v. 使躺下；埋伏 n. 长沙发；睡椅

legislator [ˈledʒɪsleɪtər] n. 立法者

monosyllable [ˈmɑːnəsɪləbl] n. 一个音节的字

famish [ˈfæmɪʃ] v. 使挨饿；感到饿

dolce vita 奢华放纵的生活方式

dehydrated [diːˈhaɪdreɪtɪd] adj. 脱水的

convalescence [ˌkɑːnvəˈlesns] n. 渐愈；恢复期

yawn [jɔːn] v. 打呵欠；张开

sermon [ˈsɜːrmən] n. 布道；讲道

slumber [ˈslʌmbər] n. 睡觉；睡眠

tax [tæks] v. 使负重担 n. 责备；谴责

lullaby [ˈlʌləbaɪ] n. 摇篮曲；催眠曲

rekindle [ˌriːˈkɪndl] v. 重新点燃；再点火

heuristics [hjuˈrɪstɪks] n. 启发式教学法

miasma [miˈæzmə, maɪˈæzmə] n. 瘴气；不良影响

apathy [ˈæpəθi] n. 无兴趣；漠不关心

fatalism [ˈfeɪtəlɪzəm] n. 宿命论；天数

insomnia [ɪnˈsɑːmniə] n. 失眠

Part 2 补充单词/词组

fetus [ˈfiːtəs] n. 胎儿

cesarean=cesarean section 剖腹产

The fetus's position was not right and therefore, the baby was delivered by cesarean section.

parturition [ˌpɑːrtʃəˈrɪʃn] n. 分娩；生产

Colostrum contains antibodies and immune substances and is produced after parturition.

draft [dræft] v. 起草；派遣；征兵 n. 草稿；气流；一口（烟酒）；汇票；拉网 adj. 草拟的；桶装的；载重的

Do you think the founding father drafted the constitution?

I felt a cold draft from nowhere when I passed that empty room at night.

She has the last draft on her cigarette before going to prison.

Is the Heineke on draft or is it bottled?

Donkeys and mules are draft animals.

herring [ˈherɪŋ] n. 鲱鱼

Fishermen found some herrings in a draft of fish.

drafty [ˈdræfti] adj. 通风的；通风良好的

The main hall is vast and drafty.

pant [pænt] v. 喘气；渴望 n. 喘气

We were panting by the time we reached the summit.

Dogs pant in hot weather.

She pants for becoming a singer.

pants [pænts] n. 裤子

homily [ˈhɑːməli] n. 说教；布道

The priest delivers his homily on a portion of the Bible.

We must listen to our manager's homilies about how to work more efficiently.

nous [naʊs] n. 常识；处世才能；机敏

These doctors are long on expertise but short on everyday nous.

If you have a little nous, you will not sell drugs in front of the police station.

His nous in the battle has been merited.

Nous often comes with age and experience.

repentance [rɪˈpentəns] n. 忏悔；后悔

metanoia [metəˈnɔɪə] n. 发自内心的改变

Confession, repentance, and metanoia are required before you enter Heaven.

pococurante [ˌpoʊkoʊkʊˈrænti] n. 冷漠之人 adj. 漫不经心的；冷淡的

He has a pococurante attitude toward the miserable.

resigned [rɪˈzaɪnd] adj. 认命的；已辞职的

James accepted the order with a resigned sigh.

The servant follows the master's instruction in a resigned manner.

He was resigned to the fact that the rest of his life would be carried out in prison.

impassioned [ɪmˈpæʃnd] adj. 充满激情的；慷慨激昂的

She gave me a long, impassioned kiss.

The teacher delivered numerous impassioned speeches.

whirl [wɜːrl] v. 旋转；急驶 n. 尝试

Turkey dancers are good at whirling round and round.

swirl [swɜːrl] v./n. 旋动

My eyes watch your fingers as you swirl them around in the puddle with a youthful sense of intrigue.

There is a swirl in the lake.

vortex [ˈvɔːrteks] n. 旋涡；旋风

The corrupted official was sucked into the vortex of a political storm.

The Germans had been drawn into the vortex of World War One.

maelstrom [ˈmeɪlstrəm] n. 大漩涡；骚乱

The ship was drawn into a treacherous maelstrom.

He was caught in a maelstrom of emotions after his wife ran away with another man.

Italy was gradually sucked into the maelstrom of World War Two.

Britain was dragged into the maelstrom of American politics.

terpsichorean [ˌtɜːpsɪkəˈriːən, -ˈkɔːriən] n. 舞蹈家 adj. 舞蹈的

There are some fete terpsichoreans on the stage.

native [ˈneɪtɪv] n. 本地人；土著 adj. 天生的；出生地的

The performance of native terpsichoreans was fantastic.

nativist [ˈneɪtɪvɪst] n. 本土文化保护者；先天论者

Several nativists called for the preservation of Maya traditions.

Nativists believed that certain abilities are innate to an individual and need not be gained through experience.

regale [rɪ'geɪl] v. 使喜悦；宴请 n. 佳肴

The historian regaled us with tales.
The master regales his guests over six-course meals.
We overate in the regale hosted by my father-in-law.

dreamland ['driːmlænd] n. 梦境

Noetic experience in the dreamland which is mystical can influence our health, our behavior, and our lives.

lag [læg] v. 落后；滞后 n. 减弱；衰退；延迟

For a month, the scandal never lagged.
The lag between World War One and World War Two is about twenty-one years.

diminution [ˌdɪmɪ'nuːʃn] n. 缩小；减少

The recession caused the diminution of corporate dividends.
The rapid diminution of endangered species sends out an alert.

effectual [ɪ'fektʃuəl] adj. 有效果的；有法律效力的

The medicine is effectual, I am restored to full health now.

ineffectual [ˌɪnɪ'fektʃuəl] adj. 无效果的；徒劳无益的

However, it was ineffectual.

duenna [djuː'enə] n. 女保姆

The duenna has adequate experience of babysitting.

blasé [blɑ'zeɪ] adj. 玩厌了的；无动于衷的

Television views have become blasé to politicians' empty promises.
The serial killer has a blasé attitude to life.

entomological [ˌentə'mɑːlədʒɪkəl] adj. 昆虫学的

The scientist conducted medical entomological research.

Part 3 识记单词 / 词组

torporific [ˌtɔːpə'rɪfɪk] adj. 引起麻痹的；失去知觉的

spoor [spʊr] n. 足迹；嗅迹

indolence ['ɪndələns] n. 懒散；懒惰

languish ['læŋgwɪʃ] v. 憔悴；烦恼

somatic cell 体细胞；营养细胞
disinclination [ˌdɪsˌɪnklɪˈneɪʃn] n. 不太乐意
a draft horse 一匹役用马
resign [rɪˈzaɪn] v. 辞职；放弃；勉强接受
impassion [ɪmˈpæʃən] v. 激起……的热情；使激动
dividend [ˈdɪvɪdend] n. 好处；被除数
integration [ˌɪntɪˈgreɪʃn] n. 集成；综合
weave [wiːv] v. 编写；编造 n. 织法；织物
weaver [ˈwiːvər] n. 织布者
warp and weft 经织和纬织
anaemia [əˈniːmiə] n. 贫血症
debility [dɪˈbɪləti] n. 衰弱
legislature [ˈledʒɪsleɪtʃər] n. 立法机关；立法部
legislative [ˈledʒɪsleɪtɪv] n. 立法权 adj. 立法的
puddle [ˈpʌdl] v. 搅泥浆；在水坑中嬉戏

Lesson 30

Part 1 主力单词/词组

outdo [ˌaʊtˈduː] v. 胜过；超过
Self-realization outdoes money-earning.
In the twilight of his career, he was about to be outdone.

surpass [sərˈpæs] v. 超过；优于
The expectation of that candidate seems to surpass others.

outshine [ˌaʊtˈʃaɪn] v. 比……更出色；比……更优异
Supernovas outshine all other stars.
The mother outshone her daughter.

overshadow [ˌoʊvərˈʃædoʊ] v. 遮阴；使失色
Public opinions overshadow bona fide aesthetic value.

eclipse [ɪˈklɪps] v. 使黯然失色 n. 蚀；黯然失色

Her sublime beauty eclipsed other stars.

His reputation has fallen into eclipse due to the mismanagement of the company fund.

outstrip [ˌaʊtˈstrɪp] v. 超过；胜于

After years of practicing in the mountain, my kung fu has outstripped my master's.

transcend [trænˈsend] v. 超越；超出……的限度

Music transcends the boundary of race and nationality.

Extraterrestrial technology transcends the understanding of human scientists.

transcendent [trænˈsendənt] adj. 超然的；卓越的

outclass [ˌaʊtˈklæs] v. 比……更高级；远高于

He battled gamely, outclassing other generals.

overhaul [ˈoʊvərˌhɔːl, ˌoʊvərˈhɔːl] v. 赶上；超过；彻底检修 n. 全面检查

The most imposing Surinamese swimmer was overhauled by a Canadian in the freestyle.

The experienced mechanic overhauls the airplane engine.

The car was overhauled with a stringent inspection.

The president overhauls his new policy.

outpace [ˌaʊtˈpeɪs] v. 比……走得快

His progress outpaces others.

trump [trʌmp] v. 胜过；打出王牌 n. 王牌；有效手段

His offer trumped others'.

• Words in sentences 句中单词 / 词组 •

self-realization [ˌself ˌriːələˈzeɪʃn] n. 自我实现

twilight [ˈtwaɪlaɪt] n. 黄昏时分；晚期

expectation [ˌekspekˈteɪʃn] n. 期望

candidate [ˈkændɪdət, ˈkændɪdeɪt] n. 候选人

bona fide 真正的；真诚的

extraterrestrial [ˌekstrətəˈrestriəl] adj. 外星的；地球外的

gamely [ˈgeɪmli] adv. 勇敢地；不屈地

imposing [ɪmˈpoʊzɪŋ] adj. 壮观的；给人深刻印象的

Part 2 补充单词 / 词组

first aid 急救

defibrillator [diːˈfɪbrɪleɪtər] *n.* 电击器
The doctor administered first aid and used a defibrillator.

taut [tɔːt] *adj.* 拉紧的；绷紧的；整洁的
She pulled the rope taut.
The principal's face was taut when someone mentioned his mistress's name.
The kitchen is clean and taut.

incorporate [ɪnˈkɔːrpəreɪt] *v.* 包含；加上；使具体化；体现
We will incorporate Eric's concept in this design.

integrate [ˈɪntɪɡreɪt] *v.* 使……成整体
The founder of this religion integrated Taoism and Buddhism together.

sapphire [ˈsæfaɪər] *n.* 蓝宝石 *adj.* 蔚蓝色的
The rare sapphire she wears represents the life of ultimate luxury.

ultimate [ˈʌltɪmət] *n.* 极限；顶点；基本原则 *adj.* 最后的；根本的
The ultimate fate of the captives has not been sealed.
The ultimate aim of this training is to rescue the hostage harmlessly.

ultimatum [ˌʌltɪˈmeɪtəm] *n.* 最后通牒；最后结论
The Japanese commander gave the U.S. military an ultimatum to surrender immediately or die.
Toxicologists did not reach an ultimatum about what substance caused the victim's death.

stringent [ˈstrɪndʒənt] *adj.* 严格的
There are few things we can do with a stringent budget.

Part 3 识记单词 / 词组

a stringent money market 一个银根紧缩的金融市场
imposing valley 壮观的山谷
twilight years 晚年
homosexuality [ˌhoʊməˌsekʃuˈæləti] *n.* 同性恋
homosexual [ˌhoʊməˈsekʃuəl] *n.* 同性恋者 *adj.* 同性恋的

bisexual [ˌbaɪˈsekʃuəl] *n.* 双性恋者 *adj.* 双性恋的
pansexual [pænˈsekʃuəl] *n.* 泛性恋的人 *adj.* 泛性恋的
counterproductive [ˌkaʊntərprəˈdʌktɪv] *adj.* 反生产的；使达不到预期目标的
parturifacient [pɑːˌtʊrəˈfeɪʃnt] *adj.* 接生的
colostrum [kəˈlɑːstrəm] *n.* 初乳
arise [əˈraɪz] *v.* 出现；起身
subtropical [ˌsʌbˈtrɑːpɪkl] *adj.* 亚热带的
subtropics [ˌsʌbˈtrɑːpɪks] *n.* 亚热带
belch [beltʃ] *v.* 打嗝；喷嚏 *n.* 打嗝
burp [bɜːrp] *v.* 打嗝 *n.* 饱嗝儿
lid [lɪd] *v.* 给……盖盖子 *n.* 盖子；限制
noetic [noʊˈetɪk] *adj.* 心智的；智力的
entre nous 要保守秘密；不要对别人说
arthropod [ˈɑːrθrəpɑːd] *n.* 节肢动物
passionate [ˈpæʃənət] *adj.* 热情的；易怒的
eye socket 眼窝
socket [ˈsɑːkɪt] *v.* 将……装入插座 *n.* 插座；插孔
lagging [ˈlæɡɪŋ] *n.* 绝热材料
defibrillate [diˈfɪbrɪleɪt] *v.* 电击
defibrillation [diːˌfɪbrɪˈleɪʃn] *n.* 电击
fibrillation [ˌfɪbrɪˈleɪʃn] *n.* 纤维性颤动
soma [ˈsoʊmə] *n.* 体细胞；细胞体
toxicologist [ˌtɑːksɪˈkɑːlədʒɪst] *n.* 毒物学家

Lesson 31

Part 1 主力单词 / 词组

self [self] *v.* 接近 *n.* 自己；私利 *adj.* 同一的；纯净的

She shows her best self at the conference.

The celebrity's public self will not be the same as her private self.

self-reflection [ˈselfrɪˈflekʃən] n. 反省
The election fiasco has urged the party to engage in profound self-reflection.

self-aggrandizement [ˌselfəˈgrændɪzmənt] n. 自我膨胀
A procession of professors was accused of self-aggrandizement.

self-ordained [ˈselfɔːˈdeɪnd] adj. 自封专家的
She experienced an epiphany of God and became a self-ordained emissary of God.

self-opinionated [ˌself əˈpɪnjəneɪtɪd] adj. 刚愎自用的
The cantankerous old man is self-opinionated and narrow-minded.

self-denial [ˌself dɪˈnaɪəl] n. 克己；忘我

self-awareness [ˌself əˈwernəs] n. 自我意识
Asceticism and stoicism are the practices of self-denial and renunciation of worldly pleasure in order to attain a higher degree of self-awareness and transcend one's spirituality and intellectuality.

self-mortification [ˈselfˌmɔːtɪfɪˈkeɪʃən] n. 苦修；禁欲
After losing his wife, he plunged into a life of austerity and self-mortification as an eremite.

self-righteous [ˌself ˈraɪtʃəs] adj. 自以为是的

self-gratification [ˌself ˌgrætɪfɪˈkeɪʃn] n. 自我满足；自我放纵
Some people relish instant self-gratification without regard to its consequences.

• Words in sentences 句中单词 / 词组 •

fiasco [fiˈæskoʊ] n. 完全失败；尴尬的结局

procession [prəˈseʃn] n. 行列；队伍

epiphany [ɪˈpɪfəni] n. 显灵；灵机一现

emissary [ˈemɪseri] n. 使者；密使

cantankerous [kænˈtæŋkərəs] adj. 爱生气的；不太好相处的

narrow-minded [ˈnæroʊˈmaɪndɪd] adj. 心胸狭窄的；偏执的

asceticism [əˈsetɪsɪzəm] n. 禁欲主义

stoicism [ˈstoʊɪsɪzəm] n. 苦修主义
renunciation [rɪˌnʌnsiˈeɪʃn] n. 声明放弃；弃绝
worldly [ˈwɜːrldli] adj. 世间的；世俗的　adv. 俗气地；追名逐利地
spirituality [ˌspɪrɪtʃuˈæləti] n. 灵性；精神性
plunge [plʌndʒ] v. 全心投入；骤然下降　n. 暴跌；跳入
austerity [ɔːˈsterəti] n. 简朴（的生活）
eremite [ˈerəˌmaɪt] n. 隐士
relish [ˈrelɪʃ] v. 享受　n. 调味品

Part 2 补充单词/词组

immolate [ˈɪməleɪt] v. 宰杀……作祭品
Religious followers immolated their cherished possessions to God so that He will bring them good fortune.
The cult leader would animate his worshipers to immolate them on the altar.
Why should I be immolated in the movie?

sterilize [ˈsterəlaɪz] v. 使无菌；使绝育
These towels have been sterilized.

gainsay [ˌɡeɪnˈseɪ] v. 否认；反对
There is no gainsaying she is the best ice skater.
I will not gainsay she is beautiful and gorgeous.

anthracite [ˈænθrəsaɪt] n. 无烟煤

combust [kəmˈbʌst] v. 燃烧

bituminite [bɪtjuːmɪnaɪt] n. 烟煤；沥青煤
Anthracite combusts more cleanly than bituminite.

combustible [kəmˈbʌstəbl] adj. 可燃的
Paper and wood are combustible materials.

propellant [prəˈpelənt] n. 推进物；推动者

kerosene [ˈkerəsiːn] n. 煤油；火油

binder [ˈbaɪndər] n. 黏结剂；纸夹；保证书

plasticizer [ˈplæstəˌsaɪzər] n. 塑化剂

The ingredients of rocket propellants include kerosene, binder, plasticizer…etc.

mortify [ˈmɔːrtɪfaɪ] v. 使……受辱

She was mortified by his insolent attitude.

superimpose [ˌsuːpərɪmˈpoʊz] v. 使（尤指图片、文字等）叠加

Christopher superimposed a white rose on the original picture.

The book cover had a picture of a unicorn superimposed on an ancient battle scene.

welt [welt] v. 毒打；加沿条于…… n. 毒打；鞭痕；沿条

The master welted his slaves for pleasure.

I can see the welt of a scar on her thigh.

Let me give him a welt with my baseball bat.

The tailor attaches welts to the sleeves.

opine [oʊˈpaɪn] v. 表达；发表

People should opine anything they want without fear.

Part 3 识记单词 / 词组

self-examination [ˌself ɪɡˌzæmɪˈneɪʃn] n. 自我反省

self-abasement [ˈselfəˈbeɪsmənt] n. 自卑；自谦

self-abandoned [ˈselfəˈbændənd] adj. 自暴自弃的；放肆的

self-abuse [ˌself əˈbjuːs] n. 自责

self-flattery [ˈselfflˈætərɪ] n. 自吹自擂；自我粉饰

self-glorification [ˈselfˌɡlɒrɪfɪˈkeɪʃən] n. 自己赞颂自己

self-importance [ˌself ɪmˈpɔːrtns] n. 觉得自己很重要

self-administer [ˈselfədmˈmɪstər] n. 自我给药

self-appointed [ˌself əˈpɔɪntɪd] adj. 自封的

self-proclaimed [ˌself prəˈkleɪmd] adj. 自称的

self-promotion [ˌself prəˈmoʊʃn] n. 自我营销

self-propelling [ˌselfprəˈpelɪŋ] adj. 自己驱动的

self-propulsion [ˌselfprəˈpʌlʃn] n. 自己推动

self-assurance [ˌself əˈʃʊrəns] n. 自信

Lesson 31

self-assertive [ˌself əˈsɜːrtɪv] *adj.* 自作主张的
self-conscious [ˌself ˈkɑːnʃəs] *adj.* 局促不安的；害羞的
self-deception [ˌself dɪˈsepʃn] *n.* 自欺
self-effacing [ˌself ɪˈfeɪsɪŋ] *adj.* 不爱出风头的；谦虚的
self-deprecating [ˌself ˈdeprəkeɪtɪŋ] *adj.* 自我贬低的；自谦的
self-doubt [ˌself ˈdaʊt] *n.* 自我怀疑
self-employed [ˌself ɪmˈplɔɪd] *adj.* 自己经营的
self-evident [ˌself ˈevɪdənt] *adj.* 不证自明的
self-explanatory [ˌself ɪkˈsplænətɔːri] *adj.* 不解自明的
self-executing [ˈselfˈeksəˌkjutɪŋ] *adj.* 自动生效的
self-exile [ˌself ˈeksaɪl] *n.* 自我流放
self-expression [ˌself ɪkˈspreʃn] *n.* 自我表现；自我表达
self-feeder [ˈselfˈfiːdə] *n.* 自动给料器
self-financing [ˌself ˈfaɪnænsɪŋ] *adj.* 自筹经费的
self-flagellation [ˌself ˌflædʒəˈleɪʃn] *n.* 自责；自罚
self-fulfilling [ˌself fʊlˈfɪlɪŋ] *adj.* 自我实现的
self-serving [ˌself ˈsɜːrvɪŋ] *adj.* 追逐私利的
self-interest [ˌself ˈɪntrəst, ˌself ˈɪntrest] *n.* 自身利益
self-giving [ˌself ˈɡɪvɪŋ] *adj.* 无私的；舍己为人的
self-governed [ˈselfˈɡʌvənd] *adj.* 自治的
self-hatred [ˈselfˈheɪtrɪd] *n.* 自我憎恨
self-loathing [ˌself ˈloʊðɪŋ] *adj.* 自我憎恨的
self-hypnosis [ˈselfhɪpˈnəʊsɪs] *n.* 自我催眠
self-ignite [ˌself ɪɡˈnaɪtɪd] *v.* 自燃
self-image [ˌself ˈɪmɪdʒ] *n.* 自我形象
self-immolation [ˈselfˌɪməʊˈleɪʃən] *n.* 自我牺牲
self-imposed [ˈselfɪmˈpəʊzd] *adj.* 自己决定的
self-improvement [ˌself ɪmˈpruːvmənt] *n.* 自我改善
self-incriminating [ˌselfɪnˈkrɪmɪneɪtɪŋ] *adj.* 自证有罪的
self-induced [ˌself ɪnˈduːst] *adj.* 自己导致的
self-indulgence [ˌself ɪnˈdʌldʒəns] *n.* 自我放纵
self-inflicted [ˌself ɪnˈflɪktɪd] *adj.* 施加于自身的

self-justification [ˌself ˌdʒʌstɪfɪˈkeɪʃn] n. 自我辩解

self-knowledge [ˌself ˈnɑːlɪdʒ] n. 自知之明

self-limitation [ˈselflɪmɪtˈeɪʃn] n. 本身的限制

self-love [ˌself ˈlʌv] n. 自爱

self-made [ˌself ˈmeɪd] adj. 自制的；白手起家的

self-mastery [ˈselfˈmɑːstəri, -ˈmæs-] n. 自制；克己

self-control [ˌself kənˈtrəʊl] n. 自我控制

self-restraint [ˌself rɪˈstreɪnt] n. 自制

self-possessed [ˌself pəˈzest] adj. 镇静的

self-motivated [ˈselfˈməʊtiveitid] adj. 自我激发的

self-mutilation [ˈselfˌmjuːtiˈlaɪʃən] n. 自残

self-parody [ˈselfpˈærədi] n. 自我嘲弄

self-perpetuating [ˌself pərˈpetʃueɪtɪŋ] adj. 能使自身永久存在的

self-pity [ˌselfˈpiti] n. 自怜；自悯

self-pollination [ˈselfˌpɒləˈneɪʃn] n. 自授花粉

self-portrait [ˌself ˈpɔːrtrət] n. 自画像

self-preservation [ˌself prezərˈveɪʃn] n. 自保

self-protection [ˌself prəˈtekʃn] n. 自卫

self-reliance [ˌself rɪˈlaɪəns] n. 倚靠自己

self-renunciation [ˌself rɪˌnʌnsiˈeɪʃn] n. 放弃权力或财产以利他人

self-replicating [ˈselfrˈeplɪkeɪtɪŋ] adj. 自体复制的

self-reproach [ˈselfrɪˈprəʊtʃ] n. 自责

self-respect [ˌself rɪˈspekt] n. 自尊

self-righting [ˈselfˈraitɪŋ] adj. 自动回到原来位置的

self-rising [ˌself ˈraɪzɪŋ] adj. 自然发酵的

self-sacrifice [ˌself ˈsækrɪfaɪs] n. 自我牺牲

self-seeker [ˈselfˈsiːkə] n. 利己主义的人

self-service [ˌself ˈsɜːrvɪs] n. 自助

self-starter [ˌself ˈstɑːrtər] n. 做事主动的人

self-sterile [ˌselfˈsteraɪl] adj. 自体不育的

self-fertile [ˈselfˈfɜːtaɪl] adj. 自体能育的

self-sufficient [ˌself səˈfɪʃnt] adj. 自给自足的

self-sustaining [ˌself sə'steɪnɪŋ] *adj.* 能自己养活自己的
self-talk ['selftɔk] *n.* 自言自语
self-tapping ['self'tæpɪŋ] *adj.* 自动攻丝的
self-taught [ˌself 'tɔːt] *adj.* 自修的
self-tender [self 'tendər] *n.* 公司用高价买回公司的股票
self-willed ['selfwɪld] *adj.* 固执的；任性的
self-winding [self 'wɪndɪŋ] *adj.* 自动上发条的
self-worth [ˌself 'wɜːrθ] *n.* 自我价值

Lesson 32

Part 1 主力单词 / 词组

dire ['daɪər] *adj.* 非常糟的；危急的；极端的
My financial situation is often dire. I have no property, but I have a Father in Heaven.
After the hurricane, the school is in dire need of repair.
Do not create a dire situation to duel with a professional killer.

abysmal [ə'bɪzməl] *adj.* 极糟的；深不可测的
Due to the lack of practice, his dancing performance was abysmal.
Turn a blind eye to abysmal ignorance.

consummate ['kɑnsəˌmeɪt, kən'sʌmɪt, 'kɑnsəmɪt] *v.* 使完美；使圆满；完成 *adj.* 完美无缺的；圆满的
The narcissist talked to me with consummate arrogance.
His consummate skill allows him to stand out among the laity.
The salesman consummates the deal within an hour.

egregious [ɪ'griːdʒɪəs] *adj.* 惊人的；过分的
That is an egregious error.

unwholesome [ˌʌn'hoʊlsəm] *adj.* 不道德的；不健康的
The supplier was deemed fraudulent and unwholesome.

woefully [ˈwoʊfəli] adv. 极其

The oxygen supply is woefully inadequate in a sinking submarine.

execrable [ˈeksɪkrəbl] adj. 极坏的；恶劣的

Living conditions were execrable in the refugee.
His execrable behavior is a telltale sign of his selfishness.

woe [woʊ] n. 灾难；悲伤

Woe betides him if he dares to challenge his superior.

consummately [ˈkɒnsəmɪtli] adv. 至上地；完成地

consummation [ˌkɒnsəˈmeɪʃn] n. 完善；圆满成功

• Words in sentences 句中单词/词组 •

hurricane [ˈhɜːrəkeɪn] n. 飓风；暴风雨；爆发
duel [ˈduːəl] v. 决斗 n. 斗争
turn a blind eye 假装没看到
narcissist [ˈnɑːrsɪsɪst] n. 自恋者
fraudulent [ˈfrɔːdʒələnt] adj. 诈骗的；欺骗的
submarine [ˌsʌbməˈriːn, ˈsʌbməriːn] n. 潜艇
telltale sign 指示标记
betide [bɪˈtaɪd] v. 发生

Part 2 补充单词/词组

carat [ˈkærət] n. 克拉

She wears a three-carat diamond and an eighteen-carat gold ring.

frustrate [ˈfrʌstreɪt] v. 挫败；阻挠 adj. 受挫的；无效的

abyss [əˈbɪs] n. 深渊；困境

He was frustrated and stood on the edge of an abyss.

discourage [dɪsˈkɜːrɪdʒ] v. 使灰心；使沮丧

I discourage you from believing he is a devil.

Lesson 32

dispirit [dɪˈspɪrɪt] v. 使气馁；使沮丧

The team became dispirited after two consecutive losses.
We can defeat the dispirited army more easily.
It was a dispiriting holiday when a typhoon occurred.

unnerving [ˌʌnˈnɜːrvɪŋ] adj. 使人紧张不安的

The haunted house is unnerving.

unnerve [ˌʌnˈnɜːrv] v. 使气馁；使焦躁

Coronavirus has unnerved residents.
Plunging oil prices unnerve the market.

under the weather 身体不舒服

recover [rɪˈkʌvər] v. 重新获得；恢复；挽回；弥补

I had been under the weather for a couple of days, but now I have recovered.

weather [ˈweðər] v. 使受日晒雨淋；使风化；经受住 n. 天气；暴风雨 adj. 上风的；迎风的

The boat weathered a storm safely.
The boss has weathered several financial crises.

moiety [ˈmɔɪəti] n. 部分；一半

Greed, fame, and fortune have consumed the moiety of human souls.

narcissism [ˈnɑːrsɪsɪzəm] n. 自我陶醉；自恋

Trump's narcissism makes him unfit for office.

blatant [ˈbleɪtnt] adj. 公然的；明目张胆的

The governor appears to be a blatant liar by addressing coal as clean coal.

collier [ˈkɑːliər] n. 矿工；煤商；煤船

coal [koʊl] v. 加煤；烧成炭 n. 煤

The ship unloaded colliers at the American port for mining coals.

telltale [ˈtelteɪl] n. 指标；告密者；计数器 adj. 搬弄是非的；泄露秘密的；警报的

The withdrawal of foreign investment is a telltale of a plunging stock market.
The telltale told the teacher the whereabouts of his classmate's magazine.

recuperate [rɪˈkuːpəreɪt] v. 恢复；复原

The injured soldiers need more time to recuperate.

The government tries to recuperate traditional culture.

clinic [ˈklɪnɪk] n. 诊所；会诊；临床

rehabilitate [ˌriːəˈbɪlɪteɪt] v. 使……康复；(使)复职
The clinic doctor rehabilitates drug addicts.
He has rehabilitated his left leg which had been injured in a car accident.
Zoe tried to rehabilitate her image from the sex scandal by doing volunteer work.

habilitate [həˈbɪləteɪt] v. 使适应；就职；穿衣；准备挖矿的钱及设备
Lucas has habilitated at the University of Michigan-Ann Arbor.

Part 3 识记单词 / 词组

consummate diamond 完美无瑕的钻石
narcissistic [ˌnɑːrsɪˈsɪstɪk] adj. 自恋的
recuperation [rɪˌkuːpəˈreɪʃn] n. 恢复；复原
rehabilitation [ˌriːəˌbɪlɪˈteɪʃn] n. 复原
elysium [iˈlɪziəm] n. 乐园；天堂
elysian [ɪˈliːʒən] adj. 极乐的；天堂般的
kickback [ˈkɪkbæk] n. 回扣
deem [diːm] v. 认为
standout [ˈstændaʊt] n. 优秀而显著的人物；坚持己见者
recuperator [rɪˈkjuːpəreɪtə] n. 恢复者；复进机
outpatient [ˈaʊtpeɪʃnt] n. 门诊病人
mysticism [ˈmɪstɪsɪzəm] n. 神秘主义
heresy [ˈherəsi] n. 异端邪说
scammer [ˈskæmər] n. 诈骗的人
monastic [məˈnæstɪk] n. 修道士 adj. 修道士的；禁欲的
delude [dɪˈluːd] v. 欺骗；蒙骗
mislead [ˌmɪsˈliːd] v. 把……引入歧途
misdirect [ˌmɪsdəˈrekt, ˌmɪsdaɪˈrekt] v. 给……指错方向；写错地址
misdirection [ˌmɪsdɪˈrekʃən, -daɪ-] n. 指示错误；指导错误

Lesson 33

Part 1 主力单词/词组

beneficent [bɪˈnefɪsnt] *adj.* 慈善的；有益的

He is beneficent to the poor.
She is beneficent in the dispensation of her money to the needy.
She is kind and beneficent.

beneficial [ˌbenɪˈfɪʃl] *adj.* 有用的；有益的

Having younger first, second, and third basemen and the shortstop in the infield will be beneficial.
The essence of Deep Ecology is to ask deeper questions...We ask which society, which education, which form of religion is beneficial for all life on the planet as a whole. (Arne Naess, Norwegian philosopher and author)

salutary [ˈsæljəteri] *adj.* 有益的；健康的

You should learn salutary lessons instead of playing video games.

constructive [kənˈstrʌktɪv] *adj.* 建设性的；构造出的

The Norwegian government has a monopoly on the truth and constructive criticisms.

advantageous [ˌædvənˈteɪdʒəs] *adj.* 有利的

I have always had a horror of them, to the point where I once refused a very advantageous offer of marriage because the gentleman wore a wig. (Élisabeth Vigée-Lebrun, French portraitist)

salubrious [səˈluːbriəs] *adj.* 清洁而有益健康的；环境宜人的

He has some salubrious habits such as exercising and consuming fruits and vegetables every day.
Hot springs are salubrious.

• Words in sentences 句中单词/词组 •

shortstop [ˈʃɔːrtstɑːp] *n.* 游击手
infield [ˈɪnfiːld] *n.* (棒球场地的) 内场
monopoly [məˈnɑːpəli] *n.* 独占；垄断

Part 2　补充单词/词组

bootless [ˈbuːtlɪs]　*adj.* 无用的；无利可图的
The investigator returned home after a bootless search.
I will not participate in this bootless project.

get over...　从疾病或令人不快的事中恢复过来
My client's remark irritates me, but I have to get over it. I want to get the deal done.

quiddity [ˈkwɪdəti]　*n.* 本质；实质；怪癖；不重要或细微的差别
The drama reflects each character's quiddity.
The ragged old man has some quirks and quiddities.

asteroid [ˈæstərɔɪd]　*n.* 小行星；海星　*adj.* 星状的

catastrophic [ˌkætəˈstrɑːfɪk]　*adj.* 灾难性的；悲惨的
The collision of an asteroid on Earth would be catastrophic.

sporotrichosis [ˌspɔːroutriˈkousis, spɔ-]　*n.* 孢子丝菌病

granulomatous [ˌgrænjuˈlɔmətəs]　*adj.* 肉芽肿的
Asteroid bodies in sporotrichosis are believed to be a granulomatous disease.

jurisprudent [ˌdʒuərisˈpruːdənt]　*n.* 法律学家　*adj.* 精通法律学的
He is an authoritative jurisprudent.

jurisprudence [ˌdʒurisˈpruːdns]　*n.* 法律学；法律体系
The professor has been studying jurisprudence for a decade.

wig [wɪg]　*v.* 斥责；痛骂　*n.* 假发
Can you imagine that I, with my love of the picturesque, could ever tolerate a wig?

wiggle [ˈwɪgl]　*v.* 扭动　*n.* 摆动
The dog wiggles its tail.

simpleton [ˈsɪmpltən]　*n.* 傻子；蠢人

bimbo [ˈbɪmboʊ]　*n.* 头脑简单的美人

derogatory [dɪˈrɑːgətɔːri]　*adj.* 诋毁的；贬低的
"Simpleton" and "bimbo" are considered derogatory words.

Lesson 33

trichome [ˈtrɪkoʊm, ˈtraɪkoʊm] *n.* 毛状体

sticky [ˈstɪki] *adj.* 黏的；泥泞的

The trichomes of this plant are sticky and expand when wet.

viscous [ˈvɪskəs] *adj.* 黏稠的

Viscous lava flows very slowly.

caterpillar [ˈkætərpɪlər] *n.* 毛毛虫

secretion [sɪˈkriːʃn] *n.* 分泌；分泌作用；隐藏

The caterpillar will release a poisonous, viscous secretion while being attacked.

viscid [ˈvɪsɪd] *adj.* 黏的；半流体的

Honey becomes more viscid at low temperatures.

extensile=extensible *adj.* 可延长的；可扩张的

glutinous [ˈɡluːtənəs] *adj.* 黏的；黏稠的

Anteaters have extensile, glutinous tongues suitable for catching ants.

tensil strength 抗张强度；抗拉强度

elasticity [ˌɪlæˈstɪsɪti, ˌɪlæ-] *n.* 弹性；伸缩性

woolen [ˈwʊlən] *n.* 毛织品；羊毛织物 *adj.* 羊毛制的；羊毛的

High tensile strength and elasticity give woolen textile the ability to retain shape.

bludgeon [ˈblʌdʒən] *v.* 用棍棒打；恫吓 *n.* 棍棒

I will not choose a bludgeon as my weapon.

paten [ˈpætn] *n.* 圣餐盘；圆形平盘

consecration [ˌkɑːnsɪˈkreɪʃn] *n.* 授任仪式；神圣化

I see chalices and patens in the consecration.

divorce [dɪˈvɔːrs] *v.* 分离；离婚 *n.* 离婚

If they divorce, she might get disenfranchised.

Part 3 识记单词/词组

take advantage of sth 利用……；占……的便宜

lause [loz] n. 占便宜的人

peeve [pi:v] v. (使) 恼怒

pet peeve 不能忍受的事

prenuptial agreement 婚前协议

asteroid belt 小行星带

medical jurisprudence 法医学

catastrophe [kə'tæstrəfi] n. 大灾难；大灾祸

granuloma [ˌgrænjə'loumə] n. 肉芽肿

granulation [ˌgrænjə'leɪʃən] n. 粗糙

granule ['grænju:l] n. 细粒

granular ['grænjələr] adj. 粒状的

granulose ['grænjuləus] adj. 由颗粒构成的

granulosis [ˌgrænju'lousɪs] n. 微粒子病

viscosity [vɪ'skɑ:səti] n. 黏质；黏性

viscidity [vi'sidəti] n. 黏性；黏质

secrete [sɪ'kri:t] v. 分泌；藏匿

disenfranchise [ˌdɪsɪn'fræntʃaɪz] v. 剥夺……的公民权

disenfranchisement [ˌdɪsɪn'fræntʃaɪzmənt] n. 剥夺公民选举权

baseman ['beɪsmən] n. 守垒员

outfield ['aʊtfi:ld] n. 外场；边境

nuptial ['nʌpʃl] n. 婚礼 adj. 婚姻的；结婚的

prenuptial [pri:'nʌpʃəl] adj. 结婚前的

Lesson 34

Part 1 主力单词 / 词组

detrimental [ˌdetrɪ'mentl] adj. 有害的；不利的

We talk about restructuring instead...We are <u>prolonging</u> the pains... I think this is <u>detrimental</u>. (Pehr G. Gyllenhammar, Swedish business executive)

The detrimental effect of excessive drinking should be noticed.

detriment [ˈdetrɪmənt]   n. 危害；损害

False information is a detriment to the public at large.

harmful [ˈhɑːrmfl]   adj. 有害的

The sense and feeling of diffidence have become harmful to us.

insidious [ɪnˈsɪdiəs]   adj. 逐渐累积的

Air pollution has an insidious effect on our health.

deleterious [ˌdeləˈtɪriəs]   adj. 有毒的；有害的

Human activities have deleterious impacts on the overall environment.

pernicious [pərˈnɪʃəs]   adj. 有害的；恶性的

Pornography has a pernicious influence on society.

baneful [ˈbeɪnfl]   adj. 有害的；使人苦恼的

The baneful notions of envy and jealousy appear to be intrinsic.

bane [beɪn]   n. 根源；灾星；致命毒药

His birth proves to be more of a bane than a boon for mankind. He invented a nuclear bomb at the end.

nuisance [ˈnuːsns]   n. 恼人的事物

What a nuisance.

The naughty kid who always plays video games very loudly while I am studying has been a nuisance.

noxious [ˈnɑːkʃəs]   adj. 对身体或道德有害的；令人讨厌的

Noxious fumes issue out from the factory.

obnoxious [əbˈnɑːkʃəs]   adj. 令人讨厌的；粗鲁无礼的

Don't make yourself obnoxious by bringing up unpleasant subjects and pinpointing others' faults thoroughly.

hazardous [ˈhæzərdəs]   adj. 危险的

The refinery emits a hazardous gas.

baleful [ˈbeɪlfl]   adj. 有害的；威胁的

The crops withering is one of the baleful effects of soil pollution.

The dog looks at me with a baleful stare.

noisome [ˈnɔɪsəm] *adj.* 有害的；有恶臭的

His noisome remark about my appearance stuck with me for years.
This noisome steerage should be sterilized.
The noisome garbage stinks.

fume [fjuːm] *n.* 烟雾；发怒

fumigate [ˈfjuːmɪgeɪt] *v.* 熏蒸；烟熏

Fumigating, flooding, and torching porcupine burrows are prohibited in this forest.

fumigation [ˌfjuːmɪˈgeɪʃn] *n.* 烟熏法

hazard [ˈhæzərd] *v.* 使遭受危险 *n.* 危险物

pestilent =pestilential *adj.* 致命的；危害社会的

pestilence [ˈpestɪləns] *n.* 有害的事物；瘟疫

● Words in sentences 句中单词/词组 ●

prolong [prəˈlɔːŋ] *v.* 延长；拖延

pornography [pɔːrˈnɑːgrəfi] *n.* 色情读物

notion [ˈnoʊʃn] *n.* 观念

intrinsic [ɪnˈtrɪnzɪk, ɪnˈtrɪnsɪk] *adj.* 固有的；本质的；内部的

boon [buːn] *n.* 提高生活质量的东西；有用之物

subject [ˈsʌbdʒɪkt, ˈsʌbdʒekt] *v.* 使臣服；征服 *n.* 学科；主题；臣民 *adj.* 臣服的；被征服的 *adv.* 在……条件下

pinpoint [ˈpɪnpɔɪnt] *v.* 准确指出 *n.* 极小的点

wither [ˈwɪðər] *v.* 枯萎；衰弱

stink [stɪŋk] *v.* 散发恶臭 *n.* 恶臭

porcupine [ˈpɔːrkjupaɪn] *n.* 豪猪

burrow [ˈbɜːroʊ] *v.* 挖巢穴；挖地道 *n.* 动物巢穴；地道

Part 2 补充单词/词组

rationale [ˌræʃəˈnæl] *n.* 根本原因；基本原理

You can create a rationale for anything.

cough [kɔːf] v. 发出噗噗声 n. 咳嗽

aerosol [ˈeərəsɑːl] n. 溶胶；浮质；喷雾器

Although both spread via respiratory droplets in coughs and sneezes, coronaviruses do not transmit very efficiently as aerosols, as flu does.

vinyl chloride 氯乙烯

Aerosol pesticides contain vinyl chloride.

aerosolize [ˈeərəuˌsəlaɪz] v. 雾化

The machine aerosolizes the drug, mixing it with a solution.

extrinsic [eksˈtrɪnzɪk, eksˈtrɪnsɪk] adj. 非固有的；外在的

You have to consider any extrinsic factors which might affect our business.

The extrinsic event changed the entire course of history.

abusive [əˈbjuːsɪv] adj. 辱骂的；滥用的；折磨的

She underachieves because of extrinsic factors, such as having an abusive family and breaking up with her boyfriend.

seat-of-the-pants 凭经验的；凭感觉的

Most decisions are seat-of-the-pants judgments.

begrudge [bɪˈɡrʌdʒ] v. 嫉妒；羡慕；吝惜

I begrudged her the chance to become the wife of that handsome man.

The miser who begrudged money wouldn't donate a single dime.

lucre [ˈluːkər] n. 金钱；利润

He begrudged her success and the lucre she had.

antiseptic [ˌæntɪˈseptɪk] n. 抗菌剂；防腐剂 adj. 无菌的；冷淡的；整洁而呆板的

The nurse used an antiseptic to kill bacteria.

He treated his wound with an antiseptic.

mouthwash [ˈmaʊθwɔːʃ] n. 漱口水

He uses an antiseptic mouthwash to deal with his bad breath.

aseptic [ˌeɪˈseptɪk] n. 防腐剂 adj. 无菌的；冷漠的；超然的

Doctors wearing aseptic white clothes use antiseptic surgical instruments.

septic [ˈseptɪk] adj. 腐败性的；败血症的

septic system 化粪池系统

The septic system is far below the international standard.

spew [spju:] v. 喷出；呕吐

These factories spew noxious fumes and dump toxic waste.

yeoman ['joumən] n. 文书军士；侍从；自耕农

The navy yeoman discovered the corruption and got dispatched in the open sea.

interdict ['ɪntərdɪkt] v. 阻断；封锁 n. 禁止；禁令

Drug shipment has been interdicted.

The government interdicts supply routes to the enemy.

interdiction [ˌɪntər'dɪkʃn] n. 禁止；禁令

firearm ['faɪərɑːrm] n. 火器；枪支

Interdiction of drugs and firearms is common in most Asian countries.

steerage ['stɪrɪdʒ] n. 客轮的统舱；操舵；指导

He won his reputation by effective steerage of the company.

veer [vɪr] v. 改变方向 n. 转向

The global economy veered downward after the trade war.

semiconductor ['semikəndʌktər] n. 半导体

The boss veered his business into the semiconductor industry.

yoke [joʊk] v. 结合；匹配 n. 轭；束缚

Chinese Yuan (CNY) has been yoked to America's.

The rebels threw off the yoke of England.

oxen ['ɑːksn] n. 牛（复数）

The farmer yoked the two oxen together

reek [riːk] v. 发臭；散发蒸汽（或浓烟）；带有…… n. 臭气

His clothes reek of vodka.

The temple is reeking of incense.

The butcher's hands were reeking with blood.

steer [stɪr] v. 驾驶；指导 n. 阉牛

I can steer the ship by the compass at night.

worn-out [ˌwɔːrn ˈaʊt] *adj.* 过时的；筋疲力尽的；磨破的

The colonial status is a worn-out, by-gone thing.

Part 3 识记单词/词组

worn-out clothes　磨破的衣服

outworn [ˈaʊtwɔːrn] *adj.* 用旧的；废弃的

bygone [ˈbaɪɡɒn] *n.* 过去；以往　*adj.* 过去的；以往的

begone [bɪˈɡɒːn] *v.* 走开；滚开

emit [iˈmɪt] *v.* 发出；发射

emission [ɪˈmɪʃn] *n.* 排放物　*v.* 排放

septic tank　化粪池

septic shock　败血性休克

sepsis [ˈsepsɪs] *n.* 败血病；腐败作用

vomit [ˈvɑːmɪt] *v.* 呕吐　*n.* 呕吐物

repayment [rɪˈpeɪmənt] *n.* 偿还

repossess [ˌriːpəˈzes] *v.* 收回；取回（尤指房产）

impair [ɪmˈper] *v.* 损害；损伤

impairment [ɪmˈpermənt] *n.* 损伤

polyvinyl chloride　聚氯乙烯

vinyl [ˈvaɪnl] *n.* 乙烯基

chloride [ˈklɔːraɪd] *n.* 氯化物

filthy lucre　不义之财

cause a stink　引起轩然大波

in default of something or somebody　缺少了某人或某物

default judgement　缺席判决

moral bankruptcy　道德沦丧

be subject to sth　遭受……；承受……

subject to sth　取决于……；视……而定

in the mdist of sth　正当……的时候；在……之中

the prohibition era　禁酒时期

antiseptic insulation　防腐绝缘

antiseptic metal　防腐金属

create/kick up/raise a stink　制造事端；滋事

Lesson 35

Part 1 主力单词 / 词组

inspire [ɪnˈspaɪər] *v.* 启发；吸入气体
I was inspired by a mantra to overlook temporal life.

inspired [ɪnˈspaɪərd] *adj.* 有创造力的；优秀的；受启发的
After years of traveling in Europe, she has become a combination of polyglot, practical mystic, heretical saint, and inspired genius.

inspiration [ˌɪnspəˈreɪʃn] *n.* 灵感；鼓舞

inspirational [ˌɪnspəˈreɪʃənl] *adj.* 给予灵感的；鼓舞人心的

enlighten [ɪnˈlaɪtn] *v.* 启发；启蒙
His persuasive rhetoric has enlightened all of us.

edify [ˈedɪfaɪ] *v.* 教化；启迪
My sermon was designed to edify the souls of men.
I have heard too much of the edifying legends of Buddha since my childhood.

afflatus [əˈfleɪtəs] *n.* 灵感；神悟
I had an afflatus by God in my dream.

enlightenment [ɪnˈlaɪtnmənt] *n.* 启蒙运动；启迪

edification [ˌedɪfɪˈkeɪʃn] *n.* 启迪；教诲

• **Words in sentences 句中单词 / 词组** •

mantra [ˈmɑːntrə, ˈmæntrə] *n.* 佛经或印度教的真言

polyglot [ˈpɑːliɡlɑːt] *n.* 通晓多种语言的人；内有多种语言的书 *adj.* 多种语言的

mystic [ˈmɪstɪk] *n.* 神秘主义者

heretical [həˈretɪkl] *adj.* 异教徒的

saint [seɪnt]　*n.* 圣人；圣人般的人
rhetoric ['retərɪk]　*n.* 花言巧语；修辞学
Buddha ['buːdə, 'bʊdə]　*n.* 佛；佛陀

Part 2　补充单词 / 词组

eureka [juˈriːkə]　*n.* 优铜　*int.* 我发现了；我找到了

eureka moment　顿悟时刻
Edison had his eureka moment to invent the light bulb after thousands of failures.

saga ['sɑːgə]　*n.* 传说；冒险故事
The author described a lockdown in an ongoing small-town saga.

lockdown ['lɑːkdaʊn]　*n.* 严防禁闭（期）；一级封锁
Saudi Arabia reimposed national lockdown after cases spike.

mind-boggling ['maɪnd bɑːɡlɪŋ]　*adj.* 令人极为惊讶的
The permutations of all public transportation fares were mind-boggling.

cogent ['koʊdʒənt]　*adj.* 使人信服的；切实的
I will believe you if you give me a cogent explanation.

inveigle [ɪnˈveɪɡl]　*v.* 说服

scam [skæm]　*v.* 欺诈；诓骗　*n.* 骗局；诡计
The beautiful woman inveigles me into plotting the scam.

locution [ləˈkjuːʃn]　*n.* 说话法；习用语
I know her birthplace by her locution.
We are taught to avoid slang and parochial locution in a formal meeting.

linguist ['lɪŋgwɪst]　*n.* 语言学者；通晓数种外语的人

logophile [lɒˈɡəfaɪl]　*n.* 喜欢字词的人

epitaph ['epɪtæf]　*n.* 墓志铭；碑文
Linguists and logophiles tried to figure out words on the ancient epitaph.

philology [fɪˈlɑːlədʒi]　*n.* 语言学；文献学
She got a Ph.D. in Roman philology.

plot [plɑːt]　*v.* 密谋；绘图　*n.* 密谋；情节；图表

They plotted to overthrow the French government which is unwise.
The plot of that movie is simple and blank.
He plots the projected cost of the company compared with last year.

rotund [rou'tʌnd]　*adj.* 圆的；洪亮的；夸张的

He called my name with his rotund voice.

loaf [louf]　*v.* 游荡　*n.* 一条（面包）

Matthew used a rotund loaf of bread as a weapon to hit a dog.

combination [ˌkɑːmbɪ'neɪʃn]　*n.* 混合；组合；联盟

permutation [ˌpɜːrmju'teɪʃn]　*n.* 重组；排列；彻底或根本的改变

The image was created by a virtually infinite stream of combinations and permutations of other pictures.

tarantula [tə'ræntʃələ]　*n.* 鸟蛛；狼蛛

I slept happily last night on top of a bin of cacao beans, having first searched the shed with a flashlight for snakes, tarantulas, and scorpions. (Peter Matthiessen, U.S. novelist and travel writer)

cobweb ['kɑːbweb]　*v.* 陷阱；圈套　*n.* 蜘蛛网；蜘蛛丝

The unjust law is like a cobweb where flies are caught.

gossamer ['gɑːsəmər]　*n.* 蛛丝；薄纱

The old temple was full of gossamer.
The gossamer of youth's dreams seems to be tenuous.

gossamery ['gɔsəməri]　*adj.* 轻而薄的

I use a gossamery white vein as a curtain.
She bought a gossamery stocking.

signboard ['saɪnbɔːrd]　*n.* 招牌；布告板

The signboard fell and gouged a car.

gouge [gaudʒ]　*v.* 凿；诈骗　*n.* 凿子；凿成的槽（孔、洞）

He tortured the prisoner and gouged his eyes out.
She tries to gouge her father's money as much as possible.

projectile [prəˈdʒektl]　*n.* 射弹；抛射体　*adj.* 抛射的；投掷的

A spear is a projectile weapon.

spume [spjuːm]　*v.* 使像泡沫般喷出　*n.* 泡沫

Spumes float on the coastal ocean.

geyser [ˈgaɪzər]　*n.* 喷泉；间歇泉

Yellow Stone Park sends its geyser spumes skyward without surcease.

timbre [ˈtæmbər]　*n.* 音色；音质

The timbre of her voice is remarkably high.

verbalize [ˈvɜːrbəlaɪz]　*v.* 以言语表述；唠叨

It is hard to verbalize her feeling.

Part 3　识记单词 / 词组

flare [fler]　*v.* 使闪耀；使张开　*n.* 加剧；恶化

disabuse [ˌdɪsəˈbjuːz]　*v.* 使省悟；消除错误的想法

isotropic [ˌaɪsəˈtrɑːpɪk]　*adj.* 等向的

simulation [ˌsɪmjuˈleɪʃn]　*n.* 仿真；模拟

rhetorician [ˌretəˈrɪʃn]　*n.* 演说家；修辞学家

linguistics [lɪŋˈgwɪstɪks]　*n.* 语言学

linguistic [lɪŋˈgwɪstɪk]　*adj.* 语言的；语言学的

bilingual [ˌbaɪˈlɪŋgwəl]　*n.* 通晓两种语言的人　*adj.* 双语的

multilingual [ˌmʌltiˈlɪŋgwəl]　*n.* 使用多种语言的人　*adj.* 使用多种语言的

tone up　（身心的）正常状态

tone color　音色；风格

combine [kəmˈbaɪn]　*v.* 组合；化合

emulation [ˌemjuˈleɪʃn]　*n.* 仿真；竞争

poison [ˈpɔɪzn]　*v.* 使恶化　*n.* 毒药；毒素

microbe [ˈmaɪkroʊb]　*n.* 微生物

figurehead [ˈfɪgjərhed]　*n.* 有名无实的首脑；名义上的领袖

Lesson 36

Part 1 主力单词 / 词组

concurrently [kən'kɜːrəntli] *adv.* 同时地；会合地
The colonel landed his ground troop on the beach with paratroopers concurrently.
The two treatments can run concurrently with each other without any side effects.

simultaneously [ˌsaɪml'teɪniəsli] *adv.* 同时地
The scandal has been broadcasting on every TV channel simultaneously.

synchronous ['sɪŋkrənəs] *adj.* 同时的；同步的
The synchronous arrivals of his girlfriend and his mother pose him the question of whom he should pick up first.

synchronize ['sɪŋkrənaɪz] *v.* 使同步；使同时
The drummer synchronized the rhythm with other band members' instruments.

concomitant [kən'kɑːmɪtənt] *adj.* 同时发生或出现的；伴随物的
Anxiety and depression are concomitant problems of our contemporary fast-pacing society.
Whoever reaches the age of 18 is concomitant with responsibility as an adult.

instantaneously [ˌɪnstən'teɪniəsli] *adv.* 即刻；突如其来地

• Words in sentences 句中单词 / 词组 •

colonel ['kɜːrnl] *n.* (陆军或空军) 上校
paratrooper ['pærətruːpər] *n.* 伞兵
scandal ['skændl] *n.* 丑闻
rhythm ['rɪðəm] *n.* 节奏；规律

Part 2 补充单词 / 词组

intellectual property rights 知识产权
Patents and intellectual property rights are incorporeal properties.

corporal [ˈkɔːrpərəl] n. 下士 adj. 肉体的

Corporal punishment in the prison of Vietnam is severe.

A corporal committed suicide and the commander fired his superior.

ailment [ˈeɪlmənt] n. 病痛

Corporal ailments usually come with advancing age.

corporeal [kɔːrˈpɔːriəl] adj. 肉体的；物质的

Cars and houses are corporeal properties.

Biological needs such as hunger, thirst, and sex are corporeal cravings.

incorporal=incorporeal adj. 无实体的；精神的

I felt an incorporeal spirit helping me while I stayed in the mountain.

remedy [ˈremədi] v. 补救；去除 n. 治疗法；药物

The medicine can remedy hypertension.

A drastic measure would be taken to remedy the situation.

There is no remedy for the new disease.

remedial [rɪˈmiːdiəl] adj. 治疗的；矫正的

The cough is remedial.

The remedial work is for the nonfunctioning car.

International students need remedial classes in writing.

irremediable [ˌɪrɪˈmiːdiəbl] adj. 不治的；不可挽回的

The irremediable mistake he made has cost us dearly.

remediable [rɪˈmiːdiəbl] adj. 可治疗的

The problem is severe but remediable.

circulatory [ˈsɜːrkjələtɔːri] adj. 血液循环的

respiratory [ˈrespərətɔːri] adj. 呼吸的

circulatory and respiratory systems

cadence [ˈkeɪdns] n. 节奏；抑扬顿挫

I enjoy the relaxed cadence of my retired life.

paraleipsis=paralipsis n. 假省笔法

Using paralipsis might make the essay more interesting.

"We need say nothing of" and "not to mention" are phrases of paraleipsis.

broach [broutʃ]　*v.* 提出；突然横转　*n.* 凿子；胸针
Why do you broach this controversial subject?
The whale broached for breathing.

lopsided [ˌlɑːpˈsaɪdɪd]　*adj.* 倾向一侧的；平衡的
The sailors broached the boat suddenly and it became lopsided.

hound [haʊnd]　*v.* 追踪；纠缠　*n.* 猎犬；卑劣的人
The hound has lop ears.

lop [lɑːp]　*v.* 砍；剪　*n.* 小树枝　*adj* 下垂的
They lopped twigs regularly.

legitimate [lɪˈdʒɪtɪmət]　*adj.* 合法的；嫡出的

controvertible [ˌkɒntrəˈvɜːtɪbl]　*adj.* 可争论的；质疑的
The legitimacy of his business remains controvertible.

incontrovertible [ˌɪnkɑːntrəˈvɜːrtəbl]　*adj.* 无可争辩的；无疑的
His death is incontrovertible.

ichthyology [ˌɪkθiˈɑːlədʒi]　*n.* 鱼类学

ornithology [ˌɔːrnɪˈθɑːlədʒi]　*n.* 鸟类学
She has specialized in both ichthyology and ornithology.

Part 3　识记单词 / 词组

lance [læns]　*v.* 用柳叶刀割开；急速前进　*n.* 长矛
lance corporal　一等兵
canalize [ˈkænəlaɪz]　*v.* 加宽；加深
respirator [ˈrespəreɪtər]　*n.* 口罩；防毒面具
ichthyofauna [ˌɪkθiəˈfɔːnə]　*n.* 鱼类区系
ornithologist [ˌɔːrnɪˈθɑːlədʒɪst]　*n.* 鸟类学家；鸟类爱好者
ail [eɪl]　*v.* 使苦恼　*n.* 病痛；苦恼
respiration [ˌrespəˈreɪʃn]　*n.* 呼吸
legitimacy [lɪˈdʒɪtɪməsi]　*n.* 合法性
shift...ground　改变……的立场

Lesson 37

Part 1 主力单词 / 词组

ostensible [ɑːˈstensəbl]   *adj.* 表面上的；假装的

Their ostensible aim is to raise money for charity, but their real goal is to make a profit for themselves.

The truce is just an ostensible reconciliation.

so-called [ˌsoʊ ˈkɔːld]   *adj.* 所谓的；号称的

So-called friends will disappear when you are in trouble.

putative [ˈpjuːtətɪv]   *adj.* 一般认定的；推定的

The putative leader of that gang was arrested yesterday.

plausible [ˈplɔːzəbl]   *adj.* 貌似真实的；花言巧语的

They give me a plausible reason for finding the treasure in a remote mountain.

A plausible salesman can often reach their sales target in time.

surface [ˈsɜːrfɪs]   *v.* 浮出水面   *n.* 表面；表层   *adj.* 表面的；肤浅的

on the surface   表面上；外表上

On the surface, he looked very calm.

• Words in sentences 句中单词 / 词组 •

charity [ˈtʃærəti]   *n.* 慈善事业；慈善

truce [truːs]   *n.* 休战；停战

gang [ɡæŋ]   *n.* 帮派

Part 2 补充单词 / 词组

implausible [ɪmˈplɔːzəbl]   *adj.* 难以置信的；不合情理的

The dog eating your homework is an implausible excuse.

Her testimony was purely fictional, implausible.

woodcutter [ˈwʊdkʌtər] *n.* 樵夫；伐木工人

hinterland [ˈhɪntərlænd] *n.* 偏僻地区；河岸等的后方地区

The woodcutter lives in a mountainous hinterland.

timber [ˈtɪmbər] *v.* 用木材建造 *n.* 木材；横梁

Japan has impressive reserves of timber.

standardize [ˈstændərdaɪz] *v.* 使标准化

The manufacturing process has been standardized.

measure up 符合标准

The products measure up with EU regulations.

reconciliation [ˌrekənsɪliˈeɪʃn] *n.* 和解；调解；一致；甘愿

She bought her girlfriend a gift in hopes of a reconciliation.

I sought reconciliation with my rival.

The reconciliation of his action with his high-standard morality is obvious.

reconcile [ˈrekənsaɪl] *v.* 使和好；使和解；使一致；调解；调停

America reconciles disputes between Japan and South Korea over trade and sea border issues.

Your statement should reconcile with your behavior.

She won't reconcile herself to be merely a servant.

reconcilable [ˈrekənsaɪləbl] *adj.* 可和解的；一致的；兼容的

The differences between the two sisters can be settled and are reconcilable by their mother.

compatible [kəmˈpætəbl] *adj.* 能共处的；兼容的

Is it possible that freedom is compatible with order, that individual liberty is reconcilable with obedience to the law?

irreconcilable [ˌɪrekənˈsaɪləbl, ɪˈrekənsaɪləbl] *adj.* 不能和解的；不兼容的

The demands from both sides are opposite and irreconcilable.

demolish [dɪˈmɑːlɪʃ] *v.* 毁坏；破坏

The irreconcilable enemy refused to communicate and intended to demolish our capital city to the ground.

incompatible [ˌɪnkəmˈpætəbl] *adj.* 不兼容的；矛盾的

Their personalities are incompatible.

scuttle [ˈskʌtl] *v.* 凿沉；放弃；破坏；急促奔跑 *n.* 天窗；小舱口；筐

He scuttled the boat.

The peace talk was scuttled by Israel.
Thieves scuttled off at the sight of the police.
The factory worker brought me a scuttle of coal.

raise [reɪz]　*v.* 养育；种植；增加；举起；筹集　*n.* 高地；加薪

I raise money for charities that help sick children.
Please raise your hands if you have questions.

furtive [ˈfɜːtɪv]　*adj.* 偷偷摸摸的

His furtive action has raised suspicion.

caesura [siˈzjʊərə]　*n.* 句读；中断

This is a day that yawns like a caesura: quiet since dawn, and wearily drawn out. (Osip Mandelstam, Russian poet, writer, and translator)

dispensation [ˌdɪspenˈseɪʃn]　*n.* 分配；管理；特许；免除

The judge likes her and grants a dispensation from the rule.

Part 3　识记单词 / 词组

compatibility [kəmˌpætəˈbɪləti]　*n.* 兼容性
furtive glance　偷偷瞧一眼
in real terms　实际地；事实上
beneficent bacteria　益生菌
reconcile dispute　调解纠纷
rough around the edges　不太好；不太完美
real earnings　实际收入

Lesson 38

Part 1　主力单词 / 词组

antiquated [ˈæntɪkweɪtɪd]　*adj.* 过时的；陈旧的

The general has intended to replace antiquated weapons with contemporary ones.
Nobody knows better than the historian how much courage it still takes to tell the truth

about American Canadian relations, and how near the surface these antiquated but latent prejudices are still to be found. (Chester Bailey Martin, Canadian historian)

old-fashioned [ˌould'fæʃnd]　*adj.* 老式的；过时的

The thatch of the village house radiates old-fashioned style.

outworn [ˌaut'wɔːrn]　*adj.* 过时的；废弃的

Outworn organizations are not half as malignant as worn-out causes. (Eldridge Cleaver, U.S. writer and civil rights activist)

worn-out [ˌwɔːrn 'aut]　*adj.* 过时的；很疲累的；磨损的

The worn-out party is better than outworn causes.

outdated [ˌaut'deɪtɪd]　*adj.* 过时的；旧式的；落伍的

Life is making us abandon established stereotypes and outdated views, it is making us discard illusions. (Mikhail Gorbachev, Russian statesman)

passe [pæ'seɪ]　*adj.* 过时的；（女子）已过青春妙龄的

The music was fashionable in the past but passe in the present.
She is just a passe star.

• Words in sentences 句中单词/词组 •

latent [ˈleɪtnt]　*adj.* 潜在的；隐性的

prejudice [ˈpredʒudɪs]　*v.* 对……有偏见　*n.* 偏见

thatch [θætʃ]　*n.* 稻草屋顶

malignant [məˈlɪɡnənt]　*adj.* 恶性的；恶意的

cause [kɔːz]　*v.* 引起；造成　*n.* 事业；目标；原因

stereotype [ˈsteriətaɪp]　*v.* 对……有成见；对……形成模式化的看法　*n.* 刻板印象

statesman [ˈsteɪtsmən]　*n.* 政治家

Part 2　补充单词/词组

proportionate [prəˈpɔːrʃənət]　*v.* 使成比例；使相称　*adj.* 成比例的

Each stakeholder will receive a proportionate share of the profits.

The bonus is proportionate to your efforts.

disproportionate [ˌdɪsprə'pɔːrʃənət] *adj.* 不成比例的

But it's too easy, and the effect is disproportionate to the effort.

excrescence [ɪk'skresns] *n.* 瘤；自然长出物（如指甲、头发）；丑陋不堪之物

eyesore ['aɪsɔːr] *n.* 难看的东西；眼中钉

The dilapidated old building in which nobody lives is a hideous excrescence(eyesore) in the city.

excise ['eksaɪz, ɪk'saɪz] *v.* 切除；删除 *n.* 货物税；国内消费税；执照税

warty ['wɔːti] *adj.* 有疣的；有树瘤的

A surgical doctor excised a warty excrescence on his arm.

graft [græft] *v.* 嫁接；(滥用政治权力进行)贪污；受贿 *n.* 嫁接用的枝条（或芽）；移植的皮肤（或骨骼）

sting operation 卧底行动（设圈套，诱人入罪）

The police who launched a sting operation pretended to be a client to catch a drug dealer.

excision [ɪk'sɪʒn] *n.* 被切除物

infarct [ɪn'fɑrkt] *n.* [医] 梗塞

He performed a surgical excision of the damaged heart muscle and infarcts.

expressionless [ɪk'spreʃənləs] *adj.* 无表情的

deadpan ['dedpæn] *adj.* 毫无表情的；脸无表情的

He remains deadpan, expressionless.

vogue [voʊg] *n.* 流行；流行物

There is a magazine called "Vogue".

It is charming to totter into vogue. (Horace Walpole, British writer)

There is a new vogue for fluorescent shoes this year.

ritzy ['rɪtsi] *adj.* 时髦的；豪华的

I don't need your ritzy advice about with whom I should make friends.

There is a ritzy nightclub.

scrap [skræp] *v.* 报废 *n.* 碎片；破烂；少量

The old vehicle was scrapped for recycling.

The plan was scrapped due to lack of preparation and manpower.

indict [ɪnˈdaɪt]　*v.* 控告；起诉

You can't indict her only with a scrap of evidence.

efficacy [ˈefɪkəsi]　*n.* 效力；功效

The efficacy of this vaccine is unknown, therefore it is still in the trial period.

efficacious [ˌefɪˈkeɪʃəs]　*adj.* 有效的；灵验的

The treatment is efficacious at present.

buttock [ˈbʌtək]　*v.* 用腰摔　*n.* 屁股（常复数）；船尾

The skin was removed from his buttock and grafted onto his face.

cower [ˈkaʊər]　*v.* 抖缩；畏缩

The little kid cowered beneath a white sheet hoping the monster would leave soon.

Part 3　识记单词/词组

state of the art　最先进的科技；（艺术的）先锋派

cutting-edge [ˌkʌtɪŋ ˈedʒ]　前沿的；最前沿的

leading-edge [ˈliːdɪŋˌedʒ]　（技术上）最先进的

trailblazing [ˈtreɪlbleɪzɪŋ]　*adj.* 领导性的；带头的

malignant tumor　恶性肿瘤

excrescent [ɪkˈskresənt]　*adj.* 异常生长的；多余的

blow sth out of proportion　对（事情或问题）小题大做

wart [wɔːrt]　*n.* [医] 疣；[植] 树瘤

weaponry [ˈwepənri]　*n.* 武器（总称）；兵器

goof [ɡuːf]　*v.* 弄错

a left hook　左勾拳

indictment [ɪnˈdaɪtmənt]　*n.* 控诉

cast a spell　施魔法；念咒语

cast a vote　投票

cast your mind back　回想……；追忆……

cast doubt/ suspicion on sb/sth　使对……产生怀疑

cast aspersions on sb/sth　诽谤……；诋毁……
cast a look/ glance/smile　看一眼（瞅一眼；冲……一笑）
cast an/your eye over sth　对……匆匆浏览
cast light on sth　使……更易理解

Lesson 39

Part 1　主力单词 / 词组

accidental [ˌæksɪˈdentl]　*n.* 偶然；非主要的特征；意外的效果　*adj.* 意外的；偶然（发生）的

These men as teachers, irrespective of accidental differences, are doing mighty work in uprooting bigotry and prejudice toward minorities.

There is no reason to assume that the universe has the slightest interest in intelligence—or even in life. Both may be random accidental by-products of its operations like the beautiful patterns on a butterfly's wings. The insect would fly just as well without them. (Arthur C. Clarke, British writer and scientist)

happenstance [ˈhæpənstæns]　*n.* 偶然事件

Happenstance is what life is all about in this chaotic world depicted in this novel.

coincidence [koʊˈɪnsɪdəns]　*n.* 巧合；一致

You stepped on my foot in the ball. Once was happenstance. Twice was a coincidence. The third time, I thought you did it deliberately.

coincidental [koʊˌɪnsɪˈdentl]　*adj.* 巧合的；同时发生的

The collision is not coincidental but premeditated.

coincidentally [koʊˌɪnsɪˈdentəli]　*adv.* 巧合地

They rendezvoused each other in a movie theater coincidentally.

coincident [koʊˈɪnsɪdənt]　*adj.* 同时发生的；一致的

The plunge of bitcoin was coincident with the inhibition announcement of electronic money in China.

The stake of an appendix surgeon is not always coincident with that of patients.

incidental [ˌɪnsɪˈdentl] *n.* 伴随事件　*adj.* 偶然发生的；伴随发生的

There was an incidental catch of shrimps while I came after small fish.
Risks are incidental to firefighters.

incidental to　伴随……而来的

Social obligations are incidental to the corporation's revenue.

fortuitous [fɔrˈtuɪtəs] *adj.* 偶然发生的；巧合的（有利的事）

The fortuitous ricochet of the ball hit the goal.
Many scientists have made fortuitous discoveries.
Humans arose, rather, as a fortuitous and contingent outcome of thousands of linked events, any one of which could have occurred differently and sent history on an alternative pathway that would not have led to consciousness. (Stephen Jay Gould, U.S. geologist and writer)

adventitious [ˌædvenˈtɪʃəs] *adj.* 偶然的；外来的

The physical attributes of dodo birds are more attributable to external or adventitious causes.
The two strangers have an adventitious resemblance.

serendipitous [ˌserənˈdɪpətəs] *adj.* 偶然发现的

Newton made a serendipitous discovery of universal gravity by a falling apple.

serendipity [ˌserənˈdɪpəti] *n.* 幸运

He won the boxing match by his incessant practice, not by serendipity.

sleeper [ˈsliːpər] *n.* 出乎意料地获得成功的人（或事物）；儿童睡衣；婴儿睡袋；卧铺

windfall [ˈwɪndfɔːl] *n.* 被风吹落的果实；意外的收获

- **Words in sentences 句中单词 / 词组**

irrespective [ˌɪrɪˈspektɪv] *adj.* 与……无关的
uproot [ˌʌpˈruːt] *v.* 根除；把……赶出家园
bigotry [ˈbɪɡətri] *n.* 偏见（很强的）
ball [bɔːl] *n.* 大型舞厅

premeditated [ˌpriːˈmedɪteɪtɪd] *adj.* 预谋的
bitcoin [ˈbɪtˌkɔɪn] *n.* 比特币
inhibition [ˌɪnhɪˈbɪʃn, ˌɪnɪˈbɪʃn] *n.* 禁止；压抑
stake [steɪk] *v.* 以……下注 *n.* 股份；赌注
appendix [əˈpendɪks] *n.* 阑尾；附录；附加物
surgeon [ˈsɜːrdʒən] *n.* 外科医生
shrimp [ʃrɪmp] *n.* 小虾
firefighter [ˈfaɪərfaɪtər] *n.* 消防员
ricochet [ˈrɪkəʃeɪ] *v.* 弹开 *n.* 弹回的球
contingent [kənˈtɪndʒənt] *n.* 代表团；偶然事件 *adj.* 偶然的
dodo bird 嘟嘟鸟
external [ɪkˈstɜːrnl] *n.* 外形；外观 *adj.* 外面的；外部的
resemblance [rɪˈzembləns] *n.* 相似（人或物的表面）
incessant [ɪnˈsesnt] *adj.* 持续不断的

Part 2　补充单词/词组

banyan [ˈbænjən] *n.* 榕树

adventitious root 不固定的根

Banyan has adventitious roots growing from the nodes of its branches.

contingent on 依……而定的

Your experience of life is not contingent on changing phenomena.

steppingstone [ˈstepɪŋ stoʊn] *n.* 跳板

springboard [ˈsprɪŋbɔːrd] *n.* 跳板

He uses his father's connection as a steppingstone/springboard for the future.

gravitate towards/to sth/sb 吸引到……

Women gravitate toward strong powerful men.

Public attention gravitates to her impeachment.

gravitate [ˈɡrævɪteɪt] *v.* 被吸引到；受吸引而参加；受重力作用

Political power gravitated into the hands of the army.

doppelganger [ˈdɑːplgæŋər, ˈdɑːplgeŋər] *n.* 面貌极相似的人；同姓名的人

The village has been haunted by a doppelganger of the demised prisoner who was wrongly executed.

I saw Steve's doppelganger at a dancing pool.

Part 3　识记单词 / 词组

externality [ˌekstɜːrˈnæləti] *n.* 外部性；伴随的结果

externalize [ɪkˈstɜːrnəlaɪz] *v.* 使具体化；把……归于外因

externalization [ɪkˌstɜːnəlaɪˈzeɪʃən, -lɪˈz-] *n.* 外表化；具体化

internal [ɪnˈtɜːrnl] *adj.* 内部的；内心的

internality [ˌɪntəˈnæləti] *n.* 内在；内在性

internalize [ɪnˈtɜːrnəlaɪz] *v.* 使藏在心底；使（习俗、准则等经吸收同化而）内在化

internalization [ɪnˌtɜːrnələˈzeɪʃn] *n.* 内在化

linkage [ˈlɪŋkɪdʒ] *n.* 联系；连锁

attributable [əˈtrɪbjətəbl] *adj.* 由……引起的

pell-mell [ˌpel ˈmel] *adj.* 匆忙的　*adv.* 凌乱地

welter [ˈweltər] *v.* 翻滚；浸湿　*n.* 混乱

welterweight [ˈweltərweɪt] *n.* （拳击或其他运动）次中量级（选手）

strew [struː] *v.* 撒；使散落；铺盖；点缀

inhibit [ɪnˈhɪbɪt] *v.* 禁止；顾忌

uninhibited [ˌʌnɪnˈhɪbɪtɪd] *adj.* 自由的；无拘无束的

append [əˈpend] *v.* 附加

premeditate [priːˈmedɪteɪt] *v.* 预先考虑；预谋

premeditation [ˌpriːmedɪˈteɪʃn] *n.* 预谋

depilate [ˈdepəleɪt] *v.* 除……的毛；使脱毛

depilation [ˌdepɪˈleɪʃən] *n.* 脱毛

epilate [ˈepəleɪt] *v.* （以化学、物理或放射物质）除毛

stakeholder [ˈsteɪkhoʊldər] *n.* 持股人；赌金保管人

jackpot [ˈdʒækpɑːt] *n.* 累积赌注；（赌博中）累积奖金

rendezvous [ˈrɑːndɪvuː, ˈrɑːndeɪvuː] *v.* 约会　*n.* 集结地

Lesson 40

Part 1　主力单词 / 词组

proportional [prəˈpɔːʃnl]　*adj.* 成比例的；对应的
Weight is proportional to food consumption.
It is irrefutable that academic success is proportional to the narrowness of one's field of study.
Pluto's gravitational force is proportional to its mass.

corresponding [ˌkɔːrəˈspɑːndɪŋ]　*adj.* 一致的；通信的
The fluctuation of oil prices is corresponding to the consumer price index.
The corresponding increase stemmed in part from the tax cut.
I hire a corresponding secretary to answer my e-mails.

commensurate [kəˈmenʃərət]　*adj.* 相当的；相称的
Your workload is commensurate with your salary.
Military power is often commensurate with economic strength.

correlate [ˈkɔːrəleɪt]　*v.* 使互相关联
Crime correlates with income.

correlation [ˌkɔːrəˈleɪʃn]　*n.* 相互关联；交互作用
He studies the correlation between diet and longevity.

• Words in sentences 句中单词 / 词组 •

irrefutable [ˌɪrɪˈfjuːtəbl, ɪˈrefjətəbl]　*adj.* 无可辩驳的
pluto [ˈpluːtoʊ]　*n.* 冥王星
consumer price index　物价指数
strength [streŋθ]　*n.* 力量；强项；（酒等的）浓度；人数

Part 2　补充单词 / 词组

innocuous [ɪˈnɑːkjuəs]　*adj.* 无害的；不会冒犯的
This is innocuous gossip.

prank [præŋk] *v.* 装饰；打扮   *n.* 恶作剧
The innocuous prank went away.

conducive [kənˈduːsɪv] *adj.* 有益的；有帮助的
Fruits and vegetables are conducive to health.

default [dɪˈfɔːlt, ˈdiːfɔːlt] *v.* 未履行；拖欠；默认   *n.* 预置值
If you default on your mortgage repayment, the bank will have your house repossessed.

the bane of sth   祸根；灾星；麻烦或不幸的根源
Coronavirus has been the bane of China recently.
My family is the bane of my entire life.

intuit [ɪnˈtuːɪt] *v.* 凭直觉感到
The detective intuits a connection between two crimes.

intuition [ˌɪntuˈɪʃn] *n.* 直觉
In the end, most decisions are based on intuition and faith. (Nathan Myhrvold, U.S. business executive)

midst [mɪdst] *n.* 中间；当中   *prep.* 在……中
It limits the ideas...impairs the mental vigor and narrows the outlook of those who are reared and educated in our midst. (Stephen Leacock, British-born Canadian writer and economist)

platonic [pləˈtɑːnɪk] *adj.* 柏拉图（哲学）的；理想的
They transformed their affection into a platonic relationship.
The concept is platonic but not practical.

red-handed [ˌred ˈhændɪd] *adj.* 正在作案的
He was caught red-handed.

neology=neologism   *n.* （发明）新词；新义
Neology is the practice of coining new words or phrases.
The contemporary newspaper appears to be more tolerant of the use of neologisms.

cyborg [ˈsaɪbɔːrg] *n.* 半机械人；电子人

strength of purpose   达成目标的决心
She shows great strength of purpose in the cyborg research project.

irrefragable [ɪˈrefrəgəbl] *adj.* 不可争辩的；不能反驳的
The irrefragable evidence of our eyes can prove he is a killer.

hireling ['haɪərlɪŋ] n. 受雇者 adj. 为金钱工作的
These hirelings have no concern for morality.

reflex ['riːfleks] v. 使经受反射 n. 反射（作用）；本能的反应；倒影 adj. 反射作用的
These exercises will strengthen your muscles and reflex.

chili pepper n. 红番椒
Chili peppers are made in varying strengths to cater to customers' different tastes.

stipend ['staɪpend] n. 津贴；养老金
He receives a small stipend as an intern in a hospital.

stipendiary [staɪ'pendieri] n.（牧师、教师、公职人员等）受俸给者 adj. 领薪金的
He is not a boss but a stipendiary public servant.

Part 3 识记单词/词组

plutonic [pluː'tɑnɪk] adj. [地] 火成岩的

pluton ['pluːtɔn] n. 火成岩

Haiti ['heɪti] n. 海地（位于拉丁美洲）

paperback ['peɪpərbæk] n. 平装本 adj. 平装（本）的；纸面装订的

hardcover ['hɑːrdkʌvər] n. 精装书 adj. 精装书的

cybernetics [ˌsaɪbər'netɪks] n. 人工头脑学；（计算机）控制学；神经机械学

cybernetic [ˌsaɪbər'netɪk] adj. 人工头脑学的

retronym ['retroʊnɪm] n. 衍生新词（因科技发展产生的）

hoi polloi 庶民；草民

the masses 群众；平民

the mass of sth ……的主要的部分

the mass of the people 大多数的人

mass number 原子量

mass defect （物理）质量亏损

defect ['diːfekt, dɪ'fekt] v. 逃跑；叛逃 n. 缺陷

defection [dɪ'fekʃn] n. 背叛；不履行义务

plato's love 精神恋爱

coin [kɔɪn] *v.* 铸造（货币） *n.* 硬币
coinage [ˈkɔɪnɪdʒ] *n.* 铸币；新造词语

Lesson 41

Part 1 主力单词 / 词组

consecutive [kənˈsekjətɪv] *adj.* 连续的；连贯的
The team won eight consecutive times.
The Scouts have survived for seventeen consecutive days without ration or sustenance.

successive [səkˈsesɪv] *adj.* 连续的；相继的
The trait of obesity can be found in their successive generations.
The life of an honest man must be an apostasy and a perpetual desertion...For the man who wishes to remain faithful to truth must make himself continually unfaithful to all the continual, successive, indefatigable renascent errors. (Charles Pierre Péguy, French writer and poet)

sequential [sɪˈkwenʃl] *adj.* 时序的；相继的；构成连续镜头的
The invited scholar explained Mesopotamia culture in sequential order from 3000 BC.
The absorption of information is not processed in linear, sequential steps.

serial [ˈsɪriəl] *n.* 电视连续剧 *adj.* 连续的；（重罪案犯或重案）连环的
The novelist wrote a thriller about a run-away serial killer hiding in this neighborhood.

concatenation [kɒnˌkætəˈneɪʃn] *n.* 一系列相关联的事物（或事件）
He suddenly came to realize who was behind the scenes after a concatenation of events.
A mammoth can be brought back to life by a concatenation of relevant technologies.
The isle is a concatenation of steep headlands and treacherous rugged cliffs strewn with weathered stones from boulders to pebbles.

concatenate [kɒnˈkætəneɪt] *v.* 把（一系列事件、事情等）联系起来 *adj.* 连接的；联系在一起的
The detective concatenates these events to puzzle out the perpetrator's motive.

sequence [ˈsiːkwəns] *n.* 顺序；[数] 数列；连续；片段；插曲

in sequence 顺次

Lesson 41

> • Words in sentences 句中单词 / 词组 •

the Scouts　童子军
ration［ˈræʃn］　n.（尤指在分配物短缺时的）配给量；合理的量；口粮
trait［treɪt］　n. 特征；少许
obesity［oʊˈbiːsəti］　n. 肥胖；臃肿
apostasy［əˈpɑːstəsi］　n. 叛教；变节；脱党
perpetual［pərˈpetʃuəl］　adj. 长期的；永恒的
indefatigable［ˌɪndɪˈfætɪɡəbl］　adj. 不懈的；不眠不休的
renascent［rɪˈneɪsnt］　adj. 新生的；复兴的
Mesopotamia［ˌmesəpəˈteɪmɪə］　n. 美索不达米亚
linear［ˈlɪniər］　adj. 线的；连续的
thriller［ˈθrɪlər］　n. 惊悚的小说、电影或戏剧
isle［aɪl］　n. 岛
steep［stiːp］　v. 浸泡　adj. 陡峭的
headland［ˈhedlənd, ˈhedlænd］　n. 向水中突出的陆地；畦头未耕的一条地；岬
treacherous［ˈtretʃərəs］　adj. 凶险的；不忠的
boulder［ˈboʊldər］　n. 卵石；大圆石
pebble［ˈpebl］　v. 用卵石铺（走道等）；用卵石连续扔　n. 小卵石；水晶
puzzle out　推测出

Part 2　补充单词 / 词组

permutate［pəˈmjuːteit］　v. 置换
The engineers permutate several designs and functions of a race car.

simulate［ˈsɪmjuleɪt］　v. 模仿；冒充　adj. 假装的；模仿的
The computer can simulate the trajectory of the missile.
The killer simulated insanity in the courtroom.

trajectory［trəˈdʒektəri］　n. 轨道；发展轨迹
He is truly fortunate if you see the trajectory of his life.

dissimulate [dɪˈsɪmjuleɪt] *v.* 掩饰；装假

To know how to dissimulate is the knowledge of kings. (Cardinal Richelieu, French churchman and statesman)

She dissimulates her sorrow with a gentle smile.

simulacrum [ˌsɪmjuˈleɪkrəm] *n.* 影像；相似物

The large school is a simulacrum of society.

The painting of skeleton pedestrians is a simulacrum of posthumous life.

A movie is a simulacrum of life.

sustenance [ˈsʌstənəns] *n.* 食物；营养；精神支撑

demise [dɪˈmaɪz] *v.* 遗赠；让位 *n.* 死亡；倒闭

He drew sustenance from Christianity after his son's demise.

corpulent [ˈkɔːrpjələnt] *adj.* 肥胖的

The lane is too narrow for a corpulent woman to pass.

apostate [əˈpɑːsteɪt] *n.* 叛教者；变节者 *adj.* 变节的

There are always some traitors and apostates in history.

apostatize [əˈpɑːstəˌtaɪz] *v.* 叛教；脱党；变节

Many Christians were apostatized by his coercion.

germane [dʒɜːrˈmeɪn] *adj.* 有密切关系的；适当的

Pollution is an environmental problem mostly germane to the factory.

rubble [ˈrʌbl] *n.* 碎石；瓦砾堆

He was crushed under rubble after the bombing.

Part 3 识记单词 / 词组

perpetuate [pərˈpetʃueɪt] *v.* 保持；使永存

perpetuation [pəˌpetʃuˈeɪʃən] *n.* 永存不朽；永久化

the Guides   女童子军

a scout around   （尤指为寻找某物而）扫视；快速查看

Scout's honor   保证；童子军誓言

perpetual fear   长期的恐惧

perpetual student   一直都是学生

linear relationship 直接联系
serial drama 连续剧
television serial 电视连续剧
founding father 开国者；创立人
cofounder [koʊˈfaʊndər] n. 共同创始人
to steep sth/ in sth 把某物浸泡在某物中

Lesson 42

Part 1 主力单词 / 词组

random [ˈrændəm] *adj.* 随机的　*n.* 随意；偶然的行动

It is hard to track the perpetrator when the attack is random.
If chance is defined as an event produced by random motion without any causal nexus, I would say there is no such thing as chance.
The traits between sea turtles and tortoises diverge either at random or as a result of natural selection.
These strangers wandered away at random.

arbitrary [ˈɑːrbɪtreri] *adj.* 随机的；独裁的

It is the dictator's arbitrary decision to kill all the suspects regardless of innocence.
The taxonomist tried to categorize species with arbitrary qualities into taxa.

desultory [ˈdesəltɔːri] *adj.* 随意的；漫无目的的

Our sins are tawdry, our virtues childlike, our revolts desultory and brief, our submissions formal and frequent. (Sean Ó'Faoláin, Irish writer)
The showgirl enjoys desultory shopping in the department store.
The infantry is subjected to desultory fire from the enemy's position.

indiscriminate [ˌɪndɪˈskrɪmɪnət] *adj.* 随机的；不加判断的

The killing seems to be indiscriminate, not based on religion or gender.
Indiscriminate and predatory lending led to the subprime mortgage problem.

aleatory [ˈeɪliətɔːri] *adj.* 随机的

Aleatory mutations might create the strongest species which adapts to the environment perfectly.

inadvertent [ˌɪnədˈvɜːrtnt] *adj.* 没计划的；随机的

The manslaughter is inadvertent.

The mountaineer has an inadvertent encounter with a rattlesnake in the Rocky Mountains.

inadvertence [ˌɪnəd'vɜːrtns]　*n.* 没注意；疏忽

A misstatement by a politician was made through inadvertence or mistake.
He was guilty of inadvertence.

haphazard [hæp'hæzərd]　*adj.* 偶然的；无计划的

The haphazard use of antibiotics is to be thoroughly condemned by practitioners.
The haphazard development of the city has made the city map like shattered glasses.

● Words in sentences 句中单词/词组 ●

perpetrator [ˈpɜːrpətreɪtər]　*n.* 犯罪者；行凶者
tortoise [ˈtɔːrtəs]　*n.* 乌龟；行动迟缓的人（或物）
diverge [daɪˈvɜːrdʒ]　*v.* 分歧；偏离
wander [ˈwɑːndər]　*v.* 徘徊；随意地走
taxonomist [tækˈsɔnəmist]　*n.* 分类学者
taxa [ˈtæksə]　*n.* 分类（复数）；类群
showgirl [ˈʃoʊgɜːrl]　*n.* 歌舞女演员
infantry [ˈɪnfəntri]　*n.* 步兵（统称）
predatory [ˈpredətɔːri]　*adj.* 食肉的；掠夺性的；好色成性的
subprime [ˌsʌbˈpraɪm]　*adj.* 次贷的
mutation [mjuːˈteɪʃn]　*n.* 突变
manslaughter [ˈmænslɔːtər]　*n.* 杀人；过失杀人
mountaineer [ˌmaʊntnˈɪr]　*n.* 登山者
rattlesnake [ˈrætlsneɪk]　*n.* 响尾蛇
antibiotics [ˌæntɪbaɪˈɑːtɪks]　*n.* 抗菌素
practitioner [prækˈtɪʃənər]　*n.* 医疗从业人员

Part 2　补充单词/词组

condemn [kənˈdem]　*v.* 谴责；宣判；迫使……接受困境；宣告使用……不安全

This condemned building is not safe.

chattel [ˈtʃætl] *n.* [律]动产；私人财产

real estate 不动产；房地产

He inherited some chattels and real estate from his father.

nexus [ˈneksəs] *n.* 联结；(事物、思想等之间的) 关系；焦点

The celebrity becomes the nexus of the 2019 casting scandal.

There is a nexus between poverty and crime.

Beijing has become a nexus of real estate investment.

acoustics [əˈkuːstɪks] *n.* 声学

He studies a nexus of theories related to acoustics.

acoustic [əˈkuːstɪk] *n.* 传音效果；音响效果 *adj.* 声音的；听觉的（乐器）

delicate [ˈdelɪkət] *n.* 微妙的形势 *adj.* 脆弱的；清淡的

The nexus between teachers and parents is delicate.

delicacy [ˈdelɪkəsi] *n.* 慎重；精细；脆弱（尤指稀有昂贵的）

They moved very carefully due to the delicacy of the ceramic vase.

She talks to her most important client with great delicacy.

glaze [gleɪz] *v.* 给……装玻璃；给……上光；给（食物）表面浇糖汁；变呆滞 *n.* 光油

The chef glazed the donut with butter.

His eyes glaze over at the mention of her name.

ceramic [səˈræmɪk] *n.* 陶瓷制品 *adj.* 陶器的

The ceramic has been glazed.

gather [ˈgæðər] *v.* 收集；渐增；猜想 *n.* 皱眉；衣褶

I gathered that she would return soon at his hour.

pollen [ˈpɑːlən] *n.* 花粉

nectar [ˈnektər] *n.* 花蜜；果汁饮料

Bees gather nectar and pollen from flowers.

ambrosia [æmˈbrouʒə] *n.* 美味的食物；甜点

upshot [ˈʌpʃɑːt] *n.* 结局；(分析或论证的) 要点；(射箭比赛的) 最后一射

The upshot is we find the treasure despite the difficulty.

The upshot of this conference is that we won't import any goods from Australia.

corollary [ˈkɔːrəleri] *n.* 必然的结果；伴随物；明显的推论

The increase in applying unemployment compensation is a corollary of recession.
Jealousy is a corollary of love.

vivisection [ˌvɪvɪˈsekʃn] *n.* 活体解剖

He was decried by the public for his vivisection project.

sting [stɪŋ] *v.* 螫；叮 *n.* 刺；蜇伤

A bee stung me.

stitch [stɪtʃ] *v.* 缝；编结；固定 *n.* 针脚；缝合伤口的针线；一件衣服；一块布

The nurse stitched the cut on his forearm.

Part 3 识记单词/词组

antibiotic [ˌæntibaɪˈɑːtɪk] *n.* 抗生素 *adj.* 抗生的；抗菌的

resistance [rɪˈzɪstəns] *n.* 抗药性

tetracycline [ˌtetrəˈsaɪklɪn] *n.* 四环素（抗生素）

penicillin [ˌpenɪˈsɪlɪn] *n.* 盘尼西林；青霉素

streptomycin [ˌstreptəˈmaɪsɪn] *n.* 链霉素

probiotic [ˌproʊbaɪˈɑːtɪk] *n.* 益生菌；益生素

biotic [baɪˈɑːtɪk] *adj.* 有关生命的；生物的

rifle [ˈraɪfl] *v.* 快速搜寻；偷窃；猛踢（足球） *n.* 步枪

desultory speech 随意的演讲

aleatory business 投机的生意（如开赌场）；赌场

aleatory contract 投机的合约

aleatory music 多种乐器随意组成的音乐

subprime mortgage 次贷按揭

subprime loan 次贷贷款

subprime lending 次贷借款

mutate [ˈmjuːteɪt] *v.* 改变；变化

mutant [ˈmjuːtənt] *n.* 突变体

adaption [əˈdæpʃn] *n.* 适应性
slaughter [ˈslɔːtər] *v.* 屠宰　*n.* 杀
categorization [ˌkætəgərəˈzeɪʃn] *n.* 分门别类；编目方法
red tape　繁文缛节；官僚作风
rattle [ˈrætl] *v.* 烦扰；使慌乱；(使)发出尖厉的敲击声　*n.* (连续重复的)嗒嗒声；嘎嘎声
decry [dɪˈkraɪ] *v.* 公开谴责
social gathering　社交聚会
gathering cry　战斗召集令

Lesson 43

Part 1　主力单词 / 词组

subsequent [ˈsʌbsɪkwənt] *adj.* 随后的；接着的；后来的
They have reached the conclusion in subsequent discussions.
The bomb exploded subsequent to our departure from the barn.
The subsequent businessman made a flippant remark about the ecological catastrophe.

succeed [səkˈsiːd] *v.* 随后出现；成功；继承
The rebellion was succeeded by oppression.
The royal troop succeeded in warding off their barbaric invaders.
He succeeded his father as a warrior.

success [səkˈses] *n.* 成功；成功者

afterwards [ˈæftərwərdz] *adv.* 后来；以后
He had dinner at a fancy restaurant and afterwards we watched a myriad of twinkling stars on a mountain top.

in the wake of　随着；仿效
The prime minister stepped down in the wake of the sex scandal.
Mayan culture has been annihilated in the wake of conquistadors and soldiers.

wake [weɪk] v. 醒来；叫醒   n. 尾流；航迹（航行的船只等留下的）；守灵

in the aftermath of 在……之后

A multitude of relics had been obliterated in the aftermath of the Cultural Revolution.

> • Words in sentences 句中单词 / 词组 •
>
> **barn** [bɑːrn] n. 谷仓；粮仓
> **flippant** [ˈflɪpənt] adj. 轻率的；浮夸的
> **ecological** [ˌiːkəˈlɑːdʒɪkl] adj. 生态的；环保的
> **rebellion** [rɪˈbeljən] n. 叛乱
> **ward off** 避开；阻止
> **barbaric** [bɑːrˈbærɪk] adj. 野蛮的
> **myriad** [ˈmɪriəd] n. 无数；极大数量   adj. 多种的；无数的
> **twinkling** [ˈtwɪŋklɪŋ] adj. 闪烁的；闪亮的   n. 瞬间；转眼
> **prime minister** 首相
> **scandal** [ˈskændl] n. 丑闻
> **annihilate** [əˈnaɪəleɪt] v. 彻底摧毁
> **conquistador** [kɑːŋˈkiːstədɔːr] n. 西班牙征服者（16世纪前往美洲并占领墨西哥和秘鲁）
> **relic** [ˈrelɪk] n. 遗物；圣物
> **obliterate** [əˈblɪtəreɪt] v. 彻底毁掉；覆盖；淹没

Part 2 补充单词 / 词组

infernal [ɪnˈfɜːrnl] adj. 地狱的；恶魔的

Will you please stop making that infernal noise? I am trying to concentrate.

mutilate [ˈmjuːtɪleɪt] v. 切断；毁坏

The victim has been mutilated. It is an infernal crime.

mutilation [ˌmjuːtɪˈleɪʃn] n. 毁损

roam [roʊm]　*v.* 在……漫步　*n.* 闲逛

My soul roams in the infernal regions of the dead.

torture [ˈtɔːrtʃər]　*v.* 虐待；拷打　*n.* 拷问；折磨

The master tortured slaves with infernal cruelty.

minatory=minatorial　*adj.* 威吓的；恫吓的

The dog gave me a minatory look as if it were going to bite me.

plumb [plʌm]　*v.* 探索；使垂直　*n.* 铅锤；垂直　*adj.* 垂直的　*adv.* 恰恰；正

The architect has to make sure the wall is plumb.

He was shot plumb in his left leg.

The psychologist plumbs the mystery of human feelings.

prophylactic [ˌproʊfəˈlæktɪk]　*n.* 预防药；预防法　*adj.* 预防疾病的

The effective prophylactic that the professor created is still being used as an antibiotic.

sadist [ˈseɪdɪst]　*n.* 虐待狂者

sadistic [səˈdɪstɪk]　*adj.* 虐待狂的

It is bound up with hatred, jealousy, boastfulness, disregard of all rules and sadistic pleasure in witnessing violence, in other words, it is war minus the shooting. (George Orwell, British writer)

Part 3　识记单词 / 词组

blockbuster [ˈblɑːkbʌstər]　*n.* (书、影片、大炸弹) 非常成功

cudgel one's brains　冥思苦索；绞尽脑汁

wrongdoing [ˈrɔːŋduːɪŋ]　*n.* 做坏事

prologue [ˈproʊlɔːɡ]　*n.* 开场白；序言

epilogue [ˈepɪlɔːɡ]　*n.* 结语；收场白

coda [ˈkoʊdə]　*n.* 终曲；结尾乐段

exofficio [ˌeksəˈfɪʃiˌoʊ]　*adj.* 依据职权的　*adv.* 当然地

impugn [ɪmˈpjuːn]　*v.* 责难；抨击

impugnment [ɪmˈpjuːnmənt]　*n.* 责难

cudgel [ˈkʌdʒl]　*n.* 棍棒　*v.* 用棍棒打

belabor [bɪˈleɪbər]　*v.* 打一顿；责骂

fulminate [ˈfʊlmɪneɪt]　*v.* 严厉批评；爆炸　*n.* 烈性炸药

fulmination [ˈfʌlməˈneiʃən] *n.* 严厉谴责；爆炸

inveigh [ɪnˈveɪ] *v.* 猛烈抨击；强烈抗议

exodus [ˈeksədəs] *n.* 外出；移居国外；大批离开

fidelity [fɪˈdeləti] *n.* 忠诚；精确；保真度

lambent [ˈlæmbənt] *adj.* 闪烁的；轻轻摇曳的；巧妙的（表达）

glint [glɪnt] *v.* 闪闪发光

hackle [ˈhækl] *v.*（做假发时的）梳理；乱劈 *n.* 颈羽；脾气；危险

reiterate [riˈɪtəreɪt] *v.* 重做；重申

reiteration [riːˌɪtəˈreɪʃən] *n.* 重申

remnant [ˈremnənt] *n.* 残余；残存者

blur [blɜːr] *v.* 变模糊；弄脏

the power vacuum 权力真空

vacuum [ˈvækjʊəm] *v.* 用吸尘器清扫 *n.* 真空；空白；与世隔绝

leave sth in your wake （离开某地）留下（麻烦或一片混乱等）

Lesson 44

Part 1 主力单词 / 词组

deliberate [dɪˈlɪbərət] *v.* 慎重考虑；仔细讨论 *adj.* 故意的

Poking me with his middle finger is a deliberate attempt to provoke conflict.
It's a deliberate decision to choose to study abroad.
The grand jury has deliberated for two weeks before reaching a verdict.

advertent [ədˈvɜːtənt] *adj.* 注意的；留心的

Graffiti is advertent wrongdoing.

intentional [ɪnˈtenʃənl] *adj.* 有意图的；故意的

Recalling the diagnoses and prescriptions given by my father's doctors and comparing them with this new knowledge of modern medicine, it gradually dawned on me that Chinese doctors were nothing more than quacks, whether intentional or unwitting. (Lu Xun, Chinese writer)

Lesson 44

on purpose 故意

Probation was denied because the judge suspected he did it on purpose.

• Words in sentences 句中单词 / 词组 •

grand jury 大陪审团

verdict [ˈvɜːrdɪkt] n. 判决

prescription [prɪˈskrɪpʃn] n. 处方；命令；规定

quack [kwæk] v. 呱呱叫 n. 庸医

unwitting [ʌnˈwɪtɪŋ] adj. 不知道的；不知情的 n. 冒牌医生；江湖医生

probation [proʊˈbeɪʃn] n. 缓刑；试用期

Part 2 补充单词 / 词组

obstetrics [əbˈstetrɪks] n. 产科医学

gynecology [ˌɡaɪnəˈkɑːlədʒi] n. 妇科学

parturient [pɑrˈtjʊrɪənt] adj. 分娩的；生产的

The nurses of obstetrics and gynecology take care of parturient women in the hospital.

obstetrician [ˌɑːbstəˈtrɪʃn] n. 产科医师

gynecologist [ˌɡaɪnəˈkɑːlədʒɪst] n. 妇科医生

She is an obstetrician and gynecologist helping manage deliveries and treat women's diseases.

flaneur [flɑːˈnə:] n. 游手好闲者

He has been called a flaneur roaming around the city aimlessly.

weft [weft] n. 纬线；薄云层

The weft is a horizontal thread.

The color of the weft was determined while threads were spun.

loom [luːm] n. 织布机

The clothes are made by warp and weft of the loom.

spacecraft [ˈspeɪskræft] n. 宇宙飞船；航天器

The spacecraft can warp space and time for space travel.

warp [wɔːrp]　*v.* 扭曲；变形　*n.* 扭曲；变形；（织布机上的）经线；拖船索

His judgment was warped by prejudices.

There is a warped drawer under the wooden desk.

sedative ['sedətɪv]　*n.* 镇静剂

Sedatives are drugs used to reduce nervous tension or induce sleep.

sedate [sɪ'deɪt]　*v.* 给……服镇静剂　*adj.* 安静的；沉着的

syringe [sɪ'rɪndʒ]　*v.* 注射；洗净　*n.* 注射器；冲洗器

The nurse sedates an irritating person with a syringe.

sedentary ['sednteri]　*adj.* 需要久坐的；惯于久坐不动的；不迁徙的

Accounting is a sedentary job.

Sedentary birds will not migrate.

barnacle ['bɑːrnəkl]　*n.* 藤壶（小甲壳动物，附着于水下岩石或船底等处）

hermaphrodite [hɜːr'mæfrədaɪt]　*n.* 阴阳人　*adj.* 雌雄同体；两性的

Most sedentary barnacles are hermaphrodites.

symptom ['sɪmptəm]　*n.* 症状；征兆

somatic [so'mætɪk]　*adj.* 身体的；细胞体的

He has neither a somatic disorder nor any symptoms of having one.

valetudinarian ['vælə,tjʊdn'erɪən]　*n.* 体弱多病的人　*adj.* 体弱多病的

The doctor told the valetudinarian about his health issues in detail.

trek [trek]　*v.* 远足；徒步旅行　*n.* 艰苦跋涉

The elderly are valetudinarians unfit for a trek and unable to be tasked with handiwork.

disincline [ˌdɪsɪn'klaɪn]　*v.* 不乐意

She is disinclined to work laboriously.

laborious [lə'bɔːriəs]　*adj.* 费力的；艰苦的

start over　重新开始

Otherwise, you have to start over.

magistrate ['mædʒɪstreɪt]　*n.* （审理轻微案件的）地方法官

plaintiff ['pleɪntɪf]　*n.* 原告

defendant [dɪˈfendənt] *n.* 被告
The magistrate first asks the plaintiff and then the defendant.

incendiary [ɪnˈsendieri] *n.* 纵火犯；燃烧弹；煽动者　*adj.* 能燃烧的；煽动的
Paper and wood are incendiary material.
The speeches Hitler delivered were usually incendiary.

reprieve [rɪˈpriːv] *v.* 撤销……的死刑　*n.* 缓刑；暂缓
The judge gave him a reprieve by considering the circumstance.
The new king reprieved prisoners under the death sentence.

mountebank [ˈmaʊntɪbæŋk] *v.* 走江湖；行骗　*n.* 江湖医生；江湖骗子
Remember to save the file. A gang of city swindlers and mountebanks try to rip the rural old lady off.
He mountebanked her love for money.

prescribe [prɪˈskraɪb] *v.* 开（药方）；命令；规定
The financial expert prescribes numerous strategies for investors.
Don't prescribe me to do something stupid.
We should obey whatever the law prescribes.

seasoned [ˈsiːznd] *adj.* 经验丰富的；老练的
The seasoned expert speaks with a magisterial tone.

magisterial [ˌmædʒɪˈstɪriəl] *adj.* 地方法官的；权威的；傲慢的
The magisterial system has to be examined.

Part 3　识记单词 / 词组

provocation [ˌprɑːvəˈkeɪʃn] *n.* 激怒；引起

evasion [ɪˈveɪʒn] *n.* 规避；借口；逃税

evasive [ɪˈveɪsɪv] *adj.* 逃避的；难以捉住的

the jury　陪审团

probate [ˈproʊbeɪt] *v.* 遗嘱检验

take evasive action　（尤指在战争中飞机、军舰等的）规避动作

juror [ˈdʒʊrər] *n.* 陪审员；评审员

the jury is (still) out　（答案或观点）尚不明确；悬而未决

daily [ˈdeɪli] n. 日报
islander [ˈaɪləndər] n. 岛上居民
unquoted share　未上市的股票
underdog [ˈʌndərdɔːg] n. 弱势群体；被认为会输的人（打架或竞赛）
ventriloquist [venˈtrɪləkwɪst] n. 腹语术者
ventral [ˈventrəl] n.（昆虫的）腹面　adj. 腹部的
dorsal [ˈdɔːrsl] adj. 背部的；背侧的
lateral [ˈlætərəl] v. 横向传球　n. 侧音　adj. 侧面的；横向的
secretiveness [sɪˈkriːtɪvnɪs] n. 隐匿；保密

Lesson 45

Part 1　主力单词 / 词组

deceive [dɪˈsiːv] v. 欺骗；蒙骗
There is no illness which it cannot counterfeit perfectly…If it is capable of deceiving the doctor, how should it fail to deceive the patient? (Marcel Proust, French novelist)
The young man was deceived by her beautiful appearance and noble mien.

mendacity [menˈdæsəti] n. 谎话
Like a daily diet, we have heard too much of political mendacity.

mendacious [menˈdeɪʃəs] adj. 说谎的；虚伪的
The peace talk with the regime is mendacious and unreliable.
I have heard a lot of your mendacious tales.

cheat [tʃiːt] v. 欺骗；作弊　n. 骗子
She cheated at cards and no one wanted to play with her.

chicanery [ʃɪˈkeɪnəri] n. 欺骗；欺诈
environmental pollution, political chicanery, and corruption

delude [dɪˈluːd] v. 欺诈
Don't delude yourself. Mary is dead. There is no way to resurrect her.

cajole [kəˈdʒoʊl] v. (以甜言蜜语) 诱骗

I cajoled the little kid into throwing away my garbage for me.

He cajoles money from his father.

cajolery [kəˈdʒoʊləri] n. 谄媚；甜言蜜语的欺骗

There is a mixed strategy of cajolery and threat.

coax [koʊks] v. 哄骗；劝诱 (哄骗某人做某事)

She finally bought the jewel after a great deal of coaxing and flattering.

swindle [ˈswɪndl] v. 骗取 (钱财)；诈骗

The businessman swindled investors into buying unquoted shares.

The accounting malpractice of Lehman Brothers was a big open swindle.

wheedle [ˈwiːdl] v. 哄骗；用花言巧语说服

The advertisement wheedled us into the service of the Vietnam army again. You can be a hero at war, nevertheless, possibly a dead one.

inveigle [ɪnˈveɪɡl] v. 诱骗

The swindler tries many schemes to inveigle a rich lady.

He used the money to inveigle these girls into prostitution.

insinuate [ɪnˈsɪnjueɪt] v. 使迂回地潜入；骗弄；含沙射影地说

The company has insinuated moles into opponents' top brass.

He tries to insinuate himself into her affections, just for money, definitely not unrequited love.

insinuation [ɪnˌsɪnjuˈeɪʃn] n. 暗暗进入；巧妙巴结；暗示；间接的讽刺

Rumors, speculations, and insinuations have been circulating concerning the company's insider trading.

worm your way/yourself into 逐渐骗取信任

The untouchable Indian managed to worm himself into the party of the rich.

legerdemain [ˈledʒərdəmeɪn] n. 很有技巧的欺骗 (借着隐藏真相)；巧妙的手法

That is his political legerdemain. Actually, he has no concern for them at all after the election.

The magician performs ventriloquism and legerdemain to impress the audience.

duplicity [duːˈplɪsəti] n. 表里不一

I can't charge him for duplicity unless I can prove it despite his secretive behavior.

double-cross [ˌdʌbl ˈkrɔːs]　*v.* 欺骗　*n.* 欺骗行为

He double-crosses his accomplice setting him up by calling police to arrest him.
We often see a last-minute double-cross in the movies.
Double-crossing and backbiting are very normal in the political arena.

bilk [bɪlk]　*v.* 欺骗；赖账；逃避；阻碍

The telephone scammer bilked people out of their life savings.
He jumped off the balcony to bilk his creditors and pursuers.
Their hopes of returning home safely were bilked when the ship was broken.

cozen [ˈkʌzən]　*v.* 哄骗；诈骗；欺骗

Frauds usually choose elderly people to cozen their money.

> • Words in sentences 句中单词 / 词组 •
>
> **mien** [miːn]　*n.* 态度；风采；样子
> **resurrect** [ˌrezəˈrekt]　*v.* 使复活；使起死回生
> **unquoted** [ˈʌnˈkwəʊtɪd]　*adj.* 未上市的
> **malpractice** [ˌmælˈpræktɪs]　*n.* 营私舞弊
> **Vietnam** [ˌviːetˈnɑːm]　*n.* 越南
> **mole** [məʊl]　*n.* 内奸；痣；鼹鼠
> **top brass**　*n.* 高层；（尤指）高级军官
> **insider trading**　内线交易
> **ventriloquism** [venˈtrɪləkwɪzəm]　*n.* 腹语术；口技
> **secretive** [ˈsiːkrətɪv]　*adj.* 遮遮掩掩的
> **backbiting** [ˈbækbaɪtɪŋ]　*n.* 背后诽谤；背后中伤
> **arena** [əˈriːnə]　*n.* 竞技场
> **creditor** [ˈkredɪtər]　*n.* 债主；债权人；贷方

Part 2　补充单词 / 词组

dissemble [dɪˈsembl]　*v.* 掩饰；假装

The spin artist dissembles to care about the underdog to mislead people to vote for him.

venal [ˈviːnl] adj. 能收买的；贪赃枉法的

The venal financial expert disseminated misinformation about the stock market.

The businesswoman bought off venal police in Venezuela.

political venality 政治贪腐

The president attempted to get rid of political venality.

unvarnished [ˌʌnˈvɑːrnɪʃt] adj. 无掩饰的；坦率的；未涂漆的

But the best and safest method...is to tell the plain unvarnished truth. (Max Frisch, Swiss dramatist and novelist)

notwithstanding [ˌnɑːtwɪθˈstændɪŋ, ˌnɑːtwɪðˈstændɪŋ] adv. 尽管如此 prep. 尽管

Formosa is a great, beautiful island of China notwithstanding.

mulct [mʌlkt] v. 诈骗；课以罚金

Joking is the third-best method of hoodwinking people. French authorities mulcted aboriginals for their land with fake diamonds.

The judge mulcted me 300 dollars for speeding.

neurosis [nʊˈroʊsɪs] n. 神经官能症；神经症

Neurosis has an absolute genius for malingering.

malingerer [məˈlɪŋɡərə] n. 装病的人

I think she is a healthy malingerer.

feign [feɪn] v. 假装；模仿；发明

unfeigned [ʌnˈfeɪnd] adj. 不假装的；真诚的

He cordially gazed upon the girl with unfeigned admiration.

peninsula [pɪˈnɪnsələr] n. 半岛

Yemen is located in the south of the Arabian Peninsula.

archipelago [ˌɑːrkɪˈpeləɡoʊ] n. 群岛

He goes fishing in a Japanese archipelago.

canard [ˈkænɑːrd] n. 谣言；误传

The coronavirus won't spread to humans proved to be a canard.

normalize [ˈnɔːrməlaɪz] v. 使常态化；使合标准

tie [taɪ] v. 系；拴；打成平手 n. 领带；绳索；束缚；关系

The state normalizes ties with Tajikistan.

stratagem [ˈstrætədʒəm] *n.* 策略；诡计

Ming Kong is a master of stratagem in the Three Kingdoms Period.

Part 3 识记单词/词组

cozenage [ˈkʌzənidʒ] *n.* 哄骗；诈骗

hoodwink [ˈhʊdwɪŋk] *v.* 诈骗

deceit [dɪˈsiːt] *n.* 欺骗；诡计；狡诈行为

deceitful [dɪˈsiːtfl] *adj.* 欺诈的；使人误解的

deceive yourself 自欺欺人

cheat death 死里逃生

cheat on sb 对（丈夫或妻子）不忠

cheat sb out of sth 骗取；诈取

swindler [ˈswɪndlər] *n.* 骗钱的人

insinuate yourself into sth 钻营

venality [viːˈnæləti] *n.* 贪赃枉法；腐败

varnish [ˈvɑːrnɪʃ] *v.* 装饰；粉饰；涂清漆

a family concern 家族企业

Vietnamese [ˌvjetnəˈmiːz, viˌetnəˈmiːz] *n.* 越南人；越南语 *adj.* 越南人的；越南语的

resurrection [ˌrezəˈrekʃn] *n.* 复活；复苏

The Resurrection 耶稣复活节

malinger [məˈlɪŋɡər] *v.* 装病

backbite [ˈbækˌbaɪt] *v.* 中伤

opponent [əˈpoʊnənt] *n.* 对手

Lesson 46

Part 1 主力单词/词组

quotidian [kwoʊˈtɪdiən] *adj.* 每日的；日常的

Should I tell you everything in quotidian details?

Drinking coffee is my quotidian routine.

The still countryside is full of quotidian drabness.

circadian [sɜːrˈkeɪdiən]　*adj.*（动植物的）昼夜的；约一日的；约 24 小时的（节律、周期）

Shifting sleep schedules constantly will affect circadian rhythm and hormone levels.

daily [ˈdeɪli]　*adj.* 一天的

We shall never be wholly civilized until we remove the treadmill from the daily job. (Henry Ford, U.S. car manufacturer).

> • Words in sentences 句中单词 / 词组 •
>
> **routine** [ruːˈtiːn]　*n.* 惯例；习惯　*adj.* 常规的；例行的
> **drabness** [ˈdræbnɪs]　*n.* 单调乏味
> **hormone** [ˈhɔːrmoʊn]　*n.* 荷尔蒙；激素
> **treadmill** [ˈtredmɪl]　*n.* 繁重的工作；跑步机；踏车

Part 2　补充单词 / 词组

circadian rhythm　生理节奏

out of whack　出毛病的；不正常的

Being devoid of proper sleep will throw your circadian rhythm out of whack.

debridement [dɪˈbriːdmənt]　*n.* 坏死组织的除去；边缘切除（术）

morbidity [mɔːrˈbɪdəti]　*n.* 病态；发病率

Debridement is essential to lower the morbidity of the wounded soldier.

morbid [ˈmɔːrbɪd]　*adj.* 病态的；可怕的；令人厌恶的

These plants with withered leaves are in a morbid condition.

buzzkill [ˈbʌzˌkɪl]　*n.* 令人扫兴的人或事

His morbid curiosity is a buzzkill.

Part 3　识记单词 / 词组

drab [dræb]　*adj.* 单调的；乏味的；缺乏色彩的；平淡的

circadian clock　生理时钟
debride［dɪˈbraɪd］　v. 清创（除去坏死的组织）
drudgery［ˈdrʌdʒəri］　n. 辛苦无聊的工作
invigorate［ɪnˈvɪɡəreɪt］　v. 使精力充沛；使活跃
vivacity［vɪˈvæsəti, vaɪˈvæsəti］　n. 活泼；活力
vivacious［vɪˈveɪʃəs, vaɪˈveɪʃəs］　adj. 活泼迷人的
vim［vɪm］　n. 活力；热情
vitality［vaɪˈtæləti］　n. 活力；生气
revitalize［ˌriːˈvaɪtəlaɪz］　v. 使复活；使复兴
revitalization［ˌriːˌvaɪtələˈzeɪʃn］　n. 复兴；复苏
laid-back［ˌleɪd ˈbæk］　adj. 懒散的；悠闲的
vibrant［ˈvaɪbrənt］　adj. 活跃的；热情洋溢的
high-spiritedness　活泼
baby boom　婴儿潮
love serenade　爱的小夜曲
languid pace　迟缓的脚步

Lesson 47

Part 1　主力单词 / 词组

hebdomadal［hebˈdɒmədəl］　adj. 每星期的
The newspaper is hebdomadal.
We have paid a hebdomadal visit to the orphanage since last year.

weekly［ˈwiːkli］　adj. 每周一次的
A well-adjusted executive is one whose intake of pep pills overbalances his consumption of tranquilizers just enough to leave him sufficient energy for the weekly visit to the psychiatrist. (Arthur Motley, U.S. business executive)

- **Words in sentences 句中单词 / 词组**

orphanage [ˈɔːrfənɪdʒ]　n. 孤儿院

intake [ˈɪnteɪk]　n. 摄入量；吸入；（尤指学院或大学的）招生人数；（空气、液体或气体的）输入口

pep [pep]　n. 精力；热情

Part 2　补充单词 / 词组

modulate [ˈmɑːdʒəleɪt]　v. 调整；控制；缓和；使变调
I have to modulate my voice for that high-pitched song.

modulation [ˌmɑːdʒəˈleɪʃn]　n. 调节；调音；调幅
The broadcast station installs frequency-modulation carrier systems.

thicket [ˈθɪkɪt]　n. 灌木丛
Young deer are kept hidden in thickets, camouflaged by their dappled markings.

Part 3　识记单词 / 词组

hebdomad [ˈhebdəˌmæd]　n. 一周；七天

carapace [ˈkærəpeɪs]　n. 甲壳

overbalance [ˌoʊvərˈbæləns]　v. 失去平衡

tranquilizer=tranquiliser　n. 镇定剂；止痛药

narcotic [nɑːrˈkɑːtɪk]　n. 催眠药；毒品　adj. 催眠药的；麻醉剂的

anesthetic [ˌænɪsˈθetɪk]　n. 麻醉剂　adj. 麻醉的

dachshund [ˈdɑːkshʊnd]　n. 腊肠狗

pay a visit　（通常指短时间的）拜访；访问

sojourn [ˈsoʊdʒɜːrn]　n. 逗留；旅居

pep talk　鼓舞士气的讲话

Lesson 48

Part 1 主力单词 / 词组

unwitting [ʌnˈwɪtɪŋ] *adj.* 不知道的；未觉察的；无意的

He helps the wrong guy and becomes an unwitting accomplice.

My discovery was this: I had become the victim of a vast, amorphous, unwitting, unconscious conspiracy to prevent me from doing anything whatever to change the university's status quo. (Warren Bennis, U.S.educationalist and writer)

unaccountably [ˌʌnəˈkaʊntəbli] *adv.* 难以解释地

She smiles unaccountably as if possessed.

The urbane gentleman has behaved unaccountably bad recently.

unbeknownst [ˌʌnbɪˈnoʊnst] *adv.* 不知道地 *adj.* 不知道的

She stayed a night with him, unbeknownst to her mother.

He snuck out the backdoor of the classroom unbeknownst.

• Words in sentences 句中单词 / 词组 •

accomplice [əˈkɑːmplɪs] *n.* 共犯；同谋

amorphous [əˈmɔːrfəs] *adj.* 无固定形状的；不定形的

possess [pəˈzes] *v.* 控制；支配（欲望或想法）；拥有；影响

urbane [ɜːrˈbeɪn] *adj.* 温文尔雅的

Part 2 补充单词 / 词组

quid pro quo *n.* 交换条件；交换物；报酬

There must be a quid pro quo corruption involved.

cop [kɑːp] *v.* 遭受；忍受 *n.* 警察

get away 逃脱

Dirty cops didn't do anything, they deliberately let the gangster leader get away.

condone [kənˈdoʊn]　v. 饶恕；纵容
The major will not condone any violence.

Part 3　识记单词 / 词组

unconscious [ʌnˈkɑːnʃəs]　adj.（想法或感情）无意识的；潜意识的；（尤指因头部受伤）昏迷的

subconscious [ˌsʌbˈkɑːnʃəs]　adj. 下（潜）意识的；意识模糊的

unaccountable [ˌʌnəˈkaʊntəbl]　adj. 无法理解的；无须对……作出解释的；不必对……负责的

unbeknown [ˌʌnbɪˈnoʊn]　adj. 不为人知的

forgiving [fərˈɡɪvɪŋ]　adj. 宽容的

sneak [sniːk]　v. 偷偷地走　n. 潜行；打小报告的人　adj. 暗中进行的

sneaker [ˈsniːkər]　n. 运动鞋

morph [mɔːrf]　v.（使）图像变形　n.（动植物的）变种

mesomorph [ˈmezəmɔːrf, ˈmiːzəmɔːrf]　n. 体育型体质者

the status quo　现状

quid [kwɪd]　n. 一英镑；咀嚼物

quo warranto　责问某人根据什么行使职权的令状

sneak a look/glance at sb/sth　很快地看……一眼

get away with it　做（错事）而未被惩罚；做（坏事）而未被发觉

Lesson 49

Part 1　主力单词 / 词组

obvious [ˈɑːbviəs]　adj. 明显的
She makes her crush on me obvious by sending me chocolates.
One of the most obvious facts about grown-ups to a child is that they have forgotten what it is like to be a child. (Randall Jarrell, U.S. author and poet)

evident [ˈevɪdənt]　adj. 明显的
It is evident he will betray us since he took the enemy's money.

apparent [ə'pærənt] adj. 明显的
My boss fired me for no apparent reason.

manifest ['mænɪfest] adj. 明显的
I like your manifest charming personality.
His flair was manifested in math.

conspicuous [kən'spɪkjuəs] adj. 显眼的
There are monarch butterflies with conspicuous colors.

palpable ['pælpəbl] adj. 明显的；可感知的；触摸得到的
Pressure has been palpable for days preceding the college entrance exam.

salient ['seɪliənt] adj. 突出的；显著的
Please summarize salient points of this regional conflict for the commander.

striking ['straɪkɪŋ] adj. 明显的
She bears a striking resemblance to her sister.

overt [oʊ'vɜːrt, 'oʊvɜːrt] adj. 公开的；明显的
Occupying our land is an overt act of invasion.
Overt criticism embarrasses people invariably.

demonstrable [dɪ'mɑːnstrəbl] adj. 可被证实的；明显可见的
Bill Gates' remarkable success is demonstrable.
Pungent air pollution from chemical factories can have demonstrable effects at very great distances.

• Words in sentences 句中单词 / 词组 •

crush [krʌʃ] v. 摧毁；弄皱 n. 拥挤的人群；热恋的对象
betray [bɪ'treɪ] v. 背叛
flair [fler] n. 天分；眼光；鉴别力
invasion [ɪn'veɪʒn] n. 侵略
invariably [ɪn'veriəbli] adv. 总是
pungent ['pʌndʒənt] adj.（气味）刺鼻的；（话语或文章）尖刻的；敏锐的

Part 2 补充单词/词组

wont [wɔːnt] *v.* 使习惯于 *n.* 习惯 *adj.* 习惯的

Cosmus, Duke of Florence, was wont to say of perfidious friends, that " We read that we ought to forgive our enemies, but we do not read that we ought to forgive our friends. " (Francis Bacon, English philosopher, statesman, and lawyer).

perfidious [pərˈfɪdiəs] *adj.* 背信弃义的；不诚实的

The perfidious principal breached the contract.

perfidy [ˈpɜːrfədi] *n.* 背信弃义；不诚实

We all railed and despaired at British perfidy.

She is a victim of her colleague's perfidy.

unwonted [ʌnˈwoʊntɪd] *adj.* 不习惯的；不同寻常的；少有的

I am unwonted to the food in the desert region.

We felt strange about her unwonted kindness. Was there something wrong?

ursine [ˈɜːrsaɪn] *adj.* 熊的；像熊的

He has a tiger's back and an ursine waist.

command [kəˈmænd] *v.* 命令；指挥；控制 *n.* 控制权；掌握

She has a good command of spoken French.

I would like to talk to someone who is in command.

acrid [ˈækrɪd] *adj.* 刺激的；辣的；苦的；刻薄的

She is an acrid critic.

acrimony [ˈækrɪmoʊni] *n.* 刻薄；讽刺

Acrimony over the election made the reconciliation for both parties almost impossible.

No issues have been so steeped in acrimony and controversy in terms of personal privacy and national security.

acrimonious [ˌækrɪˈmoʊniəs] *adj.* 激烈的；充满火药味的

They had an acrimonious fight with gangsters.

gingerly [ˈdʒɪndʒərli] *adv.* 小心翼翼地；极为谨慎地

The president dealt gingerly with the immigration issue.

We walked gingerly on the ice.

barrister [ˈbærɪstər] *n.* 律师

The judge asked barristers from both sides to approach the bar.

hibernal [haɪˈbɜːrnl]　*adj.* 冬天的；寒冷的

eczema [ɪɡˈziːmə, ˈeksɪmə]　*n.* 湿疹

He contracted hibernal eczema.

hibernation [ˌhaɪbərˈneɪʃn]　*n.* 冬眠

The snake emerges from hibernation with the return of warm weather.

hibernate [ˈhaɪbərneɪt]　*v.* 冬眠

Bears hibernate in winter.

embarrass [ɪmˈbærəs]　*v.* 使难堪；使尴尬；妨碍；使（问题）复杂化

She was embarrassed by a faux pas.
Overeating embarrassed digestion.

vernal [ˈvɜːrnl]　*adj.* 春天生长的；青春的

The poet appreciates vernal flowers and autumnal breeze.

knoll [noʊl]　*n.* 圆丘；小丘

Students have to pass a knoll to their dormitory.

ginger [ˈdʒɪndʒər]　*v.* 用姜调味　*n.* 姜　*adj.* 姜黄色的

shallot [ʃəˈlɑːt]　*n.* 青葱；红葱头

acridity [æˈkrɪdəti]　*n.* 辛辣；苦；苛刻；刺激；腐蚀性

The chef used ginger and shallot to remove the acridity of the corn.

Part 3　识记单词/词组

mesa [ˈmeɪsə]　*n.* 台地；平顶山

flautist [ˈflɔːtɪst, ˈflaʊtɪst]　*n.* 横笛吹奏者；笛子手

blindfold [ˈblaɪndfoʊld]　*v.* 蒙住……的眼睛　*n.* 眼罩；蒙眼布

summary [ˈsʌməri]　*n.* 摘要；结局

corm [kɔːrm]　*n.* 球茎

bear market　熊市（空头市场）

bull market　牛市（行情看涨的市场）

a helluva teacher　一个很好的老师

draw lots　抽签

sb's lot=the lot of sb　（某人的）生活状况；命运

Lesson 50

Part 1 主力单词 / 词组

prior to 在……之前

The witness disappeared prior to trial.
The scepter of Pharaoh was missing prior to the auction.
She had been drinking prior to the crash.

prior [paɪər] *adj.* 先前的

Do you have a prior history of heart attack or any other allergies?
The calculus course requires prior knowledge of precalculus.

precede [prɪˈsiːd] *v.* 处在……之前；在先

Diagnosis precedes treatment. (Russell John Howard，British surgeon)

predate [ˌpriːˈdeɪt] *v.* 在……之前；掠食；捕食

The ancient handicraft predates the Qing dynasty.

antecede [ˌæntɪˈsiːd] *v.* 在……之前

Dinosaur antecedes mankind.

• Words in sentences 句中单词 / 词组 •

trial [ˈtraɪəl] *v.* 测试　*n.* 审判；试用　*adj.* 试验的；试制的
scepter [ˈseptər] *n.* 权杖；统治权；王权
pharaoh [ˈferoʊ] *n.* 法老
heart attack 心脏病发作；心力衰竭

Part 2 补充单词 / 词组

parapet [ˈpærəpɪt, ˈpærəpet] *n.* 矮护墙；女儿墙

The nomadic tribe fired arrows and crossed the village's parapet.

rampart [ˈræmpɑːrt] *n.* 防御土墙；堡垒

The rampart of enmity was erected when the lady knew he was a libertine.
They build ramparts and excavate ditches preparing for war.

truce [truːs] *n.* 停战；休战协定

We agreed to a truce and signed the armistice.

predate on 以……为食

Birds predate on insects.

ken [ken] *n.* 知识范围；理解范围；视野；眼界

An unmanned boat drifts into our ken.
The alien technology is so complicated beyond my ken.

allergic [əˈlɜːrdʒɪk] *adj.* 过敏的

hypersensitive [ˌhaɪpərˈsensətɪv] *adj.* 过敏症的

She is allergic(hypersensitive) to pollen.

Part 3 识记单词/词组

prior [ˈpraɪər] *adj.* 在先的；在前的；居先的；更重要的
prior [ˈpraɪə] *n.* 犯罪前科
allergy [ˈælərdʒi] *n.* 过敏；反感；厌恶
allergen [ˈælərdʒən] *n.* 过敏原
auction [ˈɔːkʃn] *v.* 拍卖 *n.* 拍卖
antecedent [ˌæntɪˈsiːdnt] *n.* 祖先；先例 *adj.* 先前的
preceding argument 先前的论述

Lesson 51

Part 1 主力单词/词组

cooperate [kouˈɑːpəreɪt] *v.* 合作

For finding the missing person, I have cooperated with locals.

Lesson 51

In order to be true to one's conscience and true to God, a righteous man has no alternative but to refuse to cooperate with an evil system. (Martin Luther King, U.S. civil rights leader)

The merger between the two leading manufacturers will be much easier if the two presidents cooperate.

collaborate [kəˈlæbəreɪt] *v.* 合作；通敌

The firefighters collaborated with the residents to extinguish the fire.

symbiosis [ˌsɪmbaɪˈoʊsɪs] *n.* 共生；有利

The entrepreneur has tried to create a symbiosis between corporate interests and employees' initiatives.

in tandem 协作；合作；同时

Our navy will attack the invaders in tandem with our north ally.

tandem [ˈtændəm] *n.* 协力车

cooperation [koʊˌɑːpəˈreɪʃn] *n.* 合作

cooperative [koʊˈɑːpərətɪv] *n.* 合作社 *adj.* 合作的

coordinate [koʊˈɔːrdɪneɪt] *v.* 协作

coordination [koʊˌɔːrdɪˈneɪʃn] *n.* 统筹

coordinator [koʊˈɔːrdɪneɪtər] *n.* 统筹者

symbiotic [ˌsɪmbaɪˈɑːtɪk] *adj.* 共生的

• Words in sentences 句中单词 / 词组 •

merger [ˈmɜːrdʒər] *n.* (机构或企业的) 合并

entrepreneur [ˌɑːntrəprəˈnɜːr] *n.* 企业家；创业者

initiative [ɪˈnɪʃətɪv] *n.* 倡议；新措施；积极性

Part 2 补充单词 / 词组

merge [mɜːrdʒ] *v.* 使 (公司等) 合并；使同化

Oil and water can't merge together.

The investment bank merged the two companies.

confluence [ˈkɑːnfluəns] *n.* (河流的) 汇流点；(人或物的) 汇合

China is marked by a confluence of cultural traditions.
The murder took place at the confluence of the Volga and Kazanka rivers.

conflate [kən'fleɪt]　*v.* 把……合并；把……混淆

The editor conflates the two articles.
Lanzhou is a city of conflated races, cultures, and religions.

misfortune [ˌmɪs'fɔːtʃən]　*n.* 不幸

He gloated over others' misfortune.

schadenfreude ['ʃɑːdnfrɔɪdə]　*n.* 幸灾乐祸

He laughed at his misfortune and spoke with a tone of schadenfreude.

mishap ['mɪshæp]　*n.* 不幸事故；灾难

Some officials should be held accountable for the tragic mishap that could have been prevented.
His negligence of public safety occasioned the mishap.

hapless ['hæpləs]　*adj.* 不幸的

I commiserated this hapless South American nation.
George Harrison is a sweet sort of hapless character who doesn't have a mean bone in his body. (Madonna, U.S. pop singer and film actor)

misadventure [ˌmɪsəd'ventʃər]　*n.* 不幸的遭遇

Media scandals always periodically engulf a celebrity or a politician over tactless remarks or sexual misadventures.

mammoth ['mæməθ]　*n.* 猛犸象；庞然大物　*adj.* 庞大的

A string of financial misadventures bankrupted an international mammoth corporation.

stranded ['strændɪd]　*adj.* 处于困境的

The ship went through a series of misadventures and became stranded outside the coast of a deserted island.

perverse [pər'vɜːrs]　*adj.* 堕落的；故意作对的；倔强的；刚愎自用的

gloat [ɡloʊt]　*v.* 幸灾乐祸；沾沾自喜

They are gloating over their victory in the battle.

Part 3　识记单词 / 词组

nautical ['nɔːtɪkl]　*adj.* 航海的；海员的

harbor [ˈhɑːrbər]　v. 携带（细菌等）　n. 港口
moor [mʊr]　v. 停泊；被固定；被系住　n. 无树的荒野
shoal [ʃoʊl]　v. 变浅；驶入（浅水等）　n. 浅水处；沙洲
strand [strænd]　v. 使搁浅　n. 海滨；股
unkempt [ˌʌnˈkempt]　adj. 不整洁的
manicure [ˈmænɪkjʊr]　n. 指甲护理；美甲
heir [er]　n. 继承人
frisson [ˈfriːsəʊn]　n. 震颤；战栗
pedicure [ˈpedɪkjʊr]　n. 足部护理；足部美甲
entrepreneurial [ˌɑːntrəprəˈnɜːriəl]　adj. 企业家的
drunken [ˈdrʌŋkən]　adj. 酒醉的
gabble [ˈɡæbl]　v. 急促而含糊地说话　n. 急促不清的话
petal [ˈpetl]　n. 花瓣
inversion [ɪnˈvɜːrʒn]　n. 反向；倒装法
transnational [ˌtrænzˈnæʃnəl, ˌtrænsˈnæʃnəl]　adj. 跨国的；多国的
haplessly [ˈhæplɪsli]　adv. 运气不好地；不幸地
pervert the course of justice　妨碍司法公正；枉法
wring [rɪŋ]　v. 拧干；绞干
wring sth from sb　强迫（某人）交出……
wring sth out of sb　说服（某人）给予……
rip-off [ˈrɪp ɔːf]　n. 敲诈行为；索价过高的物品
to the extent that　达到……地步

Lesson 52

Part 1　主力单词/词组

annually [ˈænjuəli]　adv. 每年地
The house price rises annually by perusing fiscal reports.

annual [ˈænjuəl]　*n.* 年刊；年鉴；一年生植物　*adj.* 一年一度的

Soldiers on the frontline are celebrating their annual reunion.

per annum　每年

The seafood trading company imports lobsters worth 3 million dollars per annum.
twenty guineas per annum

● Words in sentences 句中单词 / 词组 ●

fiscal [ˈfɪskl]　*adj.* 财政的

guinea [ˈɡɪni]　*n.* 基尼（英国的旧金币）

Part 2　补充单词 / 词组

epistle [ɪˈpɪsl]　*n.* 书信（尤指写得严肃且带有教训意味的信函）

Her father penned a lengthy epistle to her.
The epistle to his student was couched in the most elegant language.

missive [ˈmɪsɪv]　*n.* 公文

The missive laid beside him was from his lovely daughter.
She delivered a missive to her boyfriend.

annuity [əˈnuːəti]　*n.* 年金；年金保险投资

People who are over 65 years old can receive a civilian annuity of 3000 each year.

exultant [ɪɡˈzʌltənt]　*adj.* 兴高采烈的

But our hero was not so spineless. He was always exultant. This may be proof of the moral supremacy of China over the rest of the world. (Lu Xun, Chinese writer)

exult [ɪɡˈzʌlt]　*v.* 狂喜；欢欣鼓舞

Soldiers exulted in their victory.

epistolary [ɪˈpɪstəleri]　*adj.* 书信的；书信体的

love affair　恋爱关系；风流事

He reveled in his epistolary love affairs.

bicameral [ˌbaɪˈkæmərəl]　*adj.* 两院制的

Representatives [reprɪˈzentətɪv]　*n.* 众议院

the Senate　参议院

The nation has a bicameral legislature comprised of the House of Representatives and the Senate.

orthography [ɔːˈθɑːgrəfi]　*n.* 正确拼写；拼字法

algebra [ˈældʒɪbrə]　*n.* 代数

arithmetic [əˈrɪθmətɪk]　*n.* 算法；计算

fortification [ˌfɔːrtɪfɪˈkeɪʃn]　*n.* 防御工事；设防

Youth are boarded, clothed, booked, furnished with pocket-money, provided with all necessaries, instructed in all languages living and dead, mathematics, orthography, geometry, astronomy, trigonometry, the use of the globes, algebra, single stick (if required), writing, arithmetic, fortification, and every other branch of classical literature.

ethnology [eθˈnɑːlədʒi]　*n.* 人种学；民族学

She studies archaeology and ethnology at Rice University.

ethnographic [ˌeθnəˈgræfɪk]　*adj.* 人种志的

The epistolary, and ethnographic evidence reveals repeated journeys of the ship between Brazil and Spain.

antediluvian [ˌæntɪdɪˈluːviən]　*adj.* 很久以前的；过时的

Archaeologists couldn't understand the antediluvian language.

outmoded [ˌaʊtˈmoʊdɪd]　*adj.* 过时的

The antediluvian car was outmoded.

Part 3　识记单词/词组

the House of exultation　欢乐之家

board sth up　用木板封闭（门窗）

fortress [ˈfɔːrtrəs]　*n.* 要塞；堡垒

strongpoint [ˈstrɔŋpoint, ˈstrɔːŋ-]　*n.* 要塞；防御据点

blitz [blɪts]　*v.* 用闪电战空袭　*n.* 闪电战；急袭

blitzkrieg [ˈblɪtskriːg]　*n.* 闪电战

pincer [ˈpɪnsər]　*n.* 钳子；螯

pincer movement　钳形攻势

armistice [ˈɑːrmɪstɪs]　*n.* 休战；休战（或停战）协议

peruse [pə'ruːz] v. 研读；细阅；随便翻阅
perusal [pə'ruːzl] n. 细读
cameral ['kæmərəl] adj. 立法或司法机构的
cameralistic [ˌkæmərə'lɪstɪk] adj. 财政或经济的
board [bɔːrd] v. 上船 n. 薄木板；董事会
furnish ['fɜːrnɪʃ] v. 提供；装修；配备家具
geometric [ˌdʒiːə'metrɪk] adj. 几何（学）的；成几何级数增加的
fortify ['fɔːrtɪfaɪ] v. 筑防御工事；（在肉体、精神等方面）增强
biannual [baɪ'ænjuəl] adj. 一年两次的
biennial [baɪ'eniəl] adj. 两年一次的
biennial plant 两年开一次花的植物
millennial [mɪ'leniəl] adj. 一千年的
millennium [mɪ'leniəm] n. 一千年
centennial [sen'teniəl] n. 百周年纪念 adj. 百年的
ethnography [eθ'nɑːɡrəfi] n. 人种志；人种学

Lesson 53

Part 1 主力单词 / 词组

inevitable [ɪn'evɪtəbl] adj. 不可避免的；必然发生的
It is inevitable that every creature will meet its end.
An inevitable occurrence due to the action of immutable natural laws. (Ambrose Bierce, U.S. writer and journalist)
The carefully packaged persona of the old-time movie star resembles nothing so much as the carefully packaged persona of today's politician. Was it not inevitable that the two would at last coincide in one person? (Gore Vidal, U.S. novelist and essayist)

unavoidable [ˌʌnə'vɔɪdəbl] adj. 无法避免的

inescapable [ˌɪnɪ'skeɪpəbl] adj. 不可避免的
The inescapable fact is the ubiquitous haze.

inexorable [ɪnˈeksərəbl]   *adj.* 无法改变的；不为所动的

He was inexorable to our admonition and decided to carry out the mission alone.

ineluctable [ˌɪnɪˈlʌktəbl]   *adj.* 无法躲避的

A fortune teller said that his premature death was preordained and ineluctable.

The impending war seemed to be an ineluctable fate.

perforce [pərˈfɔːrs]   *adv.* 必定；一定

China's trading to the U.S. was perforce curtailed due to a higher tariff.

The weariest nights, the longest days, sooner or later must perforce come to an end.

(Baroness Orczy, Hungarian-born British novelist and playwright)

I perforce fell swooning at the news of getting admitted by MIT.

If you help me, I will perforce help you.

> • Words in sentences 句中单词 / 词组 •
>
> **immutable** [ɪˈmjuːtəbl]   *adj.* 不可改变的
> **ubiquitous** [juːˈbɪkwɪtəs]   *adj.* 无处不在的
> **haze** [heɪz]   *n.* 霾
> **fortune teller**   算命师
> **premature** [ˌpriːməˈtʃʊr, ˌpriːməˈtʊr]   *adj.* 过早的；不成熟的

Part 2 补充单词 / 词组

armament reduction   裁减军备

Our view coincides with the matter of armament reduction.

armament [ˈɑːrməmənt]   *n.* 军备；武器装备；军事力量；军队

reduction [rɪˈdʌkʃn]   *n.* 减少；[摄影术] 减薄

hazy [ˈheɪzi]   *adj.* 模糊的；有薄雾的

She has only a hazy recollection of her childhood.

unwarranted [ʌnˈwɔːrəntɪd]   *adj.* 未经授权的；无根据的

impinge [ɪmˈpɪndʒ]   *v.* 干涉；侵犯

The police's unwarranted arrest impinges my rights.

pervert [pər'vɜːrt]   v. 曲解；使反常；腐蚀
Media often perverts others' messages for money.

garble ['ɡɑːrbəl]   v. 断章取义；篡改；歪曲
They garbled the spice to maintain the original flavor of the cuisine.
The sample has been contaminated and the genetic information may be garbled.

babble ['bæbl]   v. (婴儿)牙牙学语；喋喋不休   n. 嘈杂声
The politician babbled incoherently avoiding direct answers.
He babbled out the secret after getting drunk.

splay [spleɪ]   v. 张开
The ballet dancers splayed their legs.

jabber ['dʒæbər]   v. 快而含糊地说
They gabbed and jabbered like a bird singing, but I didn't get it.

invert [ɪn'vɜːrt]   v. 使反向；使上下颠倒   n. 同性恋者   adj. 转化的
The lens inverted the image.
The clerk was fired for mistakenly inverting the priorities of important guests.
He inverted the room number 9 to 6.

Part 3 识记单词/词组

suntan lotion   防晒油

suntan=tan   n. (皮肤)晒黑

sunburn ['sʌnbɜːrn]   n. 晒伤

an impermeable membrane   一层不透气的薄膜

membrane ['membreɪn]   n. 薄膜；细胞膜

cornea ['kɔːrniə]   n. 眼角膜

eyelid ['aɪlɪd]   n. 眼睑；眼皮

conjunctiva [ˌkɑndʒʌŋk'taɪvə]   n. 结膜(眼睛上覆盖的一层膜)

iris ['aɪrɪs]   n. 虹膜；鸢尾属植物

sclera ['sklɪrə]   n. 巩膜；眼白

astigmatic [ˌæstɪɡ'mætɪk]   adj. 散光的

refract [rɪˈfrækt] *v.* 使（光线）折射；使产生折射

refraction [rɪˈfrækʃn] *n.* 折射（程度）；折射角

Lesson 54

Part 1 主力单词 / 词组

palatable [ˈpælətəbl] *adj.* 美味的；可以接受的
It is a palatable wine.
The courtesy of the Chinese makes them palatable, versus the Turks who show none.
The referendum seems to be politically palatable.

delectable [dɪˈlektəbl] *adj.* 美味的；非常迷人的
It is a delectable cake.
Her delectable smile is an irresistible lure.
She looks at me like I am very delectable.

yummy [ˈjʌmi] *adj.* 美味可口的；性感的
The chef prepared yummy and nutritious dishes from his familial recipe.

luscious [ˈlʌʃəs] *adj.* 香甜的；甘美的；汁液丰富的

succulent [ˈsʌkjələnt] *adj.* 多汁的
There are spirit decanters, luscious cantaloupe, and succulent watermelon in the tantalus.

• Words in sentences 句中单词 / 词组 •

courtesy of 承蒙……的允许；因为

versus [ˈvɜːrsəs] *prep.* 与……相比；以……为对手；对……诉讼案中

referendum [ˌrefəˈrendəm] *n.* 全民公投

irresistible [ˌɪrɪˈzɪstəbl] *adj.* 不可抵抗的；制服不了的

lure [lʊr] *v.* 诱惑 *n.* 鱼饵

nutritious [nuˈtrɪʃəs] *adj.* 营养丰富的；营养价值高的

familial [fəˈmɪliəl] *adj.* 家庭的；家族的；（遗传学术语）遗传的

spirit [ˈspɪrɪt]　*n.* 烈性酒；精神；勇气
decanter [dɪˈkæntər]　*n.* （装饰用）玻璃酒瓶
cantaloupe [ˈkæntəloup]　*n.* 哈密瓜

Part 2　补充单词 / 词组

paterfamilias [ˌpætərfəˈmɪliæs]　*n.* 一家的男主人；大家长
The paterfamilias exercised his authority over his wife and kids.

esprit de corps　团队精神
These basketball players showed great esprit de corps.

esprit [eˈspriː]　*n.* 精神；勃勃生气；机敏
The singer in the concert has an infectious esprit that captivates audiences.

atavism [ˈætəˌvɪzəm]　*n.* 隔代遗传；返祖现象；复古
The propensity toward violence is the result of atavism, a reversion to a more primitive state of human development.
The building of red brick is an architectural atavism.

hash [hæʃ]　*v.* 切碎；推敲　*n.* 拼凑
Police intend to hash out the difference between these crimes.
He made a hash of the entire project.

cherry [ˈtʃeri]　*n.* 樱桃；樱桃树　*adj.* 樱桃红的
The chef hashed some roast beef and put it on the top of the cherry pie.

bask [bæsk]　*v.* 取暖；晒太阳；（在某种环境或气氛中）感到适意
She went to the beach to bask in the sun.

bel esprit　多才多艺的人

bluestocking [ˈbluːstɑːkɪŋ]　*n.* 女学者；炫耀学问的女人
The bel esprit attacked the bluestocking's pedantry.

Part 3　识记单词 / 词组

delectation [ˌdiːlekˈteɪʃn]　*n.* 愉悦；高兴

unpalatable [ˌʌnˈpælətəbl] *adj.* 难以下咽的；令人不快的；让人难以接受的

tasteless [ˈteɪstləs] *adj.* 无味道的；没有品味的；格调不高的

atavistic [ˌætəˈvɪstɪk] *adj.* 隔代遗传的；返祖的；原始的

atavist [ˈætəvɪst] *n.* 呈现返祖性之动物或植物

a discriminating palate　一名有鉴赏力的专家

discriminating [dɪˈskrɪmɪneɪtɪŋ] *adj.* 有鉴赏力的；有品味的

palate [ˈpælət] *n.* 有品味的专家

a familial disease　一种家族病

materfamilias [ˌmeɪtərfəˈmɪliəs, ˌmɑːtərfəˈmɪliəs] *n.* 家中的母亲；一家的女主人

talk turkey　坦率认真地谈话

turkey [ˈtɜːrki] *n.* 火鸡；失败（之作）；傻瓜

popsicle [ˈpɑːpsɪkl] *n.* 冰棒

lollipop [ˈlɑːlipɑːp] *n.* 棒棒糖

vintage [ˈvɪntɪdʒ] *adj.*（葡萄酒）上等的；最典型的；古老的　*n.*（优良品牌的）葡萄酒；酿造年份；葡萄收获或酿酒季节

vintage wine　上等的葡萄酒

turk [tɜːrk] *n.* 土耳其人

resist [rɪˈzɪst] *v.* 抵抗

resistance [rɪˈzɪstəns] *n.* 抵抗；反抗；阻力；电阻

lure of fame and money　名利的诱惑

nutrition [nuˈtrɪʃn] *n.* 营养物质；营养学

undernutrition [ˌʌndənʊˈtrɪʃn, ˌʌndənjʊˈtrɪʃn] *n.* 营养不良

tantalus [ˈtæntələs] *n.* 玻璃酒柜

basketry [ˈbæskɪtri] *n.* 编制篮子的技艺；篮子（总称）

Lesson 55

Part 1　主力单词 / 词组

circa [ˈsɜːrkə] *prep.* 大约（只可指时间）

The museum was built circa 1999.

The investigator looked at this vague, undated photo that his father left circa 1945.

approximately [ə'prɑːksɪmətli] *adv.* 大约

I can't remember how much we have spent exactly, but approximately 500 dollars.

round about 大约

We can meet at round about eight-thirty in front of the theater.

approximate [ə'prɑːksɪmət, ə'prɑːksɪmeɪt] *adj.* 近似的；大致的；相似的

Part 2 补充单词 / 词组

endogenous [en'dɑːdʒənəs] *adj.* 内源的；内生的

She suffered from endogenous depression.

There are porcine endogenous retroviruses found in these swine.

The plant has endogenous roots.

exogenous [ek'sɑːdʒənəs] *adj.* 外成的；外生的

There are exogenous roots produced by leaves.

The wound was deteriorated by exogenous infections.

There are some exogenous factors causing obesity.

Part 3 识记单词 / 词组

exact [ɪɡ'zækt] *v.* 迫使；强求 *adj.* 准确的

exact revenge 绝地报复

revenge [rɪ'vendʒ] *v.* 替……报仇 *n.* 报复

retrovirus ['retroʊvaɪrəs] *n.* 逆转录病毒

endogamy [en'dɑːɡəmi] *n.* 同族结婚

endogeny [en'dɑːdʒəni] *n.* 内生性；内长性

porcine ['pɔːrsaɪn] *adj.* （像）猪的

swine [swaɪn] *n.* 猪；卑贱的人；下流坯

Lesson 56

Part 1 主力单词 / 词组

suggest [səˈdʒest] *v.* 建议

The psychiatrist suggested to a doctor to imprison the unstable psycho.

When a lot of remedies are suggested for a disease, that means it can't be cured. (Anton Chekhov, Russian playwright and short-story writer)

advocate [ˈædvəkeɪt, ˈædvəkət] *v.* 提倡；支持 *n.* 支持者；提倡者；辩护律师

He advocates abolishing capital punishment.

propose [prəˈpoʊz] *v.* 建议；提出；提名；求婚；计划

She proposed to take a serious investigation immediately.

Tom was proposed as principal.

proposition [ˌprɑːpəˈzɪʃn] *v.* 提案；建议 *n.* 观念；提议

Do you both agree on the proposition that the more you earn, the happier you are?

propound [prəˈpaʊnd] *v.* 建议；提出

The project of civilizing Africans has been propounded by many missionaries.

canvass [ˈkænvəs] *v.* 提出来讨论；游说；拉选票；征求意见

The safety of food and beverage was canvassed many times.

The party canvassed the problem of an aging society and pension.

His supporting rate dropped five percent during pre-election canvassing.

The ballots were thoroughly canvassed in the presidential election. Every vote counts.

China canvassed support among silk-road nations.

The gubernatorial nominee didn't show up, but his supporters were actively canvassing on his behalf.

Do you think robocall for canvassing support is kind of annoying?

• **Words in sentences 句中单词 / 词组** •

imprison [ɪmˈprɪzn] *v.* 监禁

unstable [ʌnˈsteɪbl] *adj.* 不稳定的

pension [ˈpenʃən] n. 养老金
vote [voʊt] n. 选票 v. 投票；选举；进行表决
gubernatorial [ˌɡjuːbənəˈtɔːriəl] adj. 州长的
nominee [ˌnɑːmɪˈniː] n. 被提名者
robocall [ˈroʊbəkɔːl] n. 自动语音电话

Part 2 补充单词 / 词组

misnomer [ˌmɪsˈnoʊmər] n. 不恰当的用词
It is a misnomer to call a deer a horse.

retina [ˈretɪnə] n. 视网膜
The uneven refraction leads to some light rays focusing on the retina, other light rays focusing in front of or behind the retina.

astigmatism [əˈstɪɡmətɪzəm] n. 散光
Astigmatism is a defect in the outer curvature on the surface of the eye that causes light rays to refract unevenly inside the eye resulting in blurred vision.

contrarian [kənˈtreriən] n. 持相反观念的人；做法与一般大众想法相反的投资人（例如：买冷门股票）
The true contrarian isn't interested in what others are doing at all. (Robert Heller, British management writer)

observer [əbˈzɜːrvər] n. 观测者；观察员；遵守者
She is an independent, contrarian observer.

astronomer [əˈstrɑːnəmər] n. 天文学家

orion [oʊˈraɪən] n. 猎户座

telescope [ˈtelɪskoʊp] n. 望远镜
Astronomer observes Orion with a telescope in the observatory.

exponent [ɪkˈspoʊnənt] n. 支持者；说明者；从事者（优秀的）；指数
She was one of the foremost exponents of Darwinism.
She is an exponent of painting.

pyrotechnics [ˌpaɪrəˈtekniks] n. 各种烟火；烟火制造术；烟火使用法
We observed the National day with pyrotechnics and a parade.

cryobank [ˈkraɪəʊbəŋk]　*n.* 精子库；精液冷库
The elite deposits his sperm in a California cryobank.

cryobiology [ˌkraɪoʊbaɪˈɑːlədʒi]　*n.* 低温生物学
Cryobiology denotes the study of life at low temperatures.

Part 3　识记单词 / 词组

do away with sth　摆脱；废除
do away with sb　干掉；杀死
capital punishment　死刑
missionary [ˈmɪʃəneri]　*n.* 传教士
canvas [ˈkænvəs]　*n.* 帆布；油画布；油画
under canvas　在帐篷里
preelection [ˌpriːiˈlekʃən]　*adj.* 选举前的
ballot [ˈbælət]　*n.* 选票　*v.* 投票；进行无记名投票
turnout [ˈtɜːrnaʊt]　*n.* 产量；投票人数；出席人数
observatory [əbˈzɜːrvətɔːri]　*n.* 天文台；气象台
pyrotechnic [ˌpaɪrəˈteknɪk]　*adj.* 烟火的；灿烂的
pyrotehcnist [ˌpaɪrəˈteknɪst]　*n.* 烟火制造者
firework [ˈfaɪərwɜːrk]　*n.* 烟火；爆竹；花炮
pyrogenic [ˌpaɪrəˈdʒenɪk]　*adj.* 高热所产生的；火成的
pyromania [ˌpaɪroʊˈmeɪniə]　*n.* 纵火狂
pyromaniac [ˌpaɪroʊˈmeɪniæk]　*n.* 放火狂　*adj.* 放火狂的

Lesson 57

Part 1　主力单词 / 词组

recur [rɪˈkɜːr]　*v.* 反复出现；再次发生；求助
I can't get you out of my head, your image constantly recurring to me.
The symptom recurs.

Outbursts from protesters have been a recurring feature since the verdict came out.

recrudescence [ˌriːkruːˈdesns] *n.* (通常是指比较不好的事情的) 复发

The recrudescence of the civil war in Syria has ravaged the country.
The recrudescence of her mental illness alarms us.

resurface [ˌriːˈsɜːrfɪs] *v.* 再度浮出水面；重铺路面；又发生

The confrontation between the government and guerrilla resurfaces.

reappear [ˌriːəˈpɪr] *v.* 再出现

He reappears after having been gone for hours.

resurge [rɪˈsɜːrdʒ] *v.* 复苏；再度风靡；（尤指快速有力地）移动

The feeling for her has resurged after seeing her eyes glittering with affection in the photos.

resurgence [rɪˈsɜːrdʒəns] *n.* 再现；再起；复活

The GDP number shows the resurgence in economic activities.

resurgent [rɪˈsɜːrdʒənt] *adj.* 复活的；复苏的 *n.* 复活的人

The economic growth and resurgent national pride lead the country to contend with a superpower.

- Words in sentences 句中单词 / 词组 -

symptom [ˈsɪmptəm] *n.* 症状；征兆
outburst [ˈaʊtbɜːrst] *n.* （情感、力量等的）爆发；（火山等的）喷发
confrontation [ˌkɑːnfrənˈteɪʃn] *n.* 对抗；冲突
guerrilla [ɡəˈrɪlə] *n.* 游击队

Part 2 补充单词 / 词组

a solar eclipse 一次日食

A solar eclipse is a recurrent theme of nature.

confront [kənˈfrʌnt] *v.* 遭遇；对抗；使对质

I decide to confront my deepest fear at the innermost recess of my heart.

racism [ˈreɪsɪzəm] *n.* 种族主义；种族歧视

The synagogue shooting has incurred the wrath of racism.

Part 3 识记单词/词组

recurrent [rɪˈkɜːrənt] *adj.* 一再发生的；周期性的

recurrence [rɪˈkɜːrəns] *n.* 反复

raise the alarm 发出警报；警告

ring/sound alarm bell 敲警钟；发出危险信号

false alarm 假警报；虚惊

alarm clock 闹钟

fire alarm 火警报警器

burglar alarm 防盗报警器

alarm call （旅馆等中的）叫醒服务电话

mane [meɪn] *n.* (马、狮等的) 鬃毛

protester [prəˈtestər] *n.* 反对者

protest [ˈproʊtest, prəˈtest] *v.* 反对 *n.* 抗议

feature [ˈfiːtʃər] *v.* 特写；以……为特色；给……以显著的地位 *n.* 特写（报纸或杂志的）；专题节目（电视或广播的）；正片（电影）

synagogue [ˈsɪnəɡɑːɡ] *n.* 犹太教堂

ravage [ˈrævɪdʒ] *n.* 蹂躏 *v.* 劫掠

glitter [ˈɡlɪtər] *v.* 闪烁；闪光 *n.* 吸引力；魅力；诱惑力

hog [hɔːɡ] *n.* 猪；（船底、龙骨等的）中部的拱起 *v.* 拱起

boar [bɔːr] *n.* 野猪；公猪

peccary=javelina *n.* 野猪（原产美洲热带的）

Lesson 58

Part 1 主力单词/词组

regarding [rɪˈɡɑːrdɪŋ] *prep.* 关于；就……而言

By avarice and selfishness, and a groveling habit, from which none of us is free, of regarding the soil as property...the landscape is deformed. (Henry David Thoreau, U.S. writer)

But even regarding History as the slaughter-bench at which the happiness of peoples, the wisdom of States, and the virtue of individuals have been victimized—the question involuntarily arises—to what principle, to what final aim, these enormous sacrifices have been offered. (G. W. F. Hegel, German philosopher)

concerning [kənˈsɜːrnɪŋ] *prep.* 关于；有关

The matter concerning top secrets should have been concealed.

apropos [ˌæprəˈpoʊ] *adj.* 适合的　*prep.* 就……而言；关于

Apropos what you said I thought you were smart.
Tuxedo is apropos for formal occasions.

given that 鉴于；由于

Given that she is a genius, she wins the math contest easily.

given [ˈɡɪvn] *adj.* 规定的；特定的　*prep.* 鉴于（一定发生的）；以……而言

Given her age, she plays guitar quite well.

in relation to 和……有关的

I will give you three gifts in relation to clothing.

with respect to 就……而言

The two cups are similar with respect to color and shape, but not material.

in light of 鉴于

In light of serious air pollution, factories are asked to shut down temporarily.

vis-à-vis [ˌviːz ɑːˈviː] *n.* 面对面的人；地位（或职务、身份）相应的人　*adj.* 面对面的　*prep.* 相对于；关于

China's products are cheaper vis-à-vis Germany's.
I would like to talk to you, vis-à-vis.
She went to a movie theater with her vis-à-vis.
The constitution gives absolute power to the federal government vis-à-vis the states.

> • Words in sentences 句中单词/词组 •
>
> **avarice** [ˈævərɪs] *n.* 贪婪；贪得无厌
> **involuntarily** [ɪnˌvɑːlənˈterəli] *adv.* 无心地；偶然地
> **tuxedo** [tʌkˈsiːdoʊ] *n.* 晚礼服

Part 2 补充单词 / 词组

freehold [ˈfriːhould] n. 可终身保有的不动产 adj. 可终身保有的

leasehold [ˈliːshould] n. 租赁权；租赁之地产（或房屋）；租赁物 adj. 租赁的

Lands are freehold in the U.S. but leasehold in China.

ingénue [ˈændʒənu] n. 纯真少女；剧中纯真少女的演员

The director brought the talented ingénue to the forefront of the screen.

cupidity [kjuːˈpɪdəti] n. 贪心

He is a victim of my cupidity.

bench [bentʃ] n. 长凳；法官席；（英国议会的）议员席；场边的运动员休息区

A bench trial is a trial by judge, as opposed to a trial by jury.

behoove [bɪˈhuːv] v. 适合

The nice weather behooves us to go picnic.

enormity [ɪˈnɔːrməti] n. 穷凶极恶

The judge sentenced me to the death penalty regarding the enormity of the crime that I had committed.

The spy was caught by circulating pamphlets that bared the enormity of Nazi offenses in the occupied area.

similitude [sɪˈmɪlɪtuːd] n. 相像；相像的人；类似物；比喻

There are some similitudes between Beijing and Tokyo.

I see the striking similitude in these murder cases.

bisque [bɪsk] n. 浓菜汤；碎果仁冰淇淋

The dinner was served with a lagniappe of freshly made beef bisque.

lagniappe [lænˈjæp, ˈlænjæp] n. 小赠品；小费

The hotel owner gave us a key ring as a lagniappe.

forefront [ˈfɔːrfrʌnt] n. 最前方；最前线；中心（活动、兴趣等的）；最重要的事

Corporate revenue is at the forefront of the boss's mind.

dissimilitude [ˌdɪssɪˈmɪlɪtjuːd] n. 不同；不同之处

Do you notice the dissimilitude between the two beetles?

body double 替身

The movie used real actors, not body doubles, in order to create a sense of verisimilitude.

verisimilitude [ˌverɪˈsɪmɪlɪtuːd] n. 貌似真实；逼真的事物

The horror novel meticulously created an air of verisimilitude.
The vicissitudes of their African adventure were recounted with verisimilitude.

verisimilar [ˌverəˈsɪmələr] adj. 好像是真的

He was famous for his verisimilar acting as a young lady.

Part 3 识记单词 / 词组

given to 以……而言；经常做；习惯于……

forensic [fəˈrenzɪk, fəˈrensɪk] adj. 法医的；法庭的；辩论的

forensics [fəˈrenzɪks] n. 法医检验；法医鉴定技术；辩论练习（用作单数）；辩论学

bench trial 法官审判

suitor [ˈsuːtər] n. (女子的) 求婚者；追求者；有收购意向者；起诉人

meticulous [məˈtɪkjələs] adj. 严密的；小心翼翼的

avaricious [ˌævəˈrɪʃəs] adj. 贪心的

grovel [ˈɡrɑːvl] v. 卑躬屈膝；匍匐前进；爬行

deform [dɪˈfɔːrm] v. 使变形；使扭曲

deformity [dɪˈfɔːrməti] n. 身体畸形；发育异常

slaugther bench 屠宰台

victimize [ˈvɪktɪmaɪz] v. (尤指因种族、性别或信仰的原因) 使受害；使迫害

victimization [ˌvɪktɪməˈzeɪʃn] n. 受害；迫害

involuntary [ɪnˈvɑːlənteri] adj. 非本意的；无心的；无意识的

expertise [ˌekspɜːrˈtiːz] n. 专家意见

nail-biter [ˈneɪlˌbaɪtə] n. 充满悬念的电影；扣人心弦的体育比赛

suitable [ˈsuːtəbl] adj. 适合的

conceal [kənˈsiːl] v. 隐藏

walk-on [ˈwɔːk ɑːn] (戏剧的) 跑龙套的演员；临时队员

impound [ɪmˈpaʊnd] v. 扣押；没收

beetle [ˈbiːtl] n. 甲虫

with (all due) respect 恕我直言（用于正式场合礼貌地表示异议）；冒昧地说；斗胆直言

by all means 好的（表示许可）；当然可以

by no means 决不；一点都不

to whom it may concern （用于正式信函开头处）敬启者

be of concern 很重要；有重大影响

of your own accord 出于你的自愿

with on accord 一致同意地

respect sb's wishes 尊重（某人）的意愿

respectability [rɪˌspektəˈbɪləti] n. 值得尊敬；体面

pay your respects 拜访；（向死者）表示敬意；告别

Lesson 59

Part 1 主力单词 / 词组

charm [tʃɑːm] v. 吸引；迷住 n. 魅力；吸引力；护身符；咒语；小挂件；小饰物

With her charm and sanguine personality, she is persona grata in the Lawyer's Guild.

Those who have never dwelt in tents have no idea either of the charm or of the discomfort of a nomadic existence.

The charm is purely romantic, and consequently very soon proves to be fallacious. (Vita Sackville-West, British poet and novelist)

Conversation...is the art of never appearing a bore, of knowing how to say everything interestingly, to entertain with no matter what, to be charming with nothing at all. (Guy de Maupassant, French writer)

charisma [kəˈrɪzmə] n. 超凡的个人魅力；超凡的气质；非凡的领导力；领导魅力

We adore her charisma dearly.

Faith is a charisma not granted to all, instead, man has the gift of thought, which can strive after the highest things. (Carl Gustav Jung, Swiss psychoanalyst)

vivacity [vɪˈvæsəti, vaɪˈvæsəti] *n.* 活泼

The painting of sunflowers in which a maiden was reposing displayed with beauty and vivacity. In the guise of an aperitif, the cults have prepared a human sacrifice to test black magic and recited an exuberant ode of Lucifer to honor the vivacity of the underworld.

vivacious [vɪˈveɪʃəs, vaɪˈveɪʃəs] *adj.* 活泼的；快活的

The leading actress assumes the role of a gay and vivacious personality.
She is young, vivacious, and smart.

effervesce [ˌefəˈves] *v.* 兴高采烈；冒泡；起沫；兴奋

Teachers should effervesce with enthusiasm and passion while teaching students.

effervescent [ˌefərˈvesnt] *adj.* 冒泡的；沸腾的；兴奋的

He is a bossy, effervescent clerk who often forgets his place.

effervescence [ˌefəˈvesəns, -ənsi] *n.* 愉快

His tempest of passion perished in its own effervescence at the sight of her safe return.

• Words in sentences 句中单词/词组 •

sanguine [ˈsæŋgwɪn] *adj.* 乐观的（有自信的）

persona grata *n.* 受欢迎的人

nomadic [noʊˈmædɪk] *adj.* 游牧民族的

fallacious [fəˈleɪʃəs] *adj.* 错误的；谬误的

entertain [ˌentərˈteɪnər] *v.* 款待

guise [gaɪz] *n.* 外表（尤指为了欺骗而装出的）；伪装

exuberant [ɪgˈzuːbərənt] *adj.* 热情洋溢的；丰富的；浮华的；精力充沛的；充满活力的

lucifer [ˈluːsɪfər] *n.* 魔鬼；撒旦

the underworld （希腊神话中的）阴间

Part 2 补充单词/词组

vantage [ˈvæntɪdʒ] *n.* 优势；有利地位

From my vantage point, Trump should be impeached but not removed.

cultish [ˈkəʊltɪʃ] *adj.* 狂热的

Trump's preaching seems to be a cultish thing.

sanguinary [ˈsæŋɡwɪneri] *adj.* 流血的；血腥的；好杀戮的

The sanguinary scenes of the movie left the audience a vivid impression.

postprandial [ˌpoʊstˈprændɪəl] *adj.* 餐后的

Someone says having a postprandial smoke would be as happy as a god.

aperitif [əˌperəˈtiːf] *n.*（尤指餐前的）开胃酒

digestif [ˌdiːʒeˈstiːf] *n.* 助消化的酒

The restaurant served aperitif and postprandial digestif.

stroll [stroʊl] *v.* 散步；溜达 *n.* 闲逛

I would like to take a postprandial stroll with you.

tempest [ˈtempɪst] *v.* 使骚动；使激动 *n.* 暴风雨；暴风雪

The rumor of his death caused a tempest in a small town.

diva [ˈdiːvə] *n.*（歌剧的）女主唱者；一流女艺人（电影、戏剧等的）；自以为是的女人

They paid the fashion diva as their company's spokesperson.

pettifogger [ˈpetɪˌfɔɡər] *n.* 骗人的律师

The pettifogger is the worst curse.

impresario [ˌɪmprəˈsɑːrioʊ] *n.* 演出者；经理人（歌剧、乐团等的）

A symphony orchestra conductor and an opera impresario will collaborate together to pull off the show.

Part 3　识记单词 / 词组

temptuous relationship　常吵架的夫妻关系

cult [kʌlt] *n.* 异教；邪教；膜拜仪式；狂热；迷信者

pettifog [ˈpetɪˌfɑːɡ] *v.* 诈骗

raconteur [ˌrækɑːnˈtɜːr] *n.* 健谈者；擅长讲故事的人

amulet [ˈæmjʊlət] *n.*（戴在身上的）护身符；避邪物

juju [ˈdʒuːdʒuː] *n.* 护符

vantage ground 优越地位
vantage point 有利位置
this vale of tears 人生苦海
the ode of love 爱的颂歌
divalent [daɪˈveɪlənt] *adj.* 二价的
divalent compound 二价化合物
spokesperson [ˈspoʊkspɜːrsn] *n.* 发言人；代言人
malediction [ˌmæləˈdɪkʃn] *n.* 诅咒；坏话
heap [hiːp] *v.* 堆积 *n.* 堆积；许多
persona non grata 不受欢迎的人
impresario [ˌɪmprəˈsɑːrioʊ] *n.* 演出者；经理人
tent [tent] *n.* 帐篷
nomad [ˈnoʊmæd] *n.* 游牧民族
fallacy [ˈfæləsi] *n.* 谬见；谬论

Lesson 60

Part 1 主力单词/词组

mankind [mænˈkaɪnd] *n.* 人类
Had the Japanese reconnaissance aircraft found the U.S. aircraft carrier first, the history of mankind might have been different.
Mankind is resilient: the atrocities that horrified us a week ago become acceptable tomorrow. (Joseph Heller, U.S. novelist.)

homo sapiens 人类；智人
Homo sapiens have unquenchable curiosity.

hominid [ˈhɑːmɪnɪd] *n.* 人类；原始人类 *adj.* 原始人类的
They have excavated hominid fossils for two years.

sapient [ˈseɪpiənt] *n.* 智人 *adj.* 聪明的；智人的
My mentor always gives me valuable insights and sapient advice.
The sapient boss earned a lot of money.

Lesson 60

> **● Words in sentences 句中单词 / 词组 ●**
>
> **reconnaissance** [rɪˈkɑːnɪsns]　*n.* 侦察
> **aircraft** [ˈerkræft]　*n.* 飞机
> **aircraft carrier**　航母
> **resilient** [rɪˈzɪliənt]　*adj.* 适应性强的；有弹性的
> **unquenchable** [ʌnˈkwentʃəbl]　*adj.* 无法满足的；无法停歇的
> **fossil** [ˈfɑːsl]　*n.* 化石

Part 2　补充单词 / 词组

stamina [ˈstæmɪnə]　*n.* 精力；耐力；雄蕊
The stamina of Arabic thoroughbreds has been underestimated.

aghast [əˈɡæst]　*adj.* 惊骇的；吓坏的
The princess was aghast at the thought of marrying the ailing old king.
The official was aghast at the idea of overthrowing the government.

ghastly [ˈɡæstli]　*adj.* 可怕的；苍白的；极大的　*adv.* 极大地
The ghastly battlefield was full of dead bodies.
I don't mind your small negligence but I do mind the ghastly mistake.
The judge gave him a severe punishment for the ghastly crime he committed.

quench [kwentʃ]　*v.* 喝水解渴；用水灭火；满足
Drink tea to quench your thirst.

slake [sleɪk]　*v.* 消解；平息；使满足
Lime slakes spontaneously in moist air.

humus [ˈhjuːməs]　*n.* 腐质土壤；腐殖质
Black humus is very fertile.

gory [ˈɡɔːri]　*n.* 血污的；残酷的
I was appalled by the gory crime scene.

hirsute [ˈhɜːrsuːt]　*adj.* 有鬃毛的；多毛的

shaggy [ˈʃæɡi] *adj.* (毛发等) 粗浓的；长满粗毛的

He has a hirsute chest and shaggy eyebrows.

Part 3 识记单词 / 词组

resilience [rɪˈzɪliəns] *n.* 弹回；弹性；恢复力

thoroughbred [ˈθɜːroʊbred] *n.* 纯种动物；良好教养的人 *adj.* 纯种的；有良好教养的

horrify [ˈhɔːrɪfaɪ] *v.* 使震惊；使感到恐怖

horror [ˈhɔːrər] *n.* 恐惧；震惊

appall [əˈpɔːl] *v.* 使惊恐；使胆寒

ailing [ˈeɪlɪŋ] *adj.* 生病的

excavate [ˈekskəveɪt] *v.* 挖掘

excavation [ˌekskəˈveɪʃn] *n.* 挖掘

exhume [ɪɡˈzuːm] *v.* 掘出（尸体）；重新引用

exhumation [ˌekshjuːˈmeɪʃn] *n.* 发掘；掘墓

unearth [ʌnˈɜːrθ] *v.* 掘出；发现；揭露

Lesson 61

Part 1 主力单词 / 词组

insatiable [ɪnˈseɪʃəbl] *adj.* 无法满足的；贪得无厌的

An ambitious man has an insatiable hunger for success.
Americans were originally thrifty, big business persuaded them to become consumers instead, insatiable, richer but more vulnerable. (Theodore Zeldin, British historian)
Oligarchy was established by men with a certain aim in life: the good they sought was wealth, and it was the insatiable appetite for money-making to the neglect of everything else that proved its undoing. (Plato, Greek philosopher)

unquenchable [ʌnˈkwentʃəbl] *adj.* 难抑制的；不能消灭的

The scholar has an unquenchable thirst for knowledge, willing to go the extra mile in her search.

False accusation only proves he has a pretty unquenchable taste for notoriety.
He will do anything for you with his unquenchable love.

> • Words in sentences 句中单词 / 词组 •
>
> **thrifty** [ˈθrɪfti] *adj.* 节俭的
> **oligarchy** [ˈɑːləɡɑːrki, ˈoʊləɡɑːrki] *n.* 寡头统治的政府；寡头政治的执政集团
> **undoing** [ʌnˈduːɪŋ] *n.* (失败、垮台、破产的) 原因；解开
> **thirst** [θɜːrst] *n.* 口渴
> **go the extra mile** 付出比别人期望中还要大的努力
> **notoriety** [ˌnoʊtəˈraɪəti] *n.* 恶名；丑名

Part 2 补充单词 / 词组

sate [seɪt] *v.* 充分满足；过分给与；使饱享
The outcome sates their curiosity.
A sufficient supply of food should sate their hunger.

satiety [səˈtaɪəti] *n.* 饱足；厌腻
We ate too much beyond the point of satiety.

pass by 不注意；忽视或避免接触
Passing by the suspicious informer will be a good idea.

frugal [ˈfruːɡl] *adj.* 节约的

thrifty [ˈθrɪfti] *adj.* 节俭的
He was too generous to be frugal, too kindhearted to be thrifty, too honest to live above his means. (Vernon Parrington, U.S. educator)

skimp [skɪmp] *v.* 克扣；对……不够用心
At the end of the month, I almost ran out of money and had to skimp on my expenses to make ends meet.
Parents shouldn't skimp on their children's education.

skimpy [ˈskɪmpi] *adj.* 吝啬的；缺乏的；太小的
The restaurant served me a skimpy steak.

invulnerable [ɪnˈvʌlnərəbl] *adj.* 不会受伤害的；刀枪不入的

The fortress is extremely strong, invulnerable to all kinds of attacks.

overeat [ˌouvərˈiːt] *v.* (使)吃得过多

I overate the cake and became satiated.

Part 3 识记单词/词组

satiate [ˈseɪʃieɪt] *v.* 充分满足；使厌腻 *adj.* 充分满足的；使厌腻的
satiable [ˈseɪʃɪəbl] *adj.* 可满足的
notorious [nouˈtɔːriəs] *adj.* 恶名昭著的
thrift [θrɪft] *n.* 节俭
frugality [fruˈɡæləti] *n.* 节俭；朴素
originator [əˈrɪdʒɪneɪtər] *n.* 创作者
stratocracy [strəˈtɑːkrəsi] *n.* 军阀统治
oligarch [ˈɑːləɡɑːrk, ˈoʊləɡɑːrk] *n.* 寡头成员
oligarchic [ˌɑːlɪˈɡɑːkɪk] *adj.* 寡头政治的；少数独裁政治的
neglectful [nɪˈɡlektfl] *adj.* 疏忽的；不注意的
remiss [rɪˈmɪs] *adj.* 疏忽的
savant [səˈvɑːnt] *n.* 学者；专家

Lesson 62

Part 1 主力单词/词组

carry out 执行；完成；带走

The team carried out the mission.
She conjured up a way to carry out her task efficiently.

perform [pərˈfɔːrm] *v.* 执行；履行；表演

As a daily routine, they perform maintenance work.

operate [ˈɑːpəreɪt] *v.* 操作；经营；动手术；(在某地)采取军事行动

Does the intelligence agency still operate?

Lesson 62

execute [ˈeksɪkjuːt]   *v.* 实施；(依法) 处决

Please execute this plan according to my instruction.

undertake [ˌʌndərˈteɪk]   *v.* 做；答应

You left this strenuous work for me to undertake.

The concert organizer undertook that they would raise the price of the admission ticket.

effect [ɪˈfekt]   *v.* 实现；实行；生效   *n.* 效果；影响；财产

The chief politician who worships jingoism effects some major military reforms to recruit more soldiers.

• **Words in sentences 句中单词 / 词组** •

intelligence agency   情报机构
strenuous [ˈstrenjuəs]   *adj.* 费力的；热情的；有活力的
jingoism [ˈdʒɪŋɡoʊɪzəm]   *n.* 沙文主义；侵略主义

Part 2 补充单词 / 词组

celestial [səˈlestʃl]   *adj.* 天的；天空的

terrestrial [təˈrestriəl]   *adj.* 地球的；尘世的

God has founded the celestial and terrestrial countries.

incunabula [ˌɪnkjʊˈnæbjʊlə, ˌɪnkjʊˈnæbjələ]   *n.* 摇篮期；古版本

These invaluable Roman incunabula with ancient scripts might turn into ash at any time.

tertiary [ˈtɜːrʃieri, ˈtɜːrʃəri]   *n.* 第三系   *adj.* 第三的；第三期的

Historians classified the industries as primary, secondary, or tertiary industries.

extraterrestrial [ˌekstrətəˈrestriəl]   *adj.* 外星的

Scientists conduct an extraterrestrial experiment

traverse [ˈtrævɜːrs, trəˈvɜːrs]   *v.* 横越；穿过；[法律] 正式否认   *n.* 横越；横切线；障碍物；横 (大) 梁；[法律] 正式否认   *adj.* 横越的

The salesman traversed the state for promoting his product.

The wild horses traversed the Kherlen River.

I make traverses down the steep mountain.

The victim traversed the defendant's allegation.

troupe [tru:p]　　*v.* 巡回演出　　*n.* 表演团；（演员、歌手等的）班子

philanthropist [fɪ'lænθrəpɪst]　　*n.* 慈善家

The Canadian troupe travestied these corrupted politicians as philanthropists in their play.

philanthropy [fɪ'lænθrəpi]　　*n.* 慈善；慈善行为；慈善事业

debtor ['detər]　　*n.* 借方；债务人

The creditor felt he had enough philanthropy for the debtor.

Part 3　识记单词/词组

carry out　　打包的酒菜
for effect　　哗众取宠
to that effect　　大意是……
in effect　　实际上；事实上
conjure sth up　　变出……
conjure sb up　　念咒召唤出（鬼魂等）
conjure ['kʌndʒər]　　*v.* 念咒召唤（神灵、魔鬼等）；用魔术变出；想起
execute a will　　执行一份遗嘱
take effect　　起作用
arduous ['ɑːrdʒuəs]　　*adj.* 艰难的；费力的
terrestrial gravitation　　地球引力
terrestrial interest　　名利心
jingoist ['dʒɪŋɡəʊɪst]　　*n.* 沙文主义的人
incunabulum [ˌɪŋkjuː'næbjuləm]　　*n.* （在欧洲指1500年前所印的）初期刊本；古版书
incunable [ɪn'kjunəbəl]　　*n.* 古书之一册

Lesson 63

Part 1　主力单词/词组

attract [ə'trækt]　　*v.* 引诱；诱惑

The government provides tax-free zones to attract foreign capital.

Paradoxes are useful to attract attention to ideas. (Mandell Creighton, British churchman and historian)

captivate [ˈkæptɪveɪt] v. 使着迷；蛊惑
I was captivated by her unparalleled beauty.

fascinate [ˈfæsɪneɪt] v. 使着迷；蛊惑
Having been fascinated by this great outer-space discovery, I determine to be an astronaut one day.

enamor [ɪˈnæmər, enˈæmər] v. 使倾心；使迷恋
The emeritus of botany has become enamored of rural life.
I was enamored by the free, academic atmosphere of college life.

enthrall [ɪnˈθrɔːl] v. 迷住；吸引住；奴役
His responsibility enthralled him to work harder.

allure [əˈlʊr] v. 吸引；诱惑 n. 魅力
Such a golden opportunity allures me.

lure [lʊr] v. 诱惑 n. 鱼饵；诱饵
He has spent a great deal of time luring animals into a trap.

magnetize [ˈmægnətaɪz] v. 迷住；使有磁性；紧紧吸引
The celebrity magnetizes teenagers greatly.

tempt [tempt] v. 引诱；诱惑；使感兴趣
A salesman tempted me to buy more stuff.

entice [ɪnˈtaɪs] v. 诱惑
The restaurant has enticed customers to come by offering free breakfast.

entrance [ˈentrəns, ɪnˈtræns] v. 使着迷；进入 n. 入口；通道；（演员的）入场
The gorgeous woman has entranced many men.

beguile [bɪˈgaɪl] v. 吸引；迷住（用骗的方式）
Mermaids beguiled sailors with singing prior to dispatching them.

mesmerize [ˈmezməraɪz] v. 吸引；着迷（全神贯注）
Children were mesmerized by this storyteller concerning the adventure in Africa.

bewitch [bɪˈwɪtʃ] v. 对（某人）施魔法；令（某人）心醉；入迷
I was bewitched by the magician's outstanding performance.

She stammered by his bewitching presence.

seduction [sɪˈdʌkʃn]   *n.* 诱惑；教唆；诱惑物；有魅力的东西

The seduction of power makes ambitious men go to a greater extent beyond the moral boundary.

enchant [ɪnˈtʃænt]   *v.* 附上魔法；使陶醉

I was enchanted with her smile.
The weapon has been enchanted with a fire attribute.

beckon [ˈbekən]   *v.* 吸引；引诱；(向……) 点头

The captain beckoned us to come on board.
The lush forests beckon and enchant us.
A life in politics appeared to beckon.

- **Words in sentences 句中单词 / 词组**

  unparalleled [ʌnˈpærəleld]   *adj.* 无双的
  astronaut [ˈæstrənɔːt]   *n.* 航天员
  botany [ˈbɑːtəni]   *n.* 植物学
  mermaid [ˈmɜːˌmeɪd]   *n.* 美人鱼
  sailor [ˈseɪlə]   *n.* 水手
  boundary [ˈbaʊndri]   *n.* 疆界
  lush [lʌʃ]   *adj.* 植被茂盛的；令人愉悦的；美味的

Part 2 补充单词 / 词组

disenchant [ˌdɪsɪnˈtʃænt]   *v.* 使清醒；使不抱幻想

Let me disenchant you.

disenchantment [ˌdɪsɪnˈtʃæntmənt]   *n.* 不再着迷；不抱幻想；醒悟

Another year of disenchantment with South Korea's involvement in disputed islands in no way altered the president's determination to take back the islands.

disenchanted [ˌdɪsɪnˈtʃæntɪd]   *adj.* 不再着迷的；不再抱幻想的

The military commander was disenchanted that it's impossible to break the siege in front of an immense enemy.

rebarbative [rɪˈbɑːrbətɪv]　*adj.* 令人讨厌的；难看的

The slandering part-time job on the internet is nasty and rebarbative.

acute [əˈkjuːt]　*adj.* 敏锐的

parallel [ˈpærəlel]　*v.* 使平行；与……平行　*n.* 平行（曲）线；纬线；相似处　*adj.* 平行的；相同的

The attribute of acute smell is an obvious parallel between wolves and dogs.

parallelism [ˈpærəlelɪzəm]　*n.* 平行；相似；对应；对句法；平行度

Ancient poetry has parallelism of lines.

celibate [ˈselɪbət]　*n.* 独身者；独身主义者　*adj.* 独身的

He who doesn't like children that much is a celibate.
The priests and nuns lead a celibate life.

celibacy [ˈselɪbəsi]　*n.* 独身生活；禁欲

She has maintained celibacy since her husband died.

spatial [ˈspeɪʃl]　*adj.* 空间的；太空的

The geometry of the architecture is meant to create a sense of great spatial depth.

dispatch [dɪˈspætʃ]　*v.* 杀死；派遣；发送；快递；迅速处理　*n.* 新闻稿；快电

I received an urgent dispatch sent by the German general who asked us to send more reinforcement.

oligarch [ˈɑːləgɑːrk, ˈoʊləgɑːrk]　*n.* 寡头执政者

One of the major shareholders includes this Russian oligarch.

seclusion [sɪˈkluːʒn]　*n.* 与世隔绝

I enjoy a life of seclusion and solitude.

Part 3　识记单词/词组

seduce [sɪˈduːs]　*v.* 勾引

captivation [ˌkæptɪˈveɪʃən]　*n.* 迷惑；吸引人之物；出神的状态

fascination [ˌfæsɪˈneɪʃn]　*n.* 迷惑；妖力

repel [rɪˈpel]　*v.* 使厌恶；逐回；击退；抗御

repellent [rɪˈpelənt] *n.* 驱虫剂　*adj.* 令人厌恶的

magnetosphere [mægˈnitəsfɪr] *n.* 磁气圈

be tempted...　想要（某物）；想做（某事）

tempt fate/providence　玩命；冒不必要的危险

a wonderful future beckon　美妙的前程在招手

capital goods　资本货物

argumentative [ˌɑːrgjuˈmentətɪv] *adj.* 好争论的

disputant [ˈdɪspjutənt] *n.* 辩论者　*adj.* 争论的

disputatious [ˌdɪspjuːˈteɪʃəs] *adj.* 好争论的

jibe [dʒaɪb] *v.* 嘲笑　*n.* 嘲弄

gibe [dʒaɪb] *v.* 嘲笑　*n.* 愚弄

lowercase [ˌloʊərˈkeɪs] *n.* 小写字母　*adj.* 小写字母的；用小写字母写的

enthuse [ɪnˈθuːz] *v.* 使充满热情；兴奋地说

paradox [ˈpærədɑːks] *n.* 自相矛盾的情况

paradoxical [ˌpærəˈdɑːksɪkl] *adj.* 自相矛盾的

acuity [əˈkjuːəti] *n.*（听力、视力、思维等的）敏锐；灵敏度

stammer [ˈstæmər] *v.* 口吃

solitude [ˈsɑːlətuːd] *n.* 独居

spatial awareness　空间意识

oligarchy [ˈɑːləgɑːrki, ˈoʊləgɑːrki] *n.* 寡头政治；寡头政治的国家

pocket [ˈpɑːkɪt] *v.* 侵吞；放入口袋；忍受；抑制　*n.* 钱；财力

Lesson 64

Part 1　主力单词/词组

based on　基于；以……为前提

The charge is based on a flat fee rather than billable hours.
The ransom is based on the threat of killing the hostage.

predicate [ˈpredɪkət, ˈpredɪkeɪt] *v.* 断言　*n.* 谓语

Lesson 64

predicate on 基于；以……为前提

The relativity theory is predicated on two interrelated assumptions.

contingent on 视……而定

To be successful is contingent on several factors.

provided/providing that 如果；只要

The project can be finished on time provided that everybody works hard.

given [ˈgɪvn] *n.* 假设 *adj.* 给与的；给定的 *prep.* 考虑到

They finished their exam at a given time.

Given the intricate nature of diplomacy, they have done a good job.

It is a given pointing your finger at the moon will induce bad luck.

prerequisite [ˌpriːˈrekwɪzɪt] *n.* 先决条件 *adj.* 必备条件的

Public support is a prerequisite to winning the presidential election.

requisite [ˈrekwɪzɪt] *n.* 必要的东西 *adj.* 必要的

Bringing a bottle of water is a requisite before climbing this mountain.

What are the requisite skills for this occupation?

sine qua non 必要条件

Accurate spelling and grammar are the sine qua nons of learning English.

subject to 依……而定；易遭受……

The mission can be carried out subject to the final approval of the commander.

repose on 休息

Your speculations reposed on false information.

depend on 依……而定

It depends on the weather conditions as to whether or not we can go on our picnic.

rely on 依赖；指望

Often relying on their law enforcement privilege, the police hector, and torture the poor innocent into a confession.

bedrock [ˈbedrɑːk] *n.* 基础；床岩；底部 *adj.* 基础的；根本的

Freedom of speech is a bedrock of democracy.

dint [dɪnt] *v.* 由于；凭借 *n.* 凹痕；凹坑

He succeeded by dint of hard work and strong will.

• **Words in sentences 句中单词 / 词组** •

flat fee　固定收费率
billable hours　以小时计价
ransom　['rænsəm]　n. 赎金
assumption　[ə'sʌmpʃn]　n. 假设
intricate　['ɪntrɪkət, 'ɪntrɪkɪt]　adj. 错综复杂的
diplomacy　[dɪ'ploʊməsi]　n. 外交
law enforcement　执法
hector　['hektər]　v. 威吓　n. 威吓者

Part 2　补充单词 / 词组

given to　倾向
He is not given to anger that often.

unerringly　[ʌn'ɜːrɪŋli]　adv. 准确地
The pilot bombed the target unerringly, but they kept saying he attacked the wrong target.

morganatic　[ˌmɔːrgə'nætɪk]　adj. 通婚的

marriage　['mærɪdʒ]　n. 结婚；婚礼
The prince had a morganatic marriage with his servant.

conjugal　['kɑːndʒəgl]　adj. 结婚的；配偶的
Their conjugal bliss lasted for a decade.
His wife fought for the right to conjugal property after being divorced.

conjugate　['kɑːndʒəgeɪt]　v. 使结合；使成对　n. 结亲　adj. 结合的
The blood cells conjugate with others of the same type.

connubial　[kə'nuːbiəl]　adj. 结婚的；夫妇的
I enjoyed the serenity of our connubial life.

nubile　['nuːbl, 'nuːbaɪl]　adj. 适婚年龄的
A fan stalked a nubile starlet.

miser [ˈmaɪzər]　*n.* 守财奴；吝啬鬼

He is a miser and always gets over on me.

niggard [ˈnɪgərd]　*n.* 吝啬鬼　*adj.* 吝啬的

The niggard never donates anything to the needy.

niggardly [ˈnɪgərdli]　*adv.* 小气地；很少量地

The company increased pension niggardly and paltrily.

carafe [kəˈræf]　*n.* 玻璃水瓶

The waitress pours wine from the carafe.

Part 3　识记单词/词组

off base　大错特错的
have all bases covered　全部覆盖
touch base (with someone)　与（某人）取得联系
interrelate [ˌɪntərɪˈleɪt]　*v.* 关联
occupation [ˌɑːkjuˈpeɪʃn]　*n.* 职业
privilege [ˈprɪvəlɪdʒ]　*v.* 给予……特权　*n.* 特权；豁免权
unerring [ʌnˈɜːrɪŋ]　*adj.* 确实的；没有错的

Lesson 65

Part 1　主力单词/词组

slaughter [ˈslɔːtər]　*v.* 屠杀　*n.* 大屠杀；屠宰；暴力的杀人

Bombing serves nothing, but slaughters innocent people and breeds more hatred which nourishes terrorists to carry out the suicidal bombing.
A lowbrow politician loves to see people sacrificed and slaughtered for the sake of amorphous patriotism and white supremacy.

homicide [ˈhɑːmɪsaɪd]　*n.* 预谋杀人

Homicide is premeditated, but manslaughter is without malice aforethought.

matricide [ˈmætrɪsaɪd] n. 弑母（罪）；弑母者

patricide [ˈpætrɪsaɪd] n. 弑父（罪）；弑父者
We've all heard patricide and matricide every now and then. How absurd can it be?

fratricide [ˈfrætrɪsaɪd] n. 杀兄弟（姊妹）的行为
He was imprisoned for fratricide.

liquidate [ˈlɪkwɪdeɪt] v. 杀；清偿
If you don't pay your debt, you might be liquidated by the debt-liquidating company.

murder [ˈmɜːrdər] v. 谋杀 n. 谋杀者
Walking down the street rather late at night, females have become soft targets of the men on the prowl, from muggings to murders.

assassinate [əˈsæsɪneɪt] v. 暗杀
So-called military commander targeting is actually an assassination.

massacre [ˈmæsəkər] v. 大屠杀 n. 屠杀者
Genocide is an ethnic massacre or a religious bloodbath.

suicide [ˈsuːɪsaɪd] n. 自杀
He committed suicide after breaking up with his beloved girlfriend.

execute [ˈeksɪkjuːt] v. 实现；演奏；使生效；处死
The official was executed for embezzlement of 1 billion dollars.

fratricidal [ˌfrætrɪˈsaɪdl] adj. 杀兄弟（姊妹）的；杀同胞的

genocide [ˈdʒenəsaɪd] n. 种族灭绝；灭种的罪行

commit suicide 自杀

● Words in sentences 句中单词/词组 ●

serve [sɜːrv] v. 接待；提供 n. 发球
innocent [ˈɪnəsnt] adj. 无辜的
breed [briːd] v. 饲养（动物）；交配；繁殖；招致 n.（动植物的）品种；（人的）类型；种类

hatred [ˈheɪtrɪd] n. 恨
nourish [ˈnɜːrɪʃ] v. 滋养
terrorist [ˈterərɪst] n. 恐怖分子
suicidal [ˌsuːɪˈsaɪdl] adj. 自杀的
lowbrow [ˈloʊbraʊ] n. 庸俗的人 adj. 肤浅的
sake [seɪk, ˈsɑːki] n. 缘故
patriotism [ˈpeɪtriətɪzəm] n. 爱国主义
white supremacy 白人优势；白人至上主义
manslaughter [ˈmænslɔːtər] n. 非预谋杀人
malice [ˈmælɪs] n. 恶意
every now and then 偶尔；有时
absurd [əbˈsɜːrd] adj. 荒谬的
debt [det] n. 债务；恩义
soft target 易下手的目标
prowl [praʊl] v. 潜行跟踪 n. 跟踪者
ethnic [ˈeθnɪk] adj. 民族的
bloodbath [ˈblʌdbæθ] n. 大屠杀
embezzlement [ɪmˈbezlmənt] n. 挪用（公款）；侵占公款罪

Part 2 补充单词/词组

machine gun 机关枪
We've dispatched the contingent to attack an airport. However, they were dispatched by a machine gun later on.

chauvinist [ˈʃoʊvɪnɪst] n. 沙文主义者
The open-minded woman has difficulty with her husband's chauvinist views.

arrear [əˈrɪr] n. 欠债；待完成的工作
I spend a vacation for a month and then arrears of work have piled up.

lectern [ˈlektərn] n. 读经台；讲台
The lecturer walked over to the lectern, referring to his notes.

podium [ˈpoʊdiəm] *n.* 讲台；乐队指挥台

The conductor on the podium was so engrossed while conducting.

peroration [ˌperəˈreɪʃn] *n.* 演讲的结语；慷慨激昂的讲话

His peroration stressed the importance of free trade.

harangue [həˈræŋ] *v.* 高谈阔论；慷慨陈词 *n.* 热烈的演说

I couldn't endure this tiresome, incessant harangue so I fell to sleep for a while.

multistory [ˈmʌltiˌstɔːri] *adj.* 好几层的

The multistory house is due west.

Caucasian [kɔːˈkeɪʒn] *n.* 高加索人；白种人 *adj.* 高加索地方的；白种人的

The dead man is a Caucasian.
Most Europeans have a Caucasian complexion.

swarthy [ˈswɔːrði] *adj.* 黑黝黝的；黑皮肤的

Africans have swarthy skins.

trivial [ˈtrɪviəl] *adj.* 琐碎的

Will you stop pestering me with trivial things?

sanctimonious [ˌsæŋktɪˈmoʊniəs] *adj.* 道貌岸然的；伪善的；假装圣洁的

The teacher is a sanctimonious hypocrite.

Part 3 识记单词/词组

serve...up 向……提供

serve sb right （某人）活该

for God's sake 看在上帝的面子上

provident measure 有先见之明的措施

backup plan 备案

inbred [ˌɪnˈbred] *adj.* 近亲繁殖的

purebred [ˈpjʊrˈbred] *adj.*（动物）纯种的

thoroughbred [ˈθɜːroʊbred] *adj.*（马）纯种的

well bred 有教养的；（马、狗等）血统好的

serve time 服刑

if my memory serves me right 如果我没记错的话

serve sth out 继续工作；担任职务（直到事先规定的时间）

trillion [ˈtrɪljən] *n.* 万亿

chauvinism [ˈʃoʊvɪnɪzəm] *n.* 沙文主义

fascist [ˈfæʃɪst] *n.* 法西斯主义者

fascism [ˈfæʃɪzəm] *n.* 法西斯主义

malicious [məˈlɪʃəs] *adj.* 恶意的

aforethought [əˈfɔːrθɔːt] *adj.* 事先考虑的

afterthought [ˈæftərθɔːt] *n.* 事后的考虑或想法；后来添加的东西

absurdity [əbˈsɜːrdəti] *n.* 可笑；不合理；荒谬的行为或事物

mugging [ˈmʌɡɪŋ] *n.* 行凶抢劫

peculation [ˌpekjuˈleɪʃən] *n.* 盗用公款

embezzle [ɪmˈbezl] *v.* 盗用

arrearage [əˈrɪərɪdʒ] *n.* 欠款

Lesson 66

Part 1 主力单词/词组

serene [səˈriːn] *adj.* 宁静的；平和的；晴朗的；清澈的
Under the serene sky, I see my reflection from the lake.

tranquil [ˈtræŋkwɪl] *adj.* 宁静的；平和的
We walked along the tranquil shoreline of the lake reminiscing our old school golden days.

tranquility=tranquillity *n.* 平静；安宁
I enjoy the silence and tranquility of the countryside at night.

calmness [ˈkɑːmnəs] *n.* 安静；冷静
You can abandon the pretense of calmness now that the police have left.

halcyon [ˈhælsiən] *n.* 神话中的鸟 *adj.* 平静的
We all enjoyed the halcyon years of prosperity.

equanimity [ˌekwəˈnɪməti] *n.* 沉着；冷静
The leader faced defeat with equanimity.

placid [ˈplæsɪd] *adj.* 宁静的；易满足的
The placid stream runs quietly.

placidity [pləˈsɪdəti] *n.* 平稳；温和
The jet flew through disturbing the placidity of the countryside.

lull [lʌl] *v.* 使安静；使入睡；哄骗使放松警戒 *n.* 暂时平静；间歇
She sings softly, lulling the baby to sleep.
The traitor lulled the king into a false sense of security.
There is an early-morning lull before the honking of the urban congested cars.

equilibrium [ˌiːkwɪˈlɪbriəm, ˌekwɪˈlɪbriəm] *n.* (心情的) 平静；平衡
I lost my equilibrium after you stole my heart.
A new equilibrium of birth rates has been reached.

aplomb [əˈplɑːm] *n.* 泰然自若
He usually faces his failure with great aplomb.

poise [pɔɪz] *v.* 使平衡；握着不动；作好准备 *n.* 镇静；自信
The victim poised himself for the press conference.
She carried a basket of apples poised on her head.
She had the perfect poise like a model.
The master poised his chopstick and gave his guest a knowing look.
The soldiers poised for battle.

poised [pɔɪzd] *adj.* 泰然自若的；平衡的
The White House is poised for impeaching the president.
The senior actor is always poised on the stage.

level-headed [ˌlevl ˈhedɪd] *adj.* 头脑冷静的
He remains level-headed while the wildfire engulfs his house.

sangfroid [sɑːŋˈfrwɑː] *n.* 冷静；沉着；镇定
The general exhibited remarkable sangfroid while he was under fire.
She faces her plight with sangfroid and calmness.

equable [ˈekwəbl] *adj.* 平和的；宁静的；同等的
She has an equable mind and would not do anything irrational.
The workers placed these big vases apart at an equable distance.

idyllic [aɪˈdɪlɪk] *adj.* 恬静的；牧歌的

The boy has an idyllic childhood in the countryside.

The couple decides to spend their summer on an idyllic Caribbean island.

imperturbable [ˌɪmpərˈtɜːrbəbl] *adj.* 沉着的；冷静的

He put out the blaze with imperturbable calm.

The chief seems outwardly imperturbable, but inside of him is furious.

• Words in sentences 句中单词 / 词组 •

shoreline [ˈʃɔːrlaɪn] *n.* 海岸线

pretense [ˈpriːtens] *n.* 假装

defeat [dɪˈfiːt] *v.* 战败；击败 *n.* 失败

jet [dʒet] *n.* 喷气飞机；喷射流（水、气等的）

traitor [ˈtreɪtər] *n.* 叛徒

chopstick [ˈtʃɑːpstɪk] *n.* 筷子

wildfire [ˈwaɪldfaɪər] *n.* (毁灭性的) 大火灾；不易扑灭的野火；散布极快的事物

engulf [ɪnˈɡʌlf] *v.* 吞没；卷入；使全神贯注

Part 2 补充单词 / 词组

market equilibrium 市场均衡

Demand, supply, and market equilibrium are the central components of microeconomics.

envoy [ˈenvɔɪ] *n.* 特使；外交使节

kinetic [kɪˈnetɪk, kaɪˈnetɪk] *adj.* 运动的；运动引起的

She is a kinetic envoy assigned a special mission by our president.

fumble [ˈfʌmbl] *v.* 乱摸；摸索；错误地处理 *n.* 漏接球

The basketball play looks rather poised but unexpectedly fumbles the ball.

grope [ɡroʊp] *v.* 触摸；摸索；探索 *n.* 探求

stagger [ˈstæɡər] *v.* 摇摇晃晃地走 *n.* 摇晃；一种不稳定形式

They grope in the dark without light and stagger like drunken men.

evangelical [ˌiːvænˈdʒelɪkl] n. 福音派教徒 adj. 福音的；福音书的；福音传道的

Young evangelicals still support the incumbent president.

protestant [ˈprɑːtɪstənt] n. 新教徒；抗议者 adj. 新教的；新教徒的；提出异议的

Evangelical Protestants have grown rapidly in recent years, reaching up to 9 million.

denomination [dɪˌnɑːmɪˈneɪʃn] n. 宗派；面额；单位（度量衡等的）

Later on, Christianity was divided into three major denominations.

defeatist [dɪˈfiːtɪst] n. 失败主义 adj. 失败主义的

His defeatist and antirevolutionary speech prevailed in the nation.

quisling [ˈkwɪzlɪŋ] n. 卖国贼

Quislings seem to overrun the patriots in Egypt.

renege [rɪˈneg] v. 食言；违约；否认；有牌而不跟

You shouldn't renege on your promise.

revolutionist [ˌrevəˈluːʃənɪst] n. 革命者 adj. 革命者的

The revolutionist was branded by Moscow as a renegade.

renovation [ˌrenəˈveɪʃn] n. 修理；恢复

The mayor approves the renovation of public buildings.

Part 3 识记单词/词组

incumbent [ɪnˈkʌmbənt] n. 在职者；现任者 adj. 在职的；现任的；有责任的

madrigal [ˈmædrɪɡl] n. 牧歌；情歌；小调；合唱歌曲

idyll [ˈaɪdl] n. 田园诗；田园乐曲；牧歌；（适于作为田园诗题材的）情景

shepherd [ˈʃepərd] v. 牧羊；指导；护送 n. 牧羊人；指导者

biplane [ˈbaɪpleɪn] n. 双翼飞机

equanimous [iˈkwænɪməs] adj. 镇定的；泰然的

serenity [səˈrenəti] n. 安详；晴朗；平静

dispassionate [dɪsˈpæʃənət] adj. 冷静的；客观的

denominate [dɪˈnɑːmɪneɪt] v. 结算；命名；称……为

halcyon days （昔日）美好的时光
dynamic equilibrium 动态平衡
dynamic [daɪˈnæmɪk] *adj.* 动态的；有活力的；动力学的；机能的；功能的
kinetics [kɪˈnetɪks, kaɪˈnetɪks] *n.* 动力学
kinetic energy 动能
kinetic temperature 动态温度
kinetic art 活动艺术
conspiracy [kənˈspɪrəsi] *n.* 阴谋
pretend [prɪˈtend] *v.* 假装；伪称（有）；试图
defeatism [dɪˈfiːtɪzəm] *n.* 失败主义
renegade [ˈrenɪɡeɪd] *v.* 背叛；变节 *n.* 背教者；反传统或反法律的人 *adj.* 背弃的
gulf [ɡʌlf] *v.* 卷入；吞没 *n.* 海湾；巨大分歧；（地面的）裂口；深渊
Persian Gulf 波斯湾
component [kəmˈpoʊnənt] *n.* 零件；成分；（机器、设备等的）构成要素 *adj.* 组成的；构成的

Lesson 67

Part 1 主力单词/词组

slander [ˈslændər] *v.* 诋毁；中伤 *n.* 诽谤（口头上的）
The captain refutes all the slanders against him.
I shall not hesitate to issue writs for libel and slander if scandalous allegations are made or repeated outside the House. (John Profumo, British politician)

libel [ˈlaɪbl] *v.* 以文字诽谤；诬蔑 *n.* 诽谤
The director filed a libel suit of two million dollars against a petroleum company's former executive.

smirch [smɜːrtʃ] *v.* 弄脏；给……抹黑 *n.* 脏污；污点
Her cloth was smirched by a splash of mud.

besmirch [bɪˈsmɜːrtʃ]   *v.* 玷污；损害

The lawyer tried to besmirch the defendant's character.

sully [ˈsʌli]   *v.* 玷污；败坏

Killing you will sully my hands. I don't want to get my hands imbrued with blood.

calumniate [kəˈlʌmnɪeɪt]   *v.* 玷污；损害

The archenemy was hated and calumniated.

mudslinging [ˈmʌdˌslɪŋɪŋ]   *n.* 诽谤；中伤

The chairman of congress starts to consider how he can prevent the meeting from deteriorating into mudslinging.

defame [dɪˈfeɪm]   *v.* 诋毁；中伤

The opposition leader was tried and convicted on charges of having defamed the chief of justice in public speeches and was sentenced to jail for eight years.

aspersion [əˈspɜːrʒən]   *n.* 诋毁；中伤

College students mischievously placarded the town with aspersions of our government's ineptitude and paralysis on corruption issues.

defile [dɪˈfaɪl, ˈdiːfaɪl]   *v.* 玷污；亵渎   *n.* 狭径；峡道（山中）

Defiling proletarian internationalism is ungrounded.
The tour guide has to know the topography of mountains and forests, ravines and defiles, and wetlands and marshes in this region.

malign [məˈlaɪn]   *v.* 诽谤；中伤   *adj.* 恶意的；邪恶的

Don't you dare malign her in her presence?
Excessive swearing in movies does have a strong, malign influence on teenagers.

discredit [dɪsˈkredɪt]   *v.* 使名誉受损；使受到怀疑   *n.* 不相信；丧失名誉

The historian was discredited by representing false antiquities.

tarnish [ˈtɑːrnɪʃ]   *v.* 诽谤；中伤；蒙受耻辱   *n.* 暗锈；无光泽

Massive whale killing has tarnished Japan's image.

blemish [ˈblemɪʃ]   *v.* 损害；破坏   *n.* 斑点；瑕疵

The sex scandal and bribery have blemished his character.

traduce [trəˈduːs]   *v.* 诽谤；背叛

The press traduces the candidate's character as always.

Lesson 67

Leaving her traduced his inner feeling.

libelous [ˈlaɪbələs]   adj. 诽谤的

calumniation [kəˌlʌmniˈeɪʃn]   n. 诽谤；谗言；中伤

calumny [ˈkæləmni]   n. 诽谤；中伤

defamation [ˌdefəˈmeɪʃn]   n. 破坏名誉；中伤；诽谤

defamatory [dɪˈfæmətɔːri]   adj. 诽谤的；破坏名誉的

defamer [dɪˈfeɪm]   n. 诋毁者

maligner [məˈlaɪnə]   n. 诽谤者

mar [mɑːr]   v. 毁损；玷污   n. 污点；缺点

• Words in sentences 句中单词/词组 •

refute [rɪˈfjuːt]   v. 驳斥
writ [rɪt]   n. 文书；[法] 令状；法院命令
scandalous [ˈskændələs]   adj. 丑闻的；诽谤的
allegation [ˌæləˈgeɪʃn]   n. 指责；指控（未经证实的）；宣称
ineptitude [ɪˈneptɪtuːd]   n. 无能；不适当
proletarian [ˌproʊləˈteriən]   n. 无产阶级者；工人阶级的人
internationalism [ˌɪntərˈnæʃnəlɪzəm]   n. 国际主义；国际性
ungrounded [ʌnˈɡraʊndɪd]   adj. 不理智的；没有依据的
topography [təˈpɑːɡrəfi]   n. 地形；地貌
ravine [rəˈviːn]   n. 峡谷；深谷
wetland [ˈwetlənd]   n. 湿地；沼泽地（面积较大）
marsh [mɑːrʃ]   n. 沼泽；湿地
swearing [ˈsweriŋ]   n. 诅咒；咒骂

Part 2 补充单词/词组

paraphernalia [ˌpærəfərˈneɪliə]   n. 相关的用具
The company manufactures the paraphernalia of people's daily lives.

drug paraphernalia 吸毒用具

The criminal was charged with possession of drug paraphernalia.

dossier ['dɔːsieɪ] *n.* 档案；卷宗

Do you have any dossiers about this violent criminal?

medical dossier 病历

The doctor requires the patient's medical dossier before diagnosing him.

tabloid ['tæblɔɪd] *n.* 小报；文摘；摘要 *adj.* 摘要的；轰动性的；庸俗的

The tabloid was sued for its libelous, defamatory review of a celebrity.

inept [ɪ'nept] *adj.* 无能的；笨拙的

The inept decision he made backfired in the end.

gulch [gʌltʃ] *n.* 峡谷；冲沟

The gulch floods in summer and dries out in winter.

gully ['gʌli] *v.* 在……上冲出沟 *n.* 冲沟；水沟

The gust swept him off a bridge and into a gully.

downpour ['daʊnpɔːr] *n.* 倾盆大雨

arroyo [ə'rɔɪoʊ] *n.* 干旱的峡谷；干涸的冲沟；小溪

The downpour turns the roads in the village into a raging arroyo.

melancholy ['melənkɑːli] *n.* 悲伤

His poetry was imbued with melancholy.

affidavit [ˌæfə'deɪvɪt] *n.* 宣誓书；口供书

He wrote an affidavit affirming the signature was authentic.

tentative ['tentətɪv] *n.* 不确定的事物 *adj.* 临时的；试验性的；不确定的

The theory is tentative, open to refutation.

Part 3 识记单词 / 词组

overdose ['oʊvərdoʊs] *v.* 使服药过量；使过分沉溺 *n.* 服药过量；药剂过量

cannabis ['kænəbɪs] *n.* 印度大麻；大麻烟原料；大麻烟

file [faɪl] *v.* 归档；提起（诉讼）；提出（申请） *n.* 档案；卷宗；（计算机的）文档

massive overdose of drugs 大量过度吸毒

refutation [ˌrefjuˈteɪʃn] *n.* 反驳；反驳的言论或意见
allege [əˈledʒ] *v.* 声称；坚持己见；主张；推诿；托言；辩称
imbrue [imˈbruː] *v.* (尤指以血) 玷污
archenemy [ɑːtʃˈenimi] *n.* 主要敌人；死敌
deteriorate [dɪˈtɪriəreɪt] *v.* 恶化；变坏
deterioration [dɪˌtɪriəˈreɪʃn] *n.* 恶化；降低；堕落
chief justice 首席法官；高等法院院长
mischief [ˈmɪstʃɪf] *n.* 恶作剧；伤害；恶意
mischievous [ˈmɪstʃɪvəs] *adj.* 有害的；恶作剧的；麻烦的
placard [ˈplækɑːrd] *v.* 张贴；公布 *n.* 布告；标语牌
paralysis [pəˈræləsɪs] *n.* 麻痹；不知所措；停顿
paralyse [ˈpærəlaɪz] *v.* 使麻痹；使瘫痪
proletariat [ˌproʊləˈteriət] *n.* 工人阶级
bourgeoisie [ˌbʊrʒwɑːˈziː] *n.* 中产阶级；中产阶级的人
bourgeois [ˌbʊrʒwɑː, ˈbʊrʒwɑː] *adj.* 中产阶级的；追求物质享受的
gorge [ɡɔːrdʒ] *n.* 峡谷；令人作呕
swamp [swɑːmp] *v.* 充斥；席卷；淹没 *n.* 沼泽；湿地
antiquity [ænˈtɪkwəti] *n.* 古物；古代
melancholic [ˌmelənˈkɑːlɪk] *adj.* 忧郁的；神经质的

Lesson 68

Part 1 主力单词 / 词组

suitable [ˈsuːtəbl] *adj.* 适合的
I never would be able to make a suitable recompense, nor to serve my girlfriend as she deserved to be served while in prison.
Such protein is not suitable for human use, but exclusively for the animal.

proper [ˈprɑːpər] *adj.* 适当的；特有的
I need to find a proper place to date.

appropriate [əˈproʊpriət, əˈproʊprieɪt] *v.* 盗用；拨（专款等） *adj.* 适合的

Students have to learn appropriate social skills.

The accountant has appropriated money from her company.

Beijing appropriates ten million dollars for the new airport and the subway.

propitious [prəˈpɪʃəs] *adj.* 吉利的；顺利的；适合的；仁慈的

The witch uses astrological signs and a religious almanac to determine a propitious time for ritual combat and sacrifice.

opportune [ˌɑːpərˈtuːn] *adj.* 合适的

The policeman has waited for this opportune moment to seize the robber while he is walking out jewelry store.

providential [ˌprɑːvɪˈdenʃl] *adj.* 天意的；正合适的；及时的

Pedestrians made a providential escape in the nick of time while the truck crashed into the spot in which they had just been standing.

due [duː] *n.* 应得之物；税款；应付款 *adj.* 预定的；应有的；合适的 *adv.* 正；真正亏欠地

The meeting is due to adjourn because the mogul has not shown up.

I am due to divulge the pirate's den while reporters come in.

Installment is due at the end of every month.

Do you pay the annual membership dues yet?

I decided to put Eric in the saddle leading the school team for the national math contest after due consideration.

felicitous [fəˈlɪsɪtəs] *adj.* 令人愉悦的；幸运的；贴切的

Your felicitous remark has won the trust of the majority.

The diplomatic crisis has to been handled in a most felicitous manner.

There is a park with a felicitous design.

The stark reality of political life is less felicitous.

felicity [fəˈlɪsəti] *n.* 幸福；（措辞等的）得体；精妙的评论

He is so in love with his wife and enjoys marital felicity.

People manage to peek through the gloom in the felicities and absurdities of real life.

The writer is well-known for his felicity.

Art and philosophy transport ordinary people into a realm of beatific felicity.

apposite [ˈæpəzɪt] *adj.* 适当的；贴切的

I can't find an apposite phrase to describe her beauty.

Lesson 68

apt [æpt]   *adj.* 合适的；有天赋的；聪明的

The TV program host is well-known for her apt quip and apposite humor.

This apt child learns very fast.

- Words in sentences 句中单词 / 词组 -

recompense ['rekəmpens]   *v.* 给报酬；赔偿   *n.* 报酬

exclusively [ɪk'sklu:sɪvli]   *adv.* 唯一地；专门地；特定地；排外地

astrological [ˌæstrə'lɑːdʒɪkl]   *adj.* 天文的；占星的

almanac ['ɔ:lmənæk,'ælmənæk]   *n.* 年历；年鉴

mogul [ˌmoʊ'ɡʌl]   *n.* 大人物；雪丘（在山坡上为增加滑雪的乐趣和难度而堆起的硬雪堆）

den [den]   *n.* 巢穴；活动室

installment [ɪn'stɔ:lmənt]   *n.* 分期付款

saddle ['sædl]   *n.* 马鞍

in the saddle   控制；掌握；骑马

stark [stɑːrk]   *adj.* 赤裸的；简单的；粗陋的；严重的   *adv.* 完全；明显地；毫无掩饰地

marital ['mærɪtl]   *adj.* 婚姻的；夫妻的

realm [relm]   *n.* 领域；王国

quip [kwɪp]   *v.* 说妙语；讥讽   *n.* 俏皮话；妙语

Part 2 补充单词 / 词组

unpropitious [ˌʌnprə'pɪʃəs]   *adj.* 不适合的；不吉利的；不顺遂的

It is a financially unpropitious time to invest during the recession.

inappropriate [ˌɪnə'proʊpriət]   *adj.* 不合适的；不恰当的

Wearing a hat inside a house is inappropriate in the United States.

cash-strapped ['kæʃ stræpt]   *adj.* 缺乏现金的

The cash-strapped institution can only recompense the lecturer with a token honorarium.

divine [dɪ'vaɪn]   *v.* 占卜；猜测   *n.* 神学者；牧师   *adj.* 神的；超人的

providence [ˈprɑːvɪdəns] n. 天意；神的安排
Whether he can be revived is at divine's providence.

improvident [ɪmˈprɑːvɪdənt] adj. 无先见之明的；不管未来的
The wastrel leads an improvident life.

overdue [ˌoʊvərˈduː] adj. 过期的；延误的
Disaster prevention programs have been overdue.

due to 由于；应归于
Our gratitude is due to soldiers who died for us.

moratory [mɔrətəri] adj. 延期偿付的；可以延期履行义务的
I have to moratory interest to the bank.

moratorium [ˌmɔːrəˈtɔːriəm] n. 延期偿付；（行动、活动的）暂停；中止
The warden received an official moratorium on the execution of the felon.

beatific [ˌbiːəˈtɪfɪk] adj. 赐与祝福的；幸福的
Her beatific smile melts my frozen heart.

beatitude [biˈætɪtuːd, biˈætətuːd] n. 幸福；祝福
"Blessed is the man who expects nothing; for he shall never be disappointed" was the ninth beatitude. (Alexander Pope, English poet)

vulgar [ˈvʌlgər] n. 庶民 adj. 粗俗的；大众的

ribald [ˈrɪbld, ˈraɪbɔːld] n. 说话粗鄙的人 adj. 猥亵的；下流的
Many people like his vulgar witticisms and the ribald songs he sings.

purview [ˈpɜːrvjuː] n. 范围；视界；要项；条款
The purview of these villagers is limited.

pertain [pərˈteɪn] v. 有关；附属；适合
The judge delivers a harsh sentence to a student because his conduct pertains to an adult's behavior.

recipient [rɪˈsɪpiənt] n. 接受者；容器 adj. 受领的；容纳的；能接受的
The heart recipient died of acute cellular rejection.

Part 3 识记单词/词组

relevant [ˈreləvənt] adj. 有意义的；适宜的

inapt [ɪn'æpt]   *adj.* 不恰当的；不熟练的
inopportune [ɪnˌɑːpər'tuːn]   *adj.* 不适当的；失去时机的
inappropriate [ˌɪnə'proʊpriət]   *adj.* 不合适的；不恰当的
heart seizure   心脏病发作
exclusive interview   独家采访
honorarium [ˌɑːnə'reriəm]   *n.* 报酬；谢礼
exclusive [ɪk'skluːsɪv]   *n.* 独家新闻；特权   *adj.* 独家采访专用的；独有的；昂贵的
astrology [ə'strɑːlədʒi]   *n.* 占星术；原始天文学
provident ['prɑːvɪdənt]   *adj.* 节俭的
abscond [əb'skɑːnd]   *v.* 潜逃；携款潜逃
elope [ɪ'loʊp]   *v.* 私奔
antelope ['æntɪloʊp]   *n.* 羚羊
plod [plɑːd]   *v.* 艰难地行走；埋头工作
revive [rɪ'vaɪv]   *v.* 使复活；使恢复；使振奋；唤醒；再生效力
diviner [dɪ'vaɪnər]   *n.* 先知；预言者
in due course   及时地
divulge [daɪ'vʌldʒ]   *v.* 泄露；透露（秘密）
blurt [blɜːrt]   *v.* 脱口说出；不假思索地说
seizure ['siːʒər]   *n.* 抓住；夺取；扣押；（病的）发作
epilepsy ['epɪlepsi]   *n.* 癫痫
epileptic [ˌepɪ'leptɪk]   *adj.* 癫痫的；患癫痫的
dismember [dɪs'membər]   *v.* 肢解；分割
orate ['oʊreɪt, ɔː'ræt]   *v.* 演讲；用演说的腔调说
oration [ɔː'reɪʃn]   *n.* 演讲
perorate ['perəˌreɪt]   *v.* 冗长地谈论
peroxide [pə'rɑːksaɪd]   *v.* 用过氧化物处理；用过氧化氢漂白   *n.* 过氧化物；过氧化氢
witticism ['wɪtɪsɪzəm]   *n.* 名言；妙语
marital leave   婚假
receiver [rɪ'siːvər]   *n.* 受领人；电话听筒；破产案产业管理人

Lesson 69

Part 1 主力单词 / 词组

exude [ɪɡˈzuːd] *v.* 展现出；慢慢流出
A police official exudes confidence to catch the fugitive.

emanate [ˈemənɪt] *v.* 产生；表现出
The leader emanates an unbridled ambition trying to conquer the whole universe.
The smell emanated from that trash can.

radiate [ˈreɪdieɪt] *v.* 散发出（热、光、感情）；辐射；从中心散开
Turning his back toward me, he radiated defiance.
The heat and light radiate from the sun.

exhibit [ɪɡˈzɪbɪt] *v.* 展出；展现出
Please don't exhibit any strange behavior, you will be gone if you decide to pull even one more stunt.

expose [ɪkˈspoʊz] *v.* 露出；揭露；暴露
The young lady loves to expose her shoulders.
They are exposed to the enemy's fire.

transpire [trænˈspaɪər] *v.* 公开；暴露出；被人所知（秘密或未知事实）；发生；（人体或植物）蒸腾；水分蒸发
The exclusive news transpired that the millions of dollars of corporate debt have been hidden in a complex web of transactions.
What will transpire for a single male doctor and a single female nurse remaining in the office all night long?
The hotter the weather, the more the plants transpire.

ooze [uːz] *v.* 渗出；缓缓流出；逐渐消失 *n.* 渗出（物）；软泥
A novelist is, like all mortals, more fully at home on the surface of the present than in the ooze of the past. (Vladimir Nabokov, Russian-born U.S. novelist, poet, and critic)
Whoever oozes with sympathy toward dissidents should be punished.
Sap oozed from the yew.

The crowd began to ooze forward from the colosseum.

effuse [ɪ'fjʊs] v. 泻出；散发
The cave effuses a strong sense of evil.
His wearing and manner effused his affluence.

effusion [ɪ'fjuːʒn] n. 泻出；流出；展露
Acute gastroenteritis and pleural effusion may induce myositis.

effusive [ɪ'fjuːsɪv] adj. 过分热情的；[地]喷发的
He received an effusive welcome from his fans.

evince [ɪ'vɪns] v. 显示；展现
The sorcerer evinced a great interest in arcane magic.
The Arabian evinced the bitterest hatred toward Jews.

• **Words in sentences 句中单词 / 词组** •

fugitive ['fjuːdʒətɪv] n. 逃犯 adj. 短暂的（想法或感觉）

at home 在家；精通

dissident ['dɪsɪdənt] n. 异议者；不同意见的人

sap [sæp] v. 使伤元气；使削弱；使耗尽 n. 汁；笨蛋；液；容易上当的人；地道

yew [juː] n. 紫杉；红豆杉

colosseum=coliseum n.（罗马）圆形竞技场

gastroenteritis [ˌɡæstroʊˌentəˈraɪtɪs] n. 胃肠炎

pleural ['plʊərə] adj. 肋膜的；胸膜的

arcane [ɑːr'keɪn] adj. 神秘的；晦涩难解的

Part 2 补充单词 / 词组

glucose ['ɡluːkoʊs, 'ɡluːkoʊz] n. 葡萄糖
The cells break glycogen down into glucose for our body to absorb more easily.

caustic ['kɔːstɪk] n. 腐蚀剂；苛性钠；焦散曲线；焦散面 adj. 有腐蚀性的；刻薄的
The bug exuded caustic liquid when it was crushed.

escapade [ˈeskəpeɪd, ˌeskəˈpeɪd] *n.* 越轨行为；冒险行为

Her latest escapade was to strip in front of the White House.

gratitude [ˈɡrætɪtuːd] *n.* 感激

He demonstrated gratitude greatly by giving his savior five million dollars.

dilate [daɪˈleɪt] *v.* 扩大；膨胀；详述

Will you dilate on the subject? I don't get it.

alliteration [əˌlɪtəˈreɪʃn] *n.* 头韵（尤指诗歌中一组词以发音相同的辅音开头）

scansion [ˈskænʃn] *n.* 韵律

The poem uses both alliteration and strict scansion.

assonance [ˈæsənəns] *n.* 准押韵；半谐音（同元音）

The prose was enlivened by alliteration and assonance.

prosody [ˈprɑːsədi] *n.* 诗体学；韵律学

The various rhythms of prosody marked his poems.

doggerel [ˈdɔːɡərəl] *n.* 打油诗；拙劣的诗 *adj.* 打油诗的

Children still recite the lousy doggerel today.

carbohydrate [ˌkɑːrboʊˈhaɪdreɪt] *n.* 碳水化合物；糖；含糖食物

starch [stɑːrtʃ] *v.* 给……上浆；使拘谨 *n.* 淀粉；淀粉类食物

Starches are carbohydrates abundant in the seeds of cereal plants.

cereal [ˈsɪriəl] *n.* 谷类植物；谷类加工食品；麦片 *adj.* 谷类的；谷类制成的

I normally have cereal for breakfast.

Part 3　识记单词 / 词组

radiation [ˌreɪdiˈeɪʃn] *n.* 辐射；放射物

radiate from 由……散发出来

myositis [ˌmaɪəˈsaɪtis] *n.* 肌炎

saliva exude 口水流出

saliva [səˈlaɪvə] *n.* 唾液

salivate [ˈsælɪveɪt] *v.* （过量地）分泌唾液

irradiate [ɪˈreɪdieɪt] v.（用光或其他辐射）照射
stunt [stʌnt] n. 特技动作；噱头
foe [foʊ] n. 敌人
unbridled [ʌnˈbraɪdld] adj. 不受控制的；无限的
defiance [dɪˈfaɪəns] n. 蔑视
defiant [dɪˈfaɪənt] adj. 公然反抗的
defy [dɪˈfaɪ] v. 藐视；使成为不可能；向……挑战
dilation [daɪˈleɪʃn] n. 扩张
tanning [ˈtænɪŋ] n. 制革法
tannin [ˈtænɪn] n. 单宁酸
alliterate [əˈlɪtəreɪt] v. 押头韵
enliven [ɪnˈlaɪvn] v. 使更有生气（或活力）
iamb [ˈaɪæmb] n. 抑扬格；短长格
pentameter [penˈtæmɪtər] n. 五音步之诗 adj. 有五音步的
carbo [ˈkɑːrboʊ] n. 含糖食物
superheated [ˌsuːpərˈhiːtɪd] adj. 过热的
pleura [ˈplʊrə] n. 肋膜；胸膜
glycogen [ˈɡlaɪkədʒən] n. 糖原；肝糖（化）；动物淀粉
sop up 吸水
sop [sɑːp] v. 湿透 n. 面包片；湿软食物；巴结用的物品（小贿）
in confidence 秘密地

Lesson 70

Part 1 主力单词/词组

substitute [ˈsʌbstɪtuːt] v. 代替 n. 替代物；代替者
Electromagnetic weapons will substitute traditional weapons pretty soon.
Artificial intelligence is no substitute for genuine human affection.
A grateful environment is a substitute for happiness. It can quicken us from without as a

fixed hope and affection, or the consciousness of a right life, can quicken us from within. (George Santayana, Spanish-born U.S. philosopher, poet, and novelist)

surrogate ['sɜːrəgət]　*v.* 替代；代理　*n.* 替代物　*adj.* 替代的；代理的

The necklace that he gave her becomes a surrogate for his presence while they are apart and she is missing him.

A new organization of matter is building up: the technosphere or world of material goods and technological devices, or the surrogate world. (Edward Goldsmith, British business executive and ecologist)

supersede [ˌsuːpərˈsiːd]　*v.* 替代；取代

Horses have been superseded by vehicles.

China's embroideries have been superseded by photographs gradually.

I shall not be satisfied unless I produce something that shall for a few days supersede the last fashionable novel on the tables of young ladies. (Thomas Babington Macaulay, British politician, historian, and writer)

supplant [səˈplænt]　*v.* 取代；代替

Traditional folk songs were inevitably supplanted by fashionable music.

Surgeons are adept at supplanting patients' organs instead of real healing.

replace [rɪˈpleɪs]　*v.* 代替；替换

Handguns can't replace bayonets, particularly when they run out of ammunition.

vicarious [vaɪˈkeriəs]　*adj.* 感同身受的；间接获得的；代理的；异位元的（身体）

I took a vicarious pleasure for her scientific achievements.

in lieu of　（以……）替代

She decided to work harder in lieu of complaining.

• Words in sentences 句中单词 / 词组 •

technosphere ['teknəusfɪə]　*n.* (人类的) 技术领域

embroidery [ɪmˈbrɔɪdəri]　*n.* 刺绣品

handgun [ˈhændɡʌn]　*n.* 手枪

bayonet [ˈbeɪənət, ˌbeɪəˈnet, ˈbeɪənɪt]　*n.* 刺刀

ammunition [ˌæmjuˈnɪʃn]　*n.* 弹药；军火

Part 2 补充单词/词组

umpire [ˈʌmpaɪər] v. 当裁判   n. 裁判员

fair play 按规则比赛

accountability [əˌkaʊntəˈbɪləti] n. 责任；有义务

The coach bought off soccer umpires making a travesty of civility, fair play, and accountability.

arbiter [ˈɑːrbɪtər] n. 仲裁者；权威人士

The old man is a great arbiter who can settle disputes from both sides.
The designer is an arbiter of fashion.

comity [ˈkɑːmɪti] n. 礼让

The comity which exists in civilized people is a good virtue.

hector [ˈhektər] v. 欺凌；威吓   n. 作威作福的人

He hectored everybody who might turn him in.
He is a small-town hector with lots of time to bully others.

swaggering [ˈswæɡərɪŋ] adj. 趾高气扬的；神气活现的；说大话的

He was considered to be a swaggering, obnoxious bully.

douse [daʊs] v. 把……浸入水中；弄熄；泼湿；急速收（帆）

They doused the campfire to prevent forest fire.

set... ablaze 焚烧……

The Satin believer doused himself with gasoline and set himself ablaze.

vicariously [vaɪˈkeriəsli] adv. 间接感受到地；替代地

I have vicariously experienced the hardships of the poor.
One of the great attractions of patriotism—it fulfils our worst wishes. In the person of our nation we are able, vicariously, to bully and to cheat. Bully and cheat, what's more, with a feeling that we are profoundly virtuous. (Aldous Huxley, British novelist and essayist)

immerse [ɪˈmɜːrs] v. 使浸没；给……施浸礼；使埋首于；使深陷

The viewer immerses themselves vicariously into the horrific settings of that movie.

tribulation [ˌtrɪbjuˈleɪʃn] n. 苦难；磨难；苦难的缘由；烦恼事

I am inclined to think that history pays its way largely in the personal satisfaction of sitting on the fence and enjoying vicariously the trials and tribulations of men and times now ended. (Avery O. Craven, U.S. historian)

vicarious victimization 间接受害

Uncertainty about where and when the next man-made fatal virus will occur generates a fear that medical experts call "vicarious victimization."

travesty ['trævəsti] n. 嘲讽；歪曲

genuine ['dʒenjuɪn] adj. 真正的；真诚的；纯种的

affect [ə'fekt] v. 做作；假装，影响；感染

She affected indifference about his departure, though deeply hurt.
The child was affected by fever.

disaffect [ˌdɪsə'fekt] v. 使不满 adj. 不忠的；不满的

The troops were disaffected by not receiving their salary.
Disaffected persons could be used by hostile nations.

disgruntled [dɪs'grʌntld] adj. 不满的

The manager received many angry phone calls from disgruntled customers.
The coach was disgruntled by their lousy performance.

invidious [ɪn'vɪdiəs] adj. 引起反感的；招致不满的

The chief of the Department of Environmental Protection is an invidious position.
Raising taxes has put the president in an invidious position.

Part 3 识记单词 / 词组

substitute teacher 代课老师

there is no substitute for sth ……是无可替代的

a surrogate mother 一位代孕母亲

buy off 收买；贿赂

civility [sə'vɪləti] n. 彬彬有礼的行为；礼貌；客气

comity of nation 国际礼让；公平办事

theatrical troupe 剧团

theatrical [θi'ætrɪkl] n. 戏剧表演；戏剧演员 adj. 戏剧的；剧场的

sit on the fence 骑墙观望；犹豫不决

trial and tribulation 考验和磨难
swagger [ˈswæɡər] *v.* 昂首阔步地走 *n.* 神气活现
blaze [bleɪz] *v.* 使燃烧；闪耀出；爆发 *n.* 火焰；火灾；光辉；猛烈的扫射
electromagnetic [ɪˌlektroʊmæɡˈnetɪk] *adj.* 电磁的
quicken [ˈkwɪkən] *v.* 鼓舞；使复活；变快；增速
affectation [ˌæfekˈteɪʃn] *n.* 做作；假装
embroider [ɪmˈbrɔɪdər] *v.* 刺绣；绣（花样）；（对故事等）润饰；渲染
selfie [selfi] *n.* 自拍
photic [ˈfoʊtɪk] *adj.* 光的
photon [ˈfoʊtɑːn] *n.* 光子
fluence [fluːns] *n.* 注量；积分通量
fluence rate 通量率
immersion [ɪˈmɜːrʒn] *n.* 沉浸；专心；陷入
zombie debtor 僵尸债务人（指无法偿还本金，只能支付每月利息的债务人）
disgruntle [dɪsˈɡrʌntl] *v.* 使不满；使不高兴

Lesson 71

Part 1 主力单词/词组

frighten [ˈfraɪtn] *v.* 恐惧；惊吓

The situation of the mudslide is frightening.
He is audacious. I don't think he will be frightened by the lurid stage shows with fake blood spurting. Lurid gossips have become a national fixation.
How loathe were we to give up our pious belief in ghosts and witches, because we liked to persecute one and frighten ourselves to death with the other. (William Hazlitt, British essayist and critic)

consternation [ˌkɑːnstərˈneɪʃn] *n.* 惊愕；惊恐

The shooting of the president caused deep consternation in the election.

consternate [ˈkɑːnstərˌneɪt] *v.* 使震惊（惊愕）

He walked out from the deserted mansion appearing consternated.

trepidation [ˌtrepɪˈdeɪʃn] *n.* 惊恐不安（担心未来）

The U.N. sees this nation's nuclear power with some trepidation.

There are a few minutes of trepidation before announcing the exam results.

apprehension [ˌæprɪˈhenʃn] *n.* 忧虑；担心；逮捕；理解

Ordinary people have some apprehensions about the galloping future.

Mom-and-pop investors' apprehension appears to have impacted the stock market.

apprehend [ˌæprɪˈhend] *v.* 拘押；理解

He apprehends that his beloved pet will die before him.

The police apprehend a thief.

The wise man apprehends the main problem.

apprehensive [ˌæprɪˈhensɪv] *adj.* 忧虑的；善于领悟的

I know something disturbs her from her apprehensive look.

We were apprehensive about your safety.

He is smart, perceptive, and apprehensive.

phobia [ˈfoʊbiə] *n.* 恐惧；惧怕

Everyone has some sort of fear or phobia.

Phobia is an intense and persistent fear of a specific thing or situation.

claustrophobia [ˌklɔːstrəˈfoʊbiə] *n.* 幽闭恐惧症

The narrow alley evokes a sense of claustrophobia.

hydrophobia [ˌhaɪdrəˈfoʊbiə] *n.* 恐水症；狂犬病

She has hydrophobia and cannot swim.

fear [fɪr] *v.* 惧怕 *n.* 害怕

Let me assert my firm belief that the only thing we have to fear is fear itself. (Franklin D. Roosevelt, U.S. president)

Disturbing public order, you should have feared for your life.

stupefaction [ˌstuːpɪˈfækʃn] *n.* 惊愕；麻木状态

Anyone's death always releases something like an aura of stupefaction, so difficult is it to grasp this irruption of nothingness and to believe that it has actually taken place. (Gustave Flaubert, French novelist)

The teacher reproves our ingratitude and stupefaction.

This feeling of stupefaction was succeeded by a grim determination to reclaim the island at all hazards.

Lesson 71

daunt [dɔːnt] v. 吓倒；使气馁；使畏缩

The sudden explosion daunted the pedestrians for a moment.

Such a threat can only daunt a man of less intrepid mind.

claustrophobic [ˌklɔːstrəˈfoʊbɪk] n. 患幽闭恐惧症的人 adj. 引起幽闭恐惧的

• Words in sentences 句中单词 / 词组 •

gallop [ˈɡæləp] v. 奔驰 n. 飞奔

mom-and-pop [ˈmɑmənˈpɑp] n. 家庭式的小店；小生意

aura [ˈɔːrə] n. 光环；气氛；预兆

irruption [ɪˈrʌpʃn] n. (感情等) 迸发；大量繁殖；侵入

grim [ɡrɪm] adj. 严厉的；无情的；坚强的；残忍的

Part 2 补充单词 / 词组

bristle [ˈbrɪsl] v. 发怒；充满；戒备 n. 粗硬短须；刷子毛

The cat bristled owing to fear.

The official bristled at his suggestion of retirement.

The city bristled with antennas.

The mouse has short bristles called whiskers.

The paintbrush's bristles were made from animal hair.

reprove [rɪˈpruːv] v. 责备；斥责

A wise man will not reprove a fool. (Anonymous, Chinese proverb)

reproof [rɪˈpruːf] n. 责备

"May I attend the party tonight?" My mother turns to me with a look of reproof and says, "You are grounded."

My teacher gave me casual commendations and few reproofs about the assignment.

landmine [ˈlændmaɪn] n. 地雷

Landmines will explode if you step on them.

superannuated [ˌsuːpərˈænjueɪtɪd] adj. 年老退休的；落伍的；废弃的

He who has been in this company for twenty years was superannuated yesterday.

A superannuated judge turns into a corrupted lawyer.
I am just a superannuated old man who has no dream.
The old designer was too superannuated to innovate something new.

detonate ['detəneɪt] v. 使爆炸；使触发

He detonated a bomb by remote control.
The distribution of medical resources detonates controversies.

impale [ɪm'peɪl] v. 刺穿；使陷入困境

spear [spɪr] v. 用矛刺 n. 矛；持矛的人

He was impaled by a spear.

Part 3　识记单词 / 词组

irrupt [ɪ'rʌpt] v. 闯入；突然冲进

superannuate [ˌsjuːpər'ænjueɪt] v. 退休；解雇；淘汰

political persecution　政治迫害

pious hope　不切实际的希望

pious ['paɪəs] adj. 虔诚的；信神的；伪善的；尽责的

xenophobia [ˌzenə'foʊbiə] adj. 惧怕外国人的

xenophobe ['zenəfəub, 'ziː-] n. 惧怕外国人的人

xenophilia ['zenəfiliə] n. 喜欢外国

xenophile ['zenəˌfaɪl] n. 喜欢外国人的人

necrosis [ne'kroʊsɪs] n. 坏疽；骨疽；颓坏；黑斑症

tumor necrosis　肿瘤坏死

alley ['æli] n. 小巷；胡同；保龄球场

lurid ['lʊrɪd] adj. 可怕的；耸人听闻的；苍白的

fixation [fɪk'seɪʃn] n. 固定行为；固定想法

spurt [spɜːrt] v. (使)喷出；(使)涌出；(使)激增

spurt of energy　激增的能量

spurt of activity　激增的活动

persecute ['pɜːrsɪkjuːt] v. (尤指宗教或政治信仰的)迫害；烦扰

persecution [ˌpɜːrsɪ'kjuːʃn] n. 迫害

episode ['epɪsoʊd] n. 事件；一节（尤指电视或广播节目的）

assertion [ə'sɜːrʃn] *n.* 断言；声明
detonation [ˌdetə'neɪʃn] *n.* 引爆；爆炸
remote control 遥控（器）

Lesson 72

Part 1　主力单词 / 词组

lucid ['luːsɪd] *adj.* 清晰的；头脑清楚的；清澈的；充满光的
We are snorkeling in the lucid sea of the San Francisco Bay.
He's a muddle-headed fool, with frequent lucid intervals. (Miguel de Cervantes, Spanish novelist and dramatist)
Ordinarily, he is insane, but he has lucid moments when he is only stupid. (Heinrich Heine, German poet)

sane [seɪn] *adj.* 心智正常的；头脑清醒的
He was sane when he wrote his will.
There is less harm to be suffered in being mad among madmen than in being sane all by oneself. (Denis Diderot, French encyclopedist and philosopher)

clarity ['klærəti] *n.* 清晰；清楚
Maintaining a sense of clarity on confusing international issues is crucial for the president.
He has momentary clarity although his illness is very serious.
The writing has been condensed and edited for clarity.

articulate [ɑːr'tɪkjuleɪt, ɑːr'tɪkjələt] *v.* 清楚地讲话；使相互连贯　*adj.* 发音清晰的
So irate was he that he was hardly articulate.
Bones more often articulate with others.

pellucid [pə'luːsɪd] *adj.* 清澈的；明白的
Pellucid prose is easy to be understood.

• Words in sentences 句中单词 / 词组 •

irate [aɪ'reɪt, 'aɪreɪt] *n.* 发怒的；生气的

Part 2 补充单词/词组

inarticulate [ˌɪnɑːrˈtɪkjələt] *adj.* 口齿不清的；难以言喻的
The doctor had to deal with the baby's inarticulate fear.
Society functions on many inarticulate rules.

alembic [əˈlembɪk] *n.* 净化；淬炼
The poem was made in the alembic of the author's own imagination.
Philosophy was percolated through the alembic of his mind.
The literature was made by the alembic of his genius.

alembicated [əlembɪˈkeɪtɪd] *adj.* 过分精炼的
The story was alembicated into an excellent allegory.

fjord=fiord *n.* 峡湾

inlet [ˈɪnlet] *n.* 小湾；小港；入口
The fjord is a narrow inlet flanked by steep mountains on either side.

probate [ˈproʊbeɪt] *v.* 遗嘱检验 *n.* 遗嘱检验
The will has to be probated before his son's inheritance.

canon [ˈkænən] *n.* 准则；法规；教规

macroeconomics [ˌmækroʊˌiːkəˈnɑːmɪks, ˌmækroʊˌekəˈnɑːmɪks] *n.* 宏观经济学
You have to understand the fundamental canons of supply and demand before studying macroeconomics.

wade [weɪd] *v.* 艰难地前进；费力地做完
We waded across a pellucid stream.

crucial point 关键点；要害
The crucial point for a successful marriage is to compromise.

crucial turning point 关键转折点
The battle of the Midway Islands was the crucial turning point of World War Two.

Part 3 识记单词/词组

lucidity [luːˈsɪdəti] *n.* 明白；透明；洞察力
articulation [ɑːrˌtɪkjuˈleɪʃn] *n.* 表达；说话；吐字

the alembic of fate 命运的造化

the alembic of grief 忧伤带来的净化

the alembic of wind 风带来的净化

sickbay ['sɪkˌbeɪ] *n.* (尤指船上的) 医务室

bay [beɪ] *n.* 海湾；限定区域；月桂树

bay for blood 要求暴力相向；要求惩罚 (某人)

at bay (动物) 被包围；走投无路

hold/keep sb/sth at bay 阻止；遏制 (令人不快的事物)

nosedive ['noʊzdaɪv] *n.* 俯冲；(价格等的) 猛跌

dive in/dive into sth 贸然投入到……之中；介入

snorkel ['snɔːrkl] *v.* 潜泳 *n.* 水下呼吸管

amplitude ['æmplɪtuːd] *n.* (声音、无线电波等的) 振幅

incline [ɪn'klaɪn] *v.* 倾向于 *n.* 斜坡

recline [rɪ'klaɪn] *v.* 向后倾；斜倚

recumbent [rɪ'kʌmbənt] *adj.* 躺着的；躺倒的

insane [ɪn'seɪn] *adj.* 疯癫的；精神失常的

insanity [ɪn'sænəti] *n.* 精神错乱；精神失常

delirious [dɪ'lɪriəs] *adj.* 精神混乱的；非常激动的

delirium [dɪ'lɪriəm] *n.* 神智不清；语无伦次；狂喜

condensation [ˌkɑːndenˈseɪʃn] *n.* 凝结；凝结物；浓缩

condensate ['kɑːndənˌseɪt, kənˈdenˌseɪt] *n.* 浓缩物

microeconomics ['maɪkroʊˌiːkəˈnɑːmɪks] *n.* 微观经济学

colossal [kəˈlɑːsl] *adj.* 巨大的

Lesson 73

Part 1　主力单词 / 词组

multitude ['mʌltɪtuːd] *n.* 大众；人群；大量；许多

The bishop addresses the multitude below.

I have many times asked myself whether there can be more potent advocates of peace upon earth through the years to come than this massed multitude of silent witnesses to the desolation of war. (George V, British monarch)

The value of history lies not in the multitude of facts collected, but in their relation to each, and in this respect an author can have no larger responsibility than any other scientific observer. (Brooks Adams, U.S. historian)

horde [hɔːrd]   n. 一大群

A horde of students rushes out of school after class.

preponderance [prɪˈpɑːndərəns]   n. 大多数；优势；优越

The United States enjoys overwhelming military preponderance.

predominate [prɪˈdɑːmɪneɪt]   v. 占优势；控制

Sparrows predominate the area.

Christianity predominated over other ancient European religions.

cohort [ˈkoʊhɔːrt]   n. 一群；同伴；追随者

The priest summoned a cohort of angels expelling a demon and dispelling his horror.

People tend to get cheated on in this age cohort.

The government resolves to hunt down the terrorist leader and his cohort.

echelon [ˈeʃəlɑːn]   n. 阶层；职权的等级；（士兵、飞机等的）梯形编队

I was wondering how people live in the upper echelon of society.

The general divided his army into three square echelons, two in front, one in the rear.

ring [rɪŋ]   v. 打电话；响起铃声；包围；环绕   n. 环（状物）；戒指环；团伙；竞技场；圆形炉盘

Don't hang around with a gambling ring or a drug ring because you might get addicted to gambling or drugs.

concourse [ˈkɑːnkɔːrs]   n. 群众；聚集；广场；宽敞的大厅

An immense concourse of sympathizing friends and neighbors accompany him to the court.

Train station passengers have to go through checkpoints before entering the concourse.

generality [ˌdʒenəˈræləti]   n. 主要部分；普遍性；概括的表述

The generality of people is unsatisfied with the economic stimulating plan.

She talked in generality, not specifically.

Lesson 73

> • Words in sentences 句中单词 / 词组 •
>
> **summon** [ˈsʌmən] v. 召唤；传唤
> **dispel** [dɪˈspel] v. 消除（恐惧、疑虑）；驱散

Part 2 补充单词 / 词组

impotent [ˈɪmpətənt] adj. 无能的；虚弱的
The impotent commander will get us all killed.

gruesome [ˈgruːsəm] adj. 可怕的；阴森的
Catholics had a great appetite for reading about gruesome diseases, specially those involving the rotting or falling off of parts of the body. (Mary McCarthy, U.S. writer)

starlet [ˈstɑːrlət] n. 崭露头角的年轻女演员；小明星；小星星
The leading actress is surrounded by a bevy of starlets.

cherub [ˈtʃerəb] n. 小天使；天真无邪的可爱儿童
Satan and fallen cherubs tried to fight Jesus but it was in vain.

cherubic [tʃəˈruːbɪk] adj. 天使的；无邪的；可爱的
She has a cherubic smile.

consort [ˈkɑːnsɔːrt] v. 陪伴；使联系 n. 配偶；随航船只；演奏者
I will not consort with such kind of people.
The king ruled in consort with his queen.
I caught a criminal, but his consorts got away.
Illustrations consort with the text for stock shareholders.

diabolical [ˌdaɪəˈbɑːlɪkl] adj. 恶魔的；残忍的
These patriots have succeeded in putting an end to the traitors' diabolical plot of using biological weapons for mass destruction.

maul [mɔːl] v. 抓伤；批评；粗手粗脚地摆弄 n. 大木槌
She was mauled by low-caste men in India.
He fell down into a cage and was mauled by a lion.
The police don't want to be mauled by the mob.

pursuant to 按照（尤指规则或法律）

pursuant [pərˈsuːənt] *adj.* 追逐的

The government continued its heavy procurement of arms from abroad pursuant to its aim of becoming the dominant military power in Aisa.

I smelled a pursuant reek from the stable.

Part 3 识记单词 / 词组

preponderant [prɪˈpɑːndərənt] *adj.* 大多数的；优势的；压倒性的
bevy [ˈbevi] *n.* 一批；一群；一团
demonic [dɪˈmɑːnɪk] *adj.* 恶魔的
the multitude (the multitudes) 人群；大众
run rings round sb 遥遥领先（某人）；出色
a preponderance of people 大多数人
bishop [ˈbɪʃəp] *n.* 主教
potent [ˈpoʊtnt] *adj.* 强有力的；有权势的；有影响的
desolation [ˌdesəˈleɪʃn] *n.* 孤寂；荒芜；荒凉

Lesson 74

Part 1 主力单词 / 词组

bother [ˈbɑːðər] *v.* 使担心；打扰 *n.* 麻烦；问题

There being two rotten candidates, I did not bother to vote.

Sorry to bother you so late at night. Did you see my kitty?

"Experts" are those who don't need to bother with elementary questions anymore—thus, they fail to "bother" with the true sources of bottlenecks, buried deep in the habitual routines of the firm, labeled "we've always done it that way." (Tom Peters, U.S. management consultant and author)

If his virtues get mixed up with personal bothers, the saint might react just like ordinary people do.

annoy [əˈnɔɪ] *v.* 使恼怒

My work is supposed to be so perfect. Nonetheless, minor quibbles really annoy me.

Lesson 74

irritate [ˈɪrɪteɪt] *v.* 使生气

importunate [ɪmˈpɔːrtʃənət] *adj.* 纠缠不休的
The importunate insurance salesman really irritates me.

choleric [ˈkɑːlərɪk] *adj.* 易怒的；暴躁的
Her mood has been cryptic, occasionally choleric.

harass [həˈræs, ˈhærəs] *v.* 骚扰
Electors were harassed and intimidated by left-wing dissidents.

harry [ˈhæri] *v.* 骚扰；攻击
Senators were harried by a new lobby.
Rebels continued to harry the village.

nettle [ˈnetl] *v.* 激怒；惹恼 *n.* 荨麻
He blamed me in front of everybody which really nettled me.

disturb [dɪˈstɜːrb] *v.* 打扰；使焦虑；使烦恼
The gossip disturbed my peace of mind.

perturb [pərˈtɜːrb] *v.* 使不安；烦扰；使混乱
The boss was perturbed by the strike of union workers.

irk [ɜːrk] *v.* 使厌烦；使恼火
Her consistent rejection irks me.

rile [raɪl] *v.* 使生气；使水混浊
Her sanctimonious tone really riles me up.

umbrage [ˈʌmbrɪdʒ] *n.* 生气；恼怒；模糊的建议；怀疑
He took umbrage at his disrespectful remark.
Some cryptocurrency zealots take great umbrage with this depreciation.

pique [piːk] *v.* 使生气；激起 *n.* 激起；生气
His liberal speech might pique conservatives.
Umbrage is a feeling of pique.
The celebrity's sly remark piques more curiosity
The first non-partisan bombast stirred my heart, the second florid declamation piqued my sense of concentration and the rest of them had me checking my watch.
He piqued himself as the moral police.

gadfly ['gædflaɪ] *n.* 有意困扰他人者；讨厌的人；形似苍蝇

There are two gadflies beside that beautiful girl.

He is nothing but a political gadfly.

gall [gɔːl] *v.* 使恼怒；磨损；烦恼 *n.* 怨恨；厚颜无耻；鲁莽

Her criticism galled me for a week.

The saddle galled my thigh.

I don't have the gall to borrow money from him twice.

rankle ['ræŋkl] *v.* 使怨恨；使痛苦；化脓

Japan's atrocity in World War Two still rankles Chinese today.

testy ['testi] *adj.* 易怒的；暴躁的

He is very testy with his servants.

badger ['bædʒər] *v.* 困扰；纠缠 *n.* 獾

cryptic ['krɪptɪk] *adj.* 隐秘的；费解的；有密码的

exasperate [ɪɡ'zæspəreɪt] *v.* 激怒；使恼火；加剧

irritable ['ɪrɪtəbl] *adj.* 易怒的；烦躁的；过敏的

importune [ˌɪmpɔːr'tuːn] *v.* 强求

irksome ['ɜːrksəm] *adj.* 使人烦恼的；令人生气的

• Words in sentences 句中单词 / 词组

quibble ['kwɪbl] *v.* 争论 *n.* 小批评

intimidate [ɪn'tɪmɪdeɪt] *v.* 威胁；恐吓

senator ['senətər] *n.* 参议员

lobby ['lɑːbi] *n.* 前厅 *v.* 游说

gossip ['ɡɑːsɪp] *v.* 说三道四 *n.* 流言

disrespectful [ˌdɪsrɪ'spektfl] *adj.* 无礼的；不敬重的

conservative [kən'sɜːrvətɪv] *n.* 保守的人 *adj.* 保守的；守旧的

sly [slaɪ] *adj.* 躲躲闪闪的；狡猾的；机智的

non-partisan [ˌnɑːn'pɑːrtəzn] *adj.* 非党派的

Lesson 74

stir [stɜːr] *v.* 搅拌；打动 *n.* 搅动；搅拌
florid [ˈflɔːrɪd] *adj.* 过分华丽的；红润的
declamation [ˌdekləˈmeɪʃn] *n.* 慷慨激昂的演讲；朗诵；大声宣布

Part 2 补充单词 / 词组

molder [ˈmoʊldər] *v.* 使腐朽；使衰退 *n.* 制模者；模；薄板坯；造型物
The smell of moldering trash was stinky.

compost [ˈkɑːmpoʊst] *v.* 将……制成堆肥 *n.* 堆肥；混合物
The odor of moldering leaf in the compost was in the air.

pedestal [ˈpedɪstl] *v.* 支持 *n.* (雕像等的) 垫座；柱脚
The statue falls from the pedestal.

mold [moʊld] *n.* 霉菌；模型；塑造

fungi [ˈfʌndʒaɪ, ˈfʌŋgaɪ, ˈfʌŋgiː] *n.* 真菌（复数）
Molds and fungi tend to grow in humid environments.

hyphae [ˈhaifi] *n.* 菌丝（复数）
Each fungus has hyphae that feed and reproduce.

fungus [ˈfʌŋgəs] *n.* 真菌；菌类植物

mycelium [maɪˈsiːliəm] *n.* 菌丝（整个的）

tubular [ˈtuːbjələr] *adj.* 管状的；管子做成的；有管的

filament [ˈfɪləmənt] *n.* 细丝；(电灯泡的) 白热丝；灯丝
Mycelium is a loose network of threadlike, tubular filaments called hyphae which form the body of a fungus.

popinjay [ˈpɑːpɪndʒeɪ] *n.* 高傲；爱装腔作势的人

bombast [ˈbɑːmbæst] *n.* 浮夸的言语；大话；空话
A popinjay replied with bombast.

hidebound [ˈhaɪdbaʊnd] *adj.* 迂腐的；保守的；皮包骨的
If you are hidebound with prejudice, if your temper is sentimental, you can go through the wards of a hospital and be as ignorant of man at the end as you were at the beginning.

The hidebound cattle need to be fed.

aristocrat [əˈrɪstəkræt]   *n.* 贵族；持贵族观点的人；（同类事物中的）佼佼者
Do you think you can win freedom by simply fighting off these hidebound aristocrats? You are too naïve.

prim [prɪm]   *v.* 使显得一本正经   *adj.* 呆板的；拘谨的；整齐的
She prims her hair before going out.
His remark was prim and proper.
The hedges surrounding the park were so prim.

primp [prɪmp]   *v.* （精心地）打扮；装饰
The star primps for an hour before getting onstage.

hidalgo [hɪˈdælˌɡoʊ]   *n.* （西班牙阶层最低的）贵族
There is an impoverished hidalgo who lived outside the town.

loosen [ˈluːsn]   *v.* 释放；松开
I loosened the laces of my shoes before I wore them.

on the loose   不受约束的；自由的
The criminal is still on the loose.

antiquarian [ˌæntɪˈkweriən]   *n.* 古董商；古文物研究   *adj.* 古文物的
There is a musty, antiquarian bookstore.

Part 3 识记单词/词组

bombastic [bɑːmˈbæstɪk]   *adj.* 夸夸其谈的；大话连篇的
aristocratic [əˌrɪstəˈkrætɪk]   *adj.* 贵族的；仪态高贵的；主张贵族统治的；势利的
apical [ˈæpɪkəl]   *adj.* 顶上的；顶点的
communal [kəˈmjuːnl]   *adj.* 公共的；社区的
communal fund   共享基金
communal life   集体生活
bottleneck [ˈbɑːtlnek]   *n.* 瓶颈；阻碍；瓶颈路段（常引起交通堵塞）
cyptocurrency [ˈkrɪptoʊˌkɜːrənsi]   *n.* 加密电子钱
ribbed [rɪbd]   *adj.* 有罗纹的

tortoise [ˈtɔːrtəs] *n.* 海龟
rayon [ˈreɪɑːn] *n.* 人造丝
jay [dʒeɪ] *n.* 松鸦；爱唠叨的人；傻瓜
declaim [dɪˈkleɪm] *v.* 慷慨陈词
rot [rɑːt] *v.* 使腐烂 *n.* 蠢事；荒唐事
can't be bothered 懒得（做）；不想费力
sexual harassment 性骚扰
a pose attitude 一种摆出的姿势
rile someone up 使某人生气
florid decoration 过分华丽的装饰
florid complexion 气色好的脸
complexion [kəmˈplekʃn] *n.* 肤色；气色
musty [ˈmʌsti] *adj.* 发霉的

Lesson 75

Part 1 主力单词/词组

squander [ˈskwɑːndər] *v.* 浪费；挥霍；糟蹋（机会）
I have squandered my time and money on circumnavigating the world.
The manager has squandered his leverage and has little control over his staff.
You just squandered this once in a lifetime opportunity.

profligate [ˈprɑːflɪɡət] *n.* 挥霍的人；低道德标准的人 *adj.* 挥霍的；低道德标准的
Our profligate consumption of wooden materials has increased global deforestation at an alarming rate.
The wasteful and profligate king had been ousted by his subjects.
He outvoted other candidates by profligate muckraking propaganda which is in a grey area of legitimacy.

profligacy [ˈprɑːflɪɡəsi] *n.* 挥霍；浪费

dissipate [ˈdɪsɪpeɪt] *v.* 逐渐浪费掉；逐渐消失

He has been dissipating his father's fortune on plush, sumptuous, lavish banquets and parties.

prodigal [ˈprɑːdɪgl] *adj.* 挥金如土的；非常浪费的

The prodigal son squanders his inheritance.

If one can call the Creator to account, then I think he ought to be faulted for being too prodigal in the creation of life and too prodigal in its destruction. (Lu Xun, Chinese writer)

wastrel [ˈweɪstrəl] *n.* 挥霍者；废品 *adj.* 浪费的；挥霍的

The wastrel disrupted his parents' placid life.

The man of means was conspicuously wastrel.

In his wastrel days, he wandered around the city.

fop [fɑːp] *n.* 纨绔子弟；过分讲究衣饰或举动的人

There is a congregation of prodigal sons, wastrels, and fops.

foppish [ˈfɑːpɪʃ] *adj.* 纨绔子弟的；矫揉造作的

dandy [ˈdændi] *n.* 花花公子 *adj.* 上等的；极好的

He is a foppish dandy who likes to flirt with young, beautiful girls.

fritter [ˈfrɪtər] *v.* 浪费；减少；消散 *n.* 油炸面团（带馅）

Frittering money is easier than saving it.

The investing capital was frittered away on grandiose schemes and unrealistic projects.

I don't want to eat that banana fritter.

• Words in sentences 句中单词/词组 •

oust [aʊst] *v.* 废黜；淘汰；取代

plush [plʌʃ] *adj.* 奢华的

lavish [ˈlævɪʃ] *adj.* 奢华的

banquet [ˈbæŋkwɪt] *n.* 宴会

inheritance [ɪnˈherɪtəns] *n.* 遗产

account [əˈkaʊnt] *v.* 报导；视为 *n.* 账户；主顾

Part 2　补充单词 / 词组

primogeniture [ˌpraɪmoʊˈdʒenɪtʃər]　*n.* 长子身份；长子继承权

He went first in the funeral process according to his primogeniture.
Some Chinese still practice primogeniture.

primogenitor [ˌpraɪməˈdʒenətər]　*n.* 始祖；祖先

Our primogenitors arrived on this island 200 years ago.

codicil [ˈkɑːdəsl]　*n.* 遗嘱的附录；附加条款

A codicil is an extra part of a will.

testator [ˈtesteɪtər, tesˈteɪtər]　*n.* 立遗嘱者；留有遗嘱者

The lawyer offers her advice to a testator.

appointee [əˌpɔɪnˈtiː]　*n.* 被任命者；被指定的财产受益人

executor [ɪɡˈzekjətər]　*n.* 执行者；实行者；遗嘱执行人

Instituted executors are the initial appointees of testators in his will, there being no other substituted executors.

Part 3　识记单词 / 词组

strike camp　拆除帐篷
on strike　参与罢工
go on strike　举行罢工
strike force　快速反应部队；快速行动部队
strike up...　开始（演奏）；开始（唱）；建立（关系）；开始（交谈）
strike sth out/through=cross out　划掉；删去（文档中无关或错误之处）
strike out　独立开创新事业
strike out at (sb/sth)　打（某人）；试图打（某人）；公开批评（某人或事）
strike sb down　使（某人）猝然死去；使（某人）病倒
strike back　反击；回击
strike sth down　裁定（某法律条文）非法
strike sb off (sth)　取消（医生、律师等）的执业资格
strike on sth　发现；想起

within striking distance　距离很近；近在咫尺；唾手可得
strike while the iron is hot　趁热打铁
be struck dumb　震惊得哑口无言
strike it rich　一夜暴富；发横财
strike it lucky　意外交好运
strike a balance　求得平衡
strike a blow against/at sth　严重伤害；沉重打击
strike a blow for sth　维护；支援；捍卫
strike a chord　引起共鸣；得到赞同；拨动心弦；使触景生情
strike a note　表达看法；传达感觉
strike at the heart of sth　攻击……的要害；沉重打击
strike an attitude　装腔作势；装模作样
strike fear/terror into sb　使（某人）极度恐惧
strike gold　（在体育比赛中）夺金
strike home　命中预定目标；达到预期效果

Lesson 76

Part 1　主力单词 / 词组

delay [dɪ'leɪ]　*v.* (使) 延迟　*n.* 延误；延期
I delayed my departure for your sake.
The storm caused some delays and postponements in the construction project.
The rapprochement might be just another of his delay tactics.

put off　推迟；拖延；脱去（衣、帽等）
Get your home assignment done today. Don't always put it off until tomorrow.

procrastinate [prə'kræstɪneɪt]　*v.* 拖延；耽搁
The referendum has been procrastinated indefinitely.
I am not allowed to procrastinate, stall, or evade the project. It has to be done on time.

Lesson 76

putter [ˈpʌtər] v. 闲荡；噗噗作响（机器慢速运转时） n.（高尔夫）轻击者

There is a trend to putter around in the house and garden.

The putter of an old tank was kind of annoying.

par [pɑːr] v. 标准杆数得分 n. 标准杆数（高尔夫球）；推杆 adj. 标准的

A good putter is needed to break par.

dawdle [ˈdɔːdl] v. 磨蹭；浪费（时间等）；闲混；偷懒；游荡

He keeps dawdling around, playing video games and putting off something that should be done.

Stop dawdling. We're about to be late for the movie.

Her idle talk with strangers in the vestibule dawdles the day away.

loiter [ˈlɔɪtər] v. 磨蹭；溜达；闲逛

He had gone to the city and loitered in the vicinity of the haunted yard.

> • Words in sentences 句中单词/词组 •
>
> **stall** [stɔːl] v. 拖延 n. 摊位；售货亭；分隔间
>
> **tank** [tæŋk] v. 彻底失败；破产 n. 罐；贮水池；池塘；战车
>
> **vestibule** [ˈvestɪbjuːl] v. 为……设置门廊；以通廊连接 n. 门厅；前厅；通廊
>
> **haunted** [ˈhɔːntɪd] adj. 闹鬼的；焦虑不安的

Part 2　补充单词/词组

doff [dɔːf] v. 脱（衣、帽等）；举帽（致意）

The citizens welcome and doff their hats to the mayor.

waterspout [ˈwɔːtərspaʊt] n. 暴雨；海龙卷；喷水器；排水口

The boat turns left, trying to avoid the waterspout.

spout [spaʊt] v. 喷出 n. 水柱

These wells spout oil day and night.

The candidate goes on spouting empty promises and bad checks.

The pipe was broken and shot out a spout of water.

propinquity [prəˈpɪŋkwəti]　*n.* 接近；亲近关系（血统上的）；类似

Territorial propinquity has given the country special interests in Mongolia.

The relative may help me for the sake of the propinquity of kin.

blizzard [ˈblɪzərd]　*n.* 暴风雪

We can go out again when the blizzard subsides.

whiteout [ˈwaɪtaʊt]　*n.* 零可见度（大雪、大雾引起的）；因白化引起的临时失明

The massive blizzard caused whiteout conditions on the road.

subside [səbˈsaɪd]　*v.* 消退；平息；跪下；躺倒

I will speak to him after his anger/ fever subsides.

He subsided into a chair, exhausted.

frostbite [ˈfrɔːstbaɪt]　*n.* 冻伤；霜害

Fire can prevent frostbite.

amputate [ˈæmpjuteɪt]　*v.* 截（肢）

His right leg got severe frostbite that had to be amputated.

vaguely [ˈveɪgli]　*adv.* （形状等）模糊不清地；（想法等）不明确地；暧昧地

Frost formed on the window. I can only see outside vaguely.

hypothermia [ˌhaɪpəˈθɜːrmiə]　*n.* 低体温症；体温过低

Neither of them has the energy to walk. If they don't make a snow shelter soon, they will suffer from hypothermia.

regulate [ˈreɡjuleɪt]　*v.* 校准；管理；制订规章

Alcohol makes a body harder to regulate temperature.

dermatologist [ˌdɜːrməˈtɑːlədʒɪst]　*n.* 皮肤学者；皮肤科医生

dermabrasion [ˌdɜːrməˈbreɪʒən]　*n.* 磨去皮肤疤痕之手术

The doctor is a famous dermatologist who specializes in dermabrasion.

pachyderm [ˈpækidɜːrm]　*n.* 厚皮动物

Hippopotamuses and elephants are pachyderm species.

domino effect　多米诺骨牌效应

Asia's recession has had a domino effect on the European Union.

Part 3 识记单词 / 词组

thermometer [θərˈmɑːmɪtər]   n. 温度计
hypo- 低的；下面的
thermo- 热的
hypodermis [ˌhaɪpəˈdɜːrmɪs]   n. 皮下组织；[植] 下皮
dermis [ˈdɜːrmɪs]   n. 真皮；皮肤
dermatology [ˌdɜːrməˈtɑːlədʒi]   n. 皮肤医学
derm [ˈdɜːrm]   n. 皮肤
regulation [ˌreɡjuˈleɪʃn]   n. 章程；法则
white out 用修正液掩盖错字
procrastination [prəˌkræstɪˈneɪʃn]   n. 拖延
frost [frɔːst]   v. 结霜   n. 严寒天气
amputation [ˌæmpjuˈteɪʃn]   n. 截肢；删除
amputee [ˌæmpjuˈtiː]   n. 被截肢者
vague [veɪɡ]   adj. 含糊的

Lesson 77

Part 1 主力单词 / 词组

lead to 造成；导致

The invasion led to the downfall of the Byzantine Empire which had wheezed to its end.
The historian's thorough investigation has led to the discovery of the hidden pyramid.

bring about 引起；导致

Desperate search does not always bring about the lost item to be found.

give rise to 造成；导致

Independent maneuvers are not resorted to, as they are believed to give rise to more problems.

result in 造成；导致

They refused to compromise which resulted in a stalemate.

occasion [əˈkeɪʒn] *v.* 造成 *n.* 场合

The global threat has occasioned this nuclear talk between Trump and Py Yong.

precipitate [prɪˈsɪpɪteɪt] *v.* 造成；陡降；派遣 *n.* 沉淀物 *adj.* 突然的

The sales failure of the iPhone precipitated retrenchment in China.

spawn [spɔːn] *v.* 产卵；造成 *n.* 卵

His fame has spawned a host of imitators and imposters.

engender [ɪnˈdʒendər] *v.* 造成；产生

The issue of abortion engendered further controversy.

trigger [ˈtrɪgər] *v.* 引起 *n.* 起因；触发器

The trigger of World War One was the assassination of the prince of an empire, carried out by an inconsequential man.

whip up 激起（强烈的情感）

The racist had tried to whip up anti-immigrant prejudice.

attribute [əˈtrɪbjuːt] *v.* 把……归因于 *n.* 特征；属性

He has attributed his success to hard work.

His resignation was attributed to bribery.

ascribe [əˈskraɪb] *v.* 归咎；赋予

He ascribed his pride to his remarkable achievement.

The presidential candidate refused to ascribe certain traits to the Latin American population.

ascription [əˈskrɪpʃn] *n.* 归属

The ascription of the domestic role to the female is common in an agricultural society.

The ascription of the ancient text to Pharaoh remains questionable.

contribute [kənˈtrɪbjuːt] *v.* 贡献

contribute to 导致；造成

Carbon dioxide contributed to global warming.

accredit [əˈkredɪt] *v.* 认可；授权；归咎于

Diplomats accredited to United Nations will not be expelled.

The doctor accredits the dim memory as a side effect of the treatment.

impute [ɪmˈpjuːt] *v.* 归咎于；归罪于；归因于；嫁祸于

He imputed his failure on the exam to bad study habits.

The psychic imputes evil to anyone who disagrees with him.

Lesson 77

court [kɔːrt]　v. 向……献殷勤　n. 法院；庭院

The unseemly jostling over who the members of the Supreme Court are has courted controversy.

cause [kɔːz]　v. 引起；导致　n. 原因；事业

We are not ashamed of what we have done, because, when you have a great cause to fight for, the moment of greatest humiliation is the moment when the spirit is proudest.

enmity [ˈenməti]　n. 仇恨；敌意

underlie [ˌʌndərˈlaɪ]　v. 是……的主因；是……的深层原因；对……有重大影响

Historical enmity toward Israel underlies this terror attack.

animadversion [ˌænəmædˈvɜːrʃən]　n. 责备；责难；批评

In the international waters, France carried out the nuclear test project under international animadversion.

● Words in sentences 句中单词 / 词组 ●

stalemate [ˈsteɪlmeɪt]　n. 僵局
retrenchment [rɪˈtrentʃmənt]　n. 紧缩开支；削减费用
a host of 很多的
imitator [ˈɪmɪteɪtər]　n. 模仿者
imposter [ɪmˈpɑstər]　n. 冒名者
controversy [ˈkɑːntrəvɜːrsi]　n. 争议；民事纠纷
inconsequential [ɪnˌkɑːnsɪˈkwenʃl]　adj. 微不足道的；不重要的
anti-immigrant [ˈæntiˈɪmɪɡrənt]　n. 反移民
bribery [ˈbraɪbəri]　n. 贿赂
dim [dɪm]　v. 使变暗淡；使变模糊　adj. 微暗的；模糊的
psychic [ˈsaɪkɪk]　n. 巫师　adj. 通灵的；超自然的
unseemly [ʌnˈsiːmli]　adj. 不合适的
humiliation [hjuːˌmɪliˈeɪʃn]　n. 羞辱；蒙羞

Part 2　补充单词 / 词组

imposture [ɪmˈpɑːstʃər]　n. 冒名行骗

Imposture requires a peculiar talent, fitness for gaining admission into the upper social classes.

controvert [ˈkɑːntrəvɜːrt] *v.* 争议；争论；反驳
The evidence controverted his story

migrant [ˈmaɪɡrənt] *n.* 移民；候鸟 *adj.* 流动的；移民的
African migrants search for jobs in Europe.
Singapore has a lot of Indonesian migrant workers.

migratory [ˈmaɪɡrətɔːri] *adj.* 迁移的；有迁居习惯（或特色）的；流浪的
Wild geese are migratory birds.

deadlock [ˈdedlɑːk] *v.* 陷入僵局 *n.* 僵局
They ended the deadlock with a compromise.

standstill [ˈstændstɪl] *n.* 停止；停顿；停滞不前
His business comes to a standstill due to the outbreak of coronavirus.

jostle [ˈdʒɑːsl] *v.* 挤；推；撞
Due to too many people during the national festival, we have to jostle our way to the gate.

gargle [ˈɡɑːrɡl] *v.* 漱口 *n.* 漱口药
He sniffed his own exhalation and gargled before a meeting.

frieze [friːz] *n.* 带状物；檐壁饰带（室内或屋顶下方墙壁的）

gargoyle [ˈɡɑːrɡɔɪl] *n.* 滴水嘴；滴水兽；形象怪异的人
The frieze of stone griffins frequently served as gargoyles surrounding Gothic architecture.

gullet [ˈɡʌlɪt] *n.* 食道；咽喉；海峡；峡谷
The words stuck in my gullet didn't come out.

parsimony [ˈpɑːrsɪmoʊni] *n.* 吝啬；过于俭省
He is not a miser and won't accept the imputation of parsimony.

Part 3 识记单词 / 词组

imputation [ˌɪmpjuˈteɪʃn] *n.* 指责；归罪；毁谤；诋毁

to wreak havoc 制造破坏或混乱

psychism [saɪˈkɪzəm] *n.* 心灵论

jostle for sth 为……竞争；争夺

Byzantine Empire 拜占庭帝国

retrench their expenditure　削减他们的费用
parsimonious [ˌpɑːrsɪˈmoʊniəs]　*adj.* 吝啬的；过于俭省的
hidden [ˈhɪdn]　*adj.* 隐藏的；不为人知的
pyramid [ˈpɪrəmɪd]　*v.* 使节节增加　*n.* 金字塔
resort to　诉诸；采取
downfall [ˈdaʊnfɔːl]　*n.* 垮台；衰败
wheeze [wiːz]　*v.* 喘　*n.* 喘息声
impasse [ˈɪmpæs]　*n.* 僵局
stale [steɪl]　*adj.* 不新鲜的；厌倦的
expenditure [ɪkˈspendɪtʃər]　*n.* 开支；耗费；花费（精力、时间或钱）
anthem [ˈænθəm]　*n.* 国歌；（团体组织的）颂歌；赞歌
patriot [ˈpeɪtriət]　*n.* 爱国者
choir [ˈkwaɪər]　*n.* 合唱队；唱诗班
hymn [hɪm]　*n.* 圣歌；赞美歌
courtship [ˈkɔːrtʃɪp]　*n.* 求爱期；恋爱期
suffrage [ˈsʌfrɪdʒ]　*n.* 选举权；投票权
griffon [ˈɡrɪfən]　*n.* 半狮半鹫的怪兽；兀鹫

Lesson 78

Part 1　主力单词 / 词组

cruel [ˈkruːəl]　*adj.* 残忍的
The crowd can be easily incited by reformers to be evil and cruel.

brutal [ˈbruːtl]　*adj.* 野蛮的；残忍的
Jews experienced a brutal and savage attack by Germans in a racial cleansing.

callous [ˈkæləs]　*adj.* 麻木不仁的；不关心他人的；长茧的
His callous comment has shocked all of us.

ruthless [ˈruːθləs] *adj.* 残酷无情的

The ruthless kidnapper ordered his accomplices to kill them all, taking no hostages as police arrived.

merciless [ˈmɜːrsɪləs] *adj.* 残忍的

Merciless oppression of peasants precipitates revolution.

> • Words in sentences 句中单词 / 词组 •
>
> **racial cleansing** 种族屠杀
> **kidnapper** [ˈkɪdnæpər] *n.* 绑架者
> **accomplice** [əˈkɑːmplɪs] *n.* 共犯；帮凶
> **oppression** [əˈpreʃn] *n.* 压迫
> **peasant** [ˈpeznt] *n.* 农民
> **revolution** [ˌrevəˈluːʃn] *n.* 革命

Part 2 补充单词 / 词组

softball [ˈsɔːftbɔːl] *n.* 垒球

Softball is a game similar to baseball but played with a larger ball.

run the gauntlet 受批评

The senator ran the gauntlet by reporters for not taking any precautions against the virus.

benighted [bɪˈnaɪtɪd] *adj.* 未开化的；陷入黑暗的

Barbarians are benighted.

There are benighted African people living in this jungle.

Benighted travelers use their torch to light the mountain path.

coalition [ˌkoʊəˈlɪʃn] *n.* 联合政府

downtown [ˌdaʊnˈtaʊn] *n.* 市中心

The party leader decided to form a coalition with downtown workers.

triumvirate [traɪˈʌmvərət] *n.* 三人执政；三头统治

They created a triumvirate to rule the country.

Lesson 78

noncommittal [ˌnɑːnkəˈmɪtl] *adj.* 不作许诺的；不表态的；不确定的

The mayor remains noncommittal about which candidate he will support.
The high-ranking military official was noncommittal on this proposal.

privy [ˈprɪvi] *n.* 厕所 *adj.* 个人的；私下的

She did not tell anyone, but I knew she was privy to insider trading.
He was in danger because he was privy to their dirty secret.

privity [ˈprɪvəti] *n.* 共同秘密

He has privity with the mayor.

police sergeant 巡佐

masquerade [ˌmæskəˈreɪd] *v.* 伪装 *n.* 掩饰

The police sergeant masquerades as a drug addict to contact a major drug dealer.

desterilize [diˈsterəˌlaɪz] *v.* 解除冻结；复用

The central bank desterilizes some gold into the market.

egregious [ɪˈɡriːdʒəs] *adj.* 非常糟的

gerrymander [ˈdʒeriˌmændə] *v.* 为党政利益改选划区 *n.* 不公正划分选区

This election is the most egregious example of gerrymander.

engage [ɪnˈɡeɪdʒ] *v.* 从事；与……建立密切关系 *adj.* 介入政治的

He is engaged to a princess.

Part 3 识记单词 / 词组

callosity [kæˈlɑːsəti] *n.* 厚厚的皮肤
cruelty [ˈkruːəlti] *n.* 残酷
callous hands 长茧的手
sports apparel 运动服装
apparel [əˈpærəl] *n.* 衣服；服装
incite [ɪnˈsaɪt] *v.* 煽动
mink [mɪŋk] *n.* 貂
contagious [kənˈteɪdʒəs] *adj.* （情感）具有感染力的；蔓延的；带传染源的；接触性传染的

Lesson 79

Part 1 主力单词 / 词组

disciple [dɪˈsaɪpl]　*n.* 门徒；学生
The master of weaponry has many disciples.
Christ himself was poor.... And as he was himself, so he informed his apostles and disciples, they were all poor, prophets poor, apostles poor.

protégé [ˈprəʊtəʒeɪ]　*n.* 门徒
The maverick has regarded himself as a protégé of William.

apprentice [əˈprentɪs]　*n.* 学徒
He serves as an apprentice of a carpenter.

acolyte [ˈækəlaɪt]　*n.* 追随者；助手
He has his acolytes as well as detractors.

adherent [ədˈhɪrənt]　*n.* 追随者；拥护者
He has long been an adherent of the Communist Party.

champion [ˈtʃæmpiən]　*n.* 冠军；捍卫者
He has been a champion of human rights which abrogates the capital penalty.

advocate [ˈædvəkeɪt, ˈædvəkət]　*v.* 支持　*n.* 支持者
He is an advocate of social reform.

follower [ˈfɑːloʊər]　*n.* 追随者
The fallen angel is an avid follower of Lucifer.

myrmidon [ˈmɜːrmɪdɑn]　*n.* 盲目执行主子命令的人；忠实的追随者
These myrmidons will carry out whatever their master asks.

partisan [ˈpɑːrtəzn]　*n.* 党人；偏激的支持者；武装抗敌分子　*adj.* 忠于党派的；拥护的
The partisan of eugenics had no remorse for killing Jews.

votary [ˈvoʊtəri]　*n.* 热心者；崇拜者；信徒
The scrivener was a votary of a Muslim leader.
The dandy is a votary of worldly pleasure.

Words in sentences 句中单词/词组

maverick [ˈmævərɪk] *n.* 特立独行的人
carpenter [ˈkɑːrpəntər] *n.* 木工
detractor [dɪˈtræktər] *n.* 恶意的批评者
abrogate [ˈæbrəgeɪt] *v.* 正式废除；撤销
capital penalty 死刑
avid [ˈævɪd] *adj.* 渴望的；急切的；热衷的
eugenics [juːˈdʒenɪks] *n.* 优生学
scrivener [ˈskrɪvənər] *n.* 代书；书记；公证人

Part 2 补充单词/词组

rise above 克服；超越

tripartite [traɪˈpɑːrtaɪt] *adj.* 由三部分构成的

crossfire [ˈkrɔːsfaɪər] *n.* 困境；交叉火力；相互指责

humble [ˈhʌmbl] *v.* 使谦卑；使地位降低 *adj.* 谦逊的；简陋的

She can rise above adversity to transcend the tripartite crossfire of masculine bias, racial illogical hate, and humble origin while making her way to become a respectable manager.

masculinity [ˌmæskjəˈlɪnəti] *n.* 男子气概

The masculinity in me gets inspired by the female...I can use her as my muse.

muse [mjuːz] *v.* 沉思；沉思地凝视 *n.* 启发艺术家的人；艺术家特别的天赋

He mused what would have been if he hadn't taken sides.
The judge mused, "The innocent man should be free to go".
The artist considers his wife as his muse.

potion [ˈpoʊʃn] *n.* 一服；一剂；饮剂

To detract from history is nothing else than to pluck out the eyes of a beautiful creature and, for a medicinable potion, to offer poison to the reader's understanding.

detract [dɪˈtrækt] *v.* 减损；贬抑；使分心；转移（注意等）

He detracted from her beauty while he was in session.
Too many errors and wrong quotations detract from the quality of your essay.

detraction [dɪˈtrækʃən]　*n.* 诽谤；贬抑

messenger [ˈmesɪndʒər]　*n.* 送信人；邮递员；使者；传令员；先兆；先驱
Don't kill me. I am just a messenger.

courier [ˈkʊriər]　*n.* 信差（送递急件）；导游；情报员
A Russian courier reported to his superior at the sight of the Japanese fleet.

scribe [skraɪb]　*v.* 划出　*n.* 抄写员；文书
The Egyptian scribe recorded these ancient hieroglyphs.

Part 3　识记单词 / 词组

antiquary [ˈæntɪˌkweri]　*n.* 古物研究（或收藏）者；古董商；古籍商

love potion　爱情魔药

weaponry [ˈwepənri]　*n.* 武器

apostle [əˈpɑːsl]　*n.* 先驱者；鼓吹者；门徒

inaugural address　就职演说

inaugural [ɪˈnɔːgjərəl]　*adj.* 首次的；就职的

overbearing [ˌoʊvərˈberɪŋ]　*adj.* 专横的；自大的

overbear [ˌoʊvəˈber]　*v.* 击败；比……更重要

femininity [ˌfeməˈnɪnəti]　*n.* 女人味

affix [əˈfɪks, ˈæfɪks]　*v.* 使固定；附上　*n.* 词缀

masculinize [ˈmæskjəlɪnaɪz]　*v.* 使男子化

manhood [ˈmænhʊd]　*n.* 男子气概；男性的成年期

Lesson 80

Part 1　主力单词 / 词组

prejudge [ˌpriːˈdʒʌdʒ]　*v.* 预先判断；对……作仓促决定
Some reporters have prejudged the outcome of the investigation.

He had prejudged the case against me because I was poor and uneducated.

She was wrong for prejudging him as a malefactor.

preconception [ˌpriːkənˈsepʃn] n. 先入之见；成见

The lingering preconception of his being a fugitive was soon dispelled after his return.

preconceive [ˌpriːkənˈsiːv] v. 预设；预想

You shouldn't preconceive someone's inner thoughts by what he does.

assumption [əˈsʌmpʃn] n. 假设；臆断

Working on this assumption, we were continuing to find gold in this field.

presumption [prɪˈzʌmpʃn] n. 推测；假定；冒昧；自以为是

On the presumption of students' high intelligence, the principal made the test more onerous with his undue supervision.

premise [ˈpremɪs] n. 假设；前提

He will shoot them all on the premise that they are all terrorists.

prepossession [ˌpriːpəˈzeʃn, -ˈse-] n. 事先预想

The foreign tourists have prepossessions about life in China and think that the Chinese live in a court with great mastery of kung fu.

prepossessing [ˌpriːpəˈzesɪŋ] adj. 讨人喜欢的；有魅力的；给人好感的

By her prepossessing appearance and charisma, many people purchase clothing from her.

postulation [ˌpɒstjuˈleɪʃn] n. 假定；假设

There are discrepancies between archeological findings and theoretical postulations.

presupposition [ˌpriːsʌpəˈzɪʃn] n. 推测；假定

posit [ˈpɒzɪt] v. 假设；断定 n. 安置

Several reasons have been posited as to why figure four is so haunting for the Chinese.

• Words in sentences 句中单词/词组 •

linger [ˈlɪŋɡər] v. 逗留；徘徊

supervision [ˌsuːpərˈvɪʒn] n. 监督；管理

archeological [ˌɑːkɪəˈlɒdʒɪkəl] adj. 考古学的

Part 2 补充单词 / 词组

onerous [ˈoʊnərəs, ˈɑːnərəs] adj. 艰巨的；繁重的；负有义务的
The duties of the captain were too onerous.
The borrower met the onerous payments of thirty thousand dollars per month.

hindmost [ˈhaɪndˌmoʊst] adj. 最后面的
Every man is for himself, and the devil takes the hindmost.

undue [ˌʌnˈduː] adj. 过度的；不适当地；没到期的
You don't have to pay now. The bill is undue.
The word "undue" means excessive or inappropriate.

pert [pɜːrt] adj. 时髦的；冒失的
She is a pert girl who has many suitors.

vivify [ˈvɪvəˌfaɪ] v. 使生动；使有生气
Concrete details vivify the narrative.
The movie vivified history.

well-woven [welˈwoʊvn] adj. 编织得很好；编造得很好
He told his story, a web of well-woven lies, concocted events.

serenade [ˌserəˈneɪd] v. 为……演奏 n. 小夜曲

aubade [oʊˈbɑːd] n. 晨歌
The guitar can be played for both serenades and aubades.

pace [peɪs] v. 踱步；走来走去 n. 一步；步幅
She walked toward her lover at a sedate pace.

opus [ˈoʊpəs] n. 音乐作品；创作
The musician's final opus has won recognition from the public.

magnum opus 巨著；杰作
His magnum opus in paleontology becomes a standard reference book at many universities.

Part 3 识记单词 / 词组

prejudgment [priːˈdʒʌdʒmənt] n. 判断

prepossess [ˌpriːpəˈzes, -ˈses] v. 使预先产生；使产生好印象（或反感）；预先拥有

malefactor [ˈmælɪfæktər] n. 作恶者；罪犯；坏人
discrepancy [dɪˈskrepənsi] n. 出入；差异
curriculum vitae 简历；个人履历
curriculum [kəˈrɪkjələm] n. 课程表
curricula [kəˈrɪkjələ] n. 课程（复数）
curricular [kəˈrɪkjələr] adj. 课程的
resume [rɪˈzuːm] v. 继续；恢复职位 [ˈrezjumeɪ] n. 简历；摘要
the draft 兵役制
idler [ˈaɪdlər] n. 游手好闲者
idler gear 中间齿轮
idler pulley 惰轮；导轮
pulley [ˈpʊli] n. 滑轮；滑车
cyberflaneur = virtual flaneur 网络闲逛族
inducible [ɪnˈdjuːsəbl] adj. 可诱导的；可导致的

Lesson 81

Part 1 主力单词/词组

credence [ˈkriːdns] n. 相信；可信性；祭器台；供桌

I won't give credence to anonymous incriminatory letters.
Her disappearance lent credence to the gossip that she was the culprit behind the company's bankruptcy.
I attached little credence to the street gossip.

belief [bɪˈliːf] n. 信心；信任

There is a growing belief that he won't finish the project in time.
Everyone should be allowed to have different religious beliefs.
It is from numberless diverse acts of courage and belief that human history is shaped.

Part 2 补充单词/词组

coerce [koʊˈɜːrs] v. 强迫；迫使

coercion [koʊˈɜːrʒn] *n.* 强迫；胁迫

reprehensible [ˌreprɪˈhensəbl] *adj.* 应受谴责的

rebut [rɪˈbʌt] *v.* 反驳；揭穿

His coercion toward Ukraine is reprehensible, but he rebuts.

rebuttal [rɪˈbʌtl] *n.* 反驳；辩驳

antic [ˈæntɪk] *n.* 滑稽的动作 *adj.* 滑稽的；古怪的

pale [peɪl] *n.* 栅栏 *adj.* 苍白的

beyond the pale 在……接受范围之外

His antics in a departmental meeting are beyond the pale.

pallor [ˈpælər] *n.* 苍白的脸色

My girlfriend's pallor really concerned me.

pallid [ˈpælɪd] *adj.* 无血色的；无生气的

Her face was pallid as she encountered a ghost.

wan [wɑːn] *v.* 变苍白；呈病态 *adj.* 苍白的；病态的；微弱的

He looked rather wan after working all night.
I felt cold when the sky went wan.

delve [delv] *v.* 探究；钻研；翻找 *n.* 翻找

These professors have delved into plant biology for many years.

precaution [prɪˈkɔːʃn] *n.* 预防；预防措施

The import of his words alerted me to take precautions.

high-end [ˌhaɪ ˈend] *adj.* 高档的；尖端的

We import high-end chips from the United States.

incursion [ɪnˈkɜːrʒn] *n.* 袭击；侵略；进入

I made an incursion into the arts by accident.
A nomadic tribe made an incursion into our northern border.

Part 3 识记单词 / 词组

culprit [ˈkʌlprɪt] *n.* 过失者；责任人；罪魁祸首

candid [ˈkændɪd] *adj.* 率直的；坦诚的；直言不讳的

deterrent [dɪˈtɜːrənt] *n.* 威慑力量　*adj.* 有威慑力的
hind [haɪnd] *adj.* 后面的
hind leg 后腿
give credence to 相信；信任；使可信
lend credence to 使人相信
attach credence to sth 相信（流言蜚语、传言等）
letters of credence 到任国书
slither [ˈslɪðər] *v.* 滑行；连走带跑地滑走
multimillionaire [ˌmʌltimɪljəˈner] *n.* 千万富翁
gait [ɡeɪt] *n.* 步伐；步态
resemble [rɪˈzembl] *v.* 像；类似
contingency [kənˈtɪndʒənsi] *n.* 可能发生的事；意外事件
node [noʊd] *n.* (植物的)茎节；(线等的)交点
ramify [ˈræmɪfaɪ] *v.* (使)分枝；(使)分派；(使)纵横交错
ramification [ˌræmɪfɪˈkeɪʃn] *n.* 分枝；衍生结果
molt [moʊlt] *v.* 脱皮；脱角　*n.* 换羽期

Lesson 82

Part 1　主力单词 / 词组

stranglehold [ˈstræŋɡlhoʊld] *n.* 压制；束缚；摔跤时的犯规动作
German submarines put a stranglehold on shipping and merchant supply lines in the Strait of Gibraltar.
The state is unwilling to abandon its stranglehold on the Russian economy.

throttlehold [ˈθrɒtlhoʊld] *n.* 扼杀；压制
Trade war put a throttlehold on the nation's economy.

clampdown [ˈklæmpdaʊn] *n.* 压制；取缔；严禁；限制与控制的强行施加
The police's clampdown on gangsters went in vain because there were too many informants and moles inside the police station.

• Words in sentences 句中单词/词组

vain [veɪn] *adj.* 爱虚荣的；自负的；徒然的

Part 2 补充单词/词组

excursion [ɪkˈskɜːrʒn] *n.* 远足；涉猎；交替的移动

We went on an excursion to the northern coast of Taiwan.
I enjoyed my Greek excursions.
After an unsuccessful excursion in acting, the teacher returned to his academic life.

jaunt [dʒɔːnt] *n.* 游览；短途旅行

The family went on a five-day North America jaunt.
Would you like to have a jaunt to a mountain?

monk [mʌŋk] *n.* 修道士；僧侣

The monk disabuses his mind about his gambling habit.

monastery [ˈmɑːnəsteri] *n.* 修道院；全体修道士

She left her baby in a monastery.

cloister [ˈklɔɪstər] *v.* 使与尘世隔绝；设回廊于 *n.* 修道院；回廊

The architect cloistered the garden.

infuse [ɪnˈfjuːz] *v.* 使充满

dolor [ˈdoʊlər] *n.* 悲痛；悲哀

The painting of a lady standing alone by the winter lake was infused with dolor.

dolorous [ˈdoʊlərəs] *adj.* 悲痛的；悲哀的

She said goodbye in a dolorous tone.

a double-edged sword 双刃剑（指有利有弊的情况或行为）

There's a double-edged sword of laziness and boredom seen in the millennial population.

pretension [prɪˈtenʃn] *n.* 假装；虚荣；自称；要求；权利

She rubbed me the wrong way with her vain pretension.
His pretensions to be the general manager were unconvincing.

Let us talk turkey, without pretension.

He made the decision not to serve in the army based on his religious pretensions.

vainglorious [ˌveɪnˈɡlɔːriəs] adj. 自负的；自命不凡的
He is a vainglorious guy who always insists on being the center of attention

She obviously felt scorn for the pompous and vainglorious lecturer.

boast [boʊst] v. 自吹自擂 n. 夸耀
He boasted his past achievement.

magniloquent [mæɡˈnɪləkwənt] adj. 说大话的；自夸的
I was somewhat amused by his magniloquent boast.

magniloquence [mæɡˈnɪləukwəns] n. 夸张的话；自夸
There is no trace of magniloquence in their conversation.

fanfare [ˈfænfer] n. 号角声；夸耀；炫耀
They opened the concert with fanfare.

plaudit [ˈplɔːdɪt] n. 赞美；拍手喝彩
The lecturer has received the fanfare of plaudits.

laudatory [ˈlɔːdətɔːri] adj. 赞美的
Her work has received many laudatory comments.

Part 3 识记单词 / 词组

appetizer [ˈæpɪtaɪzər] n.（餐前的）开胃小吃

appetite [ˈæpɪtaɪt] n. 食欲；胃口；渴求

appetizing [ˈæpɪtaɪzɪŋ] adj. 开胃的

apéritif [aperitif] n.（尤指餐前的）开胃酒菜

prandial [ˈprændiəl] adj. 膳食的；正餐的

amble [ˈæmbl] v.（马）缓行；从容漫步

exuberance [ɪɡˈzuːbərəns] n. 繁茂；充溢；生气勃勃的行动

recite [rɪˈsaɪt] v. 背诵；当众吟诵

recital [rɪˈsaɪtl] n. 独奏会；朗诵会；列举

repose [rɪˈpoʊz] v. 位于 n. 休息；卧眠

repose on 依据

quietude [ˈkwaɪətuːd] n. 平静；寂静
bossy [ˈbɔːsi] adj. 爱指挥人的；专横的
tempestuous [temˈpestʃuəs] adj. 激动的
mist [mɪst] n. 薄雾；水汽；水蒸气
moisture [ˈmɔɪstʃər] n. 潮气；水分
employment rate 就业率
unemployment rate 失业率
be in sb's employ 受雇于……
be employed in doing sth 花时间做……；从事……
a conglomerate of organisms 一种有机体的混合物
practical utility 实际的应用性
generator [ˈdʒenəreɪtər] n. 发电机
rent [rent] v. 租 n. 租金；（布等上面的）破洞；裂口
giga [ˈɡɪɡə, ˈdʒɪɡə] n. 十亿

Lesson 83

Part 1 主力单词/词组

adept [əˈdept] n. 专家；能手 adj. 熟练的；擅长的
Troglodytes were adept at cave painting.
Both parties are adept at social-media manipulation and publicity warfare.
Putin has proven himself to be extremely adept in his electioneering.

good at 擅长
Oriental students are often good at math.

well-versed [ˈwelˈvɜːst] adj. 精通的；熟知的
Amorphel was a crafty, treacherous man well-versed in flattery.

skillful [ˈskɪlfl] adj. 熟练的；灵巧的；制作精巧的
The criminal skillfully maneuvered himself in hopes that the jurors would accept his debauched behavior.

proficient [prəˈfɪʃnt] adj. 熟练的；精通的

The scholar is proficient in diverse subjects.

Are you a proficient swimmer?

proficiency [prəˈfɪʃnsi] n. 熟练；精通

His English proficiency has earned him a place in the company.

adroit [əˈdrɔɪt] adj. 精明的；干练的

acumen [ˈækjəmən, əˈkjuːmən] n. 敏锐；精明

His business acumen was well matched to his brother's military talent.

conversant [kənˈvɜːrsnt] adj. 对……精通的；对……熟悉的

The doctor is conversant with zoology.

The journalist is conversant with all current topics.

virtuosity [ˌvɜːrtʃuˈɑːsəti] n. 非常擅长的技能

He has demonstrated his artistic virtuosity.

savoir-faire [ˌsævwɑːr ˈfer] n. 处世能力；机智；手腕；才干

He answered reporters' questions with his usual savoir-faire.

To be an excellent diplomat requires great savoir-faire.

tact [tækt] n. 老练；机智；圆滑

The reporter broke the news with tact.

Negotiation requires great tact.

tactful [ˈtæktfl] adj. 机智的；圆滑的；老练的

He was an influential and tactful politician.

shrewd [ʃruːd] adj. 精明的；敏锐的；奸诈的

He is shrewd enough to take on that highly demanding job.

To the public, the old president appears shrewd, nondoctrinaire, and avuncular.

I won't suggest using a sycophantic approach toward these shrewd foreign leaders.

smart [smɑːrt] adj. 聪明的；时髦的；迅速有力的；不敬的

He is too smart to have cheated on the test.

I would like to wear that smart jacket to a nice restaurant.

He is not smart to smack my face.

He is smart untimely.

Don't get smart with me.

wise [waɪz] *adj.* 聪明的；博学的

Would you like to adopt wise precautions?

sagacious [sə'geɪʃəs] *adj.* 明智的；精明的

The thief proved to be sagacious as he preemptively shouted accusations at a passerby "thief" in order to distract public attention.

judicious [dʒu'dɪʃəs] *adj.* 明断的；明智而审慎的

The businessman made judicious use of his money.

injudicious [ˌɪndʒu'dɪʃəs] *adj.* 不明智的

acumen ['ækjəmən, ə'kjuːmən] *n.* 精明；敏锐

She has considerable acumen and abnegates any idealism.

astute [ə'stuːt] *adj.* 精明的；狡猾的

An astute observer tried to discover the weapon of mass destruction.

Solomon ['sɑːləmən] *n.* 所罗门

solomonic [ˌsɔlə'mɒnɪk] *adj.* 明智判断的

I made a Solomonic decision concerning the choice of my major.

politic ['pɑːlətɪk] *v.*(贬)从事政治活动 *adj.* 明智的；有策略的；政治的

It would not be politic to ignore your boss.

It won't be politic to fire him at this point.

Words in sentences 句中单词/词组

crafty ['kræfti] *adj.* 狡猾的；诡计多端的

maneuver [mə'nuːvər] *n.* 操纵；花招；军事演习

juror ['dʒʊrər] *n.* 陪审员

debauched [dɪ'bɔːtʃt] *adj.* 糜烂的；放荡的

smack [smæk] *v.* 用巴掌打 *n.* 打巴掌

untimely [ʌn'taɪmli] *adj.* 过早的；不合时宜的

preemptively [pri'emptɪv] *adv.* 先发制人地

abnegate ['æbnɪgeɪt] *v.* 放弃（权力等）；克制（欲望等）

Part 2 补充单词/词组

prelapsarian [ˈpriːlæpˈseəriən] *adj.* 人类堕落前的；优美原始的；纯真的

The primitive forest is a prelapsarian landscape.
I had a prelapsarian romance with her in high school.

postlapsarian [pəʊstˈlæpseəriən] *adj.* 人类堕落后的

What are the differences between the prelapsarian and postlapsarian worlds?

debauch [dɪˈbɔːtʃ] *v.* 使堕落 *n.* 诱惑；放荡

Wealth has debauched these fighters to the point where they fight like girls.

leitmotif [ˈlaɪtməʊˌtiːf] *n.* 重复出现的主题；主旋律

The use of blue seems to be the leitmotif in his fashion design.
Spicy food is the leitmotif in the cuisine of Sichuan.

plangent [ˈplændʒənt] *adj.* 悲切的；悲鸣的

Plangent themes are the leitmotif in this serial.
The plangent, stentorian voice fell off to a whisper in the valley.

piquant [ˈpiːkənt] *adj.* 辛辣的；够刺激的；有趣的

I added some piquant sauce to my noodles.
Television uses piquant news to catch people's attention.

Part 3 识记单词/词组

saver [ˈseɪvər] *n.* 储蓄者；节省的东西
repress [rɪˈpres] *v.* 镇压；制止
repressive [rɪˈpresɪv] *adj.* 镇压的；制止的
reparation [ˌrepəˈreɪʃn] *n.* 可修理
reparable [ˈrepərəbl] *adj.* 可修理的；可挽回的
irreparable [ɪˈrepərəbl] *adj.* 不能修补的；不能挽回的
rumpus [ˈrʌmpəs] *n.* 喧闹
rumpus room 娱乐室
onus probandi 举证责任
collide [kəˈlaɪd] *v.* 相撞；碰撞

delude [dɪˈluːd] *v.* 欺骗；哄骗
illusion [ɪˈluːʒn] *n.* 幻觉；幻想
hostile [ˈhɑːstl, ˈhɑːstaɪl] *adj.* 不友善的；有敌意的
hostility [hɑːˈstɪləti] *n.* 敌意；对抗
oppress [əˈpres] *v.* 压迫；压制；欺压
oppressive [əˈpresɪv] *adj.* 压迫的；压制的；欺压的
demeanor [dɪˈmiːnər] *n.* 行为；举止
demean [dɪˈmiːn] *v.* 羞辱；贬低

Lesson 84

Part 1 主力单词 / 词组

utilize [ˈjuːtəlaɪz] *v.* 使用；利用；应用

I utilized coal to generate electricity.
We have to utilize every means of achieving victory.
Troops have been utilized to crack down on the riot.

employ [ɪmˈplɔɪ] *v.* 使用；利用；雇用

Military tactics have been employed in the War.
The conglomerate has employed 1200 people.
The Fox Conn Corporation expects to build a gigafactory in Wisconsin state and employ more than 10 thousand people.

• Words in sentences 句中单词 / 词组 •

crack down on 打击；制裁；处罚
tactic [ˈtæktɪk] *n.* 战术；策略
conglomerate [kənˈglɑːmərət] *n.* 联合企业（不同的企业所组成）；混合物
gigafactory [ˈgɪgəˌfæktəri] *n.* 超级工厂

Part 2 补充单词/词组

quell [kwel] *v.* 镇压；平息；消除

Eating chocolate may quell your anxiety.

utility [juːˈtɪləti] *n.* 实用性；公共设施 *adj.* 实用性的

Is the rent including utility?

riot [ˈraɪət] *v.* 暴动 *n.* 聚众闹事

The president asked the police to quell a riot.

negate [nɪˈgeɪt] *v.* 否定；取消；使无效

The teacher negates all of my achievements due to a single error of mine.

The riots and seizures in the city negate all the efforts to attract foreign investments.

negation [nɪˈgeɪʃn] *n.* 否定；反驳；对立面

The ruling by the Supreme Court was regarded as a negation of freedom of speech.

utopia [juːˈtoʊpiə] *n.* 乌托邦；空想的完美境界

The refugee camp is opposed to utopia, as a stark reality to naïveté.

shrew [ʃruː] *n.* 泼妇；悍妇

She is a shrew who likes to dominate her husband's life.

His wife is a shrew who makes his life miserable.

vixen [ˈvɪksn] *n.* 雌狐；凶悍的女人；坏心眼的女人

The heartless vixen has a sharp tongue.

The highest-ranking vixen dominates all of the foxes.

vociferous [voʊˈsɪfərəs] *adj.* 大叫大嚷的；喧嚷的

I can hear the outcry of these vociferous demonstrators.

diamondiferous [ˌdaɪəmənˈdɪfərəs] *adj.* 含钻的

The rock is diamondiferous.

disciplined [ˈdɪsəplɪnd] *adj.* 受过训练的；遵守纪律的

self-abnegation [ˌselfˌæbnɪˈgeɪʃn] *n.* 自我克制

These soldiers are highly disciplined and have a spirit of self-abnegation.

monolith [ˈmɑːnəlɪθ] *n.* 巨型独石；整块石料；庞然大物

The old computer has a monolith circuit.

logistic [ləˈdʒɪstɪk] *n.* 逻辑　*adj.* 物流的；后勤（学）的；逻辑的；计算的

logistics [ləˈdʒɪstɪks] *n.* 后勤；物流
The company has grown into a monolith of the logistics industry.

monolithic [ˌmɑːnəˈlɪθɪk] *adj.* 庞大而僵化的；独块巨石的
There are many monolithic state-run corporations in Russia.
How am I supposed to fight the trend of monolithic society?

superstate [ˈsuːpərsteɪt] *n.* 超级大国
Both nations are monolithic superstates.

Part 3　识记单词 / 词组

utopian [juːˈtoʊpiən] *adj.* 乌托邦的；空想完美主义的
ferrous [ˈferəs] *adj.* 含有的；产生的
abnegation [ˌæbnɪˈɡeɪʃn] *n.* 克制
highly-demanding 要求很高的
doctrinaire [ˌdɑːktrɪˈner] *n.* 教条主义者　*adj.* 教条主义的
sycophantic [ˌsɪkəˈfæntɪk] *adj.* 说奉承话的
sycophant [ˈsɪkəfænt] *n.* 谄媚者；谗言者；诽谤者
massive [ˈmæsɪv] *adj.* 大规模的；大量的；巨大的
a preemptive strike 一次先发制人的攻击
smart [smɑːrt] *v.* 感到剧烈疼痛　*n.* 创伤　*adj.* 精明的
intelligent [ɪnˈtelɪdʒənt] *adj.* 智慧的
Ethopia [ˌiːθɪˈəupjə] *n.* 衣索比亚

Lesson 85

Part 1　主力单词 / 词组

privation [praɪˈveɪʃn] *n.* 匮乏；贫困
His body has taken its toll during years of rationing and privation.

Constant privation of sleep has caused his hallucination.

Children live in war-torn areas often experiencing economic privation.

indigent [ˈɪndɪdʒənt] *adj.* 十分贫困的

Indian aboriginal inhabitants lead an indigent life of hunting.

impecunious [ˌɪmpɪˈkjuːniəs] *adj.* 贫穷的；没有钱的；身无分文的；一名不文的；贫困的

As an impecunious student, I can't afford to go to a prestigious university.

impoverish [ɪmˈpɑːvərɪʃ] *v.* 使变穷；消耗

Time seemed to impoverish all of us as a beautiful lady turned into an old woman.

The financial tsunami impoverished us.

Pesticide abuse has impoverished soil and destroyed habitats.

impoverished [ɪmˈpɑːvərɪʃt] *adj.* 赤贫的；恶化的

destitute [ˈdestɪtuːt] *adj.* 赤贫的；缺少的

The destitute mother can't afford her son's education.

The impoverished town is destitute of commerce.

A coward is destitute of courage.

underprivileged [ˌʌndərˈprɪvəlɪdʒd] *adj.* 贫困的；属于弱势群体的

The children in Africa being underprivileged and starving was caused by human action.

poverty [ˈpɑːvərti] *n.* 贫困；贫穷

How can a potent government be oblivious of rampant abject poverty in remote inland regions?

strapped [stræpt] *adj.* 手头紧的；贫穷的；穷困的

I am cash strapped but I can give you my psychological support.

poverty-stricken [ˈpɑːvərti strɪkən] *adj.* 穷苦的

Ethiopia is a land-locked and poverty-stricken country.

Many people think native Indians are poverty-stricken.

broke [broʊk] *adj.* 破了产的

He is broke, impecunious.

impecuniosity [ˌɪmpɪˌkjuːniˈɑːsəti] *n.* 贫穷

destitution [ˌdestɪˈtuːʃn] n. 一无所有

penury [ˈpenjəri] n. 赤贫

> ● Words in sentences 句中单词 / 词组 ●
>
> **tsunami** [tsuːˈnɑːmi] n. 海啸
> **pesticide** [ˈpestɪsaɪd] n. 农药；杀虫剂
> **abuse** [əˈbjuːs] v. 虐待；伤害 n. 滥用；辱骂
> **abject** [ˈæbdʒekt] adj. 极其苦恼的；低声下气的
> **inland** [ɪnˈlænd, ˈɪnlænd] adj. 内陆的；内地的

Part 2 补充单词 / 词组

penurious [pəˈnʊriəs] adj. 赤贫的

pauper [ˈpɔːpər] n. 贫民；穷人

tramp [træmp] v. 踏；长途跋涉 n. 流浪汉；沉重的脚步声
Tramps and paupers are often penurious.

plight [plaɪt] n. 苦难；困境 v. 保证；约定
Few people understand their plight.

rampant [ˈræmpənt] adj. 猖獗的；(狮等) 用后脚立起的；跃立的；支撑不平衡的
A rampant lion at the car window begs for meat

Part 3 识记单词 / 词组

the impoverished vagabond 赤贫的流浪者
waif [weɪf] n. 流浪者；流浪儿；流浪动物
vagrant [ˈveɪɡrənt] n. 流浪者；无业游民；乞丐
strapped financial institution 没钱的金融机构
indignant [ɪnˈdɪɡnənt] adj. 愤怒的；愤慨的
drug abuse 药物滥用；吸毒

untouchable [ʌn'tʌtʃəbl] *n.* 不可接触者 *adj.* 无法击败的；不可惩罚的
landlocked ['lændlɑːkt] *adj.* 内陆的
oblivion [ə'blɪviən] *n.* 遗忘；湮没；无知觉；不省人事
toll [toʊl] *v.* 敲（钟）；（使）缓慢而反复地鸣响 *n.* 通行费；长途电话费
tollbooth ['toʊlbuːθ] *n.* 收费站
booth [buːθ] *n.* 货摊；公用电话亭；投票站；（隔开的）小房间；（餐厅等的）雅座
rationing ['ræʃənɪŋ] *n.* 定量配给政策
hallucination [həˌluːsɪ'neɪʃn] *n.* 幻觉
war-torn ['wɔːr tɔːrn] *adj.* 遭受战争破坏的
fungicide ['fʌŋɡɪsaɪd, 'fʌndʒɪsaɪd] *n.* 杀真菌剂
nystatin ['nɪstətin, nɪs'tætɪn] *n.* 制真菌素

Lesson 86

Part 1 主力单词/词组

lack [læk] *v.* 没有；不足 *n.* 缺乏

The dog will bark at whoever lacks confidence.
The governmental organization was marked by an icy atmosphere of complete lack of cordiality.
The great curse of our modern society is not so much the lack of money as the fact that the lack of money condemns a man to a squalid and incomplete existence. (Christopher Dawson, U.S. academic)
When a man lacks mental balance in pneumonia, he is said to be delirious. When he lacks mental balance without the pneumonia, he is pronounced insane by all smart doctors. (Martin H. Fischer, German-born U.S. physician and author)

inadequate [ɪn'ædɪkwət] *adj.* 不足的；不会处理事情的

The funding is inadequate to sustain the animal preservation project and expand the reservation.

inadequacy [ɪn'ædɪkwəsi] *n.* 不充分；不足；不完全

scarcity [ˈskersəti] *n.* 缺乏；不足；萧条（时期）

A scarcity of natural resources occasioned the country to develop its trading business.

scare [sker] *v.* 吓走 *n.* 害怕；惊慌

a paucity of 缺乏；少数

He bemoans a paucity of morality in gangsters and racketeers.

a dearth of 缺乏；不足；饥荒

We can't charge him due to a dearth of evidence.

deficient [dɪˈfɪʃnt] *adj.* 不够的；不足的

The prosecutor was accused of conducting deficient investigations over espionage.

shortage [ˈʃɔːrtɪdʒ] *n.* 不足；缺少

Since the new president was inaugurated, water and power shortage have started to surface uncannily.

vacuum [ˈvækjuːm] *v.*（用真空吸尘器所做的）清扫 *n.* 真空；空白

The death of the president has led to a political vacuum and instability.

The withdrawal of U.N troops might create a security vacuum in the region.

meager [ˈmiːɡər] *adj.* 瘦的；粗劣的；不足的

She has meager legs.

The island's natural resources are meager.

The janitor only receives a meager salary to get by.

• **Words in sentences 句中单词 / 词组** •

cordiality [ˌkɔːrdʒiˈæləti] *n.* 亲切而客气的行为

squalid [ˈskwɑːlɪd] *adj.* 极其肮脏的；污秽的

pneumonia [nuːˈmoʊniə] *n.* 肺炎

physician [fɪˈzɪʃn] *n.* 医生；内科医生

reservation [ˌrezərˈveɪʃn] *n.* 野生动物保护区；预订

bemoan [bɪˈmoʊn] *v.* 悲叹

gangster [ˈɡæŋstər] *n.* 帮派分子

racketeer [ˌrækəˈtɪr] *n.* 勒索者；诈骗者

prosecutor [ˈprɑːsɪkjuːtər] n. 检察官
accuse [əˈkjuːz] v. 指控
espionage [ˈespiənɑːʒ] n. 间谍活动
inaugurate [ɪˈnɔːgjəreɪt] v. 使正式就职；为……举行就职典礼

Part 2 补充单词 / 词组

glut [ɡlʌt] v. 过度供应；吃得太饱 n. 大量；供大于求
The market is glutted with cell phones.
Aren't you on a diet? How come you glut yourself at the restaurant buffet?

overstock [ˌoʊvərˈstɑːk] v. 使进货过多 n. 过剩的库存 adj. 过量的；额外的

ware [wer] n. 商品；货物；物品；陶器
The store overstocked wares for the new year.

ample [ˈæmpl] adj. 大量的；丰富的
He has ample time, fortune, and reason to pursue that movie star.

imprecation [ˌɪmprɪˈkeɪʃn] n. 诅咒；咒语
A terrible imprecation was unfolded to his siblings.

provision [prəˈvɪʒn] v. 提供；为……提供给养 n. 规定；供给；准备金；粮食物资

mandatory [ˈmændətɔːri] adj. 强制的；法定的

precatory [ˈprekətɔːri] adj. 恳求的；希望的
Are these provisions mandatory or precatory?

witch hunt 猎巫
Before she died, the witch imprecated people who torched her in the witch hunt.

Part 3 识记单词 / 词组

excess [ɪkˈses] n. 过量；超越；超过
surplus [ˈsɜːrplʌs] n. 多余；过剩；资金盈余 adj. 多余的；过剩的

imprecate [ˈɪmprɪˌkeɪt] v. 诅咒

uncannily [ʌnˈkænɪli] adv. 奇怪地；神秘地

uncanny [ʌnˈkæni] adj. 奇怪的；神秘的

unfold [ʌnˈfoʊld] v. 展开；摊开；呈现

fold [foʊld] v. 折叠；垮台 n. 褶痕；（事业）失败

folder [ˈfoʊldər] n. 文书夹

vacuum cleaner 真空吸尘器

colony [ˈkɑːləni] n. 殖民地；群落

colonize [ˈkɑːlənaɪz] v. 使殖民地化；将……建为殖民地

colonist [ˈkɑːlənɪst] n. 殖民地开拓者；殖民地居民

aftermath [ˈæftərmæθ] n.（战争、事故、不快乐事情的）后果；创伤

cock [kɑːk] v. 上翘；扣（枪的）扳机 n. 公鸡；龙头；活栓；风信标；主要人物

fluff [flʌf] v. 使起毛；使松散；演奏错（音符等） n.（织物上的）绒毛；蓬松物（如一团头发、尘团等）

fluffy [ˈflʌfi] adj. 蓬松的；空洞的

a fluffy kitten 毛茸茸的小猫

fluffy hair 蓬松的头发

kitten [ˈkɪtn] n. 小猫 v. 产小猫

kittenish [ˈkɪtnɪʃ] adj. 小猫似的；嬉耍的

Lesson 87

Part 1 主力单词 / 词组

unceasing [ʌnˈsiːsɪŋ] adj. 持续不断的

Constant and unceasing upheaval serves nothing, but a god-sent punishment.
My service to my people is part of the discipline to which I subject myself to in order to free my soul from the bonds of the flesh...For me the path of salvation leads through the unceasing tribulation in the service of my fellow countrymen and humanity. (Mahatma Gandhi, Indian national leader)

Lesson 87

incessant [ɪn'sesnt]　*adj.* 持续的；不懈的
I was bogged down by reporters' interminable, incessant questioning.

unremitting [ˌʌnrɪ'mɪtɪŋ]　*adj.* 持续的；不懈的
The candidate delivered his speech with great panache against a backdrop of unremitting drizzle.

unrelenting [ˌʌnrɪ'lentɪŋ]　*adj.* 不停歇的；不屈不挠的
In the tropical forest, we've experienced unrelenting sultry.

relentless [rɪ'lentləs]　*adj.* 不间断的；残酷的；无情的
His relentless pursuit of her has backfired.

unflagging [ˌʌn'flæɡɪŋ]　*adj.* 永不减弱的
They overcame adversity with their undiminished will and unflagging passion to win.

unabating [ˌʌnə'beɪtɪŋ]　*adj.* 不减的
I have no intention to harbor unabating paranoia and suspicion about others' motives.

interminable [ɪn'tɜːrmɪnəbl]　*adj.* 无休止的；冗长不堪的
The forest is enormous, and its path seems to be interminable.
Pandemics in this situation give rise to interminable disputes.

• Words in sentences 句中单词 / 词组 •

upheaval [ʌp'hiːvl]　*n.* 动荡；剧变
fellow ['feloʊ]　*n.* 同事；男孩；研究生　*adj.* 同事的；同类的；同情况的
bog [bɑːɡ]　*n.* 沼泽
bog down　陷入
backdrop ['bækdrɑːp]　*n.* 背景；背景幕布
sultry ['sʌltri]　*adj.* 湿热的；闷热的
backfire [ˌbæk'faɪər]　*v.* 产生反效果
undiminished [ˌʌndɪ'mɪnɪʃt]　*adj.* 强壮的；重要的；不减的
paranoia [ˌpærə'nɔɪə]　*n.* 疑神疑鬼

Part 2　补充单词 / 词组

panache [pə'næʃ, pə'nɑːʃ]　*n.* 大气磅礴；潇洒；气派；羽饰
He played the role of the entrepreneur with great panache.

The ranger has a panache on his hat.

abate [ə'beɪt]　　*v.* 减少；减弱

The agony is abated by the medicine.

abatement [ə'beɪtmənt]　　*n.* 减弱；减轻；减少

bate [beɪt]　　*v.* 抑制；减少；振翅飞翔

He has to bate his curiosity in order to refrain from opening the present.

He is very stubborn and will not bate a jot of his dignity to accept her help.

The falcon bates and flies to the sky.

subtract [səb'trækt]　　*v.* 做减法；减去；去掉

They subtract one from the other.

The years that a woman subtracts from her age are not lost.

subtraction [səb'trækʃn]　　*n.* 扣除；减法

dwindle ['dwɪndl]　　*v.* 减少；缩小

The tumult dwindled to a calm in the end.

locust plague　　蝗灾

The crop supply has dwindled owing to the locust plague.

purvey [pər'veɪ]　　*v.* （大量）供给

The United States has purveyed soybeans for many years.

purveyor [pər'veɪər]　　*n.* 伙食承包人；提供者

The United States has been calling Mexico "the world's greatest purveyor of drugs."

The teacher is the sole purveyor of knowledge in this small village.

relent [rɪ'lent]　　*v.* 让步；同意；缓和；减弱

The dealer had refused to compensate for product defects and relented only after being threatened with a lawsuit.

The pandemic did not relent after six months.

Part 3　识记单词 / 词组

drizzle ['drɪzl]　　*v.* 细细地滴入　　*n.* 毛毛雨

paranoid ['pærənɔɪd]　　*adj.* 偏执的；多疑的

veniality [ˌviːni'æliti]　　*n.* 可宽恕

impure [ɪm'pjʊr]　　*adj.* 不纯洁的；掺杂的

impurity [ɪmˈpjʊrəti]　*n.* 杂质；污染物
populist [ˈpɑːpjəlɪst]　*n.* 平民主义者　*adj.* 民粹主义的；平民主义的
altitude [ˈæltɪtuːd]　*n.* 海拔；高度；高等
longitude [ˈlɑːndʒɪtuːd]　*n.* 经度
longitudinal [ˌlɑːndʒəˈtuːdɪnl]　*adj.* 经度的；纵向的
purge [pɜːrdʒ]　*v.* 净化；肃清
chastisement [tʃæˈstaɪzmənt, ˈtʃæstɪzmənt]　*n.* 惩罚
raid [reɪd]　*v.* 袭击；打劫
raider [ˈreɪdər]　*n.* 抢劫者；洗劫者

Lesson 88

Part 1　主力单词 / 词组

rational [ˈræʃnəl]　*adj.* 理性的；合理的
She is not being rational by fighting a lion with bare hands.
Learning had not increased our knowledge of good and evil but intensified and made more rational and deadly our greed for gain. (Jan Carew, Guyanese-born novelist, actor, and newspaper editor)

tenable [ˈtenəbl]　*adj.* 站得住脚的；可维持的
The reason for releasing me is not tenable any longer since the victim is dead.
The trade war hurts Asia as well as Europe but that doesn't seem to be politically tenable for the presidential voters.
Encampment on the open plain was not tenable but the higher ground was.
The managerial position is tenable for three years.

reasonable [ˈriːznəbl]　*adj.* 合理的；理智的

• Words in sentences 句中单词 / 词组 •

bare [ber]　*v.* 使赤裸；露出；揭露　*adj.* 赤裸的；最基本的
managerial [ˌmænəˈdʒɪriəl]　*adj.* 管理的

Part 2 补充单词/词组

beyond a reasonable doubt 证据确凿的；确实的
The prosecutor has no proof beyond a reasonable doubt and will not insist to press the charge.

the bare minimum 最低限度的；少量的
She eats only the bare minimum to stay alive.

rapacious [rəˈpeɪʃəs] *adj.* 贪婪的；巧取豪夺的；劫掠的
The prostitute has a rapacious appetite for money.
His soldiers are rapacious and licentious like bandits.
Which animal do you think is more rapacious between the coyote and the fox?

rapacity [rəˈpæsəti] *n.* 贪婪；贪得无厌

covetous [ˈkʌvətəs] *adj.* 贪心的；垂涎的
The covetous person always wants someone else's property.

missile [ˈmɪsl] *n.* 飞弹；导弹；投射物；投射武器 *adj.* 可发射的；可投掷的
Spears and grenades are missile weapons.

avocation [ˌævəˈkeɪʃn] *n.* 副业；兴趣；爱好
Teaching is his vocation and car repairing is his avocation.

Part 3 识记单词/词组

illogical [ɪˈlɑːdʒɪkl] *adj.* 不合逻辑的
self-defeating 自我挫败的；弄巧成拙的
bare...heart/soul 打开……的心扉
intensify [ɪnˈtensɪfaɪ] *v.* 加强；增强
intensification [ɪnˌtensɪfɪˈkeɪʃn] *n.* 强化；加紧
psychosis [saɪˈkoʊsɪs] *n.* 精神病
psychotic [saɪˈkɑːtɪk] *n.* 精神病患者 *adj.* 精神病的
psycho [ˈsaɪkoʊ] *n.* 精神病人
psychopath [ˈsaɪkəpæθ] *n.* 精神病患者

psychopathic [ˌsaɪkə'pæθɪk] *adj.* 精神病的
sociopath ['soʊsioʊpæθ] *n.* 反社会的人；不爱社交的人
purgation [pɜːr'ɡeɪʃən] *n.* 清洁；净化；通便
laxative ['læksətɪv] *adj.* 通便的　*n.* 泻药
lax [læks] *adj.* 松弛的；腹泻的

Lesson 89

Part 1　主力单词/词组

complex [kəm'pleks, 'kɑːmpleks] *n.* 复合物；情结；复句　*adj.* 复杂的
A complex of welfare programs puzzles many civilians.
She has a complex about her birthmark on her left face.
Virility is a complex word.
You can do some exercises in the sports complex.
A complex mixture of chemicals creates this glue.
She has a complex about cockroaches.

complexity [kəm'pleksəti] *n.* 复杂性；难题
The complexity of life itself makes it difficult for scientists to trace its origin.

complicate ['kɑːmplɪkeɪt] *v.* 使复杂化；使恶化；并发（病）
The bacteria infection complicates his illness.

complicated ['kɑːmplɪkeɪtɪd] *adj.* 复杂的；难懂的；结构复杂的
The story is really complicated with many twists.

complication [ˌkɑːmplɪ'keɪʃn] *n.* 使更复杂化的事物；并发症
The peace talk of denuclearization stalled when complications arose.

sophisticated [sə'fɪstɪkeɪtɪd] *adj.* 精于世故的；复杂的
She is neither sophisticated nor nonchalant.

sophistication [səˌfɪstɪ'keɪʃn] *n.* 世故；复杂；高水平
The diplomat has shown considerable sophistication and restraint in winning support from foreign countries.

intricate [ˈɪntrɪkət, ˈɪntrɪkɪt]　*adj.* 错综复杂的

The mechanism of the Rolex watch is extremely intricate and precise.

ravel [ˈrævl]　*v.* 使……更复杂；解开

The intervention of foreign nations ravels the peace talks.

It takes time to ravel out all the threads.

unravel [ʌnˈrævl]　*v.* 弄清；阐明；解开（线团等）；破坏

The old-fashioned horsehair sofa...was the homely instrument of the original scheme of psychotherapy, of psychoanalysis, the science of the unraveling of the tangled skeins of the unconscious mind. (H. D., U.S.-born British poet and writer)

labyrinthine [ˌlæbəˈrɪnθɪn, ˌlæbəˈrɪnθiːn]　*adj.* 曲折复杂的

The insurance salesman tricks his customer to sign that labyrinthine contract.

The insurance contract is usually labyrinthine in order to not compensate for the insured.

labyrinth [ˈlæbərɪnθ]　*n.* 迷宫；曲径；令人迷惑的东西

Japanese had made a complex labyrinth of tunnels in this island.

tapestry [ˈtæpəstri]　*n.* 复杂多样的事件；花毯（手织的）

A tapestry of his personal life and romance has caught the media's attention.

Human existence is only a single thread in the tapestry of the universe.

Turkish tapestry is famous for its motif.

The weft threads pass over and under alternate warp threads creating the image of a tapestry.

imbroglio [ɪmˈbroʊlioʊ]　*n.* 复杂的情节；纠葛

The political imbroglio over the northern borders dissolved quietly.

• Words in sentences 句中单词 / 词组 •

virility [vəˈrɪləti]　*n.* 男子气概；生殖力；活力

trace [treɪs]　*v.* 追查出　*n.* 痕迹；微量；缰绳

twist [twɪst]　*v.* 使弯曲；缠绕；扭伤　*n.* 转折；转动；曲解

insured [ɪnˈʃʊrd]　*n.* 被保险人（物）　*adj.* 已投保的

Turkish [ˈtɜːrkɪʃ]　*adj.* 土耳其的

thread [θred]　*v.* 通过；装软片于　*n.* 线；线状物；一丝

Lesson 89

Part 2 补充单词/词组

ingress ['ɪŋgres] n. 入口；入境；准许进入

She has the right to ingress.

egress ['iːgres] n. 出口；外出

The main egress has been blocked off. Perhaps the incendiary wants them to burn alive.

virile ['vɪrəl] adj. 有男子气概的；强壮的；有生殖力的

Women usually like strong, virile men.

glue [gluː] v. 胶合 n. 胶水

cohesive [koʊ'hiːsɪv] adj. 有黏着力的；凝聚性的；有结合力的

Glue is cohesive.

cohesion [koʊ'hiːʒn] n. 凝聚；附着；[物] 内聚力；团结力

They defeated the enemy due to superior morale and great cohesion.

motif [moʊ'tiːf] n. 图案；式样；主题

odyssey ['ɑːdəsi] n. 漫长而惊险的旅程；精神探索

The recurring motifs in movies are criminal violence and space odyssey.

residue ['rezɪduː] n. 残渣；残余物；剩余财产

toxaphene ['tɒksəfiːn] n. 毒杀芬（非广效性杀虫剂）

insidious residues of DDT, toxaphene, and chlordane

sieve [sɪv] v. 过滤；筛分；筛选 n. 筛子；筛网；过滤器；嘴松的人

The soil was sieved to remove pebbles.

mesh [meʃ] v. 紧密配合；互相协调；被缠住 n. 网线；网状物；陷阱；啮合

The manatee's upper and lower teeth mesh together, forming a sieve.
The farmer covered the strawberry bushes in a nylon mesh to keep the birds from eating the fruit.
They set up a political mesh for the presidential candidate.

due diligence 应有的小心；小心的调查

He investigates the matter with due diligence.

The financial minister exercises all due diligence for the well-being of countrymen.

prospectus [prəˈspektəs] （学校的）简章；募股章程；介绍说明文件

A prospectus containing the salient facts must be delivered to investors.

Part 3 识记单词 / 词组

an inferiority complex　自卑情结
viscose [ˈvɪskouz, ˈvɪskous]　*n.* 黏胶
nonchalant [ˌnɑːnʃəˈlɑːnt]　*adj.* 漠不关心的
nonchalance [ˌnɑːnʃəˈlɑːns]　*n.* 漠不关心；冷淡；无动于衷
trickster [ˈtrɪkstər]　*n.* 骗子
skein [skeɪn]　*n.* 一束；一绞；一群
leftover [ˈleftouvər]　*n.* 残存物；吃剩的饭菜　*adj.* 残余的；吃剩的
curdle [ˈkɜːrdl]　*v.* 凝结
chlordane [ˈklɔːrˌdeɪn]　*n.* [化] 氯丹（杀虫剂）
orchid [ˈɔːrkɪd]　*n.* 兰花；兰科；淡紫色

Lesson 90

Part 1 主力单词 / 词组

worsen [ˈwɜːrsn]　*v.* （使）恶化；（使）更糟

His illness worsens and requires immediate medical attention.
Pain is unjust, and all the arguments that do not soothe it only worsen suspicions. (Jean Baptiste Racine, French playwright)
Steel manufacturing is a signature industry in the city which has for decades been blamed for worsening air pollution.

exacerbate [ɪɡˈzæsərbeɪt]　*v.* 使恶化；使加重；使发怒

The parents exacerbate the situation as they try to bribe the witness.
The incidence of HIV infection will be exacerbated by the growing sex industry in Africa.
The scorching sun has exacerbated the drought. Snails and frogs estivate

aggravate [ˈægrəveɪt] *v.* 加重；使恶化；[口] 激怒

Lip service aggravates the haze problem and infuriates locals.
Lenient punishment only aggravates identity theft and wire fraud.

fester [ˈfestər] *v.* 变得更糟；化脓；溃烂 *n.* 加剧；恶化

It's better to express your anger immediately than let it fester inside you afterwards.
Humiliation over the Eight-Nation Alliance had led to resentment, which festered over the following decades.

• Words in sentences 句中单词 / 词组 •

HIV (human immunodeficiency virus)　人体免疫缺损病毒；艾滋病病毒
estivate=aestivate　*v.* 度夏；夏眠
lip service　只说不做
haze [heɪz]　*v.* 欺凌　*n.* 雾霾
infuriate [ɪnˈfjʊrieɪt]　*v.* 激怒
identity theft　身份盗窃
wire fraud　电汇欺诈
Eight-Nation Alliance　八国联军

Part 2　补充单词 / 词组

naive [naɪˈiːv] *adj.* 天真的

His intelligence remains questionable due to the naive comment he delivered on this serious matter.
This may sound naive, because of course any intervention runs the risk of making a bad situation worse. (Carolyn ax, *Washington Post*)

naivete [naːˈiːvteɪ] *n.* 天真

When the historian never fully realizes his ignorance—which sometimes happens to Americans—he becomes even more tiresome to himself than to others, because his naivete is irrepressible. (Henry Adams, U.S. historian)

verdant [ˈvɜːrdnt] *adj.* 碧绿的；青翠的；缺乏经验的

There are many animals in this verdant plain.
You are too verdant to deal with a sophisticated businessman.

impolitic [ɪmˈpɑːlətɪk] *adj.* 不明智的
To exact revenge toward the old man is impolitic. Why don't you wait for him to die naturally?

amok=amuck *adj.* 疯狂的；嗜杀的

dagger [ˈdæɡər] *v.* 恼怒；用短剑刺 *n.* 短剑；匕首
The gladiator runs amok with his dagger, murdering anyone in his way after hearing that his wife was killed.

berserk [bərˈzɜːrk,bərˈsɜːrk] *adj.* 狂暴的；狂怒的

witchcraft [ˈwɪtʃkræft] *n.* 巫术；魔法
The entirety of islanders has gone berserk, relying on superstition and witchcraft.

vile [vaɪl] *adj.* 卑鄙的；邪恶的；肮脏的
Attacking from behind is a vile and cowardly act.
Be careful if you have to pass the vile slum.

revile [rɪˈvaɪl] *v.* 辱骂；谩骂
His mother reviled him as an ingrate.

Part 3 识记单词 / 词组

a festering argument/dispute 愈益激化的争论 / 争端
lenient [ˈliːniənt] *adj.* 宽容的；宽大的；从轻的
leniency [ˈliːniənsi] *n.* 仁慈；宽大
prawn [prɔːn] *n.* 大虾
jumbo shrimp 大虾
crabbed [ˈkræbɪd,kræbd] *adj.* 脾气坏的；难解的
morose [məˈroʊs] *adj.* 阴郁的；孤僻的
scowl [skaʊl] *v.* 皱眉；沉下脸；（天气）变阴沉 *n.* 怒容
positive externality 正外部性
negative externality 负外部性

Lesson 91

Part 1 主力单词/词组

feasible [ˈfiːzəbl] *adj.* 可行的；可以做的；合理的

To build Rome in a single day is not feasible.

I think the plan is feasible enough to reengineer the robots.

Sanctions are now the only feasible, non-violent way of ending apartheid. The other road to change is covered with blood. (Neil Kinnock, British politician)

viable [ˈvaɪəbl] *adj.* 可实行的；能养活的；能发育的

The novelty of this product was commercially viable.

Tropical plants can form viable hybrids much more easily than animals.

The brand-new religion is viable alongside the indigenous people.

She is a viable candidate.

practicable [ˈpræktɪkəbl] *adj.* 可行的

It seems practicable to manufacture relatively low-cost plastic furniture.

There are practicable religions in the world, such as Chinese Daoism, Indian Buddhism, and western Christianity.

• Words in sentences 句中单词/词组 •

sanction [ˈsæŋkʃn] *v.* 认可；惩罚；实施制裁   *n.* 制裁；批准

apartheid [əˈpɑːrtaɪt, əˈpɑːrteɪt] *n.* 种族隔离制度

Part 2 补充单词/词组

fancy [ˈfænsi] *v.* 想象；认为；想要   *adj.* 绚丽的   *n.* 幻想

She fancies herself as an angel.

He took a fancy to that pretty girl.

The star wore fancy clothes.

fancy yourself 自以为是；自命不凡
He fancies himself as a would-be general.

fancier ['fænsɪər] n. 空想家；育种者
My uncle is a pigeon fancier, not a pigeon trainer.

fancied ['fænsɪd] adj. 空想的；虚构的；爱空想的
Fancied scenarios can't be taken seriously.
He is the most fancied candidate for the next presidential election.

fray [freɪ] v. 磨损；紧张 n. 争论；打架
The cheap pants had frayed at the edges.
Her nerves begin to fray as she became intimidated by backstage rumpus and a catty remark.
He drew his brothers into a fray with a neighbor.

fracas ['freɪkəs] n. 高声争吵；斗殴
The riot control police broke up the fracas and detained combatants during the riot.

criminal ['krɪmɪnl] n. 罪犯 adj. 犯法的
The criminal was extradited from Thailand to the United States.
Mafia is a criminal organization.

criminal offense 刑事犯罪

assault and battery 袭击和暴力伤害（罪）
Assault and battery are criminal offenses.

contagion [kən'teɪdʒən] n. 接触传染；感染
Many leading epidemiologists espouse measures of preventing contagion.

contagious [kən'teɪdʒəs] adj. 接触传染的
Fever is a contagious disease.

healing ['hiːlɪŋ] n. 治愈 adj. 治愈的
Her subtle smile brightens the darkest corners of my heart and gives me a chance of redemption, healing, and repair.

dress code 穿衣法则；着装标准

tuxedo [tʌk'siːdoʊ] n. 晚礼服
Does the fancy restaurant have a dress code? Should I wear a tuxedo?

fig [fɪg] v. 盛装；修整 n. 健康状况
The landlord figged up the old house before renting it out.

The old man who exercises every day is in fine fig.

transplant [træns'plænt,trænz'plænt]　v. 移植；使迁移；使移居　n. 移植；移植器官

We transplanted the orange tree into the garden.
The doctor is going to transplant some skin from your thigh to your face.
The surgeon made an incision in your chest and operated on a heart transplant.

ukase [juːˈkeɪz]　n. 敕令；法令；布告

He violated the company's ukase about wearing a mask during work.

promulgate [ˈprɑːmlɡeɪt]　v. 正式公布（新法律）；宣扬（思想、信仰）

An imperial ukase has been promulgated, dissolving Parliament and Legislature at once.

promulgation [ˌprɑːmlˈɡeɪʃn]　n. 颁布；公布；传播；发布

edict [ˈiːdɪkt]　n. 布告；法令

We must follow the stay-at-home edict during the outbreak of coronavirus.
The school issues an edict about how to dress properly at school.

Part 3　识记单词 / 词组

infeasible [ɪnˈfiːzəbəl]　adj. 不可实行的
impracticable [ɪmˈpræktɪkəbl]　adj. 不能实行的；行不通的
tsar [zɑːr]　n. 沙皇；独裁者
tsar's ukase　沙皇的命令
hybrid [ˈhaɪbrɪd]　n.（动植物的）杂种；混血儿；合成物　adj. 杂种的
hybridize [ˈhaɪbrɪdaɪz]　v. 杂交
hybridization [ˌhaɪbrɪdəˈzeɪʃn]　n. 杂交

Lesson 92

Part 1　主力单词 / 词组

violent [ˈvaɪələnt]　adj. 暴力的；凶残的

Convictions are offenses ranging from violent assault to criminal damage.
The opposition party organized violent demonstrations against the Supreme Court.

violence [ˈvaɪələns] *n.* 暴力

vicious [ˈvɪʃəs] *adj.* 剧烈的；凶残的；恶毒的
The competition here is vicious.

intemperate [ɪnˈtempərət] *adj.* 无节制的；喝过多的；过度的
The wicked politician's outrageous and intemperate remark has shocked all of us.
The president has been condemned as an intemperate racist and extremist.

fierce [fɪrs] *adj.* 猛烈的
The battle seems to be fierce. Casualties amount to 2000.

ferocious [fəˈrouʃəs] *adj.* 凶猛的；激烈的
A ferocious beast tried to bite me.
Maybe I should use ferocious violence to teach it a lesson by beating it with a stick.

rampage [ˈræmpeɪdʒ, ræmˈpeɪdʒ] *v.* 横冲直撞；狂暴；发怒 *n.* 狂暴的行为
The hurricane rampaged through the cornfield.
Thousands of demonstrators rampaged through the park.
When the united enemy captured the forbidden city, they went on a rampage for a month, massacring more than 1000 innocent civilians and fugitive soldiers, raping approximately 100 women, plundering invaluable palace treasures, and torching the city to waste.

● Words in sentences 句中单词 / 词组 ●

conviction [kənˈvɪkʃn] *n.* 判决；判罪
the Supreme Court 最高法院
wicked [ˈwɪkɪd] *adj.* 邪恶的；有害的；顽皮的；过分的
outrageous [aʊtˈreɪdʒəs] *adj.* 骇人的；无耻的
racist [ˈreɪsɪst] *n.* 种族主义者 *adj.* 种族主义的

Part 2 补充单词 / 词组

solidify [səˈlɪdɪfaɪ] *v.* 变坚固；凝固；使团结起来
The nation donates two million dollars to France to solidify their relationship.

coagulate [koʊˈægjuleɪt] *v.* 凝结；凝固
Eggs coagulate as coddled.

plaque [plæk] *n.* 匾；装饰板；血小板；铭牌；徽章

Plaque helps coagulate blood.

coagulation [kouˌægju'leɪʃn] *n.* 凝结物；凝聚；凝固；聚集

outrage ['autreɪdʒ] *v.* 激起……的义愤；违背　*n.* 暴行；骇人听闻的行为

He has outraged the moral standard past endurance.

Public urination arbitrarily outrages public decency.

Arranged outrages and assassinations were executed by terrorists.

remark [rɪ'mɑːrk] *v.* 谈论　*n.* 话语

The public was outraged by his irresponsible remark.

sulfur ['sʌlfər] *n.* 硫磺色；黄绿色　硫（磺）

carbonic acid 碳酸

Does the hot spring contain sulfur or carbonic acid?

molten ['moultən] *adj.* 熔化的；浇铸的

Molten lava flows toward the village.

igneous ['ɪgniəs] *adj.* 火的；[地]（指岩石）火成的

igneous rock 火成岩

magma ['mægmə] *n.* 岩浆；[医]乳浆剂

Igneous rock is formed when magma cools and solidifies.

pyroxene ['paɪərɔksiːn] *n.* 辉石

olivine ['ɑːlɪˌviːn] *n.* 橄榄石

crystallization [ˌkrɪstələ'zeɪʃn] *n.* 结晶化；结晶体

The minerals of pyroxene and olivine were formed during the cooling and crystallization of magma.

obsidian [əb'sɪdiən] *n.* 黑曜石

Ancient Mayans used to make weapons and tools by obsidians which are volcanic rocks.

rhyolite ['raɪəˌlaɪt] *n.* 流纹岩

vitreous ['vɪtriəs] *adj.* 玻璃的；[解]玻璃体的

grain [greɪn] *v.* 对（皮革的）粒面进行处理；使深深渗入　*n.* 谷物；纹理；气质；粒状；结晶

Rhyolite is a fine-grained, vitreous volcanic rock containing numerous cavities that were caused by expanding gas.

granulate [ˈɡrænjəˌleɪt] *v.* 使成粒状；使……表面粗糙

rock sugar 冰糖

The machine granulates rock sugar into smaller granules.

molasses [məˈlæsɪz] *n.* 糖蜜；糖浆

I add some molasses to my bread.

Part 3 识记单词/词组

rat race　日常紧张的竞争活动；无意义的竞争
rat [ræt]　*v.* 捕鼠；背叛；密告　*n.* 鼠；卑鄙小人；叛徒；告密者
sulfur dioxide　二氧化硫（气体）
sulfuric [sʌlˈfjʊrɪk]　*adj.* 硫的；含硫的
sulfate [ˈsʌlfeɪt]　*v.* 硫酸盐化；用硫酸（盐）处理　*n.* 硫酸盐
magmatic [ˈmæɡmətɪk]　*adj.* 岩浆的
crystal [ˈkrɪstl]　*n.* 水晶；水晶饰品　*adj.* 水晶般的
crystalize=crystallize　*v.* 结晶；具体化；成形
solidification [səˌlɪdɪfɪˈkeɪʃn]　*n.* 团结；凝固；固体化
solid silver　纯银
vitreous humor　眼睛的玻璃状液
granule [ˈɡrænjuːl]　*n.* 细粒
lava [ˈlɑːvə]　*n.* 熔岩；火山岩
congeal [kənˈdʒiːl]　*v.* 冻结；凝结；瘫痪；固定
citrus [ˈsɪtrəs]　*n.* 柑橘属植物；柑橘

Lesson 93

Part 1 主力单词/词组

discuss [dɪˈskʌs]　*v.* 讨论

Have you discussed buying a pet with your parents yet?

Lesson 93

Fate has not been kind to Mrs. Browning. Nobody reads her, nobody discusses her, nobody troubles to put her in her place. (Virginia Woolf, British novelist and critic)

confer [kənˈfɜːr] *v.* 商讨；授予

Concerning the disaster-stricken area, local government has convened and conferred, but no real action has been taken.

thrash out 讨论解决

A divergence of opinion should be heard and thrashed out.

thrash sth out 研讨解决……；研讨决定……

I asked all the staff to come together to thrash the glitch out.

thrash [θræʃ] *v.* 打；痛击；摔打（谷物）；使脱粒；推敲；反复研究；剧烈扭动；翻腾

Fish thrashed about in the net.
The ship thrashed in a storm.

tete-a-tete [ˈteɪtɑːˈteɪt] *n.* 促膝谈心 *adv.* 亲密地

We confide to each other and have a tete-a-tete.

discourse [ˈdɪskɔːrs] *v.* 讲述；交谈 *n.* 演讲；谈话

The politician's discourse contains misleading insinuation that gives rise to an ethical problem.

- Words in sentences 句中单词/词组 •

disaster-stricken area 灾区
convene [kənˈviːn] *v.* 召集
divergence [daɪˈvɜːrdʒəns] *n.* 差异；分歧
glitch [ɡlɪtʃ] *n.* 小毛病；小差错；短时脉冲波形干扰
confide [kənˈfaɪd] *v.* 吐露；倾诉（秘密）

Part 2 补充单词/词组

convoke [kənˈvoʊk] *v.* 召集

The president convokes an assembly.

council [ˈkaʊnsl]　*n.* 议会；理事会；议事；商讨

The council was formally convoked to dissolve the parliament.

counsel [ˈkaʊnsl]　*v.* 商议；计划；决策；劝告　*n.* 律师；建议

I took counsel with my lawyer before filing a lawsuit.

caucus [ˈkɔːkəs]　*v.* 召开干部会议　*n.* 干部会议；核心小组；政党的地方委员会

The president caucused to discuss the urgent issue.

The caucus decided to fight for their territory.

flail [fleɪl]　*v.* 用连枷打；拼命挥动；乱动　*n.* 连枷

They were flailing sticks to drive away bats.

The wounded bird lay on the ground, flailing helplessly.

A flail is a weapon that has a metal ball attached to a handle.

intimate [ˈɪntɪmət, ˈɪntəmət, ˈɪntɪmeɪt]　*v.* 透露；暗示　*n.* 密友；知己　*adj.* 亲密的；个人隐私的

An intimate acquaintance came to my house this afternoon.

He only shares this secret with his intimate.

She intimates she will no longer serve as the company's C.E.O..

An intelligent agent intimated that the former leader was in critical condition.

neurology [nʊˈrɑːlədʒi]　*n.* 神经学

His acquaintance with neurology is profound.

dissolve [dɪˈzɑːlv]　*v.* 分解；使溶解；解散；消失　*n.* 叠化画面；解散；终止；破坏；感动；消失

The empire dissolved into several small nations.

The president has the right to dissolve the parliament.

Our marriage was dissolved, as was our business partnership.

She was dissolved in tears by a touching story.

The laws of charities were annulled and dissolved.

The mist dissolves as the sun rises.

disperse [dɪˈspɜːrs]　*v.* 分散；使散开；消失；使色散；散布；疏散；驱散；消散

The police officers dispersed the crowd.

Sunlight dispersed the fog.

The light has a dispersed nature.

The general dispersed his soldiers to defend the enemy.

dispersion [dɪˈspɜːrʒn]　*n.* 散布；离中趋势；分散；弥散

We have to stop the dispersion of foreign species.

scatter [ˈskætər]　*v.* 驱散；消散；分散；撒于……上　*n.* 散布；散播；撒播；[军] 散射

The maple leaves scattered on the ground.

A farmer scattered seeds over the soil.

She scattered her clothes everywhere. Her room was so messy.

The gangsters scattered when the police arrived.

Part 3　识记单词 / 词组

hash sth out　彻底讨论（直到找到解决办法）

to follow sb's counsel　听从某人的劝告

to keep one's own counsel　不透露自己的意见

thresh [θreʃ]　*v.* 打谷；打；反复地做；推敲；研讨

intimacy [ˈɪntɪməsi]　*n.* 亲密；关系密切；亲密的言语；性行为

imprisonment [ɪmˈprɪznmənt]　*n.* 监禁

immure [ɪˈmjʊr]　*v.* 监禁；使蛰居；使闭门不出

immurement [iˈmjuəmənt]　*n.* 监禁；禁闭

internment [ɪnˈtɜːrnmənt]　*n.*（因政治或军事原因）拘留

incarcerate [ɪnˈkɑːrsəreɪt]　*v.* 监禁

incarceration [ɪnˌkɑːrsəˈreɪʃn]　*n.* 下狱；监禁

Lesson 94

Part 1　主力单词 / 词组

ponder [ˈpɑːndər]　*v.* 仔细考虑

Pondering along the riverside, she finally decided to crack down on the military mutiny.

I gave up and retired to ponder on what could be done on the insurmountable project.

The student ponders his options.

ponderable [ˈpɑːndərəbəl]　*n.* 值得考虑的事物　*adj.* 值得考虑的；可想象的

Cooperation with France is ponderable.

ruminate [ˈruːmɪneɪt]　*v.* 沉思；长时间思考

He spent a great deal of time ruminating what she really meant.

cogitate [ˈkɑːdʒɪteɪt]　*v.* 仔细考虑；谋划

If I have to cogitate everything I do, then life will be such an ennui.

deliberate [dɪˈlɪbərət]　*v.* 仔细考虑　*adj.* 故意的

The judge deliberates before sentencing the criminal.

contemplate [ˈkɑːntəmpleɪt]　*v.* 思量；仔细考虑；凝视

Contemplating the circumstances, I believe she still loves me.

conceptualize [kənˈseptʃuəlaɪz]　*v.* 解读；构想出；形成概念

She uses illustrations and photographs to help readers conceptualize information contained in newspapers.

reconceptualize [ˌriːkənˈseptʃuəlaɪz]　*v.* 重新构想出；再解读

The products and services of the company have to be reconceptualized in this highly competitive age.

mull [mʌl]　*v.* 仔细考虑　*n.* 混乱；软薄布

The Supreme Court mulls over the option of ditching the gun-rights case.

• Words in sentences 句中单词 / 词组 •

crack down 镇压

mutiny [ˈmjuːtəni]　*v.* 反叛　*n.* 哗变

insurmountable [ˌɪnsərˈmaʊntəbl]　*adj.* （尤指问题或困难）难以克服的；不可逾越的

ennui [ɑːnˈwiː]　*n.* 无聊；厌倦

Part 2　补充单词 / 词组

imponderable [ɪmˈpɑːndərəbl]　*n.* 难以衡量的事物　*adj.* 难以估量的；难以预料的

The vastness of outer space is imponderable.

There are so many imponderable problems due to the recession.

mutinous [ˈmjuːtənəs] *adj.* 反叛的；哗变的
Mutinous crews kidnapped the captain and surrendered to the British fleet.

circumstance [ˈsɜːrkəmstæns] *n.* 情况；形势；细节；机遇；仪式；条件；详情
We were obliged to go by the force of circumstance.

refugee [ˌrefjuˈdʒiː] *n.* 难民
Refugees were victims of circumstance.

clarion [ˈklæriən] *n.* 响亮清澈的声音 *adj.* 响亮清澈的；嘹亮的 *v.* 大声宣布

clarion call 感人的号召；动人的演讲
He made the clarion call to defend our village.

pensive [ˈpensɪv] *adj.* 沉思的；忧戚的
The man stared at me with his pensive eyes.

Part 3 识记单词 / 词组

conceptualization [kənˌseptʃuəlɪˈzeɪʃn] *n.* 概念化
noncompete clause 竞业禁止条款
trumpet [ˈtrʌmpɪt] *n.* 喇叭；小号
clarinet [ˌklærɪəˈnet] *n.* 木箫；竖笛
ditch [dɪtʃ] *v.* 抛弃；遗弃 *n.* 沟渠
circumstantial evidence 间接证据；旁证
chronic [ˈkrɑːnɪk] *adj.* 长期的；慢性的
larva [ˈlɑːrvə] *n.* 幼虫
chalice [ˈtʃælɪs] *n.* 大酒杯；圣餐杯
goblet [ˈɡɑːblət] *n.* 高脚杯

Lesson 95

Part 1 主力单词/词组

entrench [ɪn'trentʃ] *v.* 确立；牢固；挖掘

The consummate happiness of fairy tales has entrenched in the hearts of many children.
Reincarnation, astrology, and supernatural phenomena are entrenched beliefs in Southeastern Asia.
The empire entrenched his control over his people.
The manager hired his classmates to entrench himself in the office.

take root in one's heart 深植内心；根深蒂固

The belief in reincarnation has taken root in these villagers' hearts.

embed [ɪm'bed] *v.* 把……牢牢嵌入

Fossils were embedded in these rocks.
Please embed these video files in your e-mail.
Childhood trauma has been embedded in his psyche.

ingrain [ɪn'greɪn] *v.* 使……深深印在脑中；给……原纱染色 *n.* 生染的纤维 *adj.* 根深蒂固的；原纱染色的

The father has ingrained his children with a deep respect for teachers.

ingrained [ɪn'greɪnd] *adj.*（观念）根深蒂固的；（尘土等）深嵌着的；难以去除的

Both sides have this deeply ingrained distrust.

• Words in sentences 句中单词/词组 •

supernatural phenomena 超自然的现象
reincarnation [ˌriːɪnkɑːr'neɪʃn] *n.* 轮回转世
psyche ['saɪki] *n.* 心灵；精神；心态

Part 2 补充单词/词组

bury [ˈberi] v. 埋葬；埋藏

The child buried a dead cat.

relative [ˈrelətɪv] n. 亲戚 adj. 相对的；相关联的

My uncles and cousins are all my relatives.

It is a matter relative to world peace.

sorrow [ˈsɑːroʊ] v./n. 悲伤

His sorrowing relatives refused to bury him unless the truth comes out.

Her sorrow reveals in her paintings.

soothe [suːð] v. 减轻；缓和

Her kindness soothes my pain and sorrow.

emollient [ɪˈmɑːliənt] n. 润肤剂 adj. 润肤的；使缓和的

I often use an emollient in winter to soothe my skin.

She used emollient words to soothe our tension.

hubris [ˈhjuːbrɪs] n. 傲慢；狂妄

His hubris in his army's capability attributes to the defeat in World War One.

no wonder 难怪

No wonder the entire crew was going down with him.

bravura [brəˈvjʊrə] n. 精湛技艺 adj. 精湛技艺的

Surviving the landing on death island was a project of boldness and foolhardiness, requiring great bravura and risking great hubris.

We saw the bravura performance of the ballet at the national concert.

Part 3 识记单词/词组

trench [trentʃ] n. 壕沟

sondage [sɒnˈdɑːʒ] n. 试掘深沟

epiphenomenon [ˌepɪfɪˈnɑːmɪnən] n. 附带现象；附带症状

astrologist= astrologer n. 占星师

occurence [əˈkʌrəns] n. 发生的事；事件；遭遇

mutable [ˈmjuːtəbl] *adj.* 可变的；会变的
march [mɑːrtʃ] *n.* 边界 *v.* 行进；共享边界
interference [ˌɪntərˈfɪrəns] *n.* 干涉；阻挠；阻碍
impingement [ɪmˈpɪndʒmənt] *n.* 影响；冲突；侵害
interferometry [ˌɪntərfəˈrɒmɪtri] *n.* 干涉仪；干涉法
maturity [məˈtʃʊrəti, məˈtʊrəti] *n.* 成熟；完成；齐备
preordain [ˌpriːɔːrˈdeɪn] *v.* 预先注定
swoon [swuːn] *v.* 昏厥；昏倒 *n.* 心醉神迷
be nominated 被提名
nominate [ˈnɑːmɪneɪt] *v.* 提名
misname [ˌmɪsˈneɪm] *v.* 误称；诋毁
propose a toast 提议为……祝酒；提议为……干杯

Lesson 96

Part 1 主力单词/词组

drive [draɪv] *v.* 开车；驱赶；驱动；猛击 *n.* 驱车旅行；驾车；传动

The war was driven by territorial disputes.
His insolent attitude drives me mad.
The storm drove them to shelter.

motivate [ˈmoʊtɪveɪt] *v.* 成为……的动机；是……的原因；推动……

Self-esteem motivates her to study hard so as to get into a prestigious university.

incite [ɪnˈsaɪt] *v.* 煽动

The insurgent incites rebellion.

entice [ɪnˈtaɪs] *v.* 诱使

Salesmen often entice customers to buy more things.

rouse [raʊz] *v.* 唤醒；使觉醒

The mentor roused him from his daydream.

At the sight of his injured compatriots rousing his courage, he furiously attacked the enemy alone regardless of consequence.

arouse [əˈraʊz]　v. 引起；唤醒；激起性欲
A lot of people, on the verge of death, utter famous last words or stiffen into attitudes...They still want to arouse admiration and adopt a pose and tell a lie with their last gasp.

provoke [prəˈvoʊk]　v. 激起；引起；挑衅
Coal incineration, which gives rise to haze, has provoked a public outcry.
The orphanage provoke memories of my childhood.

invoke [ɪnˈvoʊk]　v. 法律的引用；召唤；唤起
The antiquated defense of insanity is rarely invoked in England.
The sorcerer invoked Apollo to help us.

propel [prəˈpel]　v. 推动；驱动；推进
Fear of retribution propelled him to run away.
The North Korean military propelled the rocket into the sky.

impel [ɪmˈpel]　v. 迫使
Starvation has impelled nomads to plunder the south.

urge [ɜːrdʒ]　v. 敦促；驱策；力劝
He urged us to go to the dugout during the airstrike.
Citizens have urged the government to take drastic measures against illegal immigrants.

galvanize [ˈɡælvənaɪz]　v. 激起
The bombing of the embassy has galvanized widespread student protests.

instigate [ˈɪnstɪɡeɪt]　v. 使开始；使发生；煽动；唆使
Refusing to submit, they instigate a rebellion.

fear-mongering　散布恐慌
His fear-mongering strategy might work during the election.

goad [ɡoʊd]　v. 驱使；刺激；激怒
The WTO was designed to goad the laggards into further liberalization of trading on a worldwide basis.

touch off　激起；点燃爆炸；胜了一点点
The sex scandal had also touched off a fusillade of investigations, media inquiries, civil lawsuits, and probes by legal agencies.

elicit [ɪˈlɪsɪt]　*v.* 激起；探出；诱出

The psychiatrist tried to elicit the main cause of his patient's phobia.

elicitation [ɪˌlɪsɪˈteɪʃn]　*n.* 引出；诱出；抽出；启发

impetus [ˈɪmpɪtəs]　*n.* 动力；冲力

The government is devoid of impetus to improve conservation further.

The special government funding provided an impetus.

actuate [ˈæktʃueɪt]　*v.* 启动；激励；驱使

The robot was actuated by electricity.

She was actuated by self-interest.

actuation [ˌæktʃuˈeɪʃən]　*n.* 活动；开动

foment [foʊˈment]　*v.* 挑起；激起；煽动；热敷

The major's incompetence foments the discontent from the public.

He was accused of fomenting the Hong Kong riot

prod [prɑːd]　*v.* 刺；戳；鼓动　*n.* 催促；鼓励；提醒

The military adviser prodded the commander to leave the island.

The teacher prods us to hand in our assignment on time.

• Words in sentences 句中单词 / 词组 •

insolent [ˈɪnsələnt]　*adj.* 无礼的

insurgent [ɪnˈsɜːrdʒənt]　*n.* 叛乱者；反对派

compatriot [kəmˈpeɪtriət]　*n.* 同胞；同事

gasp [gæsp]　*v.* 喘气；倒抽一口气；上气不接下气地说　*n.* 喘气

outcry [ˈaʊtkraɪ]　*n.* 强烈抗议

sorcerer [ˈsɔːrsərər]　*n.* 魔法师

plunder [ˈplʌndər]　*v.* 掠夺；侵占

dugout [ˈdʌgaʊt]　*n.* 防空洞；地下掩体；独木舟；队员座席

airstrike [ˈeɪrˌstraɪk]　*n.* 空袭；空中打击

laggard [ˈlægərd]　*n.* 落后的人；落后的事物　*adj.* 行动迟缓的；勉强的

fusillade [ˈfjuːsəlɑːd, ˈfjuːsəleɪd]　*v.* 用猛烈炮火击落；以排炮齐射　*n.* 连发；连续齐射；连续投掷

Part 2 补充单词/词组

strategical [strə'tɪdʒɪkl] *adj.* 战略的

The snake perches on a strategical position, waiting for its prey to pass by.

reverie ['revəri] *n.* 白日梦；幻想；[音] 幻想曲

The Qing Empire was aroused from a reverie of supremacy after battling with Japan.

I was lost in reverie in a train station after she said goodbye to me.

unsurpassed [ˌʌnsər'pæst] *adj.* 卓绝的；出类拔萃的

The birthday gift you gave me was unsurpassed romantic evocations of Beijing.

wizard ['wɪzərd] *n.* 男巫；术士；[口] 奇才；名家 *adj.* 男巫的；巫术的

He is a wizard at electrical engineering.

wizardry ['wɪzərdri] *n.* 巫术；魔法；高超的技能

The attorney demonstrates her wizardry in legal maneuvering.

corsair [kɔːr'ser] *n.* 海盗；海盗船

The corsairs pillaged passing merchant vessels.

pillage ['pɪlɪdʒ] *v.* 抢劫；掠夺 *n.* 掠夺物

The village was pillaged by bandits.

booty ['buːti] *n.* 战利品；掠夺物；奖品；赠品

The French general transported the booty back to France.

bootie ['buːtiː] *n.* 毛线鞋

The dog was worn green booties on its feet.

malcontent [ˌmælkən'tent] *n.* 不满现状的人；反抗者 *adj.* 不满的；不服的

Italian authorities were trying to get rid of malcontents among the many applying to leave the country.

He is one of the malcontent soldiers.

responsive [rɪ'spɑːnsɪv] *adj.* 回答的；响应的

She stared at me and I gave her a responsive glance.

The patient was not responsive to medicine.

The lawyer is very responsive to the needs of her clients.

messiah [mə'saɪə] *n.* 救世主；救星

Do you believe a messiah will come down from Heaven at the end of the world?

last-ditch [ˌlæst ˈdɪtʃ] *adj.* 最后的努力
Soldiers made a last-ditch effort to hold off the enemy.
The last-ditch resistance is likely to fail.

paean [ˈpiːən] *n.* 赞歌
She wrote a paean to the queen on her birthday.
The song is a paean to love.

maim [meɪm] *v.* 使残废；使受重伤
The missile killed no one but maimed several civilians.
Car accidents maim dozens of people every year.

determinant [dɪˈtɜːrmɪnənt] *n.* 决定因素 *adj.* 决定的
Working experience and education level are determinants of income.
Determinant factors of one's personality might rely on his childhood experience.

grotto [ˈɡrɑːtoʊ] *n.* 洞穴；石室；避暑洞室
There are countless grottoes near the mountain.

litany [ˈlɪtəni] *n.* 连祷（文）；陈词滥调
The priest chanted the Litany of the Saints.
The hotel manager received a litany of complaints.
Flooding causes a litany of problems.

extradite [ˈekstrədaɪt] *v.* 引渡
The criminal was extradited from Brazil for prosecution.

extradition [ˌekstrəˈdɪʃn] *n.* 引渡
He filed a lawsuit to avoid extradition.

extradition proceedings 引渡程序
They locked me up for two months and then started the extradition proceedings.

hap [hæp, hɑːp] *n.* 机会；幸运
The draw is purely by hap.

nasty [ˈnæsti] *adj.* 龌龊的；令人作呕的
They have played nasty tricks on each other. Now their relationship is irreparable.

modish [ˈmoʊdɪʃ] *adj.* 流行的；时髦的
A deep décolletage made the shirt more modish.

onus [ˈoʊnəs]　*n.* 责任；义务；耻辱

Legislators put the onus of national defense on the president.
The onus is on you to exhibit the extent of your suffering to the judge.
He bears the onus of causing the accident.

capias [ˈkeɪpɪæs]　*n.* 拘票

mittimus [ˈmɪtəməs]　*n.* 收监令

The capias mittimus was executed by state marshals.

Part 3　识记单词/词组

driving while intoxicated　酒后驾驶（罪）
perch [pɜːrtʃ]　*v.* 栖息；暂歇；飞落　*n.* 栖息处；位居（某职位）
carry out reprisals　进行报复
monger [ˈmɑːŋɡər]　*v.* 贩卖；制造　*n.* 商人；小贩
ironmonger [ˈaɪərnˌmɑːŋɡər]　*n.* 五金商人
ironmaster [ˈaɪərnˌmæstər]　*n.* 铁器制造业者
haven [ˈheɪvn]　*v.* 避难；为……提供避难处　*n.* 避风港
pipe dream　白日梦；幻想
retributive [rɪˈtrɪbjutɪv]　*adj.* 惩罚性的
reprisal [rɪˈpraɪzl]　*n.* 报复；报复性劫掠
retaliate [rɪˈtælieɪt]　*v.* 反击；报复
vindictive [vɪnˈdɪktɪv]　*adj.* 想复仇的；怀恨在心的
despoil [dɪˈspɔɪl]　*v.* 破坏；洗劫
maraud [məˈrɔːd]　*v.* 洗劫
marauder [məˈrɔːdər]　*n.* 洗劫者
submission [səbˈmɪʃn]　*n.* 屈服；提交；谦恭
succumb [səˈkʌm]　*v.* 屈从；屈服
illicit [ɪˈlɪsɪt]　*adj.* 非法的；违禁的
prorogue [proʊˈroʊɡ]　*v.* 使休会
prorogation [ˌproʊroʊˈɡeɪʃən]　*n.* 休会；闭会

Lesson 97

Part 1 主力单词 / 词组

forerunner [ˈfɔːrʌnər] *n.* 先驱者；前兆

Tribes are a forerunner of a nation.
The dawn is the forerunner of the rising sun.
The U.S. is a forerunner in space technology.

herald [ˈherəld] *v.* 欢迎；预兆；显示；公开 *n.* 传讯者；使者；征兆

The sprouting plants are a herald of spring.
The legion has sent a herald (messenger) rushing to the castle to ask the king for reinforcement.

harbinger [ˈhɑːrbɪndʒər] *v.* 前兆 *n.* 预示前兆的人

The denuclearization agreement is the harbinger of world peace.

bellwether [ˈbelweðər] *n.* 风向标；领导者；领头羊

The stock market is a bellwether of a country's economy.
China is considered to be a bellwether of manufacturing processes.
Prada and Louis Vuitton are bellwethers of fashion.

predecessor [ˈpredəsesər] *n.* 前任；前辈；原有事物；祖先

The compatriot missile outruns its predecessor.
The predecessor of the district attorney was dilatory and negligent which led to the reinvestigation.
The antivirus software needs to be updated to replace its predecessor.

precursor [prɪˈkɜːrsər] *n.* 先驱者；前任；反应前的化合物

Acid rain and its precursor have been brought to the fore.
During the Middle Ages, the precursors of many modern institutions were created.
The U.S. president's uncompromising manner is unlike that of his precursor.

trailblazer [ˈtreɪlbleɪzər] *n.* 开路者；先驱者

The trailblazer noticed a speck of blood on a fallen leaf.

apostle [əˈpɑːsl] *n.* 倡导者；使徒

Martin Luther King is an apostle for racial equality.

Lesson 97

spearhead [ˈspɪrhed]　*v.* 当……的先锋；带头；为……扫清道路　*n.* 矛头；枪尖；先锋

She spearheaded the archaeological project to excavate an ancient monument.

preface [ˈprefəs]　*v.* 作为……的开端；在……之前　*n.* 序言；序祷；序幕；前奏

he notes were prefaced in each chapter.
The professor prefaces his speech with a joke.
The author wrote the preface of the book concisely.
The assassination of the prince was the preface of World War Two.

prefatory [ˈprefətɔːri]　*adj.* 序文的；位于前面的

prefatory remarks　开场白

preamble [ˈpriːæmbl]　*n.* 先兆；前奏；序言；开场白

The preamble of the new Constitution stressed the equality of all people.
Brian was sent the prototype of a new product without a preamble explaining how to use it.
I take it for granted that the present question is a mere preamble—a title-page to a great tragic volume. (John Quincy Adams, U.S. president)
His early research in A.I. and biology were just a preamble to his later invention of invincible cyborgs.

• Words in sentences 句中单词 / 词组 •

sprout [spraʊt]　*v.* 使萌芽；很快地成长　*n.* 幼苗；嫩枝；年幼者
legion [ˈliːdʒən]　*n.* 军团；众多
attorney (lawyer) [əˈtɜːrni]　律师
district attorney　地方检察官
negligent [ˈneɡlɪdʒənt]　*adj.* 疏忽的；失职的
antivirus [ˈæntivaɪrəs]　*adj.* 杀毒的
to the fore　显要位置
speck [spek]　*v.* 使产生斑点；使沾上污点　*n.* 斑点；污迹；微粒；微小物；一点点

Part 2 补充单词 / 词组

dilatory [ˈdɪlətɔːri] *adj.* 拖延的；迟缓的
Brazil's rainforest wildfires were blamed on the dilatory and arrogant attitudes of the prime minister.

acidulous [əˈsɪdʒələs] *adj.* 微酸的；尖刻的；带讽刺意味的
He delivered an acidulous speech to the new president after failing the election.
India-Pakistan relations degenerated into acidulous animosities due to the boundary issue.

detestation [ˌdiːteˈsteɪʃn] *n.* 憎恨；厌恶
She alternated between affection and detestation at the sight of her lover who had cheated on her.

commentary [ˈkɑːmənteri] *n.* 社论

alternately [ˈɔːltərnətli] *adv.* 轮流地；交替地
The commentary has alternately praised, satirized, and sentimentalized U.S. settlers who had eradicated Indians.

commentariat [kəmənˈtəriət] *n.* 政治时事评论者
Messages from online commentariats were swift and largely damning.

commentator [ˈkɑːmənteɪtər] *n.* 实况播音员；注释者；评注者

mote [moʊt] *n.* 尘埃；微粒
Motes float in the shafts of sunlight.

tread [tred] *v.* 踩；踏；步行；践踏 *n.* 踏板；胎面；鞋底；轮距
The drug dealer is treading in a path leading to perdition.

perdition [pɜːrˈdɪʃn] *n.* 地狱；毁灭
They condemned the criminal to eternal perdition.
Perdition awaits him for his enormous crime.

Part 3 识记单词 / 词组

legions of fans 众多的影迷
denuclearization [diːˌnjuːklɪəriˈzeɪʃən] *n.* 去核化
denuclearize [diːˈnjuːklɪəraɪz] *v.* 非核化；解除核武器
detest [dɪˈtest] *v.* 厌恶；憎恨；讨厌

paper trail 能证明某人活动的纸质文件；纸质追踪档案
be trailing （比赛中）落后；失败；逐渐减弱到停止；逐渐消失
devil's advocate 故意唱反调的人
peculiarity [pɪˌkjuːliˈærəti] *n.* 古怪
permeate [ˈpɜːrmieɪt] *v.* 渗透；弥漫
permeable [ˈpɜːrmiəbl] *adj.* 可渗透的；可渗入的
impermeable [ɪmˈpɜːrmiəbl] *adj.* 不可渗透的；不透气的
exponentially [ˌekspəˈnenʃəli] *adv.* 指数地；快速发展地
exponential [ˌekspəˈnenʃl] *adj.* 指数的；幂的
darwinism [ˈdɑːrwɪnɪzəm] *n.* 进化论；达尔文主义
preposition [ˌprepəˈzɪʃn] *n.* 介词
reinvestigate [ˌriːɪnˈvestɪgeɪt] *v.* 重新调查

Lesson 98

Part 1 主力单词/词组

infect [ɪnˈfekt] *v.* 传染；影响
The bacterium infected half of the population.
Don't be that paranoid. You might infect our morale.
His bad mood infects all of us.

infectious [ɪnˈfekʃəs] *adj.* 传染性的；感染的
Infectious diseases have to be curbed.
Tuberculosis is an infectious and contagious disease.

contagious [kənˈteɪdʒəs] *adj.* 传染性的；接触传染的
Compassion, sympathy, and empathy are contagious.

transmit [trænzˈmɪt, trænsˈmɪt] *v.* 传播；传染
The radio wave was transmitted from that station.
It was said that AIDS (Acquired Immunodeficiency Syndrome) was transmitted amongst gay men.

contaminate [kənˈtæmɪneɪt]　v. 污染

These rivers have been contaminated by metals.

contamination [kənˌtæmɪˈneɪʃn]　n. 污染；污秽；交感

taint [teɪnt]　v. 使感染；玷污　n. 污点；败坏

The role model was tainted by his conceitedness.
Her sanguine personality was tainted by envy.
The taint of the priors causes him to lose the election.

metastasis [məˈtæstəsɪs]　n. [医] 转移

This medicine should prevent the metastasis of the chondrosarcoma.

metastasize [məˈtæstəˌsaɪz]　v. 转移

Cancer metastasized from his lung to his whole body.

● Words in sentences 句中单词 / 词组 ●

morale [məˈræl]　n. 士气
empathy [ˈempəθi]　n. 感同身受
immunodeficiency [ˌɪmjuːnoʊdɪˈfɪʃnsi]　n. 免疫缺陷
syndrome [ˈsɪndroʊm]　n. 症状
gay [geɪ]　n. 同性恋　adj. 开心的
chondrosarcoma [ˌkɒndrəʊsɑːˈkəʊmə]　n. 软骨肉瘤

Part 2　补充单词 / 词组

rheum [ruːm]　n. 分泌物；鼻黏膜感冒

The rheum was exuding from the sick turtle's eyes.

rheumatic [ruˈmætɪk]　adj. 稀黏液的；引起鼻炎的

Rheumatic diseases are the most common cause of chronic illness, according to the latest research.

Part 3　识记单词 / 词组

epidemic [ˌepɪˈdemɪk]　n. 流行性的传染　adj. 流行性的；极为盛行的

transmission [trænzˈmɪʃn, trænsˈmɪʃn] *n.* 传染；传播；变速器发射；播送；传输
cleanse [klenz] *v.* 净化；清洗；使……清洁
redeem [rɪˈdiːm] *v.* 赎回；救赎；拯救；弥补
metaplasia [ˌmetəˈpleɪʒə] *n.* 组织的变形
hyperplasia [ˌhaɪpərˈpleɪʒə] *n.* [医] 增生
metaphase [ˈmetəˌfeɪz] *n.* 细胞分裂中期
metagalaxy [ˌmetəˈɡæləksi] *n.* 总星系
paranoia [ˌpærəˈnɔɪə] *n.* 疑神疑鬼；多疑
schizophrenia [ˌskɪtsəˈfriːniə, ˌskɪtsəˈfreniə] *n.* 精神分裂症
schizophrenic [ˌskɪtsəˈfrenɪk] *adj.* 患精神分裂症的；反复无常的；自相矛盾的

Lesson 99

Part 1 主力单词 / 词组

focus [ˈfoʊkəs] *v.* 使集中注意力；使聚焦 *n.* 焦点

You have to remain focused on your project.
The president focuses mainly on economic development instead of political ideology.
Sensationalism, which dominates the entire press, is the focus.
The path of the rocket orbiting Mars has the shape of a conic section—a circle, ellipse, parabola, or hyperbola—with the central body at one focus of the curve.
The environmental bureau launched a broad research program focused on pollution problems that arise when modern technology and science are introduced into massive rural areas, ravaging all sorts of creatures.

concentrate [ˈkɑːnsntreɪt] *v.* 专注；集中；提炼 *n.* 浓缩物；浓缩液；精矿

It is very difficult for me to concentrate when you play your music so loud.
I should concentrate all my resources on making a profit.
Most toxins concentrate in a fish's liver.
The national populations of some countries are concentrated in their capital cities.

concentration [ˌkɑːnsnˈtreɪʃn] *n.* 浓度；集中；专心

You have to remain focused and learn the strength of concentration.

They have obtained concentrations of uranium from raw ore.

engross [ɪnˈɡrous]　v. 使专注；使着迷

The surreal movie engrosses us all the way to the uncanny ending.
The tyrant decided the attack of his neighboring countries, completely disconnected from conscience and engrossed in his own needs and desires to expand his territory insatiably.
The film engrossed viewers.
The readers purchased engrossing novels.
People were engrossed in and enraptured by the *Harry Potter* movies.

rapt [ræpt]　adj. 全神贯注的

Children often watch cartoons with rapt attention.
Her face was rapt with pleasure and desire by a big shining diamond.

cathect [kæˈθekt]　v. 将精力集中于

She devotes her time cathecting with the subject of psychology.
You should cathect with the song while you are singing.
Nothing can distract a cathected person of arts.

cathexis [kəˈθeksis]　n. [心] 精神集中

• **Words in sentences 句中单词 / 词组** •

sensationalism [senˈseɪʃənəlɪzəm]　n. 耸人听闻；制造轰动
conic [ˈkɑːnɪk]　adj. 圆锥的
ellipse [ɪˈlɪps]　n. 椭圆形
parabola [pəˈræbələ]　n. 抛物线
hyperbola [haɪˈpɜːrbələ]　n. 双曲线
uranium [juˈreɪniəm]　n. 铀
raw [rɔː]　adj. 生的；未开采的
ore [ɔːr]　n. 矿石；矿砂
surreal [səˈriːəl]　adj. 超现实的；梦幻般的；离奇的
uncanny [ʌnˈkæni]　adj. 奇怪的；神秘的；无法解释的
enrapture [ɪnˈræptʃər]　v. 使高兴；将……奉献（给）；把……全用于

Part 2 补充单词 / 词组

architect [ˈɑːrkɪtekt] *n.* 建筑师；缔造者

in section 以截面图的方式

The architect shows the house in section.

sports section 体育版

The sports section of the magazine features an article on my brother.

section [ˈsekʃn] *v.* 切开；切断 *n.* 切割成片；切下的部分；片；区域；阶层；部门；剖面图

She sectioned a watermelon for colleagues in the business section.

coroner [ˈkɔːrənər] *n.* 验尸官

The coroner performed a dissection.

dissection [dɪˈsekʃn, daɪˈsekʃn] *n.* 切开；解剖；解剖体；仔细分析；详细查究

The detective decided to pursue a different profession after the dissection of the homicide case disturbed her.

aortic [eˈɔrtɪk] *adj.* 主动脉的

Performing an aortic surgery can be dangerous.

sherbet [ˈʃɜːrbət] *n.* 果汁牛奶冻；果汁冰沙

Sherbet is a frozen dessert.

saffron [ˈsæfrən] *n.* 藏红花 *adj.* 橙黄色的

Premium saffrons, which contain abundant antioxidants, cost around $3000 for 2 pounds.

sear [sɪr] *v.* 烧烤；打烙印；使失去感觉 *n.* 烧焦痕迹；烙印 *adj.* 干焦的

She seared a fish with saffron rice on a pan.

elliptical [ɪˈlɪptɪkl] *adj.* 椭圆形的；省略的

Elliptical galaxies have an ovoid or globular shape generally containing older stars.

ascendancy [əˈsendənsi] *n.* 优势

The politician knows how to utilize the ascendancy of the public.

The U.S. gained a firm ascendancy over the battle on the eastern front because Japan ran out of resources.

potter [ˈpɑːtər]　*v.* 闲混；虚度；消磨　*n.* 陶工；陶艺家

The rascal used to potter around in the plaza.

pottery [ˈpɑːtəri]　*n.* 陶器；陶器厂；制陶手艺

They found ancient potteries in a cave.

canny [ˈkæni]　*adj.* 精明的；机敏的；节俭的

You cannot fool with a canny boss.

devout [dɪˈvaʊt]　*adj.* 虔诚的；衷心的

She is a devout Christian.
The teacher has a devout wish for her success.

Part 3　识记单词/词组

focal point　焦点

go/run round in circles　原地兜圈；白忙

an ice cream cone　冰淇淋蛋筒

aorta [eɪˈɔːrtə]　*n.* 主动脉

session [ˈseʃn]　*n.* 会议；开庭；一段时间

summer session　暑期开课

orange-juice concentrate　橘子浓缩果汁

a mineral concentrate　精矿

a mineral deposit　矿层

mother lode　主矿脉

lode [loʊd]　*n.* 矿脉；金属矿

press a charge　指控

hyperbole [haɪˈpɜːrbəli]　*n.* 夸张的语句；修辞的夸张法

rapture [ˈræptʃər]　*n.* 很幸福；很高兴

rapture on his face　欣喜若狂

rapturous [ˈræptʃərəs]　*adj.* 兴高采烈的；狂喜的

Lesson 100

Part 1 主力单词 / 词组

relieve [rɪ'liːv] *v.* 缓解；减轻

I felt relieved at the sight of rescuers.
Gout is not relieved by a fine shoe nor a hangnail by a costly ring nor migraine by a tiara. (Plutarch, Greek biographer and philosopher)

relief [rɪ'liːf] *n.* 缓解；减轻；救济；浮雕

The exhilarating comedy provided relief from rancor.
Riot endangered international relief workers.
The picture in the church window was a relief.

mitigate ['mɪtɪgeɪt] *v.* 使缓和；减轻

German prime minister Angela Merkel has mitigated the tensions and misunderstandings concerning the treatment of Iraqi refugees residing in Germany.

alleviate [ə'liːvieɪt] *v.* 减轻；缓和

Action has to be taken to alleviate the pressing problems of inflation.

allay [ə'leɪ] *v.* 减轻；缓解

The conqueror tries to allay fear, anxiety, and rancorous feelings by offering their captives food and water.

palliate ['pælieɪt] *v.* 减轻负面影响

Candy as a placebo can palliate the child's illness but cannot cure it.

palliative ['pæliətɪv] *adj.* 缓解剂；治标药物

soothe [suːð] *v.* 抚慰；使平静；缓和；减轻

The prospect of fame and fortune might soothe the politician's irritation by slander and libel.

assuage [ə'sweɪdʒ] *v.* 缓和；减轻；满足；使安静

I have to win the case so as to assuage others' misgivings about my leadership capabilities.

appease [ə'piːz] *v.* 平息；抚慰

The country appeased its outraged minorities.

pacifist [ˈpæsɪfɪst] *n.* 和平（反战）主义者

pacify [ˈpæsɪfaɪ] *v.* 使平静；平息；安抚

You can pacify gods through worship and sacrifice.

pacification [ˌpæsɪfɪˈkeɪʃn] *n.* 平息；安抚手段；和解

lessen [ˈlesn] *v.* 减少；降低；减轻

The latest technology of nuclear generation of electricity has lessened the shortage of power.

remit [rɪˈmɪt, ˈriːmɪt] *v.* 汇款；减轻；饶恕

remission [rɪˈmɪʃn] *n.* 减轻（病情、罪行、刑期）；饶恕；豁免

His acute flu was in remission.

The judge gave him a three-month remission.

We prayed based on the remission of sins.

The scorching sun beat down on us without remission.

mollify [ˈmɑːlɪfaɪ] *v.* 使平静；抚慰

The policemen mollified the kidnappers by offering them a helicopter.

anodyne [ˈænədaɪn] *n.* 止痛剂；缓和物；镇痛剂 *adj.* 止痛的；不得罪人的；一团和气的；温和的

The dentist prescribed an anodyne for me after the removal of my tooth.

She always makes anodyne comments, not provocative at all.

painkiller [ˈpeɪnkɪlər] *n.* 止痛药

Opium, which has an anodyne property, is used as a painkiller in medical practice.

propitiate [prəʊˈpɪʃieɪt] *v.* 使高兴；安抚

They pushed him into a deep fire pit to propitiate a god.

He propitiates the business for getting a job.

propitiation [prəʊˌpɪʃɪˈeɪʃn] *n.* 挽回；和解

• Words in sentences 句中单词 / 词组 •

gout [ɡaʊt] *n.* 痛风

hangnail [ˈhæŋneɪl] *n.* 手指头的倒拉刺

migraine [ˈmaɪɡreɪn] *n.* 偏头痛

tiara [tiˈɑːrə] n. 冕状宝石头饰
rancorous [ˈræŋkərəs] adj. 很生气的；很不友善的
captive [ˈkæptɪv] n. 战俘
irritation [ˌɪrɪˈteɪʃn] n. 恼怒
scorch [skɔːrtʃ] v. 烤；(使)烧焦 n. 变色；高速疾驶；飞驰
beat down 曝晒

Part 2 补充单词/词组

immitigable [ɪˈmɪtɪgəbl] adj. 不能缓和的；不能减轻的
The pain of losing his children was immitigable.

unassuageable [ˌʌnəˈsweɪdʒəbl] adj. 无法被安抚的
She has unassuageable hatred toward her ex-husband.

unmitigated [ʌnˈmɪtɪgeɪtɪd] adj. 未缓和的；未减轻的；彻底的；全然的
The drastic change of policy leads to an unmitigated failure in his business.

rancorous debate 很生气的争论

grudge [grʌdʒ] n. 怨恨；嫌隙；妒忌
From our rancorous debate, she still holds a grudge against me.

polemicist [pəˈlemɪsɪst] n. 参与论战者
The TV polemicist has probed the boundaries of what constitutes conscience and justice.

polemical [pəˈlemɪkl] adj. 有争议性的；好争论的
The books he published were frequently polemical in content.
The author was a satiric poet and polemical writer in morality.

polemic [pəˈlemɪk] n. 争论；辩论；争论者 adj. 好争论的

nostrum [ˈnɑːstrəm] n. 万能药；秘方
Hypochondriacs squander large sums of time in search of nostrums by which they vainly hope they may get more time to squander.

second-rate [ˌsekənd ˈreɪt] adj. 二流的；平庸的
Political nostrums and social panaceas prescribed by second-rate governmental officials are

but incidentally and superficially useful.

elixir [ɪˈlɪksər]   *n.* 万灵药；长生不老药

panacea [ˌpænəˈsiːə]   *n.* 万灵药

There is no elixir or panacea in this life.

stigma [ˈstɪɡmə]   *n.* 耻辱；恶名

Victory seems to be the only elixir to wash away all the stigmas he bore.

misapprehension [ˌmɪsæprɪˈhenʃn]   *n.* 误解

The police arrested the wrong man under a misapprehension.

misapprehend [ˌmɪsæprɪˈhend]   *v.* 误会

He was misapprehended by many followers.

misprision [mɪsˈprɪʒən]   *n.* [律]官吏的失职；渎职；知情不报

The official was guilty of misprision.

rancor [ˈræŋkər]   *n.* 仇恨；剧烈的憎恶

The economic sanction increased rancor between the United States and Iran.

grudging [ˈɡrʌdʒɪŋ]   *adj.* 勉强的；不情愿的；吝啬的

She walked very slowly with grudging compliance.

He did the difficult work with grudging acceptance.

perspective [pərˈspektɪv]   *n.* 看法；观点；透视图；洞察力   *adj.* 透视的

From a political perspective, the king's move was very smart.

implacable [ɪmˈplækəbl]   *adj.* 不能安抚的；难平息的；不能减轻的

diehard [ˈdaɪhɑːrd]   *n.* 顽固分子；死硬分子   *adj.* 抵抗到底的；死硬的

The implacable diehard refuses to compromise.

The army encountered heavy resistance from diehard, implacable enemies.

louche [luːʃ]   *adj.* 不老实的；没道德的；人品可疑的；靠不住的

The young man approaches her with his louche charm.

The prostitute is a louche lover.

orifice [ˈɔːrɪfɪs]   *n.* 孔；窍；穴

He was poisoned and bled from every orifice.

Part 3 识记单词 / 词组

exacerbate [ɪgˈzæsərbeɪt]　　v. 加剧；使恶化；使加重
satirical [səˈtɪrɪkl]　　adj. 写讽刺文章的；好讽刺的
satire [ˈsætaɪər]　　n. 讽刺作品；讽刺文学；讽刺
palliative measure　　治标不治本的措施
prospective girlfriend　　未来可能的女友
snitch [snɪtʃ]　　v. 告密；打小报告；顺手牵羊
pilfer [ˈpɪlfər]　　v. 顺手牵羊
exhilarate [ɪgˈzɪləreɪt]　　v. 使高兴；使兴奋
hypochondria [ˌhaɪpəˈkɑːndriə]　　n. 疑病症；忧郁症
hypochondriac [ˌhaɪpəˈkɑːndriæk]　　n. 疑病症的人　adj. 忧郁症的

Lesson 101

Part 1 主力单词 / 词组

motley [ˈmɑːtli]　　n. 小丑；混杂物　adj. 混杂的
The antique dealer has a motley collection of ancient objects.
Soldiers wear motley garments for camouflage.

dapple [ˈdæpl]　　v. 使有斑点　n. 斑点；花斑动物　adj. 有斑点的
The fleeting clouds threw dapples of shadows in the valley.
The giraffe is a dapple.

mottle [ˈmɑtl]　　v. 使呈杂色；使显得斑驳陆离　n. 杂色；斑点
There are some mottles on the ceiling.
The painting was mottled by mold.
The smoker's teeth were mottled with brown stains.

mottled [ˈmɑːtld]　　adj. 杂色的；斑驳的；斑点的
Tortoises and turtles have mottled carapaces.

piebald [ˈpaɪbɔːld]　　n. 花斑马　adj. 斑纹的；杂色的；杂种的
The piebald dachshund is very cute.

The piebald horse has distinct white and black spots.
Her piebald ethnic background contributes to her beautiful appearance.

pied [paɪd]　*adj.* 斑驳的；杂色的；穿花衣服的

The old lady is fond of wearing pied clothes.

roan [rəʊn]　*n.* 花毛马；黑白杂色；红棕色　*adj.* 花毛的（指毛色红棕色或黑白杂色的）

There are roan calves.

Part 2　补充单词 / 词组

composite [kəmˈpɑːzət]　*n.* 合成物；菊科植物　*adj.* 合成的；复合的

The photograph is not original but composite.

anisotropic [ˌænaɪsəˈtrɑːpɪk]　*adj.* 非均质的；各向异性的

inhomogeneous [ˌɪnhoʊməˈdʒiːnɪəs]　*adj.* 不同类的；不同质的

Composites are anisotropic and inhomogeneous materials.

bubble [ˈbʌbl]　*v.* 发出沸腾声；沸腾；冒泡　*n.* 气泡；泡状物；透明圆形罩

The economic bubble creates a factitious demand.

factitious [fækˈtɪʃəs]　*adj.* 人工的；虚假的

They used factitious wooden material to lower the cost.
He cheated her with factitious friendliness.

pertussis [pərˈtʌsɪs]　*n.* 百日咳

toxin [ˈtɑːksɪn]　*n.* 毒素

microbial [maɪˈkroʊbɪəl]　*adj.* 微生物的；细菌的

infection [ɪnˈfekʃn]　*n.* 传染；传染病

Pertussis bacteria produce toxins which are poisonous chemicals interfering with the respiratory tract's ability to eliminate microbial infections.

Part 3　识记单词 / 词组

cardiac surgery　心脏手术

cardiac [ˈkɑːrdiæk]　*adj.* 心脏的；心脏病的

cardiac arrest　心脏停跳

pulmonary [ˈpʌlmənəri] *adj.* 肺的；肺病的
cardiopulmonary [ˌkɑrdɪoʊˈpʌlmənəri] *adj.* 心肺的；与心肺有关的
cardiopulmonary bypass 体外循环
take after 相像（在外貌、性格等方面）；追赶
bigot [ˈbɪɡət] *n.* 抱偏见的人；心胸狭窄的人
sumpsimus [ˈsʌmpsɪməs] *n.* 矫正
respective [rɪˈspektɪv] *adj.* 分别的；各自的
incidental expense 伴随的费用
luck into 化险为夷
contingency plan 应急计划
cryptocurrency [ˈkrɪptoʊkɜːrənsi] *n.* 加密电子货币
link (sth) up （使）建立联系；（使）结合

Lesson 102

Part 1 主力单词 / 词组

pressing [ˈpresɪŋ] *adj.* 紧迫的；迫切的

The measure was best calculated to procure relief and to supply our pressing necessities.
The regulation of financial markets is the single most pressing issue of the world economy. (Anthony Giddens, British economist.)
The need for judiciary reform was especially pressing.

urgent [ˈɜːrdʒənt] *adj.* 紧急的；急迫的；执着的；坚定的

I should respond to your urgent request quickly.

emergency [ɪˈmɜːrdʒənsi] *n.* 紧急状况

The government rolls out several emergency vaccination programs. However, the vaccines appear to be bogus.

• Words in sentences 句中单词 / 词组 •

to procure relief 获得救助

judiciary [dʒuˈdɪʃieri] *n.* 司法部；司法官；审判员 *adj.* 司法的；法院的

roll [roʊl] *v.* 启动；(使)翻滚；滚动；碾平；摇晃；(机器)运转；翻白眼

vaccination [ˌvæksɪˈneɪʃn] *n.* 接种疫苗

bogus [ˈboʊɡəs] *adj.* 假的

Part 2 补充单词 / 词组

compute [kəmˈpjuːt] *v.* 计算；估算；推断
Vendors compute the price of vegetables by weight.

diabetic [ˌdaɪəˈbetɪk] *n.* 糖尿病人 *adj.* 糖尿病的
Not everyone has to be injected with a diabetic vaccine.

Part 3 识记单词 / 词组

trivial [ˈtrɪviəl] *adj.* 琐碎的；无价值的；不重要的
roll out 推出；实行；开展
procurement [prəˈkjʊrmənt] *n.* 获得；购买
inoculation [ɪˌnɑːkjuˈleɪʃn] *n.* 接种疫苗；培育
inoculate [ɪˈnɑːkjuleɪt] *v.* 给(人、动物)接种疫苗；接种

Lesson 103

Part 1 主力单词 / 词组

excellent [ˈeksələnt] *adj.* 极好的；杰出的
The boxer was a strong man with an excellent constitution.
The king came to the throne with an excellent lineage.
The cast of that movie was excellent.

Lesson 103

outstanding [aʊtˈstændɪŋ] *adj.* 优秀的；卓越的；出众的

Mary is an outstanding all-around athlete.

terrific [təˈrɪfɪk] *adj.* 极好的

The gladiator waged a terrific duel with his opponent in an arena in Rome.

exceptional [ɪkˈsepʃənl] *adj.* 卓越的；杰出的；不同凡响的

wonderful [ˈwʌndərfl] *adj.* 极好的；绝妙的

The fable is an all-time wonderful narrative.

marvelous [ˈmɑːrvələs] *adj.* 极好的；令人印象深刻的

It's marvelous to see this famous pyramid.

premium [ˈpriːmiəm] *n.* 保险费；额外费用；减价或给小礼物 *adj.* 高昂的；优质的

The insurance premium will go up if you have a car accident.

The hotel is near a rapid train station so they might charge you a premium for the rent.

The bookstore offers 10% off as a premium for buyers.

The kid pays a premium price for his premium ice cream.

Goods shipped by air will be charged more, at a premium of 25%.

The superb cattle range produces premium milk.

stellar [ˈstelər] *adj.* 杰出的；优秀的；星球的

She is promoted for her stellar performance.

optimum=optimal *adj.* 最优的；最佳的；最高的

The pricing strategy is designed to obtain optimum benefits.

The massive audience has exceeded the auditorium's optimum capacity.

Scientists have sought a more significant breakthrough in the optimum use of rare metals.

preeminent [priˈemɪnənt] *adj.* 卓越的；显著的

The U.S. has preeminent war power.

Time magazine is designed for preeminent people.

The preeminent chef demonstrates his exquisite meal.

eminent [ˈemɪnənt] *adj.* 出众的；卓越的；明显的

He is an eminent scholar in the realm of chemistry.

Who is the most eminent artist in your country?

The mother's love toward her children is eminent.

prominent [ˈprɑːmɪnənt] *adj.* 重要的；著名的；引人注目的；突出的；显著的

She is a prominent lawyer in New York.
Big Bear Mountain is a prominent landscape.
He has prominent eyes like a fish.

primacy [ˈpraɪməsi] *n.* 首要地位；首要；至高无上；总主教职

The primacy of the Qing dynasty was ended after the Sino-Japanese War.
Both countries fought for primacy in the region.
The corporation insists on the primacy of customers' satisfaction.

primate [ˈpraɪmeɪt, ˈpraɪmət] *n.* 灵长类动物；最高阶主教（一省内的）

Primates are subjected to an experiment for human welfare.

magnificent [mæɡˈnɪfɪsnt] *adj.* 极好的；壮丽的；宏伟的

marvel [ˈmɑːrvl] *v.* 对……感到惊奇；惊叹 *n.* 奇迹；令人感到惊奇的事物（或人）

• Words in sentences 句中单词 / 词组 •

constitution [ˌkɑːnstɪˈtuːʃn] *n.* 体格；宪法；全部

lineage [ˈlɪniɪdʒ] *n.* 血统

all-around=all-round *adj.* 全能的；涵盖的

gladiator [ˈɡlædieɪtər] *n.* 角斗士

duel [ˈduːəl] *v.* 决斗；竞争（激烈的）

fable [ˈfeɪbl] *n.* 寓言；寓言故事

all-time [ˈɔːl taɪm] *adj.* 前所未有的；空前的

narrative [ˈnærətɪv] *n.* 故事；陈述

auditorium [ˌɔːdɪˈtɔːriəm] *n.* 听众席；会堂；礼堂

Part 2 补充单词 / 词组

well-rounded [ˌwel ˈraʊndɪd] *adj.* 全面的；全面发展的

I try to be well-rounded in all subjects.

pugilist [ˈpjuːdʒɪlɪst] *n.* 拳击手

pummel [ˈpʌml] *v.* (用拳头) 连续击打

He fought like an experienced pugilist, pummeling his opponent.

screed [skri:d] n. 冗长的文章（议论等）；[建] 砂浆层；（压实混凝土路的）整平板

A screed refers to a lengthy discourse.
Her screed is mainly about how to improve your life psychologically.

disfavor [dɪsˈfeɪvər] v. 疏远 n. 讨厌；冷淡；疏远

Students who incurred the teacher's disfavor were soon relegated to sit farther back in the classroom.

relegate [ˈrelɪgeɪt] v. 贬谪；放逐；降职；把……委托给

The bill has been relegated to congress for further discussion.

eugenicist [ju:ˈdʒenisist] n. 优生学家

relegation [ˌrelɪˈgeɪʃən] n. 驱逐；归属；降级；降职

The eugenicist was condemned by the relegation of the elderly and crippled people to the garbage heap of society.

at a premium 稀少；难得；超出平常价；溢价

Living space in Tokyo is at a premium owing to the overcrowded population.
These antiques of the Song dynasty are sold at a premium.

Part 3 识记单词/词组

written constitution 成文宪法
rare metals 稀有金属
First Sino-Japanese War 甲午战争
all-round athlete 全能运动员
apologue [ˈæpəˌlɒg] n. 寓言故事
parable [ˈpærəbl] n. 寓言故事
allegory [ˈæləgɔːri] n. 讽喻的故事
lick [lɪk] v. 舔；舐；蔓延（火焰）
freight [freɪt] n. 运费；货运；运送
demotion [dɪˈmoʊʃn] n. 降职
demote [diːˈmoʊt] v. 使……降级；把……降职；贬黜
bazaar [bəˈzɑːr] n. 市场（中东等国家的）；商店街；小工艺品商店；义卖市场

Lesson 104

Part 1 主力单词/词组

border [ˈbɔːrdər] v. 给……镶边；接近；与……接壤 n. 分界线；边界

Canada and Mexico have no common border.

The army was sent to the border to fight.

The illegal immigrants tried to cross the border into the United States.

The affluent couple sent out their wedding invitations with a delicate gold leaf border.

China borders Russia.

The family borders their garden with a fence.

demarcation [ˌdiːmɑːrˈkeɪʃn] n. 界线；区别

There is no clear demarcation between finance and economics.

The mountain serves as the line of demarcation.

boundary [ˈbaʊndri] n. 边界；分界线；范围

Meandering through the valley, the river marks the boundary between Germany and Poland.

frontier [frʌnˈtɪr] n. 边境；前线；新领域

Drug trafficking often takes place in China's southwestern frontier with Vietnam.

The scientific frontier of artificial intelligence has its own set of problems.

parameter [pəˈræmɪtər] n. 界限；范围；规范；因素；特征

The landed paratroops established the parameter for defense very quickly.

The parameter of the debate has been confined by their limited knowledge.

The nation studied the parameters of the North Korean missiles.

Traffic congestion and social injustice are parameters of urban life.

demarcate [ˈdiːmɑːrkeɪt] v. 给……划界

• Words in sentences 句中单词/词组 •

meander [miˈændər] v. 蜿蜒；曲折前行 n. 曲径

drug trafficking 贩毒

artificial intelligence 人工智能

Part 2 补充单词/词组

border on sth 接近于……；近乎……

His imagination borders on insanity.

intelligentsia [ɪnˌtelɪˈdʒentsɪə] *n.* 知识分子；知识界

Most intelligentsia support the reform.

crossing [ˈkrɔːsɪŋ] *n.* 十字路口；渡口；横渡；横穿

She got robbed at the crossing.
We took the boat at the crossing down the river.
Crossing this river would be very dangerous.

couple [ˈkʌpl] *v.* 连接；结合 *n.* 夫妻；一对

High inflation coupled with low income causes great dissatisfaction among civilians.
We are a perfect couple.

trailer [ˈtreɪlər] *n.* 拖车；挂车

The trailer coupled with another car.

sinuous [ˈsɪnjuəs] *adj.* 弯曲的；迂回的

The river runs a sinuous course.
The sinuous movement of the dancer's arm was fantastic.

art nouveau 新艺术运动

His painting is well-known for sinuous forms of the art nouveau style.

sinuate [ˈsɪnjuɔɪt, -eɪt, ˈsɪnjueɪt] *adj.* 弯弯曲曲的；波状的

mulberry [ˈmʌlberi] *n.* 桑树

The mulberry has sinuate leaves.

Part 3 识记单词/词组

sinus [ˈsaɪnəs] *n.* 静脉窦；下陷或凹下去的地方

center [ˈsentər] *v.* 集中 *n.* 篮球中锋

Lesson 105

Part 1 主力单词 / 词组

limit [ˈlɪmɪt]　*v.* 限制；禁止　*n.* 范围
Did you set a time limit for the marathon?
Scarce rainfall limits the growth of plants in Africa.

restrict [rɪˈstrɪkt]　*v.* 限定；约束
Censorship has restricted all the derogatory news against the government.

confine [kənˈfaɪn]　*v.* 局限在……；限制
You shouldn't confine your study only to math.

constrain [kənˈstreɪn]　*v.* 限制；约束；束缚
The values of morality constrained him from committing cruelty toward captives.

constraint [kənˈstreɪnt]　*n.* 限制；限定
Economic failings in recent years reflected the financial misjudgment and constraints imposed by its traditional system of central planning.

refrain [rɪˈfreɪn]　*v.* 抑制　*n.* 迭歌；老调
Russia refrains from taking any action against China.
They played the refrain quite well.
His licentious ex-girlfriend has become a constant refrain of his friends.

inhibit [ɪnˈhɪbɪt]　*v.* 阻止；阻碍；禁止
Barren soil inhibits the growth of plants.
They were all inhibited before beautiful ladies.

curb [kɜːrb]　*v.* 控制；抑制　*n.* 抑制；路边
The new law was intended to curb the power of the police.

forbid [fərˈbɪd]　*v.* 禁止
The wanted man is forbidden from leaving the country.

stricture [ˈstrɪktʃər]　*n.* 限制；严厉的指责；收缩；非难
Some women demonstrated a protest against Islamic strictures on their rights to vote and to

remarry in the public square.

The space exploration project has been abandoned due to budgetary stricture.

The criticism of China's hegemony in Africa had to be tempered by a stricture on Japan's own insular nationalism.

smother [ˈsmʌðər]　*v.* 抑制；窒息　*n.* 窒息状态；被抑制状态

He has to smother his rage in front of his boss.

The president smothers the health care project.

Too much care will smother kids' development.

The snow smothers the trail.

Pretentiousness stifles the earliest instincts and smothers the first breathings of the innate personality.

He was smothered by the smoke so somebody called an ambulance.

constipate [ˈkɑːnstəˌpeɪt]　*v.* 使便秘；使迟钝

The slave has been constipated for most of his life.

constrict [kənˈstrɪkt]　*v.* 约束；压缩；收缩

The tight clothes constrict my breathing.

His creativity was constricted by templates.

The cold temperature causes the blood vessels to constrict.

constriction [kənˈstrɪkʃn]　*n.* 压缩物；阻塞物

Snakes kill their prey by constriction or envenomation.

circumscribe [ˈsɜːrkəmskraɪb]　*v.* 约束；包围；为……下定义；为……划界线

Law circumscribes its citizen's behavior.

The teacher circumscribed the wrong answers.

The prison was circumscribed by tall walls.

enjoin [ɪnˈdʒɔɪn]　*v.* 禁止；命令；嘱咐

The judge enjoined traders from exporting rare metal.

The licentious novel was enjoined prior to the publication.

The prince enjoined guards to be more careful tonight.

The boss enjoined a task on his secretary.

pinion [ˈpɪnjən]　*v.* 束缚；限制　*n.* 翼梢；前翼

His ambition was pinioned by a lack of funding.

The robbers pinioned his arms behind his back.

The prisoner was pinioned to a stake under the scorching desert sun.

shackle [ˈʃækl] v. 带上镣铐；束缚；羁绊 n. 脚镣；手铐；束缚

The captives were shackled in pairs.
I tried to get rid of the shackles of poverty and racism.

stint [stɪnt] v. 节制；停止；吝惜 n. 分配的工作；工作期限

Reviewers didn't stint with their praise.
The chef normally won't stint on the butter.
Sarah spent a two-year stint as a waitress.
After a brief stint in Canada, he returned to his work in America.

restriction [rɪˈstrɪkʃn] n. 限制规定

constipation [ˌkɑːnstɪˈpeɪʃn] n. 受限制；受约束

circumscription [ˌsɜːrkəmˈskrɪpʃn] n. 区域；范围

limitation [ˌlɪmɪˈteɪʃn] n. 限制

• Words in sentences 句中单词 / 词组 •

marathon [ˈmærəθɑːn] n. 马拉松赛跑
censorship [ˈsensərʃɪp] n. 审查；审查制度
budgetary [ˈbʌdʒɪteri] adj. 预算的
temper [ˈtempər] v. 使缓和；调和；给（乐器）调音 n. 勇气；暴怒；坚韧性
pretentiousness [prɪˈtenʃəsnɪs] n. 自命不凡
innate [ɪˈneɪt] adj. 天生的；与生俱来的
template [ˈtemplət] n. 样板；模板
envenomation [inˌvenəˈmeɪʃən] n. 注射毒液

Part 2 补充单词 / 词组

agricultural bureau 农业局

incentive [ɪnˈsentɪv] n. 刺激；奖励措施；诱因；动机；刺激 adj. 刺激的；奖励的

the soil 耕作；务农
The agricultural bureau provides many incentives for farmers' return to the soil.

off-limit [ˌɔːfˈlɪmɪt] 禁止的
The house is off-limit to us because it is considered to be a crime scene.

lose someone's temper 发脾气
I won't lose my temper unless you make a rude or stupid inquiry.

temerity [təˈmerəti] n. 鲁莽；冒失
He brought her a gift to atone for his temerity.
Should I consider this misdeed in front of the tyrant to be an act of courage or temerity?

chromatic [krəˈmætɪk] adj. 半音阶的；着色的；彩色的

costive [ˈkɑːstɪv] adj. 动作迟缓的；便秘的；小气的
If you ask her to be your friend, she will become costive.

hermetic [hɜːrˈmetɪk] adj. 与世隔绝的；不透气的；神秘的
The recluse is gesturally sparing, chromatically costive, and seems to enjoy his hermetic existence.

concept [ˈkɑːnsept] n. 概念；想法

comedy [ˈkɑːmədi] n. 喜剧
His innovative concept has pushed the envelope of TV comedy.

tickle [ˈtɪkl] v. 使发痒；逗……笑；激起 n. 使人痒的东西
The two kids tickled each other joyfully.
The wool sweater tickles my neck.
The clown's antics tickled the audience.
The flag and anthem tickle our patriotism.

barren [ˈbærən] adj. 贫瘠的；无成果的
Scientists try to convert the barren desert into arable land.

arable [ˈærəbl] n. 耕地 adj. 适于耕种的
We can cultivate paddies in this arable land.

stimulus [ˈstɪmjələs] n. 刺激品；兴奋剂
They paid an extra bonus as a stimulus for production.

stimuli [ˈstɪmjulaɪ] *n.* 促进因素（复数）
Heat, light, and wind are all physical stimuli.

stimulate [ˈstɪmjuleɪt] *v.* 刺激；激励
The tax cut will stimulate economic growth.

tingle [ˈtɪŋgl] *v.* 感到刺痛；使激动 *n.* 刺痛感
My cheek tingled with her slap.
Her ears tingle due to illness.

hegemony [hɪˈdʒeməni, ˈhedʒɪmouni] *n.* 领导权；霸权；支配权；争霸；盟主权
Russia challenges the U.S.'s hegemony in the Middle East.

insular [ˈɪnsələr] *adj.* 观念狭隘的；保守的；岛的
Insular locals are not receptive to new ideas.

paramedic [ˌpærəˈmedɪk] *n.* 急救护理人员；伞兵医务员
The paramedics will arrive soon.

roughage [ˈrʌfɪdʒ] *n.* 粗食品；粗饲料
Constipation may be induced by a diet insufficient in roughage or fiber

immanent [ˈɪmənənt] *adj.* 内在的；固有的；无所不在的
I appreciate her immanent beauty.
Compassion is immanent in all individuals.
She is an almighty fighter in her immanent world.

kyphosis [kaɪˈfousɪs] *n.* 脊柱后凸症；驼背
His kyphosis is congenital.

glamor [ˈglæmər] *v.* 使有魅力；迷惑 *n.* 魅力；魔力
The glamor of Hollywood attracts many tourists.

glamorize [ˈglæməraɪz] *v.* 使有迷惑力；渲染；美化
You don't have to glamorize your romance with her.

Part 3 识记单词 / 词组

stimulant [ˈstɪmjələnt] *n.* 兴奋剂；酒；激励物 *adj.* 使人兴奋的；激励的

excitation=excitement　　*n.* 刺激；兴奋；激动
itchy [ˈɪtʃi]　*adj.* 发痒的；渴望的
itch [ɪtʃ]　*v.* 发痒；渴望　*n.* 痒；疥疮
curfew [ˈkɜːrfjuː]　*n.* 宵禁；戒严
budget [ˈbʌdʒɪt]　*v.* 谨慎花钱　*n.* 预算　*adj.* 低廉的；收费公道的
pretentious [prɪˈtenʃəs]　*adj.* 自命不凡的；自负的；狂妄的
hermetically [hɜːrˈmetɪkli]　*adv.* 密封着地
congenital [kənˈdʒenɪtl]　*adj.* 天生的；先天的
congenital disorder　先天失常；先天性疾病
push the envelope　跨越出界限
not soil someone's hands　不沾染污点
foolhardy [ˈfuːlhɑːrdi]　*adj.* 有勇无谋的；鲁莽的
glamorous life　令人向往的生活
paramedical [ˌpærəˈmedɪkl]　*adj.* 辅助医疗的
kyphotic [kaɪˈfɒtɪk]　*adj.* 后凸的；驼背的

Lesson 106

Part 1　主力单词/词组

malevolent [məˈlevələnt]　*adj.* 带有恶意的

The devil with malevolent eyes inflicts pain and suffering upon people.
There is a widespread assumption in Asia that ill-fated people can be subjected to malevolent forces distinct from their conscious minds.
The talisman was believed to frighten away malevolent spirits that caused bad luck.

ill will　恶意

Let's stop this nonsense rivalry and ill will toward each other.
The longstanding border dispute has sparked ill will between the two nations.
Malicious intention and ill will start to spring from my mind.

malicious [məˈlɪʃəs]　*adj.* 恶毒的

He has been ill-treated and therefore, his malicious intentions start coming out.

malignant [mə'lɪgnənt]   *adj.* 恶性的

A malignant tumor has cast a blight on his promising future.

hostile ['hɑːstl, 'hɑːstaɪl]   *adj.* 敌意的

Aliens remain hostile.

inimical [ɪ'nɪmɪkl]   *adj.* 不友好的；有害的

The trade war initiated by Trump is inimical to global interests.
We are surrounded by inimical countries.

• Words in sentences 句中单词 / 词组 •

talisman ['tælɪzmən]   *n.* 护身符；辟邪物；法宝

nonsense ['nɑːnsens, 'nɑːnsns]   *n.* 胡闹   *adj.* 荒谬的；无意义的

rivalry ['raɪvlri]   *n.* 竞争；对抗

longstanding [ˌlɔːŋ'stændɪŋ]   *adj.* 长时间的；长期存在的

spring [sprɪŋ]   *v.* 跳；跃   *n.* 春季；泉水；小溪

cast a blight on something   让某物蒙上阴影；对某事造成破坏

Part 2 补充单词 / 词组

benevolent [bə'nevələnt]   *adj.* 仁慈的；慈善的

malice ['mælɪs]   *n.* 恶意；害人之心

The benevolent youngsters bear him no malice.

vegetable fat   植物性脂肪

adipose ['ædɪpoʊs, 'ædɪpoʊz]   *n.* 动物性脂肪   *adj.* 脂肪的；含脂肪的

Vegetable fat is better than adipose.

abdomen ['æbdəmən]   *n.* 腹部

She is fat and has an adipose abdomen.

kiosk ['kiːɑːsk]   *n.* 凉亭；报摊

pavilion [pə'vɪliən]   *v.* 置……于亭（或帐篷）中；为……搭篷   *n.* 亭子；展示馆

The kiosk means the Turkish pavilion.

icicle [ˈaɪsɪkl] n.（屋檐等处滴水形成的）冰锥；冰柱

eave [iːv] n. 屋檐
There are icicles pendent for the eaves.

pendant [ˈpendənt] n. 吊坠；吊灯　adj. 下垂的；没决定的；突出的
They made the lantern pendent from the ceiling to celebrate the festival.
Four pendent elliptical windows make the building unique.

remain [rɪˈmeɪn] v. 仍然有；遗留；剩下
The decision remains pendent.

protrude [prouˈtruːd] v. 伸出；突出
The horse has large eyes protruding from the sides of the head.

handkerchief [ˈhæŋkərtʃɪf, ˈhæŋkərtʃiːf] n. 手帕；围巾
He tries to put the protruding white handkerchief into his pocket.

mercantile [ˈmɜːrkəntiːl, ˈmɜːrkəntaɪl] adj. 商人的；商业的
I was born into a mercantile family.
His righteousness is renowned in the mercantile cycle.

tremendous [trəˈmendəs] adj. 巨大的；惊人的；极好的
The currency has been devaluated due to tremendous mercantile pressure.

game-changing adj. 很大变化的；影响结果的
Trump made a game-changing shift in foreign policies.
The detective made a game-changing discovery to crack the murder case.

Part 3　识记单词/词组

pedant [ˈpednt] n. 书呆子；学究
merchandise [ˈmɜːrtʃəndaɪs, ˈmɜːrtʃəndaɪz] n. 商品
debacle [dɪˈbɑːkl] n. 溃败
pariah [pəˈraɪə] n. 受蔑视的人
bear witness/testimony to something　见证；作证
testimony [ˈtestɪmouni] n. 证词；证言
be (a) testimony to something　很清楚的证明

shell pendant 贝壳垂饰
protrusion [prouˈtruːʒn] *n.* 突出物
merchant [ˈmɜːrtʃənt] *n.* 商人

Lesson 107

Part 1 主力单词 / 词组

circumspect [ˈsɜːrkəmspekt] *adj.* 小心的；谨慎的
Obviously being given carte blanche as the commander is a mixed blessing. One should be more circumspect.
The investor is exceedingly circumspect.
She is very thoughtful and circumspect in spending money.

prudent [ˈpruːdnt] *adj.* 小心的；精明的；考虑周到的
You need to be prudent and provident in your use of money.
It is prudent to have a second string in a contest.
All government, indeed, every human benefit and enjoyment, every virtue, and every prudent act, is founded on compromise and barter. (Edmund Burke, Irish-born British statesman and political philosopher)

prudence [ˈpruːdns] *n.* 谨慎；慎重

circumspection [ˌsɜːrkəmˈspekʃn] *n.* 谨言慎行

• Words in sentences 句中单词 / 词组

carte blanche 绝对的自主权
mixed blessing 福祸兼有的事物；利弊并存的事物
second string 替补队员
barter [ˈbɑːrtər] *v.* 以物易物　*n.* 易货贸易

Part 2 补充单词 / 词组

brusque [brʌsk] *adj.* 寡言而无礼的
She is not polite with her brusque replies such as "Nobody likes you" and "You are very ugly".

abrupt [əˈbrʌpt] *adj.* 唐突的；陡峭的
You will get used to the senior's abrupt manner.
She makes an abrupt decision to move to New York.

obstinate [ˈɑːbstɪnət] *adj.* 固执的；倔强的；棘手的
Obstinate people can be divided into the opinionated, the ignorant, and the boorish. (Aristotle, Greek philosopher)

boorish [ˈbʊrɪʃ] *adj.* 粗鲁的
I can overlook your boorish behavior.

imprudent [ɪmˈpruːdnt] *adj.* 轻率的；不明智的
Lending a stranger money is imprudent.

blanch [blæntʃ] *v.* 使变白；使有光泽
The constant fear of being murdered has blanched her hair.
Her lip was blanched due to a lack of oxygen.
Without sunshine, leaves start to blanch.

Part 3 识记单词 / 词组

barterer [ˈbɑːrtərər] *n.* 以物易物的商人
boor [bʊr] *n.* 粗鲁的人；农民
madcap [ˈmædkæp] *n.* 鲁莽的人 *adj.* 鲁莽的
reckless [ˈrekləs] *adj.* 鲁莽的

Lesson 108

Part 1 主力单词 / 词组

diligent [ˈdɪlɪdʒənt] *adj.* 认真的；勤奋的
He is a diligent and committed officer.

It consumes three years of diligent endeavor to make the reservoir.

conscientious [ˌkɑːnʃiˈenʃəs] *adj.* 认真的；有道德的

He is a conscientious butler without whom I can't imagine.

Are you a faineant student or a conscientious one?

He doesn't agree on peace-time conscription due to conscientious grounds.

industrious [ɪnˈdʌstriəs] *adj.* 勤劳的；勤奋的

Industrious workers manufacture more products.

assiduous [əˈsɪdʒuəs] *adj.* 刻苦的；勤勉的

The assiduous antique appreciator knows each object's provenance.

studious [ˈstuːdiəs] *adj.* 认真的；有目的的；读很多书的

He is taciturn and studious.

The studious inspector leaves no stone unturned.

His studious alibi raises suspicion concerning this murder case.

sedulous [ˈsedʒələs] *adj.* 勤奋的；刻苦的；认真又小心的

There are no tasks paralleling the conscientious and painstaking effort of sedulous monographers/investigators.

The sedulous suitor constantly sends her flowers and presents.

sedulity [sɪˈdjuːliti] *n.* 勤勉；勤奋

Her sedulity finally paid off as a Fortune 500 company has decided to recruit her.

• Words in sentences 句中单词/词组 •

committed [kəˈmɪtɪd] *adj.* 有责任感的

butler [ˈbʌtlər] *n.* 男管家

conscription [kənˈskrɪpʃn] *n.* 征兵制

manufacture [ˌmænjuˈfæktʃər] *v.* 制造

appreciator [əˈpriːʃieɪtə] *n.* 鉴赏者；了解真价者

taciturn [ˈtæsɪtɜːrn] *adj.* 沉默寡言的

alibi [ˈæləbaɪ] *n.* 借口；托词

monographer [ˈmɑːnəɡrəfə] *n.* 专栏作家

suitor [ˈsuːtər] *n.* (女子的) 求婚者；有收购意向者

Lesson 108

Part 2 补充单词/词组

tacit [ˈtæsɪt] *adj.* 默许的；缄默的
He gave me a tacit consent.
She remained tacit about her family.

conscionable [ˈkɑːnʃənəbl] *adj.* 合乎良心的；公正的
Conscionable persons won't earn money by hurting others.

unconscionable [ʌnˈkɑːnʃənəbl] *adj.* 没良心的；不合理的；过多的
There is an unconscionable number of defects found in this equipment.
That unconscionable man left his wife and children without a single word.

atelier [ˌætlˈjeɪ] *n.* 工作室；画室
An atelier refers to an artist's studio.
The building contains 100 air-conditioned ateliers.

sluice [sluːs] *v.* 冲洗；开闸放水 *n.* 水闸；水门
The water plant staff sluices out the water in the reservoir.
The chef sluiced the kitchen with a hose.
The rainwater is diverted along the sluice.

gutter [ˈgʌtər] *v.* 形成沟；弄熄灭 *n.* 排水沟；阴沟；檐沟；恶劣的社会环境；道德沦落的社会最低阶层
The plumber took out some trash and sluiced the gutters with lots of water.

provenance [ˈprɑːvənəns] *n.* 起源；出处；由来
The provenance of this antique is very questionable.

Part 3 识记单词/词组

leave no stone unturned　竭尽全力；不遗余力
online suitor　网络上的追求者
floodgate [ˈflʌdgeɪt] *n.* 水闸
conscience [ˈkɑːnʃəns] *n.* 道德；良知
monograph [ˈmɑːnəgræf] *n.* 专题；专栏

Lesson 109

Part 1　主力单词 / 词组

tend to　倾向

People in northern provinces tend to drink a lot of alcohol.
Kids tend to spit saliva at their opponents if they lose a fight.
Teachers tend to favor students who achieve higher scores.

incline [ɪnˈklaɪn]　*v.* 倾向于　　*n.* 斜坡

He inclined to suspect an untenable conclusion.

prone to　易于遭受（疾病）的；趴着的（脸朝下）

The spoiled brat is prone to exaggerate, pontificate, and brag about how smart she is.

apt to　容易……

Senile people are apt to be forgetful.

proclivity [prəˈklɪvəti]　*n.* 倾向（尤指坏的）

She has a proclivity for reckless driving.

disposition [ˌdɪspəˈzɪʃn]　*n.* 性情；倾向；趋势

He has the disposition of a saint.
The president has the disposition to purchase natural gas from Russia.

propensity [prəˈpensəti]　*n.* 倾向；嗜好（尤指不良的）

She has a propensity for negligence.
Eric has a propensity to eat gluttonously.

predisposed [ˌpriːdɪˈspəʊzd]　*adj.* 易感染的；倾向的

Wounded soldiers in tropical forests are predisposed to parasites and viruses.
The leader is predisposed to negotiation and reconciliation instead of war.

predispose [ˌpriːdɪˈspəʊz]　*v.* 使……更容易；使倾向于

A good teacher predisposes children to learn and create.
Malnutrition and freezing temperature predispose the injured stranger to die in the street.

• Words in sentences 句中单词/词组 •

spit [spɪt] *v.* 吐出   *n.* 口水；烤肉叉
brat [bræt] *n.* 小孩；（尤指）顽童
brag [bræg] *v.* 吹嘘   *n.* 布莱格牌游戏（一种简化扑克）
senile ['siːnaɪl] *adj.* 老迈的；年老所致的
gluttonously ['glʌtənəsli] *adv.* 暴饮暴食地；浪费地
parasite ['pærəsaɪt] *n.* 寄生虫

Part 2 补充单词/词组

arrondissement [ə'rɔndismənt] *n.*（法国）大城市的区
There are twenty arrondissements in Paris.

schmooze [ʃmuːz] *v.* 闲谈   *n.* 闲聊

tend [tend] *v.* 照顾；倾向
She tends to socialize and schmooze with strangers at parties.

wound [wuːnd, waʊnd] *n.* 伤口
The nurse tended the patient's wound.

untenable [ʌn'tenəbl] *adj.* 站不住脚的；不能租赁的
The failure of economic reform puts the president in an untenable position.

conclude [kən'kluːd] *v.* 推断出；结束；完成
I concluded she was not the killer from her reaction to the crime scene photos.
The meeting concluded within five minutes.
My boss flew to Paris to conclude a deal.

inconclusive [ˌɪnkən'kluːsɪv] *adj.* 不确定的；无结论的；非决定性的；无结果的
The result of the river water test was inconclusive.

pontificate [pɑːn'tɪfɪkeɪt, pɑːn'tɪfɪkət] *v.* 自以为是地发表意见；目空一切地谈论   *n.* 教皇任期
The philodox pontificates as he is the Pope.

diffidence [ˈdɪfɪdəns] n. 内向；缺乏自信
Now Giant Despair had a wife, and her name was diffidence. (John Bunyan, English preacher and writer)

loudmouthed [ˈlaʊdˈmaʊðd] adj. 高声讲话的；吼叫的

braggart [ˈbrægərt] n. 吹牛的人 adj. 吹牛的；自夸的

diffident [ˈdɪfɪdənt] adj. 缺乏自信的

braggadocio [ˌbrægəˈdoʊtʃioʊ] n. 自夸；吹牛大王
A loudmouthed braggart is diffident with braggadocio.
The wrestlers intimidated his opponent with an air of swaggering braggadocio.

gambit [ˈgæmbɪt] n. 策略；险招；开场白
Israel's gambits in other areas of foreign policy are quite successful.

puberty [ˈpjuːbərti] n. 青春期；妙龄；开花期

senility [səˈnɪləti] n. 高龄；年老糊涂
The old president was suffering from the effects of senility.

cremation [krəˈmeɪʃn] n. 焚化；火葬

geriatric [ˌdʒeriˈætrɪk] n. 老年人；老年病人 adj. 老年人的；老年病学的
The geriatric canine can't run very fast.

geriatrician=geriatrist n. 老年病学专家
The geriatrician examines an old man.

gormandize [ˈgɔːrmənˌdaɪz] v. 贪吃；拼命吃
The international student is so hungry that he will gormandize whatever he happens to find in the refrigerator.

crapulent [ˈkræpjulənt] adj. 暴饮暴食的
A crapulent obese friend asked me out to a buffet for lunch.

rapport [ræˈpɔːr] n. 亲密关系；友好关系
The animal lover has an instant rapport with animals.
The teacher has a rapport with the children.

dispose [dɪˈspoʊz] v. 使倾向于；排列；安排

Timid personality disposed them not to venture further.

Legislators propose and the president disposes.

disposed [dɪˈspoʊzd] adj. 倾向的；愿意的

Why should I feel disposed to help her?

formation [fɔːrˈmeɪʃn] n. 阵型；结构；形状

He disposed his soldiers into a square formation.

totalitarian [toʊˌtæləˈteriən] n. 极权主义的

The totalitarian state is not disposed to freedom of speech.

sophomore [ˈsɑːfəmɔːr] n.（大学、高中的）二年级学生；具有二年经验者

I played golf in my sophomore year.

I am a sophomore at Stanford University.

sophomoric [ˌsɑːfəˈmɔːrɪk] adj. 二年级（学生）的；一知半解的；幼稚的

Her sophomoric behavior is like that of a child.

twaddle [ˈtwɑːdl] v. 废话；闲聊 n. 废话；闲聊

The sophomoric twaddle of the legislator wearied the locals.

cadaverous [kəˈdævərəs] adj. 死尸样的；苍白色的

tawny [ˈtɔːni] n. 黄褐色 adj. 黄褐色的

The cadaverous-looking man wore tawny clothes.

inquest [ˈɪnkwest] n. 验尸；审讯；调查死因的陪审团

The victim's mother demanded an inquest.

Therefore, the inquest has ended.

timorous [ˈtɪmərəs] adj. 极胆怯的；提心吊胆的

I reproached myself for being so timorous, not asking her out.

The squad proceeds with timorous steps toward the school shooter.

pusillanimous [ˌpjuːsɪˈlænɪməs] adj. 胆怯的；懦弱的；优柔寡断的

Barbarians threatened the cowardly, pusillanimous tyrant.

quail [kweɪl] v. 胆怯；畏缩 n. 鹌鹑；鹌鹑肉

He quailed in front of the monarch.

We have a quail for lunch in a forest restaurant.

disjointed [dɪsˈdʒɔɪntɪd]   *adj.* 不连贯的；脱臼的

She leads a moral life in a disjointed world.
The disjointed novel is very difficult to read.

dispose of sb/sth   清除；销毁；应付；解决；处理；击败；杀死

How to dispose of garbage remains a question.
It's difficult to dispose of stolen jewels.
The captain arrived to dispose of the crews' disagreements.
The martial art contender disposed of his final opponent within five minutes.

Part 3 识记单词 / 词组

cremate [ˈkriːmeɪt]   *v.* 将……烧成灰；火葬
a joint bank account   共有银行账户
joint venture   联合商业活动；联合企业
aptitude test   能力倾向测验
leech [liːtʃ]   *n.* 水蛭；寄生虫
provincial [prəˈvɪnʃl]   *n.* 外省人；乡下人   *adj.* 外地的；地方性的；朴素的
pontification [ˌpɒn.tɪfɪˈkeɪʃən]   *n.* 训话
aptitude [ˈæptɪtuːd]   *n.* 天资；天赋；才能
glutton [ˈɡlʌtn]   *n.* 贪吃的人
gluttony [ˈɡlʌtəni]   *n.* 暴食；贪吃
crapulence [ˈkræpjuːləns]   *n.* 暴饮暴食
dispose of garage/corpus/opponent   停车房 / 文集 / 对手的处理
corpus [ˈkɔːrpəs]   *n.* 身体；文集；语料库
corpse [kɔːrps]   *n.* 尸体
insulin [ˈɪnsəlɪn]   *n.* 胰岛素
timidity [tɪˈmɪdəti]   *n.* 胆小
joint [dʒɔɪnt]   *v.* 把……切成带骨的大块   *n.* 关节；接合点   *adj.* 共有的；共享的
disjoint [dɪsˈdʒɔɪnt]   *v.* 弄乱；解体；脱臼   *adj.* 不连贯的
disjoin [dɪsˈdʒɔɪn]   *v.* 分开

Lesson 110

Part 1 主力单词/词组

divergent [daɪˈvɜːrdʒənt] *adj.* 有分歧的；叉开的；扩散的

Accents are divergent from states.
They have divergent attitudes toward globalization.

disparate [ˈdɪspərət] *adj.* 截然不同的；迥然相异的

You live in a disparate world.
How can you expect them to achieve a common goal with disparate political agendas?

disparity [dɪˈspærəti] *n.* 不平等；差异

The professor highlights the growing educational and economic disparity between the rich and the poor.

vary [ˈveri, ˈværi] *v.* （使）不同；（使）呈现差异

Sport cars vary in price.
Income varies with career and educational background.

diverge [daɪˈvɜːrdʒ] *v.* 分歧；开叉；背离

Part 2 补充单词/词组

parity [ˈpærəti] *n.* 对等

Feminists have fought for parity in the workplace.
Government purchases farmer's products with parity.

be out of your league 高不可攀；高不可及

She is out of your league.

straw [strɔː] *n.* 麦秆；吸管

hut [hʌt] *v.* 使住临时营房 *n.* 简陋的小房子

The straw hut is precariously perched on a declivity of the mountain's northeastern face.

declivity [dɪˈklɪvəti] *n.* 下斜；下（斜）坡

On the declivity of a hill, we overlook the pellucid waters of a river.

boloney [bə'louni] *n.* 燻肠；愚蠢的言辞/行为

Sausage is a generic term for boloney.

generic [dʒə'nerɪk] *n.* 公共用地；公有地 *adj.* 一般的；总称的

She brought me to a generic restaurant, nothing special about it.

I don't know who manufactures this generic drug.

generically [dʒɪ'nerɪkəli] *adv.* 一般地

A malignant submicroscopic entity as a parasite in plants, animals, and bacteria, is generically called a "virus".

ulterior [ʌl'tɪrɪər] *adj.* 别有用心的；将来的；在那边的

His business proposal to the C.E.O. has an ulterior motive.

She is very smart and can calculate her opponent's ulterior actions.

disparage [dɪ'spærɪdʒ] *v.* 批判；贬低

The general has been disparaged as a traitor due to his surrender without a single fight.

humane [hju:'meɪn] *adj.* 仁慈的；人道的

Conditions in the penitentiary are more humane now.

precarious [prɪ'kerɪəs] *adj.* 不稳的；危险的

The winning is based on the reinforcement arriving in time which seems precarious.

Part 3 识记单词/词组

league champion 联盟冠军

van [væn] *v.* 用车搬运 *n.* 面包车

slope [sloʊp] *v.* 倾斜 *n.* 坡度

inhumane [ˌɪnhju:'meɪn] *adj.* 不人道的；残忍的

Lesson 111

Part 1 主力单词/词组

hardship ['hɑːrdʃɪp] *n.* 艰难；困苦；艰难情况

The remote villagers have many hardships to endure besides a shortage of water.

The salary and quality of corporate work were preferable to the hardships of sharecropping.

Farmers had suffered the brunt of the hardship. The drought seemed to be endless.

I will swallow any defeat and hardship with fortitude.

predicament [prɪˈdɪkəmənt] *n.* 困境；范畴

Mismanagement has led to the club's financial predicament.

plight [plaɪt] *n.* 苦难 *v.* 保证

There seems to be no means of escape and they have come to realize their helpless plight.

quagmire [ˈkwæɡmaɪər] *n.* 困境；沼泽地

He hired a lawyer so as to extricate him out of the legal quagmire.

mire [ˈmaɪər] *n.* 困境；沼泽地

His boondoggle/white elephant/grandiose project has drawn our company into the financial mire.

quandary [ˈkwɑːndəri] *n.* 窘境；犹豫不决

I am in a quandary.

trying [ˈtraɪɪŋ] *adj.* 令人难受的；令人烦恼的

A trying physical education lesson might yield an abundance of rewards for your health.

morass [məˈræs] *n.* 泥沼；困境

The guru attempted to solve a morass of social injustices.

The project has been impeded in a morass of economic pressure.

asperity [æˈsperəti] *n.* 苦难；严酷；粗暴；粗糙

We donate some money and try to relieve the asperity of her sorrowful life.

I don't think I can go through the asperity of the climate of the Arctic again.

My superior always talks to me with asperity.

conundrum [kəˈnʌndrəm] *n.* 难题；谜语

The graduate was faced with the conundrum of getting a job without having experience.

The supreme conundrum of our time is "What is the president up to now?"

• Words in sentences 句中单词 / 词组 •

sharecrop [ˈʃerˌkrɑp] *v.* 作佃农耕种

brunt [brʌnt]　*n.* 主要冲击；主要压力
fortitude [ˈfɔːrtɪtuːd]　*n.* 毅力
mismanagement [ˌmɪsˈmænɪdʒmənt]　*n.* 管理不善
boondoggle [ˈbuːndɑːɡl]　*n.* 耗资巨大而无意义的工作
white elephant　昂贵且无用的东西
grandiose [ˈɡrændioʊs]　*adj.* 华而不实的；不切实际的
draw [drɔː]　*v.* 拉；拖　*n.* 抽奖；平局
guru [ˈɡuːruː]　*n.* 泰斗；专家；权威

Part 2　补充单词 / 词组

noctivagant [nɔkˈtivəɡənt]　*adj.* 晚间徘徊的；夜游的
The vampire seems to be a noctivagant wanderer seeking a potential victim.

protean [ˈproʊtiən, proʊˈtiːən]　*adj.* 千变万化的；一人演几个角色的
She is a protean actress who plays several roles in this movie.

hang out　出去玩
I have to do my homework tonight, but I really want to hang out with you guys.

oval [ˈoʊvl]　*n.* 卵形（物）　*adj.* 卵形的；椭圆形的
We discovered oval pebbles downstream.

oviparous [oʊˈvɪpərəs]　*adj.* 卵生的；产卵的
Fishes are oviparous.

viviparous [vɪˈvɪpərəs]　*adj.* 胎生的
Cows are viviparous.

ovoviviparous [ˌoʊvoʊvɪˈvɪpərəs]　*n.* 卵胎生的
Great white and tiger sharks are ovoviviparous.

swallow [ˈswɑːloʊ]　*v.* 忍耐；吞咽；全盘相信　*n.* 燕子
I tried not to offend my boss and swallowed my disappointment.
I swallow my pill with water.
Swallows are always present before it rains.

raging [ˈreɪdʒɪŋ] *adj.* 猛烈的；剧烈的

The raging sea swallows the ship up.

dubious [ˈduːbiəs] *adj.* 可疑的

Your story is too dubious to swallow.

sciamachy [saiˈæməki] *n.* 自己想象的敌人；自己的影子

He conquers fear and defeats his own sciamachy.

dilemma [dɪˈlemə, daɪˈlemə] *n.* 左右为难；困境

It is such a dilemma.

Part 3 识记单词 / 词组

ovoid [ˈoʊvɔɪd] *n.* 卵形体 *adj.* 卵形的
offense [əˈfens] *n.* 触怒；罪行；过错
reward [rɪˈwɔːrd] *v.* 报答；报应 *n.* 奖品；赏金

Lesson 112

Part 1 主力单词 / 词组

aftereffect [ˈæftərɪˌfekt] *n.* 事后影响；余波

The series of seduction is a haunting rumination on love and its aftereffects.

The aftereffects of child abuse can be harrowing.

The aftereffects of civil war can still be felt.

Most people can recover from hepatitis A without any serious aftereffects.

backwash [ˈbækwɔːʃ] *n.* 余波；后果；反流

In the backwash of international sanctions, the nation has finally renounced its nuclear program.

backfire [ˌbækˈfaɪər] *v.* 适得其反

The propaganda of prosperity has backfired as people see the unemployment rate has risen.

repercussion [ˌriːpərˈkʌʃn]　n. 后果；反射（声音和光）

The decision of whether or not to pursue a master's degree will have a profound repercussion in your life.

Social upheaval is a phenomenon involving repercussions and impacts both rulers and civilians.

reverberate [rɪˈvɜːrbəreɪt]　v. 产生广泛影响；回荡

The surge in petroleum prices reverberates across the globe.

reverberation [rɪˌvɜːrbəˈreɪʃn]　n. 回响；回声

The military fiasco has delivered a reverberation over democratic nations.

resonant [ˈrezənənt]　adj. 洪亮的；引起共鸣的

The memorial of the massacre is resonant with racial hatred.

ripple [ˈrɪpl]　n. 涟漪

a ripple effect　一种连锁反应

The turnaround procedure of products will have a ripple effect on the corporation's core competence.

byproduct [ˈbaɪˌprɑːdʌkt]　n. 副产品；结果

Pollution is a byproduct of modernization.

fallout [ˈfɔːlaʊt]　n. 放射性坠尘；恶果

The unclear fallout is detrimental to living beings.

The political fallout of the president's collaboration with foreign will be significant.

backlash [ˈbækˌlæʃ]　n.（社会或政治方面的）强烈抵制

The massive demonstration shows a sign of a backlash against legalizing homosexual marriage.

The nation has been receiving a lot of backlash since the trade war, especially from farmers who are affected by the first wave.

blowback [ˈbloʊbæk]　n. 负面的反应；气流倒行

The politician's empty promise will receive blowback in the future.

ramification [ˌræmɪfɪˈkeɪʃn]　n. 后果

The lawmaker didn't foresee the unexpected ramifications of the new labor law.

Are you aware of the ramification of your decision to betray the country?

resonance [ˈrezənəns]　n. 回声

Lesson 112

• Words in sentences 句中单词/词组 •

haunting [ˈhɔːntɪŋ]　*adj.* 萦绕心头的；让人难忘的
rumination [ˌruːmɪˈneɪʃn]　*n.* 反刍；沉思
hepatitis [ˌhepəˈtaɪtɪs]　*n.* 肝炎
propaganda [ˌprɑpəˈgændə]　*n.* 政治宣传
petroleum [pəˈtrouliəm]　*n.* 石油
turnaround [ˈtɜːrnəraund]　*n.* 周转时间；改善；彻底的改变
procedure [prəˈsiːdʒər]　*n.* 程序；流程；手术
core competence　核心竞争力
foresee [fɔːrˈsiː]　*v.* 预见；预知

Part 2　补充单词/词组

hallowed [ˈhæləud]　*adj.* 神圣的
Confucius is the most hallowed saint in this nation.

concentric [kənˈsentrɪk]　*adj.* 同圆心的
Compact disks have concentric circles.

orotund [ˈɔːrətʌnd]　*adj.* （声音）响亮的；（言词）夸大的
Sensational and orotund prose are favored by reporters.

aria [ˈɑːriə]　*n.* 唱腔；抒情调；旋律
Someone who has this orotund voice and high-pitch aria should be a superstar.

side effect　副作用；未曾预料的结果
The placebo doesn't have any side effects.

exhaustion [ɪgˈzɔːstʃən]　*n.* 精疲力竭
The hallucination might merely be a side effect of fatigue and exhaustion.

harrow [ˈhæroʊ]　*v.* 折磨；使苦恼；耙地　*n.* 耙；耙地
I harrowed the field at noon.
We were harrowed by this invisible war.

renounce [rɪˈnauns]　*v.* 声明放弃；与……断绝关系　*n.* 垫牌
He decided to renounce his claim to the inheritance.

Is it legal for a father to renounce his son?
She lost her faith and renounced her belief.

prosper [ˈprɑːspər] v. 繁荣；成功

She prospers as a leading scientist.
Her business has prospered after the recession.

cymbal [ˈsɪmbl] n. 铙钹

The cymbal is a percussion instrument.

memorialize [məˈmɔːriəlaɪz] v. 纪念；向……请愿

The park stands a statue memorializing the founding father.
She memorializes her demised friend with flowers and candles.

placebo [pləˈsiːboʊ] n. 安慰剂；安慰的东西

lollypop [ˈlɒlipɒp] n. 棒棒糖

I just lost my best friend and you give lollypop as a placebo.

loll [lɑːl] v. 懒洋洋地倚靠；闲荡；耷拉

After work, she lolled on a sofa watching television.
The homeless lolls around in the park.
Dogs loll out their tongues to dissipate heat.

lounge [laʊndʒ] v. 倚；靠；消磨时间 n. 休息室；会客厅

I lounged away the day playing computer games.
I am going to wait for you in the lounge.

hammock [ˈhæmək] n. 吊床

She lounged in the hammock outside the house in the afternoon.

counterattack [ˈkaʊntərəˌtæk] v. 反击 n. 反攻

Iran is still capable of launching a devastating counterattack.

manpower [ˈmænpaʊər] n. 人力；劳动力

I don't have enough manpower to carry out the project.

workforce [ˈwɜːrkfɔːrs] n. 劳动力；劳动人口；工人

How much workforce do you need?

sundial [ˈsʌndaɪəl] n. 日晷；羽扇豆

gnomon [ˈnoʊmɑːn]　*n.* 指时针

dial [ˈdaɪəl]　*v.* 打电话；收听　*n.* 刻度盘
Sundials consist of two parts: a gnomon and a dial plane.

Part 3　识记单词 / 词组

hallow [ˈhæloʊ]　*v.* 使神圣化；敬重
unhallowed [ʌnˈhæloʊd]　*adj.* 亵渎的；邪恶的
precursor [prɪˈkɜːrsər]　*n.* 先驱者；前任
far-reaching repercussion　影响深远的后果
far-reaching [ˌfɑːr ˈriːtʃɪŋ]　*adj.* 影响深远的；波及广泛的
percussion [pərˈkʌʃn]　*n.* 打；敲；冲击
remorse [rɪˈmɔːrs]　*n.* 懊悔；悔恨
remorseful [rɪˈmɔːrsfl]　*adj.* 懊悔的
turnabout [ˈtɜːrnəbaʊt]　*n.* 彻底改变
in labor　在分娩中；在阵痛中
gnome [noʊm]　*n.* 土地神；矮人；格言

Lesson 113

Part 1　主力单词 / 词组

bemuse [bɪˈmjuːz]　*v.* 使困惑；使迷惑

bemused [bɪˈmjuːzd]　*adj.* 糊涂的；茫然的
He seemed bemused by the sound of the erratic remark.
We seemed more bemused by the shenanigans of clowns than by a war being waged half a world away in Africa.
The general was in a state of bemused silence and declined to meet the media afterwards.

confound [kənˈfaʊnd]　*v.* 使困惑；击败
The cause of death in victims still confounded the detective.

The black boxer's success confounded the expectation of only white supremacy.
The genius will confound his adversary's strategy.

baffle [ˈbæfl]　v. 使困惑；使迷惑

The drastic change in the stock market baffles many experts.

befog [bɪˈfɑːg]　v. 困惑

A cornucopia of job opportunities befogs me.

nonplus [ˌnɒnˈplʌs, ˈnɒnplʌs]　v. 使迷惑　n. 迷惑

I am slightly nonplused by the event/ by your statement.
I was nonplused by my best friend's rude reaction.
Her smile in this unforeseen tragedy nonpluses me.
The firefighter was at a nonplus whether to save people or evacuate immediately.

bewilder [bɪˈwɪldər]　v. 使迷惑；使糊涂；难住

His reaction bewildered me.

perplex [pərˈpleks]　v. 使困惑；使茫然

The riddle intrigues and perplexes us.

stupefy [ˈstuːpɪfaɪ]　v. 使麻木；使惊呆

The drug stupefies the patient.
Banality and strict rules stupefied the public servant.
Stupefying mediocrity and immaturity of cartoons weaken our kids' minds.

stupendous [stuːˈpendəs]　adj. 惊人的；了不起的；巨大的

Starvation plunged the country into the most stupendous civil war.
The most stupendous change in contemporary society is the application of technology in warfare.

befuddle [bɪˈfʌdəl]　v. 使昏迷；使迷惑

The philosophical hermeneutic befuddled some students.
The extremely high price of the salable art object has befuddled buyers since the heyday of pop art.

fuddle [ˈfʌdəl]　v. 使烂醉　n. 困惑；酗酒

The hotel waitress was fuddled by his strange request of accompanying him to walk.

muddle [ˈmʌdl]　v. 使糊涂；弄乱　n. 糊涂；混乱

A student muddled through his homework.

Everything has been in a muddle since she became the mayor.

> **Words in sentences 句中单词 / 词组**
>
> **erratic** [ɪ'rætɪk]　*adj.* 不规则的；怪异的
> **shenanigan** [ʃɪ'nænɪɡən]　*n.* 恶作剧；诡计
> **detective** [dɪ'tektɪv]　*n.* 侦探　*adj.* 侦探的；适于探测的
> **supremacy** [suː'preməsi]　*n.* 最高（至高）的地位
> **adversary** ['ædvərseri]　*n.* 对手；敌手
> **slightly** ['slaɪtli]　*adv.* 微小地；细小地
> **unforeseen** [ˌʌnfɔːr'siːn]　*adj.* 未预料到的
> **riddle** ['rɪdl]　*v.* 使布满窟窿　*n.* 谜语；费解之事
> **intrigue** [ɪn'triːɡ]　*v.* 使很感兴趣　*n.* 阴谋；诡计
> **hermeneutic** [ˌhɜːrmə'njuːtɪk, ˌhɜːrmə'nuːtɪk]　*n.* 解释学；圣经注解学　*adj.* 解释的
> **salable** ['seɪləbl]　*adj.* 价格适当的；畅销的
> **pop art**　流行艺术

Part 2　补充单词 / 词组

buffoonery [bə'fuːnəri]　*n.* 滑稽的举动

demagoguery ['deməˌɡɔɡəri]　*n.* 煽动

The shameless politician is good at performing buffoonery and demagoguery to impress the electors.

wangle ['wæŋɡl]　*v.* 用计获得　*n.* 哄骗

He was paid off and decided to wangle a fight with Harrison.

Aubrey wangles a ticket to the concert.

He wangles his way into a private party.

to wangle sth out of sb　从某人那里弄到某物

They managed to wangle money out of their grandmother.

finagle [fɪ'neɪɡl]　*v.* 欺骗；哄骗

The suspect finagled an alibi.

feculent [ˈfekjulənt]   *adj.* 不洁的；肮脏的；臭的

The haze is like a feculent fog that pervades the city.
The stifling, feculent muck can fertilize beautiful flowers.

scum [skʌm]   *n.* 浮渣；泡沫

She might be the greatest feculent scum in human civilization.

heyday [ˈheɪdeɪ]   *n.* 全盛期

In his heyday, he could walk 60 miles within a single day.

effloresce [ˌefloʊˈres]   *v.* 开花；发展；风化

Buddhism effloresced in China, not India.
The ancient monument exposed to the weather for thousands of years starts to effloresce gradually.

efflorescence [ˌefləˈresns]   *n.* 全盛期；开花；风化

The movie theater has found a new efflorescence after renovation.
His painting talent has found its efflorescence.

attenuate [əˈtenjueɪt]   *v.* 减弱；(使)纤细   *adj.* 稀薄的；细小的

Signal attenuates with distance.
The patient in a persistent vegetative state has attenuated limbs.

Part 3 识记单词/词组

air supremacy   制空权

stock exchange   股票交易

buffoon [bəˈfuːn]   *n.* 丑角；滑稽剧演员

stock [stɑːk]   *n.* 股票；存货；储备物

livestock [ˈlaɪvstɑːk]   *n.* 牲畜；家畜

to wangle sth for sb   设法为某人弄到某物

urinate [ˈjʊrɪneɪt]   *v.* 撒尿；小便

urine [ˈjʊrɪn]   *n.* 尿

feces [ˈfiːsiːz]   *n.* 粪便

fecal [ˈfiːkl]   *adj.* 排泄物的；残渣的

dung [dʌŋ]   *v.* 施粪肥于   *n.* 粪；粪肥

underachiever [ˌʌndərəˈtʃiːvə]   *n.* 发挥不佳者

efflorescent [ˌefləˈresənt] *adj.* 开花的；风化的
attenuation [əˌtenjuˈeɪʃn] *n.* 衰减；变薄
monumental [ˌmɑːnjuˈmentl] *adj.* 纪念性的；巨大的；不朽的

Lesson 114

Part 1　主力单词/词组

pivot [ˈpɪvət] *v.* 在枢轴上转动；随……转移　*n.* 关键的人物；枢纽；中心

The pivot to genetic plants presents the unintended possibility of obliterating certain bug species.

The eyewitness is the pivot for police to iron out the case.

Her foot was pivoted by a rock.

Interest rate pivots on the decision of the International Monetary Fund.

linchpin [ˈlɪntʃpɪn] *n.* 核心

Nurses are the linchpin of health care centers.

Sophisticated lawyers and eyewitnesses are the linchpins of winning cases.

cynosure [ˈsaɪnəʃʊr] *n.* 引人注目的人（或事物）

The anchor in a TV new program is the cynosure of all eyes.

The narrative paintings sold were the cynosure of famous artists around the world.

anchor [ˈæŋkər] *v.* 把……系住　*n.* 可以依靠的人；主持人；锚　*adj.* 系住的

The boat was held fast by its anchor.

The renowned general is an anchor during the war.

kingpin [ˈkɪŋpɪn] *n.* 主要的人物

The kingpin in a criminal syndicate always uses his lackeys and underlings as the scapegoats to vindicate his innocence.

fulcrum [ˈfʊlkrəm, ˈfʌlkrəm] *n.* 支柱；关键点；支点

Fox Conn corporation is the national fulcrum of cell phone manufacturing.

pivotal [ˈpɪvətl] *adj.* 关键性的；核心的

Words in sentences 句中单词/词组

iron out　解决；消除

International Monetary Fund　国际货币基金组织

syndicate　[ˈsɪndɪkeɪt, ˈsɪndɪkət]　v. 联合组成　n. 联合企业（组织）

underling　[ˈʌndərlɪŋ]　n. 手下；下属

scapegoat　[ˈskeɪpɡoʊt]　n. 替罪羊；代人受过的人

vindicate　[ˈvɪndɪkeɪt]　v. 证明；证明……正确

Part 2　补充单词/词组

patio　[ˈpætioʊ]　n. 院子；平台；天井

hinge　[hɪndʒ]　v. 用铰链连接；依……而转移　n. 铰链；关键；中枢

An outdoor patio hinges outward toward the diners.

hinge on　取决于……；以……为转移

The entire case hinges on fingerprint evidence.

in line with sth　与……相似；与……处于同等水平

consumer confidence　消费者信心指数

fair value　公允市价

The stock price of a company will be indexed in line with consumer confidence, not certainly fair value.

fair and square　诚实地；不偏不倚地

He won the election fair and square.

lionize　[ˈlaɪənaɪz]　v. 把……当成重要人物对待

She was lionized after winning an international tennis champion.

The beauty celebrity was lionized by television.

veranda=verandah　n. 阳台；游廊；走廊

She watched the sunrise on the verandah.

Lesson 114

porch [pɔːrtʃ]　*n.* 走廊；阳台；入口处
I still waited for her on the porch outside of the classroom.

plaza [ˈplæzə]　*n.* 广场；市场；购物中心；步行街
We danced in the town's plaza.

astrophysicist [ˌæstroʊˈfɪzɪsɪst]　*n.* 天体物理学家

supernova [ˈsuːpərnoʊvə]　*n.* 超级新星；超级新秀

cosmology [kɑːzˈmɑːlədʒi]　*n.* 宇宙论
The astrophysicist directed the Supernova Cosmology Project.

Part 3　识记单词/词组

pivot on　依……而定
index [ˈɪndeks]　*v.* 为……编索引　*n.* 索引
indices [ˈɪndɪsiːz]　*n.* 索引（复数）
index finger　食指
middle finger　中指
ring finger　无名指
little finger　小指
knuckle [ˈnʌkl]　*v.* 打；压；碰　*n.* 指关节；膝关节
knuckle down　认输；（向某人）屈服；开始认真工作
OEM (Original Entrusted Manufacture)　代工
lackey [ˈlæki]　*n.* 顺从的奴仆；跟班
footman [ˈfʊtmən]　*n.* 男仆
balcony [ˈbælkəni]　*n.* 阳台；露台
hallway [ˈhɔːlweɪ]　*n.* 玄关；门厅；走廊
toll plaza　道路收费区
cosmologist [kɑːzˈmɑːlədʒɪst]　*n.* 宇宙学家
nova [ˈnoʊvə]　*n.* 新星

Lesson 115

Part 1 主力单词 / 词组

refuse v. [rɪˈfjuːz] n. [ˈrefjuːs] v. 拒绝 n. 废弃物；垃圾

A common vice among artists—or rather bad artists—is a certain kind of mental cowardice because of which they refuse to take up any position whatsoever, invoking a misunderstood notion of the freedom of art, or other equally crass commonplaces. (Piero Manzoni, Italian painter and multimedia artist)

He refuses to testify against his friend.

We refuse the verdict and continue the hunger strike.

reject [rɪˈdʒekt] v. 拒绝 n. 废品

The U.S rejects humanitarian relief for African refugees.

decline [dɪˈklaɪn] v. 下降；谢绝；婉拒 n. 减少

How can you decline this offer?

abnegate [ˈæbnɪgeɪt] v. 放弃

I abnegate my education and find a job to make ends meet.

rebuff [rɪˈbʌf] v. 断然拒绝 n. 粗暴回绝

Taiwan rebuffs the proposal of secession.

spurn [spɜːrn] v. 轻蔑地拒绝；摒弃

She has spurned his flirtation and invitation to the party.

repudiate [rɪˈpjuːdieɪt] v. 拒绝接受；拒不履行（法律义务）

A diplomat repudiates denuclearization.

veto [ˈviːtoʊ] v. 否决；禁止 n. 否决权

The president of China has the right to veto U.N. proposals.

He will exercise the power of veto to any antiquated bill.

withhold [wɪðˈhoʊld, wɪθˈhoʊld] v. 隐瞒；扣留；抑制

It's too late for the president to withhold the message which has been debunked and was leaked to the public.

The tenant withheld her rent until the landlord finished the repairs.
You should withhold any communication with insiders while under investigation.
The sturdy dam should be capable of withholding the water pressure.

• Words in sentences 句中单词 / 词组 •

crass [kræs] *adj.* 不考虑他人感受的；愚蠢的

commonplace [ˈkɑːmənpleɪs] *n.* 老生常谈；口头禅 *adj.* 平凡的；陈腐的；平庸的

hunger strike 绝食；抗议

humanitarian [hjuːˌmænɪˈteriən] *n.* 人道主义者 *adj.* 人道主义的

make ends meet 勉强维持生计

secession [sɪˈseʃn] *n.* 脱离；独立

flirtation [flɜːrˈteɪʃn] *n.* 不认真对待；挑逗

landlord [ˈlændlɔːrd] *n.* 房东；地主；酒吧经理

Part 2 补充单词 / 词组

debunk [diːˈbʌŋk] *v.* 破解；拆去……的假面具

They are working to debunk what he did.

flirt [flɜːrt] *v.* 调情；摆动 *n.* 调情者

He flirts with an attractive girl in the pub.

slicker [ˈslɪkər] *n.* 骗子；雨衣

This city slicker had dalliances with several pretty girls before getting married.

dalliance [ˈdæliəns] *n.* 调情；随意涉猎；闲混

A scientist has a brief dalliance with novel writing.

flirtatious [flɜːrˈteɪʃəs] *adj.* 打情骂俏的

She is pretty and flirtatious.

denounce=denunciate *v.* 谴责；痛斥

Deforestation in Brazil has been denounced internationally which will result in global warming.

Part 3 识记单词/词组

renunciate [rɪˈnʌnsieɪt] v. 宣告放弃；宣布脱离关系 n. 克己的人

renunciation [rɪˌnʌnsiˈeɪʃn] n. 宣告放弃；放弃声明书

refusal [rɪˈfjuːzl] n. 拒绝；回绝

Ukraine [juˈkreɪn] n. 乌克兰

leak out 泄露

leakage [ˈliːkɪdʒ] n. 泄漏；漏损物；漏损量

nuclear leakage 核泄漏

get by 继续存在；过得去；逃过查验

crass remark 蠢话

crass comment 风凉话

secessionist [sɪˈseʃənɪst] n. 想独立的人

secede [sɪˈsiːd] v. 脱离；退出

denouement=denunciation n. 结局

denuclearize [diˈnʊklɪəˌraɪz] v. 无核化

Lesson 116

Part 1 主力单词/词组

talkative [ˈtɔːkətɪv] adj. 爱说话的；多嘴的

Her talkative and freewheeling style might have already offended several political conservatives.

The old fellow is quite talkative.

The South American public is passionate and talkative.

loquacious [ləˈkweɪʃəs] adj. 爱说话的；多嘴的

The loquacious priest teaches us to philosophize about the meaning of life as a vehicle for listening to one's inner voice.

voluble [ˈvɑːljəbl] adj. 滔滔不绝的

The professor was very voluble on the subject of actuarial science.

garrulous [ˈgærələs] adj. 喋喋不休的
That garrulous old man tells me a farfetched and highly improbable tale.

garrulity [gəˈruːliti] n. 喋喋不休；多嘴
She resorted to garrulity due to lack of real content in her conversation while speaking to a professor.

gibber [ˈdʒɪbər] v. 语无伦次地说；急促不清地说
The moribund vampire was gibbering, shrieking, and gnashing imprecations upon the slayer before meeting his fate.

• Words in sentences 句中单词 / 词组 •

freewheeling [ˌfriːˈwiːlɪŋ] n. 惯性滑行 adj. 随心所欲的；惯性滑行的

priest [priːst] n. 牧师

philosophize [fəˈlɑːsəfaɪz] v. 理性思考

actuarial [ˌæktʃuˈeriəl] adj. 精算的

farfetched [ˈfɑrˈfetʃt] adj. 不太可能的；牵强的

moribund [ˈmɔːrɪbʌnd] adj. 濒死的；无生气的；停滞不前的

shriek [ʃriːk] v. 尖叫 n. 尖叫

gnash [næʃ] v. 咬牙（切齿）

slayer [ˈsleɪə] n. 残杀者

Part 2 补充单词 / 词组

glabrous [ˈgleɪbrəs] adj. 光滑的（无毛的）
Frogs have glabrous skins.

pettifog [ˈpetiˌfɑːg] v. 欺骗；挑剔
He engaged in legal chicanery pettifogging his clients.

pettifogger [ˈpetiˌfɑːgər] n. 骗人的律师；挑剔的人
A lawyer without scruples is nothing more than a pettifogger.

chassis [ˈʃæsi] *n.* 车身底盘；飞机底部；起落架；底架
The new composite chassis of the Ferrari is lighter and stronger.

zombie company 僵尸企业

bailout [ˈbeɪlaʊt] *n.* 紧急（财政）援助；跳伞
A lot of zombie companies need bailouts.

fragment [ˈfrægmənt, frægˈment] *v.* 使……分开；拆分；分散 *n.* 碎片；断片
The dish fell and fragmented into pieces.
Permanent civil strife fragmented the empire into smaller, weaker kingdoms.
I could only hear fragments of your talking due to bad transmission.

fragmentation [ˌfrægmenˈteɪʃn] *n.* 分裂；破碎
Russia will not tolerate the territorial fragmentation of its nation.

snippet [ˈsnɪpɪt] *n.* 片段；摘录
I read a snippet of her poem and thought it was terrific.
The government released an audio snippet concerning a conversation with an alien.

crepitant [ˈkrepɪtənt] *adj.* 吱吱作响的
I heard a crepitant sound as I went down the metal stair.

fuliginous [fjʊˈlɪdʒənəs] *adj.* 烟幕弥漫不清的；煤烟色的
Fuliginous air pollution is evident that issues out from the chimneys of factories.

hortatory [ˈhɔrtəˌtori] *adj.* 忠告的；鼓励的
The priest delivers a hortatory sermon.

Part 3 识记单词/词组

reticent [ˈretɪsnt] *adj.* 含蓄的；寡言少语的；有保留的；谨慎的
retention [rɪˈtenʃn] *n.* 保留；节制
inner sanctum 内心不受打扰的地方
meet one's fate 死亡
preach [priːtʃ] *v.* 讲道；布道
preacher [ˈpriːtʃər] *n.* 传道士；牧师
sanctum [ˈsæŋktəm] *n.* 神圣的地方；私人不受打扰的地方
actuary [ˈæktʃueri] *n.* 精算师